Economic Displacement

Economic Displacement examines China's economic displacement of the United States in Latin America and the Caribbean (LAC), and its implications for global geopolitics. Through data analysis and case studies, Francisco Urdinez demonstrates how China has filled the economic void left by US retrenchment from 2001 to 2020. He argues that this economic shift has led to a significant erosion of US political influence in the region, affecting public opinion, elite perspective, and voting patterns in international organizations. Providing a multifaceted view of this geopolitical transformation in this timely and important book, the author offers crucial insights into the changing landscape of global influence and the future of US–China rivalry in Latin America.

Francisco Urdinez is an associate professor at the Institute of Political Science of the Pontifical Catholic University of Chile, where he also directs the Millennium Nucleus for the Impacts of China in Latin America (ICLAC) project on China's impacts in Latin America, a large three-year grant funded by the Ministry of Science of Chile. He served as a 2022–23 resident fellow at the Woodrow Wilson Center in Washington, DC. He is a fellow of the National Agency for Research and Development of Chile and his work on China's relations with the Global South has been published in *Comparative Political Studies*, the *Review of International Organizations*, the *Journal of Peace Research*, *Research & Politics*, the *Chinese Journal of International Politics*, and the *Cambridge Review of International Affairs*, among others.

Economic Displacement

China and the End of US Primacy in Latin America

FRANCISCO URDINEZ
Pontifical Catholic University of Chile

Shaftesbury Road, Cambridge CB2 8EA, United Kingdom

One Liberty Plaza, 20th Floor, New York, NY 10006, USA

477 Williamstown Road, Port Melbourne, VIC 3207, Australia

314–321, 3rd Floor, Plot 3, Splendor Forum, Jasola District Centre,
New Delhi – 110025, India

103 Penang Road, #05–06/07, Visioncrest Commercial, Singapore 238467

Cambridge University Press is part of Cambridge University Press & Assessment,
a department of the University of Cambridge.

We share the University's mission to contribute to society through the pursuit of
education, learning and research at the highest international levels of excellence.

www.cambridge.org
Information on this title: www.cambridge.org/9781009672269
DOI: 10.1017/9781009672238

© Francisco Urdinez 2026

This publication is in copyright. Subject to statutory exception and to the provisions
of relevant collective licensing agreements, no reproduction of any part may take
place without the written permission of Cambridge University Press & Assessment.

When citing this work, please include a reference to the
DOI 10.1017/9781009672238

First published 2026

A catalogue record for this publication is available from the British Library

*A Cataloging-in-Publication data record for this book is available from the
Library of Congress*

ISBN 978-1-009-67224-5 Hardback
ISBN 978-1-009-67226-9 Paperback

Cambridge University Press & Assessment has no responsibility for the persistence
or accuracy of URLs for external or third-party internet websites referred to in this
publication and does not guarantee that any content on such websites is, or will
remain, accurate or appropriate.

For EU product safety concerns, contact us at Calle de José Abascal, 56, 1°,
28003 Madrid, Spain, or email eugpsr@cambridge.org

Economic Displacement

China and the End of US Primacy in Latin America

FRANCISCO URDINEZ
Pontifical Catholic University of Chile

Shaftesbury Road, Cambridge CB2 8EA, United Kingdom

One Liberty Plaza, 20th Floor, New York, NY 10006, USA

477 Williamstown Road, Port Melbourne, VIC 3207, Australia

314–321, 3rd Floor, Plot 3, Splendor Forum, Jasola District Centre, New Delhi – 110025, India

103 Penang Road, #05–06/07, Visioncrest Commercial, Singapore 238467

Cambridge University Press is part of Cambridge University Press & Assessment, a department of the University of Cambridge.

We share the University's mission to contribute to society through the pursuit of education, learning and research at the highest international levels of excellence.

www.cambridge.org
Information on this title: www.cambridge.org/9781009672269
DOI: 10.1017/9781009672238

© Francisco Urdinez 2026

This publication is in copyright. Subject to statutory exception and to the provisions of relevant collective licensing agreements, no reproduction of any part may take place without the written permission of Cambridge University Press & Assessment.

When citing this work, please include a reference to the
DOI 10.1017/9781009672238

First published 2026

A catalogue record for this publication is available from the British Library

A Cataloging-in-Publication data record for this book is available from the Library of Congress

ISBN 978-1-009-67224-5 Hardback
ISBN 978-1-009-67226-9 Paperback

Cambridge University Press & Assessment has no responsibility for the persistence or accuracy of URLs for external or third-party internet websites referred to in this publication and does not guarantee that any content on such websites is, or will remain, accurate or appropriate.

For EU product safety concerns, contact us at Calle de José Abascal, 56, 1°, 28003 Madrid, Spain, or email eugpsr@cambridge.org

Contents

List of Figures	*page* vii
List of Tables	xi
Acknowledgments	xiii
Author's Note	xvii
List of Abbreviations	xix
Map of Latin America and the Caribbean	xxi

PART I ECONOMIC DISPLACEMENT

1	Economic Weight and Displacement: A New Framework for Understanding US–China Rivalry	3
2	China's Economic Displacement of the US in Latin America	25
3	Filling the Void: Chinese Economic Actors and the Provision of Substitute Goods	55
4	The Demand Side: Latin American Agency in Economic Displacement	79

PART II THE POLITICAL CONSEQUENCES OF ECONOMIC DISPLACEMENT

5	The Effects of Economic Displacement on Public Opinion and Political Elites	107
6	The Effects of Economic Displacement in International Organizations	132
7	The New Cold War and the Future of China–US Rivalry in LAC	163

Appendices	185
Notes	203
Bibliography	235
Index	257

Figures

1.1	The global economy's shifting center	page 4
1.2	Global trend of US–China economic weight and displacement in the world	6
1.3	Chinese economic displacement of US in Latin America by country	7
1.4	Visualizing economic weight	17
1.5	Visualizing economic displacement	20
2.1	Chinese Economic Weight Index by continent, 2000–2020	28
2.2	Components of Chinese economic weight by region, 2001–2020	29
2.3	Chinese economic weight in LAC by subregion	30
2.4	US economic weight by continent, 1989–2020	37
2.5	US economic weight by component in LAC	39
2.6	US economic weight in LAC, 1989–2020	40
2.7	American stock of FDI in LAC as a share of its stock in the world	46
2.8	Difference between US economic weight and Chinese economic weight by region	49
2.9	Evolution of the economic weight of China and the US by country in LAC	50
2.10	Chinese displacement of the US economy, measured in countries and as a share of LAC population	51
2.11	Chinese and US economic weights in the world in 2001 and 2020	53
3.1	Commodity price index	59

3.2	Average Chinese corporate and banking presence in Latin American countries	68
3.3	Top thirty leading Chinese investors and financiers by country, 2001–2020	69
3.4	Chinese actor presence and economic displacement risk over time	75
3.5	FDI preference: impact of investment attributes	78
4.1	Loans for energy infrastructure in LAC, 2001–2020	82
4.2	Argentina's energy trade balance (in US$ millions)	84
4.3	President Kirchner meets with Gezhouba Group and Electroingenieria executives, August 21, 2013	86
4.4	Share of Peruvian metal exports	92
4.5	COSCO–Volcan contract signing in 2019 in Lima	95
4.6	Chinese contributions received by Latin American governments and municipalities	99
4.7	Governor Joao Doria and São Paulo officials meet Chinese businesspeople in Beijing, 2019	100
5.1	Comparing trust in US versus China for addressing Latin American issues	109
5.2	The impact of economic displacement on trust in US versus China for Latin American problem solving, 2015	110
5.3	Perception of China versus US in addressing Latin American issues	111
5.4	The effect of economic displacement on trust in China versus US for Latin American problem solving	111
5.5	The impact of economic displacement on preference for US versus China relations, 2023	113
5.6	The influence of economic displacement on foreign policy priorities of legislators	119
5.7	The impact of economic displacement on preferred trading partner preference	119
5.8	Perceived value of China–Latin America FTA	120
5.9	The impact of economic displacement on US–Latin America FTA support by party affiliation	121
5.10	Chinese space station in Neuquén: part of China's Deep Space Network	123
6.1	China's membership in international organizations: comparison with Western countries	134

List of Figures

6.2	UNGA voting convergence: global and Latin American trends, 2001–2020	138
6.3	UNGA voting alignment: Latin American countries' proximity to China versus US	139
6.4	UNGA ideological alignment for LAC countries: US versus China, pre- and post-displacement	141
6.5	Impact of economic displacement on ideological distance from the US in UNGA voting	143
6.6	Probability of economic displacement in voting against a resolution in the UNHRC	152
6.7	Effect of economic displacement on voting in the OAS	159
6.8	Marginal effect of US economic weight conditioned by China's economic weight on a country's vote alignment with the US in the UNHRC	160
7.1	Cumulative IADB financing: Chinese versus American enterprise tenders (US$ millions)	170
7.2	Difference in the trajectories of South America and the rest of Latin America and the Caribbean	176
7.3	Trajectories of the largest economies in Latin America and the Caribbean	177
A.1	Difference between the economic weight of China and the US by country in a global sample, 2001–2020	190
B.1	Weight of each component of the index for each LAC subregion	194
B.2	Chinese Economic Weight Index by subregion (2001 = 100)	195
B.3	US Economic Weight Index by subregion (2001 = 100)	195
B.4	Continuous measurement of economic displacement by subregion	196
B.5	Dichotomous version of economic displacement by country in Latin America and the Caribbean	196
C.1	Number of Chinese actors by country in Latin America and the Caribbean	197

Tables

2.1	Variables used to operationalize Chinese economic weight	page 27
2.2	Variables used to operationalize US economic weight	36
3.1	Key arguments and their operationalization	58
3.2	First difference regression models of Chinese goods provision	70
3.3	Identifying sectors with emerging Chinese providers	72
3.4	Cox survival model for the occurrence of economic displacement	75
3.5	Sample comparison of investment project pairs	77
4.1	Loans for energy infrastructure from 2001 to 2020 (in US$ millions)	82
4.2	Chinese donations by actor type and origin	98
5.1	Main themes highlighted by legislators who voted for and against the space station project	129
6.1	UNGA resolution types: voting distribution, 2001–2022	140
6.2	Effect of economic displacement on UNGA ideological distance	142
6.3	Effect of economic displacement on UNGA resolution convergence	144
6.4	Latin American member countries of the UNHRC	149
6.5	Effect of economic displacement on vote convergence with the US in the UNHRC	151
6.6	Resolutions adopted by the Permanent Council of the OAS by roll call vote on domestic political situations, 2001–2021	157

6.7	Comparative analysis of OAS voting alignments: impact of China's economic displacement on alignment with US	158
A.1	List of Chinese companies in Forbes 500 ranking	189
B.1	Descriptive statistics of variables used to create the Chinese Economic Weight Index	193
B.2	Chinese investment stock to LAC (in US$ millions), 2001–2020	193
B.3	Descriptive statistics of variables used to create the US Economic Weight Index	194
E.1	Effect of economic displacement on Latin American public opinion	197
E.2	Preferred country for a closer relationship in public opinion	198
E.3	The influence of economic displacement on legislators' preferences	199
E.4	Legislative support for an FTA with the US	199
F.1	Resolutions with the most votes in the UNHRC	200

Acknowledgments

This book evolved from my doctoral thesis, defended in 2017 through a joint program between the University of São Paulo and King's College London. My studies were made possible by generous scholarships from the Brazilian government's National Council for Scientific and Technological Development program and the State of São Paulo's São Paulo Research Foundation (FAPESP) grant. Upon joining the Institute of Political Science at the Pontifical Catholic University of Chile (PUC Chile), I received support from the Chilean Fund for Scientific and Technological Development (Fondecyt Initiation grant 11180081) to study Chinese multilateralism and the establishment of the Asian Infrastructure Investment Bank (AIIB). This was followed by a Fondecyt Regular grant (1230307) to explore the provision of competitive economic goods between China and the United States. The Chilean Ministry of Sciences generously funded the establishment of the Millennium Nucleus for the Impacts of China in Latin America (ICLAC), a research cluster I am honored to direct, bringing together an exceptional group of researchers to address the implications of China's rise in the region (grant NCS2022_053). In 2023, I was fortunate enough to spend ten months as a resident fellow at the Wilson Center in Washington, DC, where I dedicated my full attention to advancing this book. Ironically, the argument of this book is quite telling regarding the presidential decision in the United States to close the Wilson Center in 2025.

A data-intensive book like this required vital support from assistants and students for data cleaning, systematization, and analysis. For assistance creating actor-level databases for investments, loans, and foreign aid, I am grateful to my doctoral students Andrea Freites, Luciano

Quispe, and Diego Telias, and to my research assistants (in alphabetical order) Daniel Alcatruz, Soledad Araya, Paul Barrezueta, Mariel Hidalgo, Eliana Jung, Ana Maria Llumiquinga, Nerea Palma, Gonzalo Parra Vicente Quintero, and Benjamin Zúñiga. Shicheng (Jess) Shao was my exceptional assistant during my time at the Wilson Center, and her brilliant performance continued upon my return to Santiago. Eugenio Sanchez, passionate and dedicated, has been an excellent assistant in the advanced stages of the project. I have also been fortunate to work with Margaret Myers on improving Chinese investment data that is publicly available online in Francisco Urdinez and Margaret Myers (2024), "Regional Repository of Chinese Investments in Latin America," ICLAC and Inter-American Dialogue.

During my fellowship at the Wilson Center, I held an early manuscript workshop in 2023. I am especially grateful to Cindy Arnson, Ben Gedan, Maryhen Jimenez, Julio Rios, Margaret Myers, Igor Patrick, Robert Daly, and Francisco Sagasti for their invaluable input. In January 2024, I conducted a workshop in Santiago with participation from Erik Voeten, and I received feedback from my ICLAC colleagues Maria Montt, Johannes Rehner, and Andres Borquez, among others. While in DC, I benefited from discussions with Margaret Pearson, Scott Kastner, Stephen Kaplan, Kerry Ratigan, and Myles Kahler on ideas for Chapters 1, 3, and 5. At the 2023 International Studies Association conference in Montreal, I presented progress on Chapter 6, receiving valuable comments from Alvin Camba (University of Denver) and other Global China experts. I presented Chapter 2 at the International Political Science Association conference in Buenos Aires in June 2024. Within ICLAC, I have discussed the work with leading authors in China–LAC relations, including Carol Wise, Rhys Jenkins, Evelyn Hu, and Cynthia Sanborn. I have also presented summaries of the argument to think tank audiences such as the Carnegie Endowment, Brookings Institution, the United States Institute of Peace, and the National Committee on United States–China Relations. Chapter 5 builds on an article published in the *Journal of Chinese Political Science*. I thank their editors for allowing me to use portions of this work.

Throughout this journey, I have formed friendships with co-authors who have helped me understand this fascinating topic and who have made the work more enjoyable: special thanks, in alphabetical order, to Giovanni Agostinis, David Altman, Daniela Campello, Jin Lin Duanmu, Pedro Feliu, Agustina Giraudy, Jan Knoerich, Tom Long, Gilmar Masiero, Federico Merke, Fernando Mouron, Amancio Oliveira, Janina

Onuki, Gino Pauselli, Federico Rojas, Luis Schenoni, and Diego Telias. At the project's inception, David Altman, Gabriel Negretto, Juan Pablo Luna, and Nando Rosemblatt were very generous in sharing their experience in writing an academic book from the Global South.

My wonderful colleagues at the Institute of Political Science at PUC Chile, a privileged place to work in Latin America, have been a constant support. Several read and commented on parts of the book; I thank David Altman, Catherine Reyes-Housholder, Valentin Figueroa, Cristobal Rovira, Nicole Jenne, Carsten Schulz, Juan Pablo Scarfi, and Juan Pablo Luna for their generous feedback and brainstorming sessions. During a trip organized by the Latin American Department of China's Ministry of Foreign Affairs in early 2024, I had the opportunity to exchange ideas about the book with academics from Tsinghua University, Fudan University, Hubei University, and the Chinese Academy of Social Sciences, as well as several think tanks. I am grateful to these Chinese colleagues who generously shared their opinions.

I was privileged to have Robert Dreesen at Cambridge University Press champion my project and bring his considerable expertise to bear as its editor. His support and guidance were instrumental in shaping the work and bringing it to fruition. I want to thank Sable Gravesandy, Senior Editorial Assistant, and Claire Sissen, Senior Content Manager, of Cambridge University Press. I also want to thank the two blind reviewers for the quality and warmth of their comments, and for offering constructive rather than destructive feedback. Elena K. Abbott was instrumental in helping me edit my manuscript and improve the clarity of my ideas, ensuring the book is as clear as possible. Rudy Leon compiled the book's index.

Lastly, this book could not have been written without the emotional support of my beloved family, especially my wife Beatriz, to whom this book is dedicated.

Author's Note

This book addresses one of the most pressing questions in contemporary international relations: What are the political consequences of China's growing economic power? While offering new theoretical insights and conceptual developments, this book's strength lies in its empirical analysis of how Chinese economic influence is increasingly supplanting that of the United States in Latin America. Writing a book on such a significant topic – the economic rise of China and its political effects on the Western Hemisphere – proved a substantial undertaking. The book strives to present a wealth of empirical evidence while offering a clear synthesis. Although it is an academic work, my greatest hope is that it will be read by practitioners and influence policymaking.

The book documents the effects of China's economic influence on legislative opinion and behavior, public opinion, and foreign policy actions in international organizations. A key argument is that China is achieving its objectives primarily by filling an economic void left by the United States, rather than through an intentional strategy to gain political influence. This argument has significant implications for scholars of international relations and foreign policymakers alike. Extensive documentation throughout the book illuminates the role played by China's provision of alternative goods and services in the global marketplace and demonstrates the importance of economic displacement to its rising influence. Exploring the complex interplay between intentions and results, the book highlights how the pragmatic necessities of politics often lead to unforeseen consequences and adaptations. By examining the structural shifts that have occurred in Latin America at the turn of the century, it offers important insights into the future landscape of geopolitical competition in the region and its implications for global power dynamics. Although this book covers events through the end of 2024, Donald Trump's second term makes this analysis even more urgent, as China's economic weight in Latin America is expected to grow (due to reduced demand for manufacturing in the US) while US economic influence declines (due to credit restrictions, USAID cuts, and the "Make America Great Again" mercantilist policies that affect even countries with free trade agreements with the United States).

There are at least three ways to read this book. Those interested in policy implications can read Chapters 1 and 7, and perhaps 5 or 6, depending on whether they are more interested in domestic or foreign policy. Notably, those interested in US hegemony and its loss of leadership will find the second part of the book particularly engaging. The main text is accessible to a wide audience of interested readers, but those who wish to deepen their study will find valuable details and information in the notes and Appendix. The data can also be downloaded from the author's Harvard Dataverse repository at https://dataverse.harvard.edu/dataverse/furdinez.

Abbreviations

AIIB	Asian Infrastructure Investment Bank
ALBA	Bolivarian Alliance for the Peoples of Our America
BOC	Bank of China
BRI	Belt and Road Initiative
CCCC	China Communications Construction Company
CCP	Chinese Communist Party
CDB	China Development Bank
CELAC	Community of Latin American and Caribbean States
CHEC	China Harbour Engineering Company
CIDCA	China International Development Cooperation Agency
CMOC	China Molybdenum Company
CNPC	China National Petroleum Corporation
CNSA	China National Space Administration
COSCO	China Ocean Shipping Company
CRCC	China Railway Construction Corporation
CRRC	China Railway Rolling Stock Corporation
CSG	China Southern Power Grid
DFC	US International Development Finance Corporation
FDI	Foreign direct investment
FTA	Free trade agreement
GDP	Gross domestic product
IADB	Inter-American Development Bank
ICBC	Industrial and Commercial Bank of China
IMF	International Monetary Fund
LAC	Latin America and the Caribbean
MNC	Multinational corporation

MOFCOM	Ministry of Commerce of the People's Republic of China
NDB	New Development Bank
OAS	Organization of American States
PELA	Latin American Elites Project
POE	Privately owned enterprise
PRC	People's Republic of China
SASAC	State-Owned Assets Supervision and Administration Commission
SGCC	State Grid Corporation of China
Sinosure	China Export & Credit Insurance Corporation
SOE	State-owned enterprise
UN	United Nations
UNGA	United Nations General Assembly
UNHRC	United Nations Human Rights Council
USAID	United States Agency for International Development
WB	World Bank

Map of Latin America and the Caribbean

Source: Charlip (2015).

PART I

ECONOMIC DISPLACEMENT

1

Economic Weight and Displacement

A New Framework for Understanding US–China Rivalry

Over the past two decades, there has been a marked shift in the global economic epicenter from the North Atlantic to East Asia, propelled with remarkable intensity by China's state-led mobilized globalization (Figure 1.1). This shift has not only altered economic dynamics but also redefined the locus of international power.[1] While the twentieth century was characterized as the "Atlantic century," the twenty-first century is shaping up to center on the Pacific.

China, as the world's second-largest economy, has emerged as the predominant influence in this newly established gravitational core. In 2000, only ten Chinese companies were listed among the 500 largest multinational corporations worldwide. The United States led the list with 179 companies. By 2020, this landscape had shifted dramatically; 124 of the world's largest 500 firms were Chinese, surpassing the United States (with 121) and Japan (with 53).[2] A similar trend is observable in the banking sector. In 2000, three of the top five global banks were American (Citigroup, Bank of America, and Chase), with only one Chinese bank, Industrial and Commercial Bank of China (ICBC), making the top ten. By 2020, ICBC had ascended to become the world's largest commercial bank, and the top four spots were dominated by Chinese institutions (ICBC, China Construction Bank Corporation, Agricultural Bank of China, and Bank of China).[3] Citigroup and Bank of America dropped to sixth and seventh positions, respectively, while Chase fell out of the top ten entirely.[4] Another notable indicator of China's ascent is that, since 2012, it has surpassed the United States in the annual number of intellectual property technology patents filed.[5]

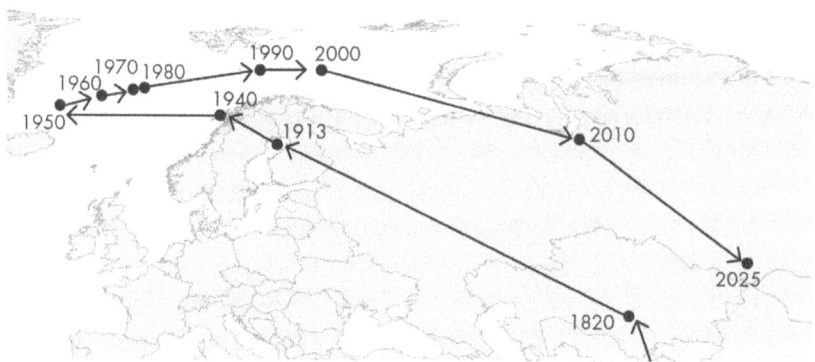

FIGURE 1.1 The global economy's shifting center
Source: Bolt and Van Zanden (2014) and The Economist (2018).
Note: The "economic center of gravity" is determined by calculating a weighted average of global locations based on their GDP in three dimensions and then projecting this point onto the nearest land surface. This method offers a tangible way to visualize the shifting focus of global economic activity. For future projections, such as the one for the year 2025, analyses have been conducted by organizations like the McKinsey Global Institute.

Pivotal policies drove the globalization of Chinese state capital starting in 1999: the Western Development Program, initiated in 1999; the Going Global policy, launched in 2000; and the Belt and Road Initiative (BRI), introduced in 2013.[6] These Chinese strategies catalyzed a significant transformation in most of the country's large state-owned enterprises (SOEs).[7] They also expanded globally, marking the rise of transnational state capital; a phenomenon denoting the ability of states to become global owners and investors, penetrate international markets, and control substantial assets beyond their national borders.[8] However, China's state-led and mobilized globalization did not unfold with uniform intensity across all target nations. While the country's economic expansion has been less intense in Europe and Oceania, it has been readily identifiable in other regions, including Africa and Asia. Over the past two decades, Chinese investments and financing have been particularly successful in addressing unmet development needs in the Global South. Due to market forces that enabled hundreds of Chinese actors to take advantage of the capital outflow following US retrenchment from 2001 to 2020, as well as the creation of economic opportunities in abandoned markets, China has capitalized on the huge demand to find substitutes for goods and services previously offered by Western actors.

This dynamic has been a prime example of what I term "economic displacement," a phenomenon where one country's economic influence surpasses that of another. In this book, I am discussing economic displacement in regard to the world's two leading economies: China and the United States. Economic displacement considers a comprehensive set of factors – total investment, trade, foreign aid, and credit – making it a robust proxy for gauging the economic weight that China and the US hold over each continent. Although measured as a dichotomous phenomenon (it either occurs or it does not occur), it is in fact a simplification of a gradual process that depends on the increasing economic weight of China and the erosion of the economic weight of the US in each country. Indeed, it is not enough to tell the story of China's rise.[9] My research shows that we must bring the concomitant contraction of the US to the front of the analysis.

As will be further explained in Chapter 2, I have developed a composite index based on trade, investment, financial flows, and aid relative to each target country's gross domestic product (GDP). This composite index enables us to measure the economic weight of both countries. If we look at the global trend, China is narrowing the gap relative to the economic weight of the US and generating displacement in much of the Global South (Figure 1.2). As China's economic weight increases and that of the United States declines, Chinese economic actors have become more significant in offering alternative economic goods. The concept of displacement thus simplifies what is actually a gradual process of alternative goods provision. For example, when a country crosses the threshold at which I consider economic displacement to have occurred, it signifies that China has become more economically influential than the United States in that specific country. At that point, China has become the primary provider of economic opportunities in the country.

Latin America and the Caribbean (LAC) presents a unique case study for understanding these global dynamics. Traditionally considered the US's sphere of influence, or "backyard," during the twentieth century, LAC yields exceptional insights as a "hard test" for understanding the ramifications of the United States' economic displacement by China due to its distinct characteristics when compared to other regions of the Global South: It is geographically and culturally distant from China, logistically challenging to access, and traditionally considered the US's sphere of influence. Moreover, it arguably has even less historical precedent for Chinese involvement than Africa or Southeast Asia. Over a period of twenty years (2001–2021), China has economically displaced the US in ten of the twelve countries of South America, a subregion that

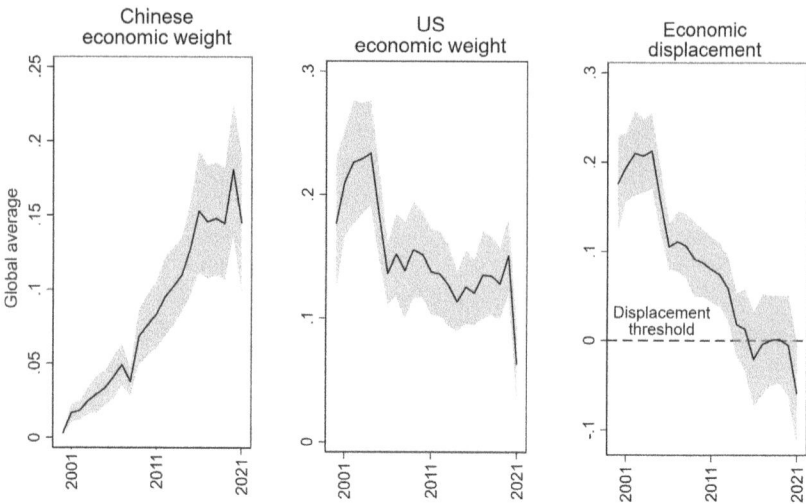

FIGURE 1.2 Global trend of US–China economic weight and displacement in the world
Source: Author's elaboration.
Note: Annual averages estimated by ordinary least squares in a global sample of 185 countries. Ninety-five percent confidence intervals in gray. The economic displacement figure on the right is calculated as the difference between the US economic weight and the Chinese economic weight for each country in each year; as indicated by the dotted line, values below it indicate that displacement has occurred.

accounts for two thirds of LAC's population and roughly 80 percent of the region's GDP (Figure 1.3). By exploring the case study of US–China economic influence in LAC, this analysis sheds light on a critical puzzle: Why has China, without surpassing the United States in global economic rankings, succeeded in economically displacing the US within its traditional sphere of influence? Moreover, what are the long-term economic and political implications of this development?

In the pages to come, I present a new theory of how Chinese economic actors have filled the economic voids left by US capital based on the demand of elite actors in target states, and I suggest what this will mean for the global economy and geopolitical influence over the next two decades. Notably, I show that China has not always capitalized politically on its economic growth. In fact, the effect of displacement is more to the detriment of US leadership than it is in favor of China. As I insist throughout this book, leadership is built and requires material resources to sustain – something the US has ceased to allocate in LAC.

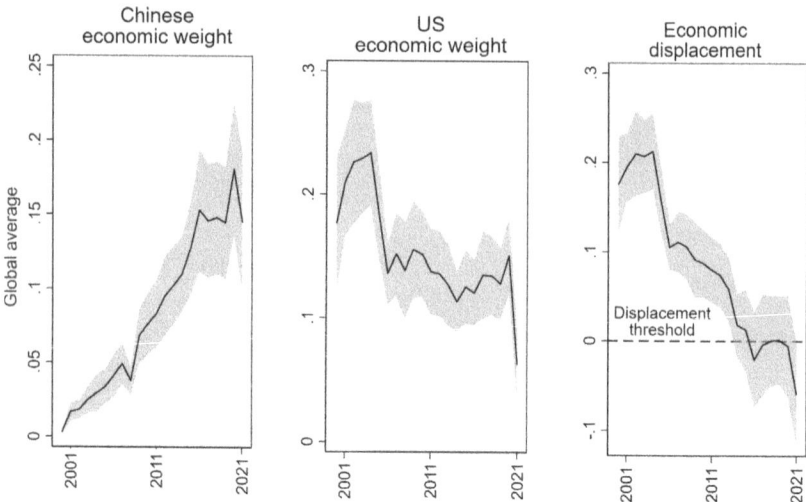

Economic Weight and Displacement 7

FIGURE 1.3 Chinese economic displacement of US in Latin America by country
Source: Author's elaboration.
Note: The figure shows which is greater, the economic weight of China (black) or the US (gray).

1.1 THE IMPACT OF ECONOMIC DISPLACEMENT IN LAC

In a new cold war, I believe that competition between the US and China will primarily be about economic power, similar to the hegemonic transition between Great Britain and the US in the eighteenth century.[10] Both China and the US will engage in competitive economic statecraft, aiming to provide public and private goods (and services) across the world. While the USSR competed militarily with the US, China has not yet reached military parity with the United States.[11] More importantly, it does not offer an ideological or moral alternative to the US.[12] Thus, the competition will continue to center around economic preeminence.

LAC provides a clear test case for how this competition will unfold. Here, I offer three broadly applicable findings related to China's economic displacement of the United States in LAC:

1. China's current economic position already represents a notable shift in global economic dynamics. If the current trend persists, China could overtake the US as the world's largest economy by 2040. Overall estimations mask a more intricate reality: In some nations, China has already or will soon displace the US in terms of its economic weight. In fact, from 2001 to 2020, China displaced the US in much of the developing world. LAC is no exception.

2. China has successfully positioned itself as a provider of alternative economic goods, thus becoming a substitute to the US in many economic sectors. This includes extending credits, making infrastructure investments, offering COVID-19 assistance,[13] and

spearheading initiatives like the Asian Infrastructure Investment Bank (AIIB) and various free trade agreements (FTAs).[14]

After World War II, American economic goods were pivotal for rebuilding Europe. The provision of American goods not only assisted in North Atlantic recovery but also established US political and economic authority in the Western Hemisphere.[15] Over the past two decades, however, in the face of considerable US retrenchment between 2001 and 2020, Chinese investments and financing have been addressing unmet developmental needs in the Global South.[16] This phenomenon, which I explain in detail in Chapters 2–4, occurred due to market forces that enabled hundreds of Chinese actors to take advantage of the capital outflow from the US and the creation of economic opportunities, or "voids," in abandoned markets. It is typically suggested that this opportunism was a strategic maneuver by China to intentionally displace the US's influence in LAC. However, this phenomenon was actually significantly driven by the demands of local elites themselves, who increasingly turned to Chinese goods as viable alternatives, especially in contexts where American options were lacking or absent. This shift underscores the pivotal role of local agency in shaping economic and geopolitical landscapes.

3. The United States is experiencing a decline in its ability to offer economic opportunities relative to China. This shift is not just economic; it has profound implications for the US's political influence and leverage on the global stage.

A key theoretical assumption of this book is that the United States' international dominance was primarily built upon the robustness of its economy. Throughout the nineteenth century, the US economy experienced extraordinary growth, propelling the country to the status of an economic superpower before it had even achieved corresponding military or political might. From 1774 to 1909, the US economy grew at an average rate of 3.9 percent per year. The period between 1897 and 1914 saw US investments abroad increase fivefold, much of which was linked to the LAC. Not surprisingly, the first American bank to open a branch abroad was not in Europe, but in Buenos Aires just before World War I.[17] This linkage was facilitated through European firms involved in colonial enterprises, as well as through direct US investments in Mexico, Cuba, Central America, and, to some extent, other regions of Latin America. The United States, which had been a net capital importer in the nineteenth century, transformed into the world's largest capital exporter by

1918. It maintained this status until 1981.[18] In the 1930s, the United States used its Export-Import Bank to provide bilateral funding to Latin American countries, partly to counter growing geoeconomic and geopolitical competition from nations like Germany. This historical precedent mirrors today's contest among major powers for influence through development support.[19]

Throughout the twentieth century, the United States' monopoly in providing both private and public goods laid the foundation for its hegemonic legitimacy. However, this monopoly has been challenged by China since 2001, and it has led to what I describe as the erosion of political influence. Political influence indicates one country's ability to shape another country's domestic agenda in its favor through public opinion, legitimacy among local political elites, and foreign policy making. The erosion of US political leadership has thus manifested as a shift away from the US in terms of (a) the preferences of the elite, (b) public opinion, and (c) political alignment within international organizations in the Global South. While China's economic weight does not always translate into Chinese political gains, I show that it certainly erodes US legitimacy.

The findings in this book show that the provision of economic goods plays a crucial role in sustaining the stability of the hegemonic system. When China commenced supplying alternative goods and services in LAC (as well as in Africa and Asia), the initial reaction from the US was positive. This development was perceived as a relief for the US, as it alleviated its responsibility for being the sole supplier of goods in these less prioritized regions. Moreover, there was an expectation that, as China's economy expanded and liberalized, it would gradually align with and support the liberal international order. Twenty years later, however, a more complex story has emerged.

I contend that the shift in economic power dynamics between the US and China has not only altered the global economic landscape but has also provided smaller, developing nations with more options and leverage in the international arena and reshaped their interactions with major powers. I see this dynamic unfolding specifically in relation to the material goods underlying so-called rationalist approaches to international affairs, such as aid, credits, infrastructure projects, and investment capital. Between 2001 and 2020, Chinese economic actors became central in the provision of specific goods and services that improved people's quality of life in the developing world, in some cases surpassing the US in importance.

Traditionally, literature on international relations distinguishes between public and private goods. However, in the context of the goods provided by China to LAC, this distinction is often blurred. In this book, the concept of public goods is treated as an ideal type, recognizing that, in reality, products often possess both public and private characteristics, making their classification far from straightforward. The majority of products generate a spectrum of effects, some of which may be global, others regional or local, and others that oscillate between public and private impacts. Chinese offerings in these regions may not neatly fit into the conventional categories of public or private goods. They can have characteristics of both, or their categorization might shift based on the political and economic dynamics at play.

This complexity around the blurry divide between public and private adds another layer to understanding the nature and impact of Chinese influence in LAC countries through the provision of various goods. For instance, consider a dam, a solar park, or a port constructed by a Chinese enterprise with Chinese financing. While these may initially appear as private goods that primarily benefit the investing entities or specific stakeholders, they also have positive externalities that extend to the general population. Their construction and operation might stimulate local economies, create jobs, or contribute to infrastructure development, yielding benefits that transcend their immediate private utility. Political elites, for their part, utilize these projects to enhance their chances of reelection and to show results to their electorate. The dual nature of such projects illustrates the complex interplay of public and private benefits in the realm of international relations and economic exchanges, particularly in the context of growing Chinese influence in various regions.

A particularly salient example of this dynamic can be found in how Chinese SOEs have executed numerous infrastructure and railway renovation projects in Latin America, often financed by loans from Chinese policy banks. The infrastructure of the San Martín line in Argentina in 2004, for example, was funded with a loan granted by the Export–Import Bank of US\$113 million for the purchase of 24 locomotives and 160 cars provided by the state-owned China Railway Construction Corporation (CRCC). Strictly speaking, these are private assets, the use of which benefits those who pay the train fare and the companies that transport products in their cars. In addition, credit must be paid back with interest, which benefits the lender. Yet while this infrastructure is a private good, it undoubtedly benefits a broad group of citizens, even those who do not consume it directly, and it would have been very difficult for the Argentinean government to finance new infrastructure or renovate existing infrastructure without Chinese players. And, indeed, once the work was completed, the positive outcomes of the project were enormous, including a reduction in emissions, a revaluation of land, and greater safety in the movement of people and goods.

COVID-19 vaccinations offer another significant example of how alternative private goods from China have served the public in LAC in significant ways. At the onset of the COVID-19 pandemic in early 2020, LAC countries were the hardest hit in the world in terms of GDP and deaths per capita. The desperation to vaccinate the population was met with a global shortage of vaccines, especially those developed by Western laboratories (which also showed the best results on human immunity). Faced with a shortage of Pfizer, Moderna, and Johnson & Johnson vaccines, Chile and Brazil negotiated the purchase of thousands of doses from the private Chinese laboratory Sinovac. The doses were paid for at market price, and it was certainly a lucrative deal for the laboratory. But the governments of Brazil and Chile managed to vaccinate the majority of their populations in time to avoid a major crisis. Were Sinovac's vaccines a second-best for the governments of these countries? They were. In a universe where Pfizer's vaccine supply had been sufficient for both rich and poor countries, Chile and Brazil would surely have chosen to buy these vaccines. But that hypothesis is immaterial against the reality these countries faced. Vaccines from Chinese laboratories were the best alternative they had.[20]

My keen interest in the competition between China and the US and the effects of displacement on the provision of goods is fundamentally connected to the US's role as the global hegemon. In scenarios where the hegemon is in decline, it tends to minimize its contribution of public goods to the lowest feasible level. This reduction is based on the expectation that the secondary powers, or followers, will step up their contributions to compensate for the shortfall; a dynamic, I argue, that is particularly evident in LAC. In LAC, the US effectively "delegated" the provision of economic goods to China, and this trend has intensified in recent years. In the long run, this shift has affected US political leadership and made countries dependent on Chinese economic goods. It has, in turn, led the US to implement a reactive policy, which I analyze in Chapter 7.

1.2 THEORETICAL INTERVENTIONS

1.2.1 The Question of Intentionality

A consistent theme throughout this book is that while China does not always successfully convert its economic influence into enhanced soft power or greater alignment in international organizations, it effectively diminishes that of the United States. Notably, this shift may not necessarily be the result of a deliberate strategy by China (something this book does not aim to prove). Rather, I suggest, it is an indirect effect of China's growing structural power in Latin America.

Past scholarship, by contrast, has placed significant emphasis on Chinese intentionality. Indeed, the idea of intentionality has had such a chokehold on discussions of Chinese statecraft that it is nearly impossible to avoid. Following the classics on economic statecraft, a number of scholars examining China's economic statecraft – most notably William Norris and James Reilly – assert that China is "purposeful" and/or "deliberate" in its use of economic tools to achieve its foreign policy objectives.[21] Their work illuminates, for example, the conditions under which Chinese corporations and banks align with the central government. On the opposite end of the spectrum, there is a rising collection of scholars urging us to abandon the assumption that all economic interactions engaged in by great powers must have strategic, diplomatic, or geopolitical motivations. There are those, furthermore, who believe it nearly impossible to deduce foreign policy objectives from official documents or interviews, since these objectives are frequently not made plain.[22] The opacity of nondemocratic regimes makes this task particularly difficult. Other scholars contend that the line between political and economic objectives is blurry in a state-controlled economy like China's.[23] Some suggest that the BRI, for example, is both an economic and political instrument, making it impossible to determine the project's "true" purpose.[24]

For scholars focused on the question of Chinese intentionality, the questions are: How can future academic debate address the challenge of proving intentionality regarding the long-term political consequences of China's economic rise? Which effects have been the result of strategy, and which have been unintended and structural? We are talking about hundreds of actors, including SOEs, privately owned enterprises (POEs), political banks, commercial banks, and provincial actors. Sometimes these actors are even competing against each other. One possibility would be to conceive of the political consequences of a state's economic rise (in this case, China's) as externalities or by-products. This approach is engaged by some of the most notable authors insisting that there is intentional strategy behind Chinese economic statecraft.[25] Another way to address the challenge of proving intentionality is to infer strategy from behavior. That is, to use inductive reasoning to assume that deliberate intentionality has led to specific political results. I myself have used this approach in the past, although it is not without problems.[26] The main concern with assuming intentions from observable results is that a strategy becomes observable only when successful. Thus, there is a confirmatory bias in which failed attempts to exert political influence go unseen. For example, what if a Chinese SOE, despite the efforts of its executives, fails to link the success of a project to the host country's support for China in a multilateral organization?

Authors generally describe the evident contradictions in Chinese foreign policy as a gradual result of the process of opening up to the world since the late 1970s.[27] Political scientist Nicholas Rühlig, for example, characterizes how the Chinese state evolved from a "rule monopolist," defined as a state able to independently make all relevant binding decisions and that maintains exclusive legitimacy and possession of the means of enforcement, into a "rule manager," which sets the frameworks within which a complex mix of states, international institutions, and private sector actors shape politics. Political scientist James Reilly, meanwhile, refers to the Chinese State as an "orchestrator," noting that, at times, it may not be listened to.[28] These authors posit the need to look at other actors affecting Chinese foreign policy beyond the state, such as private and mixed capital enterprises and international organizations.[29] Looking beyond state intentions and behaviors in the intentionality debate offers a more nuanced understanding of China's economic influence. Shifting focus to local actors and multi-stakeholder interactions provides fresh insights into the mechanisms and outcomes of economic statecraft. This approach examines how local agency and complex multi-actor dynamics shape the implementation and effects of China's economic activities.

1.2.2 The Role of Local Agency

A fundamental theoretical tenet of this book is that the efficacy of China's economic statecraft in the developing world is dependent on the agency of domestic elites. Economic statecraft is said to be effective if a strategy succeeds in turning economic means into political gains. Yet, not only has the literature remained overly focused on intentionality, it has ignored the role of the target state. In this case, I highlight how LAC countries have come to view China as a provider of goods in absolute terms and relative to the US.[30]

I contend that two factors determine how much of what China offers to target countries has been demanded by domestic actors. The first factor is the degree to which China has become an outside option as a supplier of the same goods provided by – or goods that are complementary to those provided by – other major powers. The second factor is the extent to which these goods address domestic developmental needs. The agency of consumer countries for goods offered by China can either be direct (i.e., agency exercised by the central government to procure or consume Chinese goods) or indirect. In the case of indirect agency, the central government can orchestrate companies or other subnational actors to procure or consume a good offered by China (e.g., by encouraging a national enterprise to jointly venture with a Chinese enterprise to raise needed funds to deliver necessary infrastructure, as is the case with the Chancay Port), or it can delegate procurement or consumption to large corporations or subnational governments (as when provincial governments are given autonomy to bypass national governments in negotiating investment projects or aid from China, as occurred in Brazil during COVID-19). Just as China orchestrates the action of its economic actors, as shown by James Reilly,[31] the countries that consume goods offered by China exercise agency through a multitude of actors (a dynamic discussed further in Chapter 4).

Let's take one of China's largest multinational enterprises (MNEs), Huawei, as an example. William Norris's theory, which is based on state control, suggests that states – particularly those with strong enforcement and monitoring abilities like China's – can incentivize or deter specific behaviors in firms by implementing measures that either penalize undesirable actions or reward desirable ones. Meanwhile, James Reilly's orchestration theory suggests that top leaders implement some economic statecraft initiatives while delegating authority to line ministries and government agencies. In turn, these agencies deploy orchestration techniques to mobilize and manage financial institutions, enterprises, and regional authorities. How can Norris's state control theory and Reilly's orchestration theory improve our understanding of the varying degrees of Huawei's success in penetrating markets when considering, for example, the tech giant's evident interest in expanding into foreign markets and winning bids to deploy 5G infrastructure? While some nations, such as Costa Rica, took restrictive measures against Huawei fairly early on, other Latin American countries, such as Colombia, deepened their connections with the company.[32] Similar divergences occurred between 2001 and 2020 throughout LAC in a wide range of sectors, such as energy, mining, and logistics (see Chapter 3). In this example, it is reasonable to assume that an independent variable utilized by both Norris and

Reilly – the sender's control/relationship with a specified commercial actor (in this case, China's control of Huawei) – is held constant because the corporation is the same in each location (Costa Rica and Colombia). Yet, neither the state control nor the orchestration framework explains Huawei's strategic success or failure in these two distinct countries. To put it another way, the existing frameworks fall short of offering a valuable explanation for how China's overseas economic connections influence the interests and policy decisions of other governments. Local agency, I suggest, is paramount to the equation.

China, like any other country, may want to maximize its economic resources for political aims, but the effectiveness of such efforts will rely on whether the target nation finds such resources to be in demand. Whether the target nation determines Chinese resources to be in demand, in turn, depends on whether there are any other suppliers for such resources. Foregrounding the push-and-pull of these dynamics, this book thus focuses on the area where supply and demand converge, or where proactive economic statecraft is successful in accomplishing its policy goal because there is a market for the Chinese goods delivered to the target country.

1.2.3 "Three to Tango": Toward a New Theory of Economic Statecraft

In sum, I argue that the existing literature tends to overstate the importance of senders (in our case, China) in interstate contacts impacted by the instruments of economic statecraft.[33] Recent research on China–Latin American relations demonstrates that smaller states and their domestic political interest groups can greatly diminish the economic influence of major powers.[34] Authors studying China's relations with Southeast Asian countries have also called for a more inclusive study of statecraft in which the target countries be addressed as active actors who can shape and affect the dynamics of a given relationship.[35] What we need is a theory that allows us to study the political effects of China's economic rise without having to accept the validity of the two core assumptions embedded in existing theories and frameworks: firstly, that there is always political intentionality behind the use of economic means; and secondly, that target states are passive agents. In addition, such a theory should discuss the political effects of economic influence and be empirically operationalizable in a clear manner.

To address this need, the theory presented in this book explains economic displacement as a result of the provision of alternative goods to target states (in this case, the provision of Chinese goods to LAC) and the extent to which these goods address domestic development needs. It utilizes a "three to tango" approach, emphasizing how target countries actively engage with China to fulfill their local development needs when the US does not offer good enough alternatives. This approach complements the existing literature on economic statecraft and geoeconomics, which often overlooks the role of target countries in determining the effectiveness of China's use of economic tools for political ends. It shows that as China's economic influence expanded, China emerged as a competing provider of goods; although its success in this role has varied in extent across different countries. Consequently, the United States faces increasing challenges when it comes to resonating with overseas audiences, which has led to a decline in its soft power and support within international organizations. The political effectiveness or ineffectiveness of Chinese economic means, my theory demonstrates, depends on the local demand for the economic goods offered.

1.3 DEFINING ECONOMIC WEIGHT AND ECONOMIC DISPLACEMENT

1.3.1 Economic Weight and the Concept of Structural Power

The hypothesis tested in this book is that economic displacement has the capacity to result in a country's loss of political influence in a sphere where it has been historically dominant. In order to test this hypothesis, the chapters to come introduce the concept of economic weight and define how it has contributed to the economic displacement of the US by China in LAC.

The classic definition of power in international relations (IR) is the so-called relational one. Developed by Robert Dahl and disseminated by way of the classical realism school of IR theory, it focuses on the power of A to get B to do something they would not otherwise do.[36] While similarly dyadic, Susan Strange's definition of "structural power," by contrast, emphasizes positional power – a power that does not imply intentionality. In Strange's words, "structural power [...] is the power to shape and determine the structures of the global political economy within which other states, their political institutions, their economic enterprises and (not least) their scientists and other professional people have to operate."[37] While Strange's books do not operationalize this variable, her theory of power is more useful than the classic definition for the purposes of

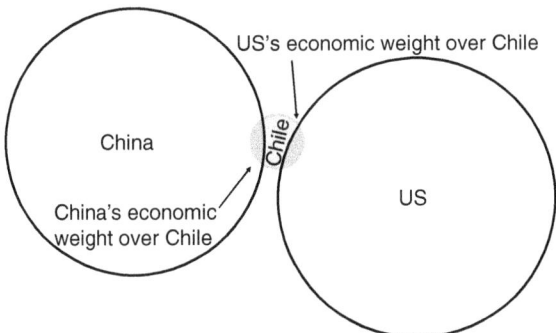

FIGURE 1.4 Visualizing economic weight

proposing a concept that (a) does not depend on China's intentionality, and (b) recognizes the agency of target countries.

Drawing on this definition of structural power, the concept I propose, "economic weight," reflects the power exerted by Country A on Country B through economic interactions. This influence is quantified based on the annual total of capital that Country B accrues from economic entities originating from Country A, adjusted in proportion to the size of Country B's economy. Significantly, this concept also encompasses the relative scale of Country A's economic capabilities in comparison to those of competing nations. In this sense, the economic weight of Country A on Country B exerts structural power on how Country C relates with Country A. Notably, this conceptualization does not presuppose any intentional outcomes on Country B as a result of these economic interactions. It focuses on the structural impact rather than the intentionality of deliberate strategy of the influencing country.

If we were to express economic weight graphically, we could think of circles representing the size of a country's economy. Let's say Country A is a small country (Chile, for example) and country B is a large country, like China. The collective impact of hundreds of Chinese economic actors engaging in economic activities within Chile can be conceptualized as having an "economic weight" on Chile's economy. The influence, or impact, of this economic weight can thus be represented visually as a shaded area of overlap, symbolizing the extent to which Chinese economic involvement permeates and influences the Chilean economic landscape. This shaded area can be compared to the weight that a third country has on Chile, which, in this book, is the United States. In Figure 1.4, for example, we see a graphic representation of Chinese and US economic weight on Chile, which in this figure looks relatively even.

Operationalizing economic weight as a positional phenomenon presents a distinct advantage: It recognizes that power is fundamentally relational rather than merely an attribute that varies over time or is specific to individual countries. Traditional measures of power, such as the widely recognized Composite Index of National Capability (CINC), tend to be unidirectional and do not account for the dyadic nature of power relations between countries.[38] This approach overlooks the reality that power is most meaningfully understood in the context of relationships.[39] Furthermore, conventional definitions often focus exclusively on power as emanating from states, disregarding the influence exerted by non-state actors. Works on structural power in domestic politics highlight this oversight in mainstream IR scholarship, noting that the IR preoccupation with the power of large states often marginalizes the significant role that the structure of global capitalism plays in elevating large firms to the status of international political actors in their own right.[40] This view has recently been recognized in the "global China" research agenda.[41] The concept of structural power is inherently interdependent, which aligns with my perspective: Power emerges from the control that firms and capital holders wield over business decisions that are critical for economic growth and how they condition other actors. This framing underscores the dependence of states on private investors, situating these non-state actors as pivotal in international power dynamics. By considering economic weight in this broader, more interconnected context, we gain a more comprehensive understanding of the multifaceted nature of power in the global political economy.[42]

In her seminal work *States and Markets*, Strange identifies four pillars that underpin a nation's power: (a) the security structure; (b) the production structure; (c) the financial structure; and (d) the knowledge structure. My concept of economic weight specifically captures a country's structural power within the realms of finance and production.[43] This focus is deliberate, as these are the domains where the current rivalry between China and the United States is most pronounced. While the US maintains a clear advantage in the security and knowledge structures,[44] competition with China is more evident and critical in the financial and production sectors. This selective emphasis allows for a more nuanced understanding of the current geopolitical dynamics, particularly in relation to the shifting balance of economic power between these two global giants. One of the strengths of my conceptual framework, which I will delve into in Chapters 3 and 4, is its capacity to incorporate the dynamics of "outside options" for target states to the traditional notions of economic statecraft. Ultimately, the effectiveness of China in converting its economic prowess into political clout, especially between 2001 and 2020, has largely depended on the extent to which it represented a viable outside option for LAC countries. Similarly, the effectiveness of US economic statecraft has weakened as China has increasingly offered alternative goods to those used instrumentally by the US. This perspective offers a nuanced understanding of the interplay between economic power and political influence in international relations.

In the discipline of international relations, there has been a debate between those who are optimistic and those who are pessimistic about the systemic effects of the China–US rivalry.[45] This debate specifically concerns the possibility of a rising China challenging US hegemony. It is therefore essential to agree on a measurable definition of key concepts, something that has not always been possible. I believe that the concept of economic weight, as I have defined it, has great potential for encompassing the competition for global influence between China and the United States because it is easily operationalizable (as I will show in Chapter 2). Moreover, it shares some of its central intuitions with other debates, such as soft balancing, forum shopping, and regime complexity, which have also been used to study the China–US rivalry.[46]

1.3.2 The Dynamics of Economic Displacement

In my approach to understanding the economic weight and competition between China and the US when it comes to providing alternative goods in the developing world, I also introduce the possibility – or potential outcome – of "economic displacement." This concept is defined as the phenomenon that occurs when the economic weight of Country A (a rising power; for instance, China) on Country B (a developing nation) surpasses the economic weight of Country C (the established power; for example, the US) on Country B. Essentially, the dynamic of economic displacement captures a shift in economic weight, highlighting the moment when one nation's economic presence and influence in another country becomes more significant than that of a competing nation. There is a very useful metaphor: As with a solar eclipse, economic displacement depends not only on both the size of the celestial bodies (the gross size of the US and Chinese economies) but also on their proximity to each target country (measured by the shaded area of economic weight). To illustrate this graphically, let us compare two moments: the year 2001 and the year 2018. If we were to express the relative economic weight of

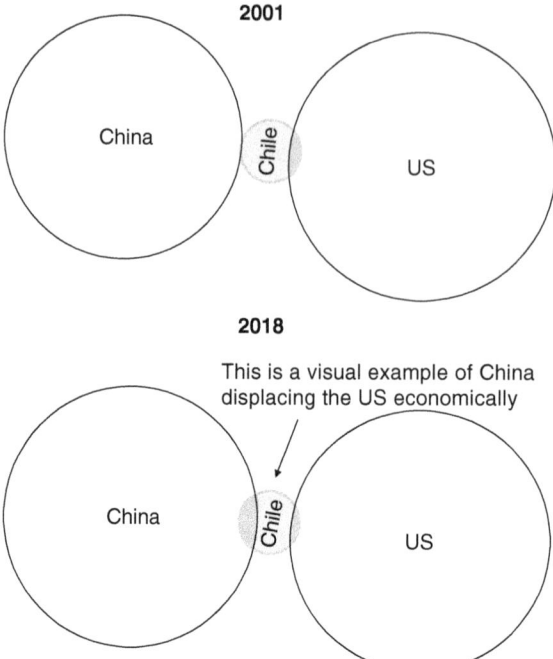

FIGURE 1.5 Visualizing economic displacement

China and the US on Chile in that year, the figure would show that the United States had a greater economic weight than China (which, in fact, had an almost nonexistent weight). On the other hand, in 2018, China's economic weight in Chile was greater than that of the US (Figure 1.5). In a side-by-side visual of these two years, we are witnessing the dynamic of economic displacement wherein China's economic weight has surpassed that of the US in Chile.

The dyadic measurement of economic weight and economic displacement allows me to account for the fact that China's economic growth has taken precedence over the pre-existing US relationship with smaller countries.[47] As China's economic weight has grown in certain countries, so has the possibility of strengthening its position vis-à-vis the US, especially when China can boast an outside option in a bargaining situation. This possibility is in play every time China provides a good that meets the needs of a smaller country and offers it on terms comparable to or better than those of the US, whether it be investments, credits, or trade opportunities. Displacement is most likely to occur, in particular, when China's economic weight has grown and the US's economic weight has diminished over time. The greater China's economic weight, the more credible it will be when a small country threatens to lean toward China instead of the US. The phenomenon of displacement is more complex than it may initially appear, however. Rather than being a sudden event, it's a gradual process that unfolds over years. This process can be measured in two ways: as a continuous variable (showing gradual change, as I illustrated in Figure 1.2) or as a discrete variable (showing distinct stages, as I illustrated in Figure 1.3). Throughout the book, I primarily use a simplified measurement, focusing on displacement as a dichotomous (yes/no) variable. This approach pinpoints the moment when China surpasses the US in economic influence.[48] However, I also present additional evidence using the continuous variable to capture the nuanced, gradual nature of the process by which China has overtaken US economic influence through the provision of alternative goods.

Notably, this trend is not irreversible. As I discuss in Chapter 2, the US has the potential to reverse its displacement by China in LAC. Thus, the long-term outcome remains uncertain; in 40 years, we could see the US reversing the trend, maintaining its current position, or being completely displaced by China. I explore the policy implications of these various scenarios in Chapter 7.

1.4 BOOK OVERVIEW

1.4.1 Data and Methodology

This book originated as an empirical inquiry aimed at answering questions for which data was not yet available. I thus started by creating the databases I needed, using the highest level of disaggregation possible (e.g., down to the company level), before scaling up to national and regional levels.[49] I have also been capitalizing on data development since around 2015.[50] As a result, this project benefits from years of systematic data collection, disaggregation, and curation on investment, trade, foreign aid, and credit. Each chapter utilizes different data tailored to its specific objective, integrating both quantitative and qualitative methods.

To measure the economic weight of China and the US, I systematized investment, aid, trade, and credit data using existing sources and my own data collection from secondary sources. An important aspect of disaggregation is to avoid the biases of nation-level statistics as much as possible.[51] For assessing the effects of economic displacement on the erosion of political influence, I relied on pre-existing survey data, covering both public opinion and the views of political elites. Additionally, I incorporated quantitative analysis of parliamentary debate texts. To evaluate the loss of political influence in international bodies, I coded data based on existing sources for the United Nations General Assembly (UNGA) as well as original data for use in relation to the Organization of American States (OAS) and United Nations Human Rights Council (UNHRC) cases. Furthermore, for two case studies on the demand for Chinese substitute goods and for insights used in the conclusion, I used qualitative data – namely, in-depth interviews with over forty politicians and business leaders – and government data obtained from public websites.

Each chapter provides detail regarding the data used, and the Appendix provides an in-depth explanation of how the original data was gathered. In addition, the data is made available to readers through an online repository for consultation.

1.4.2 Roadmap

This book consists of seven chapters, divided into two major parts. In the first part of the book, I explore the question of how China has managed to economically displace the US within its traditional spheres of influence despite not surpassing the US in global economic standings. This part is comprised of four chapters, including this one.

Chapter 2 operationalizes the concepts of economic weight and economic displacement as defined in the parts above, demonstrating how China has increased its presence in the Global South while the United States has seen a notable decline since 2001. This chapter is significant as it presents evidence that China has economically displaced the US in much of LAC; a shift attributed not only to China's growing economic influence but also to the US's decline. Chapter 3 investigates whether Chinese entities have filled the economic gaps left by the withdrawal of US actors from the region, examining the causality between the US's diminishing economic influence and the influx of Chinese economic players in the region. The chapter reveals that neither the commodity boom nor the ideology of Latin American presidents sufficiently explains China's remarkable growth. It illustrates that the rapid economic displacement of the US by China was facilitated by Chinese actors becoming alternative suppliers of goods in the region – a causal mechanism overlooked in previous analyses.

Chapter 4 presents two case studies based on qualitative evidence and in-depth interviews to explore how domestic actors in South America have exercised agency in demanding alternative goods from Chinese economic actors. Focusing on South American countries where economic displacement has been more pronounced, the chapter illustrates how political elites utilized Chinese goods to demonstrate their ability to deliver solutions to constituents. These cases show that the agency of South American states has not always been exercised directly, but sometimes through subnational actors. The first case study exemplifies top-down dynamics, examining the construction and financing of two dams in Argentine Patagonia by Chinese actors. The second case study – which focuses on the most significant port project in the hemisphere – illustrates bottom-up dynamics whereby businesses and subnational governments have engaged with China independently of traditional nation-state channels. In this instance, the Peruvian state played an orchestrating role in the project but delegated agency to local entrepreneurs, demonstrating how subnational actors can engage with China independently and how national governments can benefit from these interactions.

In Part II of the book, I ask: To what extent does economic displacement translate into a loss of the US's political leverage in other countries? Essentially, this part of the book considers the political consequences of the displacement phenomenon for US political leadership. I explore two causal paths that explain a loss of US political leverage: (a) the deterioration of the US's valuation in the domestic arena in terms of public opinion and (more importantly) the perspective of political elites; and (b) the US's increased inability to influence voting in international organizations in the international arena. The hypothesis is the same for both mechanisms: Economic displacement hampers the US's ability to exert political leverage because it dilutes the effectiveness of the use of economic incentives (i.e., sticks and carrots).[52]

In Chapter 5, I investigate the effect of economic displacement on the deterioration of US soft power in domestic politics and among political elites. To do this, I examine a multi-country survey that asks about the role of China and the US in relation to their capacity to provide solutions to the problems faced by Latin America. Then, focusing specifically on national legislators, I analyze a sample of over 2,500 legislators spanning ten years across fifteen countries to conduct an initial assessment of the impact of economic displacement on their foreign policy preferences. My analysis confirms the trend: Economic displacement erodes legislators' valuation of the United States. Meanwhile, China's economic growth empowers incumbent governments, regardless of their ideology, by allowing them to present themselves as effective managers providing development solutions to their voters; a dynamic I explore further in relation to the Argentine legislative debate on the installation of a China-controlled space station in Patagonia.

Chapter 6 examines another facet of how China's economic displacement undermines US political leverage: its capacity to generate alignment in international organizations. Existing literature has shown that China's economic rise has enabled it to form coalitions and garner support in international bodies. However, little is known about how this affects the US's ability to influence countries where economic displacement has occurred. In this context, I investigate instances within the United Nations General Assembly, the UN Human Rights Council (UNHRC), and the Organization of American States (OAS). My findings indicate that countries' alignment with the US decreases in these three forums when displacement occurs.

Chapter 7 of the book summarizes my key findings and derives three major policy lessons from them. The lessons my work illuminates may, I believe, define the future landscape of competition between China and the United States in LAC, and they are readily extended to other regions of the Global South.

2

China's Economic Displacement of the US in Latin America

This chapter undertakes the substantial task of demonstrating where and when the United States experienced economic contraction and China subsequently expanded its economic presence. This endeavor required extensive data collection and the development of a straightforward, easily replicable metric for measuring economic influence, understandable to a wide audience and other researchers. To achieve this, I created indices quantifying the economic weight of both the United States and China. These indices then served as the foundation for my calculation of economic displacement. This methodology has provided a clear, quantifiable analysis of the economic dynamics between these two major powers in the context of LAC.

To illuminate the dynamics at play, we must understand how Chinese and US economic weight evolved over time and across world regions. The next section details the methodological choices and data sources that were used to arrive at a measurement of these phenomena. In addition, I present the Economic Weight Index, which shows that China increased its influence in the Americas more than in any other region. It also shows that, since 2000, the US has reduced its influence in Latin America. Establishing these trends through data-driven analysis lays critical groundwork for the next two chapters, where I analyze the demand-side for Chinese goods in Latin America and the political consequences that economic displacement has had.

2.1 MEASURING CHINESE ECONOMIC WEIGHT

By operationalizing the Economic Weight Index for China, we can measure China's economic influence over a third country while taking into account the multitude of Chinese actors operating simultaneously. The index enables us to evaluate the diverse and concurrent activities of Chinese entities – from state-led initiatives to private-sector engagements – and offers a nuanced view of China's growing role and impact in the global economic landscape.

China's economic weight in each region of the world is calculated as the sum of a country's exports to China, aid received from China, the stock of corporate investments, and loans from policy and multilateral development banks in which China has a majority stake. The amounts expressed in US dollars were deflated to express constant values over time. In total, this sum measures the annual total of capital that Country B accrues from economic entities originating from Country A, adjusted in proportion to the size of Country B's economy. A value expressed in billions of dollars, this sum is then divided by the GDP of each country. Thus, the index is expressed as follows:

$$\text{Chinese economic weight} = \frac{\Sigma(\text{trade} + \text{aid} + \text{investment} + \text{loans})_{it}}{\text{GDP}_{it}}$$

Where t is the year and i is the country. For calculations at the regional level, both the denominator and the numerator of the units (i) are aggregated into regions (r).

For the sake of comparing the economic weight of a country across time or across regions, I have set the year 2001 as base 100. This means that all regions start the year at the value 100, and the growth or decrease of each region is relative to that year's value. For example:

$$\text{Chinese economic weight index}_{it} = \frac{\text{Chinese economic weight}_{it}}{\text{Chinese economic weight}_{i\,2001}} * 100$$

A score above 100 indicates that a region's economic weight has increased compared to 2001, while a score below 100 suggests a decrease. Specifically, a value of 200 means that the economic weight has doubled since 2001. Conversely, a value of 50 indicates that it has halved.

Table 2.1 summarizes the variables included in this index and their primary sources, providing a clear overview of the data used. For those interested in a more in-depth understanding of the data's coding and systematization, I provide detailed information in the appendix (Appendix B.1). This approach ensures transparency and replicability, allowing other researchers to understand and apply the index in their work. To compare the indexes across regions, I use the UN classifications of large regions and sub regions.[1]

TABLE 2.1 *Variables used to operationalize Chinese economic weight*

Variable	Operationalization	Years	Countries	Source
Trade	Exports to China (million US$)	2001–2020	185	United Nations Comtrade
Aid	Official Development Assistance (million US$)	2001–2020	185	Dreher et al. (2022), CIDCA, Telias and Urdinez (2021)
FDI	Chinese investments (million US$)	2001–2020	185	Scissors (2011), Dussel Peters (2020), fDi Markets, Mergr, and Urdinez and Myers (2024)
Loans	Loans by Chinese Policy Banks (CDB and Ex-Im Bank), the AIIB, and the NDB (million US$)	2001–2020	185	Dreher et al. (2022), AIIB, NDB, Ray and Myers (2023)
Size of the economy	GDP (million US$)	2001–2020	191	World Bank data

AIIB, Asian Infrastructure Investment Bank; CDB, China Development Bank; NDB, New Development Bank.

2.1.1 China's Economic Weight in LAC in Comparative Perspective

An analysis of the Economic Weight Index on a global scale, with a focus on the total sums across continents, reveals significant regional trends since 2001 (see Figure 2.1). The data clearly shows that Chinese economic growth has been substantial, ranging from 9 to 15 times its size at the start of the twenty-first century across all regions of the world. Notably, LAC emerged as the region with the most pronounced growth in comparison to 2001, highlighting a significant increase in China's economic influence there. By 2020, China's economic weight in LAC was 15 times greater than it had been two decades earlier, with the most substantial growth observed between 2010 and 2020. This dramatic increase underscores the extent of China's expanding economic presence and influence in LAC and marks a historically unprecedented shift in the region's economic landscape.[2]

Figure 2.1 shows data on a scenario that several academics have already described: from 2001 to 2021, the relationship between China and LAC reached levels never before seen.[3] Scholars frequently note that,

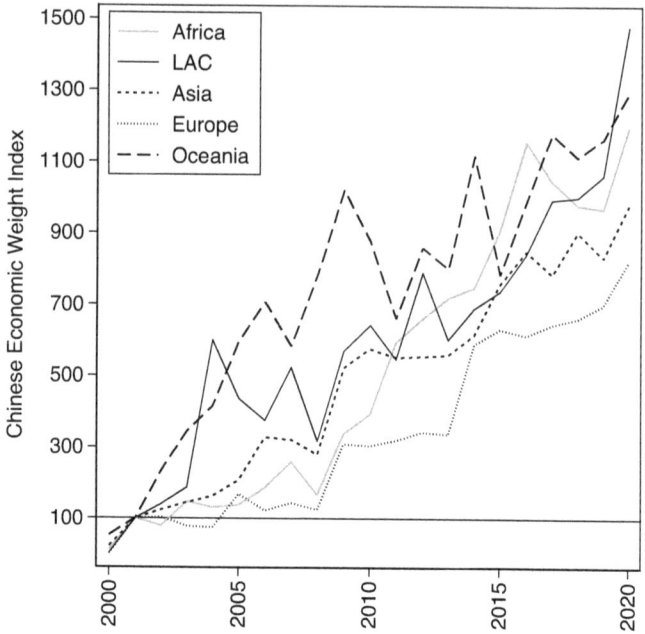

FIGURE 2.1 Chinese Economic Weight Index by continent, 2000–2020

by 2014, China had become the region's second-largest economic partner and a major foreign direct investor for most LAC countries. Several nations in the region developed strategic ties with Beijing and received substantial credit.[4] During this time, the material needs of LAC nations led to a preference for Chinese loans, which were free from the macroeconomic conditionalities typical of International Monetary Fund (IMF) loans. Chinese loans also differed from World Bank and Inter-American Development Bank (IADB) lending, which primarily focused on social services and assistance for the public sector and civil society.[5] Instead, Chinese lending concentrated on infrastructure, electricity, energy, and water projects. Between 2005 and 2020, Chinese policy banks invested a total of US$136 billion in LAC, surpassing the finance provided by the US International Development Finance Corporation (US$9.7 billion) and the World Bank (US$31.2 billion) during the same period.[6] Chinese firms became particularly active in renewable energy projects in the region, with Chinese policy banks providing six times more credit than Western banks for energy projects.[7]

When analyzing the Economic Weight Index by its individual components in LAC and other regions, trade emerges as the most significant driver

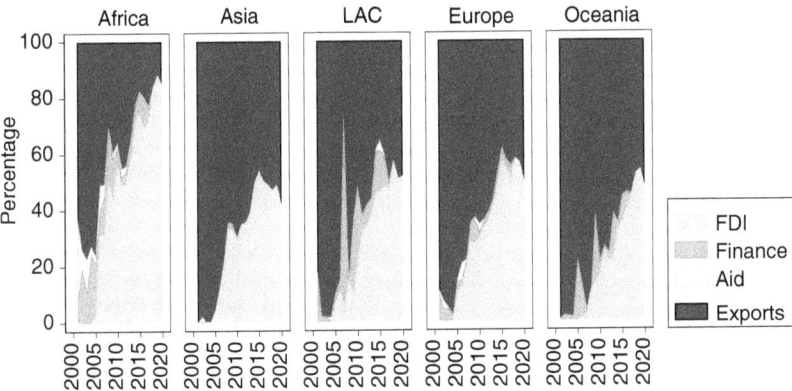

FIGURE 2.2 Components of Chinese economic weight by region, 2001–2020

of China's economic impact on the region (as depicted in Figure 2.2).[8] China's role as a major consumer of Latin American exports has been the key factor in its escalating economic weight in the region. However, it's noteworthy that China's investment stock in Latin America has also grown substantially over time, with a similar trend observed in other regions. In fact, in recent years, Chinese investment has become as relevant as trade in terms of economic influence. By 2020, the impact of China's investment in the region was comparable to that of trade, marking a significant shift in the composition of China's economic presence in LAC. Indeed, this evolution suggests a more complex and multifaceted economic relationship developing between China and LAC countries. While trade remains a crucial component, the growing importance of Chinese investment indicates a deepening and diversification of economic ties.

The other components of the index – loans and aid – have had less influence comparatively, although finance had more relevance in LAC between 2007 and 2017 than in any other region. Chinese loans from policy banks were booming until 2017, but their relevance has diminished since then. Chinese aid has remained relatively minor during the years analyzed, especially when compared to the billions of dollars circulating through trade and investment flows.

Latin America, a region comprising three distinct sub-regions – South America, Central America (including Mexico in this analysis), and the Caribbean countries – exhibits varied economic dynamics. A closer examination of the evolution of economic weight by sub-region reveals that South America has experienced the most significant growth. As depicted in Figure 2.3, this growth is more than three times the magnitude of that

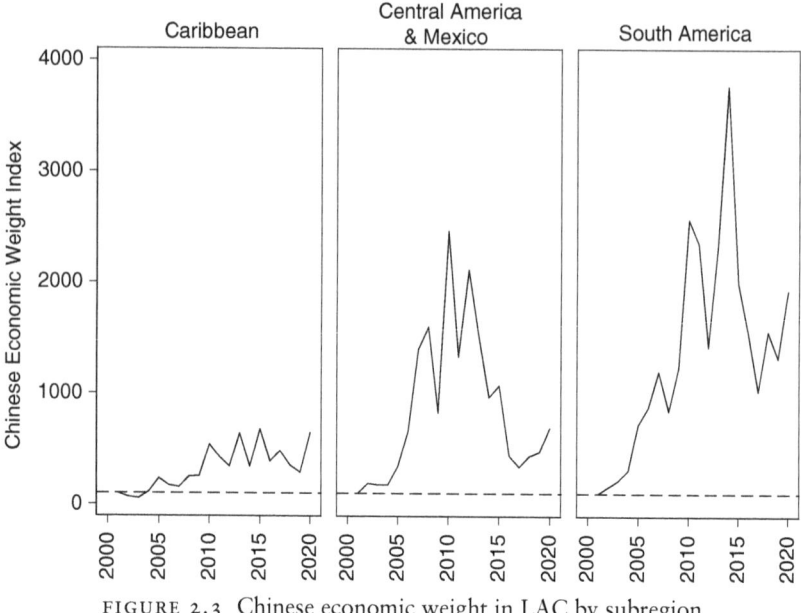

FIGURE 2.3 Chinese economic weight in LAC by subregion

seen in Central America and the Caribbean. This finding is particularly noteworthy given that, according to World Bank data, South America accounted for 82 percent of LAC's total GDP by 2020 and 67 percent of its total population. The observation suggests that "Latin America," as a unified analytical category, may not be as useful in understanding China's role in the region after all. Instead, two distinct clusters emerge:

1. South America, where China's economic weight has increased almost twentyfold over the entire period, with a peak in 2015 reaching 40 times its size in 2001.
2. Mexico, Central America, and the Caribbean, where a more moderate increase of about sevenfold is observed, with a larger observable footprint between 2008 and 2014.

This differentiation is crucial for developing a nuanced understanding of the economic dynamics within LAC as well as China's influence on the region. It highlights the need for more region-specific analyses, as the impact and nature of China's economic engagement clearly varies significantly between sub-regions.[9] Moreover, the stark contrast in China's economic weight between South America and the rest of LAC raises important questions about the factors driving these differences. Relevant factors could include variations in natural resources, trade patterns, investment opportunities, and geopolitical considerations. Future research could explore these factors to provide a more comprehensive understanding of China's differentiated economic impact across Latin America.

2.1.2 Envisioning Latin America without China's Economic Influence

What would Latin America look like without China's economic footprint? Envisioning the region without China's economic influence is challenging. However, a close approximation of such a counterfactual can be found by examining countries in the region that maintain diplomatic relations with Taiwan instead of China. This political choice effectively excludes them from direct Chinese investments, aid, and loans, while also necessitating trade via third countries, which can have significant economic implications.

To quantify this economic impact, I collaborated with Tom Long, Professor of International Relations at Warwick University, to calculate a counterfactual scenario to assess how much Chinese investment and finance Paraguay – a country with diplomatic ties to Taiwan – has potentially foregone.[10] We then subtracted the actual aid and investments received from Taiwan to arrive at what we term the "Taiwan cost." This method provides a tangible measure of the economic difference between Latin American countries where Chinese actors are active and those where they are not. For a full analysis, we then employed two distinct samples, beginning with a regional similarity-based sample consisting of twenty-five Latin American countries. This allowed for a close examination of specific dynamics and trends in China's economic influence in Latin America and provided insights that are particularly relevant to the region.

Our findings revealed that, per year and on average, Latin American countries recognizing Taiwan received approximately US$850 million less in combined investment, aid, and finance from China compared to countries recognizing China. Of course, it's important to note that this figure is an average and would vary depending on the size of the economy in question. This approach not only quantifies the potential economic implications of diplomatic choices but also highlights the significant role that China has come to play in the LAC region's economic landscape. It underscores the complex interplay between diplomatic relations and economic opportunities, suggesting that countries' political decisions regarding China and Taiwan can have substantial and measurable economic consequences.

2.1.3 Limitations in the Chinese Economic Weight Index

In the process of collecting data with which to analyze China's economic weight, I faced five key challenges that should be noted:

1. Uneven levels of data curation: The level of data curation is significantly higher for Latin America than for other continents. However, while the index for other regions could be refined, it still captures the broader trend of China's economic weight beyond LAC in figures that compare it with other regions.
2. Starting point of data collection: Data collection began in 2001, coinciding with China's increased engagement in Latin America and its accession to the World Trade Organization (WTO). Preliminary data from the 1990s showed a limited Chinese presence in Latin America, with low rankings in trade, investment, loans, and aid except in isolated cases like mining investments in Peru. The year 2001 serves as a milestone indicating the beginning of China's growing influence in the region.
3. Challenges in collecting investment data: Foreign direct investment (FDI) data was the most complex to code and the most challenging to obtain reliable values for. Economic Commission for Latin America and the Caribbean (ECLAC) reports suggest that China lagged behind the EU and the US in investment in the region, but preliminary data analysis indicates China might be the primary source of investment flows in many Latin American countries today. The data published by the Chinese government lacks transparency, often listing Caribbean tax havens as the primary recipients of Chinese investment without discriminating the final destination of investment amounts.[11] To address these challenges, I adopted a multifaceted approach to collecting data, including interviews with ECLAC officials and creating a database from various sources. Primary sources included the China Global Investment Tracker by the American Enterprise Institute and Dussel Peters's CECHIMEX FDI Monitor. These were supplemented by data from fDi Markets and Mergr, plus data collected by Urdinez and Myers. This triangulation of data, along with meticulous project-by-project analysis, led to the creation of a reliable database. According to my estimate, LAC received US$265 billion in investments from Chinese companies between 2001 and 2020, exceeding the estimate by the China Global Investment Tracker but well below what was reported by MOFCOM (see Table B.2 in the Appendix).

4. Clarity regarding Chinese credits: Distinguishing promised credits from those actually disbursed is crucial for this kind of project.[12] Due to difficulties in obtaining comprehensive data, the estimates were thus based on a combination of Ray and Myers's database and project-by-project comparison with AidChina data. Additionally, credits granted by the AIIB, which focuses mainly on Asia, as well as those taken by Brazil from the New Development Bank, were considered. Swaps in Chinese currency signed with Latin American countries were included only if activated, as in the case of Argentina. Commercial bank credits, such as those from ICBC, were not taken into account due to a lack of data on the amounts for all countries.
5. Foreign aid clarification: The definition and nature of Chinese aid differ from Western aid. The primary data source was AidChina, supplemented by information from the China International Development Cooperation Agency (CIDCA) website and data developed by Telias and Urdinez (2022) covering aid during the COVID-19 pandemic years (2020–2022).

These challenges highlight the complexity of quantifying China's economic influence in Latin America. Despite obstacles, the index offers a more comprehensive picture of China's regional footprint than previously available, revealing the significant role of Chinese investment, aid, and finance amidst data opacity.

2.2 MEASURING THE ECONOMIC WEIGHT OF THE UNITED STATES

In this section, I present the US Economic Weight Index, which I developed using a methodology analogous to that of the Chinese index. The economic weight of the US in each world region is calculated by summing up several key financial components. These include a country's exports to the US, aid received from the United States Agency for International Development (USAID), the stock of investments made by US companies, and loans from international organizations and multilateral development banks where the US holds a majority stake (plus its policy bank, the US International Development Finance Corporation (DFC)). All amounts are expressed in US dollars and have been adjusted for inflation to represent constant values over time. This aggregation provides a measure of the annual capital that a country (referred to as "Country B" in the definition) earns from economic activities associated with the US (referred to as "Country A").

To contextualize this sum within the broader economic landscape of each country, it is divided by the GDP of that country. This step ensures that the index reflects the US economic weight relative to the size of Country B's economy. As a result, the index is expressed in terms of a ratio or percentage, illustrating the proportion of a country's economic activity that is directly linked to the US. This approach allows for a nuanced understanding of US economic influence, both in absolute terms and relative to the size and capacity of each individual economy.

$$\text{US economic weight} = \frac{\sum(\text{trade} + \text{aid} + \text{investment} + \text{loans})_{it}}{\text{GDP}_{it}}$$

To facilitate a meaningful comparison of a country's economic weight over time and across different continents, the year 2001 is established as the baseline, with a base value set at 100. This year is particularly significant as it marks the beginning of the twenty-year period under analysis, in which we are focusing on the economic competition between China and the United States. The data collection for my study spans from 1989 to 2021. While my primary focus is on the period from 2001 to 2020 (to align with the timeframe of China's growing influence), having data from the previous years is crucial for establishing context. The period leading up to 2000 is especially important for understanding the baseline from which I begin my analysis.

Before the year 2000, China's role in regions like Latin America, Africa, and Europe was relatively marginal, and it did not pose a significant counterbalance to US influence. Meanwhile, the years between 1990 and 2001 represent the height of US unipolarity. During this time, the United States's considerable economic weight was reflected globally through the widespread adoption of the Washington Consensus, a set of economic policy principles that emphasized free-market capitalism. This period is thus critical for understanding the extent of US economic dominance and its influence across the world, including and particularly in Latin America. Having data that predates 2001 is also valuable because it provides a comprehensive backdrop against which the shifts in global economic dynamics can be better understood. Specifically, it illuminates the transformation of the US's economic stature in the twentieth century, setting the stage for the comparative analysis of the US and China's economic weights in the subsequent period.

By setting the year 2001 as the reference point, all continents begin the period with an index value of 100. Changes in the economic weight of each region are then measured relative to this base year's value. This means that any growth or decline in a region's economic weight is calculated in relation to its status in 2001. For instance, an index value of 150 in a subsequent year would indicate a 50 percent increase in economic weight since 2001, while a value of 80 would signify a 20 percent decrease. This approach provides a clear and standardized method for tracking and comparing the shifts in US economic influence across different regions over the two-decade period analyzed here, and it allows for an objective assessment of how the US's economic relationships with various parts of the world have evolved in the context of its competition with China. The calculation for the US's index value is as follows:

$$\text{US economic influence index}_{it} = \frac{\text{US economic influence}_{it}}{\text{US economic influence}_{i\,2001}} * 100$$

The US Economic Weight Index is operationalized using a set of variables detailed in Table 2.2. When developing this index, two primary concerns were addressed. First, ensuring that the index is sufficiently generalizable so that an equivalent index can be created for China. Second, utilizing data that are replicable by other researchers, thereby ensuring the index's scientific integrity and utility. As with the index for China, a value above 100 denotes a higher economic weight than in 2001, and a value below 100 denotes a lower economic weight. A value of 200 indicates that the economic weight is double that of 2001, and a value of 50 indicates that the economic weight is half that of 2001.

The data for the US index proved to be less challenging to compile than the data for China, mainly due to their greater accessibility and transparency. Most of the data sources for the US index are publicly available, with the exception of certain investment data. The aggregate stock data published by the Bureau of Economic Analysis (BEA), for example, are publicly accessible and were used as a primary source. However, to refine and double-check these figures, private databases were also employed. For greenfield investments, the fDi Markets database was used, while Merger and Acquisition data were sourced from Mergr. Data on USAID, meanwhile, were extracted from their Greenbooks, which include both military and economic aid, and provided a comprehensive dataset for a clear picture of the US aid landscape. Loan data were gathered from the websites of respective banks. In cases where there were no systematized databases available, the information was manually coded from annual reports and other official documents.[13]

TABLE 2.2 *Variables used to operationalize US economic weight*

Variable	Operationalization	Years	Countries	Source
Trade	Exports to the US (million US$)	1989–2020	185	United Nations Comtrade
Aid	Official Development Assistance (million US$)	1989–2020	185	USAID
FDI	US investments (million US$)	1989–2020	185	Bureau of Economic Analysis, fDi Markets, and Mergr
Loans	Loans by the Development Finance Corporation, IADB, IMF, and the World Bank, and loans provided by multilateral development banks where the US is a majoritarian shareholder	1989–2020	185	Loans from DFC, IMF, WB, and IADB
Size of the economy	GDP (million US$)	1989–2020	191	World Bank data

2.2.1 US Economic Weight in the World Between 1989 and 2020

Figure 2.4 illustrates the calculation of the US Economic Weight Index for each of the five continents as classified by the United Nations. By presenting regional values, this figure offers a visual representation of the US's economic weight across large world regions. The data reveals that, from 1989 to 2001, the US economic weight increased steadily in all regions. In some cases, such as in Africa, Asia, and Europe, the economic weight in 2001 was double or more compared to the end of the Cold War. However, it fell to a quarter or half of it in the following twenty years.[14]

The case of LAC is particularly noteworthy in the contrast between the years leading up to and the years stretching beyond the 2000s. Toward the end of the Cold War, LAC was the region where the US economic weight was strongest. Remarkably, between 1995 and 2000, US economic weight reached its peak for the three-decade period. Moreover, LAC remained the continent with the largest US economic weight until 2005, although the gap with other continents shrank. A significant shift

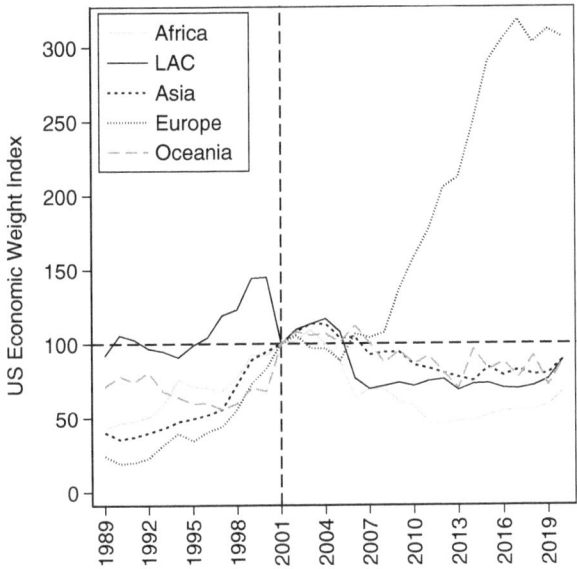

FIGURE 2.4 US economic weight by continent, 1989–2020

occurred starting in 2000, however, marked by a notable decline in economic weight. Although there was some recovery between 2001 and 2005, the US economic weight in LAC fell sharply in 2006 to three-quarters of its 2001 level and remained approximately 25 percent contracted throughout the period. It experienced only a slight recovery in 2020. Overall, the two decades following 2001 were characterized by a reduced US economic weight in LAC compared to the 2001 benchmark. This trend was not unique to LAC. Similar patterns were observed in other continents, with the stark exception of Europe.[15]

The insights gained from Figure 2.4 are critical for understanding the evolving dynamics of US economic influence globally, particularly in terms of the notable shifts in regions where the US traditionally held strong sway, such as LAC and the Global South in general. This figure also reflects a broader debate in the US regarding its international role. In recent years, there has been a growing discussion in the United States about the need for retrenchment, which refers to the intentional reduction of the overall cost of a state's foreign policy.[16] Retrenchment in foreign policy serves as a strategy for risk reduction, where states actively scale back their foreign policy commitments, temper their objectives in specific regions, and downgrade the importance of certain international issues. This approach can be a deliberate choice to minimize liabilities and exposure in the global arena. However, retrenchment can also stem from a position of limited resources, which in turn exposes vulnerabilities and necessitates a strategic recalibration of foreign policy priorities.

For the US, this idea emphasizes a shift in focus toward domestic affairs and offers a distinct contrast to its prominent international role during the 1990s. As argued by some scholars, the United States faces a longstanding tension seen throughout the twentieth century between withdrawing from and investing in the liberal international order.[17] During the Cold War, the perceived threat from communism underpinned an expansive US strategy. Even after the Soviet Union's collapse, the United States remained committed to its global role. American leaders framed the maintenance of international order as a moral imperative; a responsibility that seemed manageable in the absence of a counterbalancing superpower. This perspective allowed the US to justify its continued interventionist stance in world affairs, where it viewed itself as the primary guardian of global stability in a unipolar world.

The debate over the costs and benefits of sustaining the liberal international order has thus become increasingly prominent with the rise of China, especially since the beginning of the administration of President Trump in 2017. The resurgence of debate about the US's role in international affairs reflects changing global dynamics and the United States's reconsideration of its place on the world stage. This reconsideration has been influenced by both internal and external factors, but one prominent factor has certainly been the shifting economic powers in an evolving geopolitical landscape.

The common discourse within Washington since 2001 suggests that the US opted for retrenchment to concentrate on more immediate concerns. These included shifting the national focus to the war on terrorism, particularly in Iraq and Afghanistan. Such a redirection of attention and resources had significant implications for US engagement in other parts of the world, including Latin America. Later, under Donald Trump's administration, the concept of retrenchment took on new dimensions with the "America First" policy embodied by the slogan "Make America Great Again" (MAGA). This policy shift emphasized a further withdrawal from certain global engagements while redirecting focus toward domestic priorities and the "Pivot to Asia" strategy. These shifts reflect a reevaluation of US foreign policy that is being influenced by both the changing international landscape and domestic political considerations. They also highlight the dynamic nature of US engagement on the world stage, where it is shaped by evolving strategic objectives and global challenges.

2.2.2 US Economic Weight in LAC

When we dissect the US Economic Weight Index by component, it allows us to determine whether the contraction of US influence in LAC is attributable to any specific variable. As depicted in Figure 2.5, all variables experienced a contraction at some point between 2005 and 2008, remaining between 25 and 50 percent below their 2001 levels for much of the analyzed period. This indicates a broad-based decline across various aspects of US economic engagement in the region. A notable development occurred in 2017, where there was a significant increase in loans. This surge can likely be attributed to an outlier event: the substantial loan of US$40 billion granted to Argentina by the IMF.[18]

Analyzing the heterogeneity within LAC is as crucial for understanding US economic influence as it is for China. When examining US retrenchment in these subregions, a clear contraction in economic influence is observable. In Central America, this contraction began around the year 2000, while it became evident around 2005 in South America. But the extent of this reduction in US economic weight varies across sub-regions. Central America experienced a decrease in US influence, but it was less pronounced than the decrease in South America, where the contraction of US economic weight was much more significant, of approximately 50 percent.

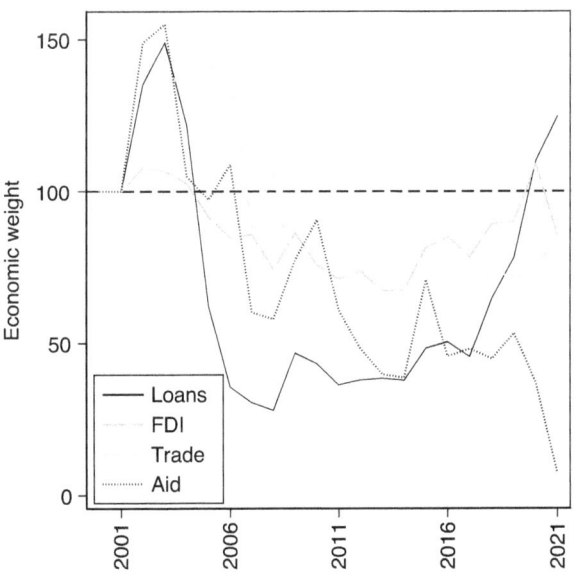

FIGURE 2.5 US economic weight by component in LAC

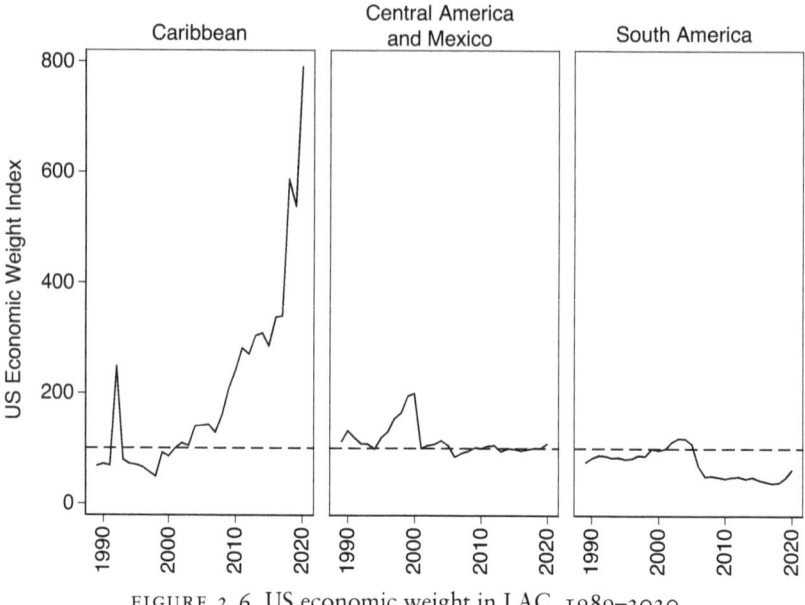

FIGURE 2.6 US economic weight in LAC, 1989–2020

Interestingly, the Caribbean's experience diverges from the other two sub-regions. Instead of a decrease, there has been an increase in US influence in the Caribbean of almost eight times over the period analyzed here. I attribute this to the Caribbean's utilization of its small islands as tax havens, which results in capital inflows. These islands' unique economic and regulatory environments have made them attractive destinations for financial activities linked to the US, thereby enhancing US economic presence in the region (Figure 2.6).[19]

2.2.3 Limitations in the Data

In my methodology for measuring US economic weight through trade, investment, aid, and financial assistance, at least two key decisions merit explanation.

2.2.3.1 *The Inclusion of the World Bank (WB) and the International Monetary Fund (IMF)*

I have chosen to consider these institutions as reflective of US economic weight. This decision is grounded in the fact that the US holds a majority share in both organizations. Historically, prior to the creation of the DFC in 2019, the WB and IMF have been pivotal financial tools through which the US exerted political pressure on other countries. This perspective is supported by numerous scholarly articles and books that discuss the influence wielded by the US in these international financial institutions.[20] The United States has exerted significant influence over international financial institutions (IFIs), including the IMF, WB, and IADB, since their inception. While it is impossible to be exhaustive, there is evidence of political co-optation of the IMF and WB by the United States practically since their creation. This influence has been particularly evident in the context of US foreign policy objectives and economic interests. For instance, political economist Noel Maurer notes that, when Argentine President Arturo Illia canceled contracts with US companies in 1963, the IMF and World Bank denied Argentina credit while the Kennedy administration cut economic and military aid.[21]

The extent of US influence became more pronounced during the 1980s. Historian Hal Brands provides compelling evidence of how the Reagan and George H. W. Bush administrations leveraged the Third World debt crisis to promote free-market reforms and extend globalization to the Global South, effectively using the IMF and World Bank as vehicles for these policies. The US actively pushed for tighter IMF conditionality and a greater focus on rolling back state involvement in economies by development banks.[22] This approach included replacing IFI officials deemed hostile to US views with those committed to free-market principles. By late 1984, sixteen Latin American countries had negotiated IMF stabilization agreements, reflecting the pervasive influence of these US-backed policies.

US influence persisted into the late 1990s and 2000s, as noted by scholars who, for example, highlight how the IMF and other IFIs increasingly linked economic assistance to a country's democratic and human rights performance.[23] The trend toward political conditionality was reinforced by events such as the *autogolpe* in Peru in 1992. Throughout these decades, the US utilized various mechanisms to exert its influence, including bilateral aid programs, Export–Import Bank credits, and its voting power within the IFIs. As the classic International Political Economy author Stephen Krasner observes regarding the IADB, it has operated within a hegemonic structure dominated by US national power capabilities despite its status as a regional multilateral bank, allowing US policymakers to pursue long-term political objectives through the institution.[24] More significantly, regarding the competition between Chinese and Western credits, scholars have observed that the World Bank often reflects US political interests as well, which adds an important dimension to the analysis of international lending practices and their geopolitical implications.[25]

2.2.3.2 *The Focus on Exports to the US Instead of Imports from the US*

The primary reason for concentrating on exports to the US is that they align with the definition of economic weight, which is interested in the flow of trade that generates foreign exchange for a country. While imports from the US are significant, they encompass not just final consumer goods but also intermediate goods used as inputs in various industries. In an alternate version of the index where both exports and imports were considered, the economic weight of the US showed minimal change, but it notably increased the economic weight of China. Therefore, in this analysis, I have opted for a more conservative approach to the index, focusing solely on exports to the US to maintain a clearer representation of economic influence based on capital inflow to a country.

One other reason not to include imports from the US and China in the calculation of economic weights has to do with the difficulty of controlling for transnational value chains.[26] Part of what China exports to Latin America is produced by American companies (iPhones, for example), which inflates the statistic.[27] This weakness of trade statistics is more applicable to the exports from China and the US to Latin America and the Caribbean than vice versa. Most of what the LAC countries export to China and the US are raw materials that are not re-exported, and even in the case of manufactures (such as those from Mexico to the US), they are consumed in the US.

The approach of focusing on exports, while not without challenges, aims to capture the economic benefits accruing to LAC export companies from their sales to China and the United States. These gains often translate into increased state revenue through mechanisms such as tariffs and taxes. Consequently, the rents generated from commodity exports are redistributed, enabling an expansion of public spending. On the whole, this strategy reflects the potential for leveraging international trade to support domestic economic objectives.

2.3 EXPLAINING THE FALL OF US ECONOMIC WEIGHT IN LAC

The ebb and flow of US economic influence in Latin America is a multifaceted narrative spanning several decades. To grasp its complexity, I believe, we must look back to 2001 as a pivotal point. Unlike China, the United States had an intense twentieth century in its Latin American relations. It maintained undisputed dominance in the region for many decades, even during the Soviet Union's peak influence. However, its relationship with

Latin America has been characterized by fluctuations, aptly described by historian Robert Pastor as resembling a whirlpool. When the US perceived no external threats in the region, it would diminish its focus on Latin America and turn its attention to other parts of the world. Conversely, at the first sign of a potential threat, the US would swiftly re-engage with a sense of urgency. This pattern led to periods where the US seemed to neglect its southern neighbors, reflecting a sharp contrast to China's more recent and steadily growing involvement in the region. The US–Latin America relationship, deeply rooted in a shared history, has been marked by periods of intense engagement followed by relative neglect, creating a complex legacy that continues to shape regional dynamics today.[28]

The "whirlpool effect" in US foreign policy historically meant that global crises, particularly in Europe or Asia, would selectively engage the US away from Latin America. However, the Cold War marked a significant shift in this dynamic: faced with perceived communist threats in the Americas, the US refocused its attention on the region. This renewed effort was articulated through George Kennan's containment policy, which outlined specific objectives for US engagement with Latin America. The goals were threefold: to secure access to raw materials, to prevent military use of the region by hostile powers (the USSR), and to counter any anti-American sentiment or mobilization in the area. This strategic reorientation underscored the importance of Latin America in the broader context of US global interests during the Cold War era.[29]

Despite these fluctuations in its level of engagement with the region, the United States consistently maintained the strongest economic influence in LAC from 1945 to the 2000s. Scholarly consensus indicates that US economic dominance in LAC far exceeded that of other global powers during these decades. It fended off the Soviet Union throughout the Cold War, weathered Japan's economic surge in the 1980s, and maintained its dominance in the face of the European Union's growing presence in the late 1990s. (China's economic influence in LAC during this timeframe was minimal.) And even as US priorities in the region shifted over time, its economic impact remained unparalleled, underlining the enduring nature of US economic hegemony in LAC throughout the latter half of the twentieth century. It was not until 2001 that the tide began to turn.

2.3.1 The Lonely Superpower (1990–2001)

The influence of the United States in Latin America during the 1990s was significant and far-reaching, as evident from various economic indicators and policy decisions. The US emerged as a "lonely superpower" during this period, and its impact on Latin American economies and politics was profound.[30] One of the key ways that the US exerted influence in Latin America was through trade and investment. US exports to Latin America skyrocketed from US$53.9 billion to US$142 billion between 1990 and 1998, while imports from Latin America also surged from US$67 billion to US$142 billion. US direct investment more than tripled – from US$70.7 billion in 1990 to US$223 billion in 1999 – with significant investments in the finance and manufacturing sectors. The North American Free Trade Agreement (NAFTA), which came into effect in 1994, further boosted trade between the US, Mexico, and Canada. Agricultural trade between the US and Mexico alone increased by 55 percent from 1994 to 2000, reaching US$11.6 billion annually. Overall trade between the two countries increased from US$100 billion in 1994 to US$170 billion in 1998.[31]

The privatization of state-owned corporations and the liberalization of economies in Latin America during the 1990s also contributed to the growing influence of the US. According to historian Thomas O'Brien, the privatization of Latin American enterprises during this period – a process that involved both domestic and international buyers – generated a significant influx of capital totaling US$220 billion.[32] US corporations, notably, expanded their operations in key sectors like manufacturing, petroleum, and finance. This expansion led to Latin America becoming the leading recipient of foreign investment among developing countries in 1999. For the first time since 1986, the region even surpassed Asia in this regard.[33] Then, a landmark event occurred when Citibank, then the largest financial conglomerate in the US, acquired Mexico's second-largest bank, Grupo Financiero Banamex Accival, for US$12.5 billion in 2001. This acquisition was the largest foreign purchase ever made by a US bank at the time, and it symbolized the pinnacle of an era of US economic growth in LAC.

During the 1990s, the United States also exerted significant influence in Latin America through economic policies associated with the Washington Consensus, which advocated for economic liberalism. These policies included measures like ending price controls, privatizing state-owned enterprises, implementing market-based interest rates, and reforming labor unions. While these policies aimed at liberalizing economies and encouraging trade and investment, they were met with considerable resistance, especially from the middle and lower classes in Latin America. These groups were particularly vulnerable to fluctuations in commodity prices and the economic adjustment policies forced to align with IMF and World Bank objectives. The US's ability to influence macroeconomic policies in Latin American countries through these organizations was thus not without controversy. It led to significant criticisms and backlash, with increased economic integration accompanied by growing socio-economic challenges and widespread resistance to US-backed policies.

2.3.2 Retrenchment and China's Growing Influence (2001–2020)

While the United States played the role of regional goods provider in Latin America for decades through financing, infrastructure, and investment, Chinese banks and enterprises have been gradually contesting this monopoly since 2001. The war on terrorism beginning in 2001 forced the US to prioritize the Middle East, respond to the formation of the Islamic State in the Arab world, and contain Russia's aggressive foreign policy, leaving Latin America as a secondary concern.[34] At the same time, the legitimacy of the OAS, the Washington Consensus, and the Free Trade Area of the Americas (FTAA) was hampered by the "Pink Tide," a shift to the left that was very critical of these institutions and channeled the discontent of the middle and lower classes.[35] During this period, governments critical of the Washington Consensus also profited from consistently high commodity prices, which enabled LAC progressive governments to pursue policies of significant state investment.[36] As a result of these overlapping trends, Chinese investments flourished while American investments shrank relative to US investments in other regions of the world.

Between 1982 and 1990, US companies had already reduced their exposure to LAC, with their investment stock in the region decreasing from 23 to 15 percent of their total global investments (Figure 2.7). While these investments rebounded in the 1990s – growing to 20 percent by the end of the twentieth century – the LAC region subsequently lost significance among US investors. The US share of investment stock in the region continually declined to just 5 percent in 2020.

Recognizing the rising influence of China, the administrations of George W. Bush and Barack Obama generally saw China's involvement in LAC as positive. Between 2006 and 2015, the US and China conducted seven bilateral discussions focusing on LAC.[37] The prevailing view in Washington was that, as the US focused its foreign policy efforts on other global regions and faced the distancing of leftist governments critical of the social impacts of the Washington Consensus, China's growing

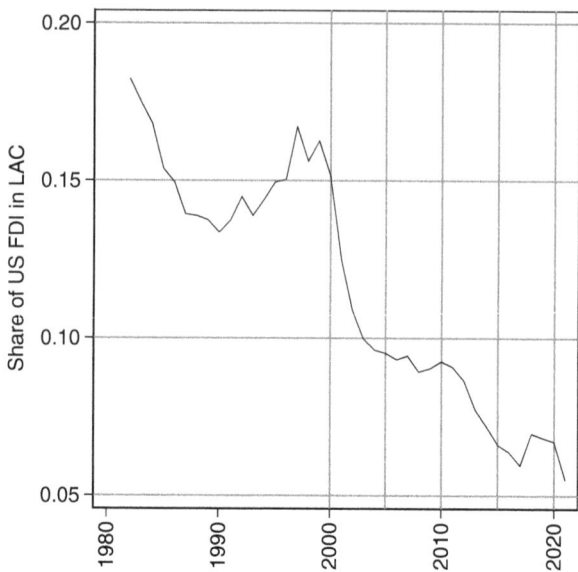

FIGURE 2.7 American stock of FDI in LAC as a share of its stock in the world
Source: Author's elaboration based on data from the US Bureau of Economic Analysis (2023) *Direct Investment by Country and Industry*.

economic ties with Latin America could promote stability in the region. This perspective held that China's engagement would not significantly disrupt the existing geopolitical balance, allowing for a deeper Sino–Latin American economic relationship that could be beneficial without fundamentally changing the established order. However, LAC leftist governments began to shift toward greater state control in the economy, aiming to reassert authority over strategic sectors, including many previously privatized US firms. This shift led to a significant withdrawal of US businesses from the region. The retreat was driven by fears of expropriation as well as by the fact that selling assets back to the government appeared more lucrative than enduring political instability.

In 2009, during Barack Obama's presidency the administration introduced the Obama Doctrine, signaling a departure from historical dominance toward establishing equal, peer-to-peer relationships.[38] This new policy reduced the conditions attached to US economic influence without proportionately increasing incentives, or "carrots." As a result, countries in the region gained more freedom to pursue alternatives to goods, services, and benefits traditionally offered by the United States. The moment marked a significant shift in US foreign policy toward

Latin America. Additionally, Obama's "Pivot to Asia" policy aimed to reclaim influence in the Asia-Pacific region, a strategic goal that had been advocated since the 1970s. It was a policy of selective engagement that focused on bolstering key alliances, notably with Japan and South Korea, and it aimed to counter China's expanding military presence in the area. During its implementation, scholars expressed concern that the shift in focus might lead the US to neglect its commitments and interests in other regions of the world. And this is, indeed, what occurred.[39]

Since the Trump administration took office in 2017, the US has not only struggled to engage effectively in Latin America, it has increasingly recognized the challenge posed by China's presence in the region now that the country's influence has increased. This began as a hesitant acknowledgment, but it has grown more frequent, with both Latin American politicians and Washington policymakers noting the change. By 2021, the endpoint of this book's timeline, Washington felt "frustrated and powerless" in its competition with China for global influence.[40] It was soon acknowledged that China's strategic focus on leveraging its economic clout, including the promotion of trade deals and infrastructure projects, gave its diplomats an advantage, particularly in LAC and African nations that felt overlooked by Washington. Moreover, US efforts to counter China's infrastructure initiatives were less accessible and underfunded, partly because traditional US diplomatic approaches had underemphasized the commercial aspect of these projects.

Gradually, the United States diminished the prominence of capital in its relationship with LAC, focusing instead on niche issues such as drug trafficking, illegal migration, and the promotion of democracy. Some historians argue that the US lost its focus on economic issues over time.[41] Others suggest that this shift may reflect a broader trend in US foreign policy. Historian Odd Arne Westad, for example, contends that rather than viewing the role of markets in US foreign policy as part of a comprehensive ideology, there have been moments when foreign policy treated the business and corporate component with disdain, considering it contrary to the purity of ideological ideals.[42] This perspective is instrumental for understanding why and how US foreign priorities reflected a reduced emphasis on Latin America. Although there have been periods when specific business interests significantly influenced American foreign interventions, a comprehensive review of historical records reveals that these have been exceptions rather than the rule.

2.4 MEASURING CHINA'S ECONOMIC DISPLACEMENT OF THE US IN LAC

In the previous sections, I have shown that (a) China increased its economic weight by 17 times between 2001 and 2020, and that (b) the US contracted its economic weight by one quarter in the same period. I have also shown that China's economic weight increased the most in South America, the LAC sub-region that accounts for 82 percent of the regional GDP and two-thirds of its population. Having discussed the reasons behind the US's contraction, I will also offer an in-depth explanation for China's rise (see Chapter 3). First, however, it is useful to address where and when Chinese economic weight displaced US economic weight and how LAC compares to other regions of the world.

In operationalizing the competition between China and the US for economic influence in the developing world, I have proposed the concept of economic displacement. As introduced in Chapter 1, economic displacement *occurs when the economic weight exerted by Country A over Country B surpasses the economic weight that Country C exerts over Country B*. LAC serves as a pivotal region for examining this shift in global power dynamics.[43] International Relations studies interested in power transitions have used similar intuitions to measure power in a comparative way, such as using the Composite Index of National Capabilities. MacDonald and Parent, for example, deal with the concept of decline, which they see as occurring when a great power "decreases its ordinal rank among the great powers." More specifically, they see decline at the point "when the rank order of great powers changes – for instance, when numbers one and two switch places – and the switch is not temporary."[44] In this regard, it is not a state's own trajectory that matters; rather, it is how this trajectory changes its position relative to others.

The concept of displacement masks a gradual trend. Since its measurement, in this case, is the difference between the economic weights of China and the US, we can observe the gradual trend in which China reduces the economic gap in each region. The period we are analyzing is crucial, as it marks a time when China impressively narrowed the gap in all regions of the world except Europe. Looking at Figure 2.8, we can see that by the late 2010s, China had displaced the US in terms of economic influence in the average country across Africa, Asia, Oceania, and LAC. The Appendix breaks this down by subregion, revealing that South America, Central Asia, Southeast Asia, West and Middle Africa, and Melanesia are the areas where this phenomenon occurred most clearly.[45]

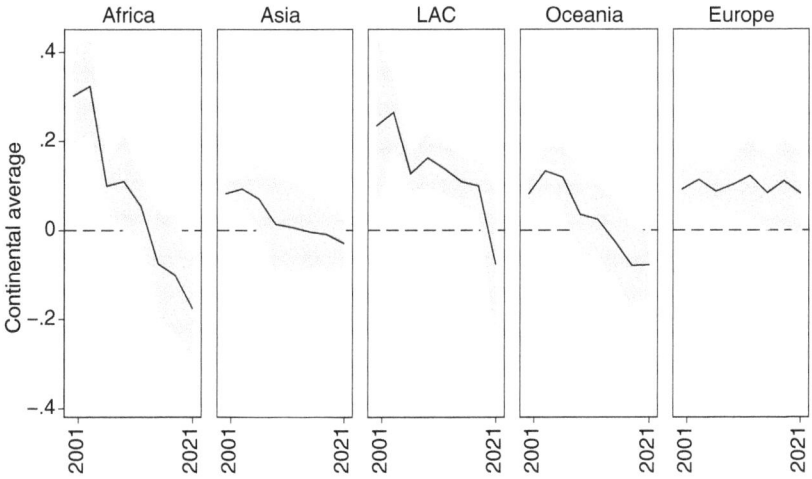

FIGURE 2.8 Difference between US economic weight and Chinese economic weight by region
Note: Values below the dotted line indicate that China has displaced the US in terms of economic influence.

This gradual shift in economic influence reflects China's growing global economic power, as well as its strategic focus on developing regions. However, while this trend is significant, economic influence is just one aspect of international relations and doesn't necessarily translate directly into political or cultural dominance.

In LAC, the shifting economic influence of China and the United States can be visualized through a grayscale representation (Figure 2.9), where shading intensity indicates relative economic weight at three points in time. This visual aid reveals China's dramatic transformation from an irrelevant actor in 2001 to a significant economic force by 2020. Countries like Argentina, Bolivia, Peru, and Brazil show clear shifts, with darkening shades in China's section indicating increased influence. However, the change isn't uniform across the region; some countries exhibit more subtle shifts that require closer examination or alternative representations to discern. This visualization effectively captures China's rapid ascent in LAC over two decades while highlighting the varied impact of its growing economic presence across different countries in the region.

Despite the gradual nature of the phenomenon, my chosen measurement of displacement is a dichotomous variable. If "D" represents the occurrence of displacement, "$Wc_{c,t}$" represents the weight of the Chinese economy on country c in year t, and "$Wa_{c,t}$" represents the weight of the

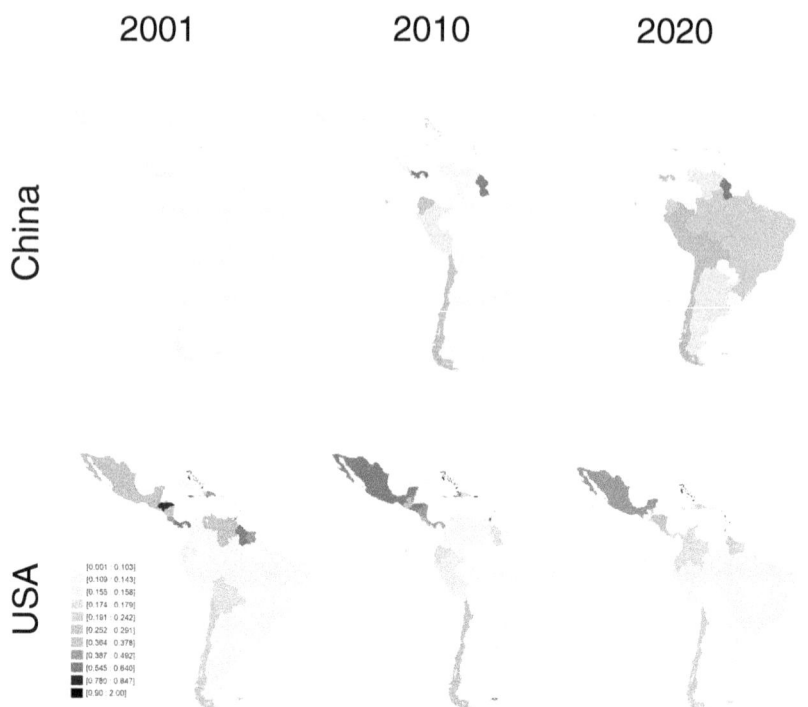

FIGURE 2.9 Evolution of the economic weight of China and the US by country in LAC

Note: The scale shows economic weight for the US and China per country.

American economy on country c in year t, then we can represent the condition of "Chinese economic weight is equal to or larger than US weight" as $[Wc_{c,t} >= Wa_{c,t}]$. We can then represent the displacement value as: $D = 1$. When we can combine these conditions into a formula, we get: $D = [Wc_{c,t} >= Wa_{c,t}] \times 1$. This formula uses the logical operator "$[Wc_{c,t} >= Wa_{c,t}]$" to check if the Chinese economic weight is equal to or greater than the American weight. If this condition is true, the operator returns 1, which is then multiplied by the displacement value of 1 to give a displacement of 1. If the condition is false, the operator returns 0, and the displacement remains at its default value of 0.

Figure 2.10 illustrates the evolution of Chinese economic displacement in the LAC region, mirroring data from Figure 1.3 in Chapter 1. In 2001, only two countries – Cuba and Dominica – had a greater Chinese economic weight compared to the US. By 2020, the number had increased to 12 countries. The graph reveals that while some countries experience

China's Displacement of the US in Latin America 51

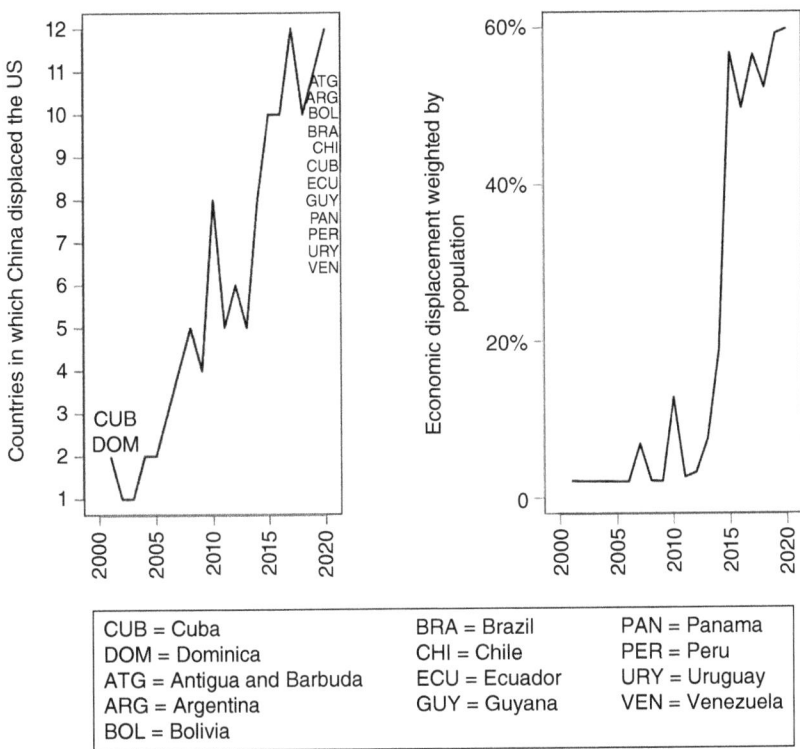

FIGURE 2.10 Chinese displacement of the US economy, measured in countries and as a share of LAC population

a consolidated shift in economic influence over time, others show more transitory changes. The significance of this displacement becomes more evident when considered in relation to population size, which serves as a proxy for economic scale. In 2000, merely 3 percent of the region's population lived in countries where China's economic weight exceeded that of the US. By 2020, this figure had surged to 60 percent, underscoring the dramatic shift in China's economic influence across the LAC region over two decades.[46]

From 2001 to 2020, several countries in LAC experienced a period where China's economic weight surpassed that of the United States and consolidated over time. The duration of this shift varied across different countries. Cuba was the most notable case, with China being the more significant economic partner throughout the entire twenty-year period. Antigua and Barbuda saw fourteen years of stronger economic ties with China, while Guyana experienced thirteen years of a more substantial

Chinese economic influence. Uruguay had eleven years of China being more economically significant. In Dominica, China held a stronger economic position for nine years. Ecuador and Peru each had eight years where China's economic importance was greater, and Venezuela and Bolivia both saw seven years of heightened economic engagement with China. Lastly, Argentina and Brazil each had six years during which China's economic weight was more pronounced than the US's weight.

2.4.1 The Difficulty of Having It Both Ways

We have already established that the dichotomous concept of displacement is a research design choice that simplifies a more complex, gradual phenomenon. The displacement threshold I've chosen allows me to confidently expect China to become an alternative goods provider in countries where the US has been displaced. However, in certain economic agendas, this can occur well before crossing the defined limit, which raises a crucial question for analysis: Is it possible for countries to increase the economic weight of both China and the US? To examine this, let's consider Brazil, a key country in LAC. Brazil is a particularly interesting case study because it is the largest economy in the region as well as the eighth largest economy in the world. Significantly, it has actively sought to diversify its economic portfolio between China and the US.

Figure 2.11 presents a global sample of 185 countries in 2001 and 2020. Each country is represented by a point, with solid squares for 2001 and solid circles for 2020. Each country is positioned in a two-dimensional space according to its unique combination of Chinese and US economic weight. The diagonal dotted line represents the threshold used in this book to consider when the US has been economically displaced by China in any given country. For Brazil, we have placed both the actual scenario (A) and two hypothetical scenarios (B) and (C) into the sample. In the real scenario, the US was displaced by China in Brazil. China's economic weight in Brazil grew from virtually 0 to almost 10 percent of its GDP, while that of the US decreased from slightly more than 10 percent to approximately 5 percent. In the hypothetical scenario B, let's imagine displacement has also occurred, but that it was due to an increase in China's economic weight without a reduction in the US's economic weight. In scenario C, let's imagine that no displacement has occurred despite growth in China's economic weight; in other words, the economic weight of both China and the US has increased.

China's Displacement of the US in Latin America 53

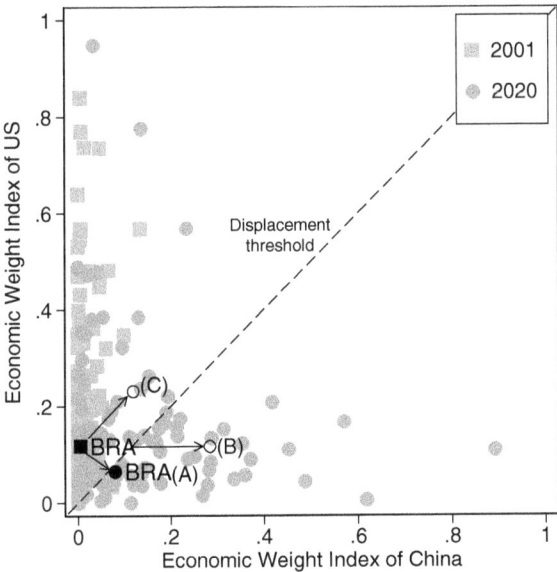

FIGURE 2.11 Chinese and US economic weights in the world in 2001 and 2020
Note: The diagonal line denotes the occurrence of economic displacement at a continental level.

Figure 2.11 shows an "L-shaped" behavior, with the center of the figure almost empty.[47] We can thus assume that during the two decades being analyzed, it was very difficult for countries to increase the economic weight of both China and the US. Ideally, of course, countries would always prefer scenario C; however, for reasons that warrant further study, this is challenging to achieve in practice. There are important policy implications and ramifications stemming from the observation that displacement (rather than having it both ways) seems to be the likely outcome when it comes to the significant growth of one country's economic weight in a given country. A discussion of the policy implications emerging from this phenomenon is presented in Chapter 7.

2.5 CONCLUSION

This chapter has operationalized the economic weight variable of the US and China in order to effectively operationalize our independent variable: economic displacement. What we see as a result is that Latin America has experienced a significant shift in its economic relationships with the world's two major powers – China and the United States – from

2001 to 2020. This shift has been most noticeable in South America. During this period, China's economic weight in the region grew 15 times, while the economic weight of the United States contracted by one fourth. This dramatic change in economic weight has largely been overlooked, as Latin America has traditionally been seen as a sphere of influence for the United States. By examining the relative economic weights of US and China over a period of two decades, this chapter has shed light on a surprising reality: an extra-regional actor, China, has displaced a historically relevant player in the region; a trend that seems prepared to continue.

3

Filling the Void

Chinese Economic Actors and the Provision of Substitute Goods

In Chapter 1, I theorized two factors that determine the demand in developing countries for goods offered by China: (a) the extent to which China can act as a substitute provider of the same goods provided by the hegemon and/or goods that complement what the US supplies; and (b) the extent to which these goods meet the needs of domestic development. Having defined and operationalized the dependent variable of economic displacement, we can now analyze these explanatory variables. First, however, it is essential to understand why some countries experienced displacement earlier than others, and why some did not experience displacement at all in the past twenty years. Between 2001 and 2020, China's economic weight grew more than 15 times in LAC, resulting in economic displacement in countries representing over 60 percent of the population. So, the question is: Why did China's economic weight grow more in some countries than in others?

If China's considerable economic rise in the Global South is interpreted as an unprecedented phenomenon, it follows that the concurrent story of the decline of US economic influence in its own sphere of influence is at best under-analyzed and at worst ignored.[1] A key theoretical assumption of this project is that the legitimacy of the US order in the Western Hemisphere has been increasingly undermined by the diminishing scope and intensity of its economic relations with countries in the region.[2] This material dimension consists of the provision of goods through capital flows, foreign aid, financial assistance, and the creation of trade opportunities that together generate economic growth, predictability, and improvements in infrastructure in LAC countries.[3] My hypothesis for why China grew more in some areas than others consists of two principles that align with the concept of economic weight defined in Chapter 2. First, the United States left an economic vacuum in the hemisphere that was filled by Chinese actors. Second, these Chinese actors provided substitute goods that reduced countries' dependency on the monopoly of US goods. Together, these dynamics triggered displacement.

More specifically, my analyses show that the decline of US economic influence in LAC created an opportunity for Chinese multinational enterprises (MNEs) and banks to establish themselves as viable alternatives. This shift occurred as Chinese capital became available to Latin American countries during periods when traditional Western financial institutions were either unable or unwilling to provide necessary funding to the region.[4] This change signifies more than just a reshuffling of economic alliances; it demonstrates China's strategic positioning to fill the economic void left by Western powers. During the period analyzed, Chinese entities often stepped in to provide financial resources when other sources were scarce, effectively establishing China as a new and significant economic partner for LAC countries. This development reflects a broader transformation in global economic dynamics, with China increasingly able to offer alternative economic engagement models to regions traditionally dominated by Western influence. Indeed, the timing and nature of China's increased economic presence in LAC underscore its ability and willingness to capitalize on shifts in the global economic landscape.

The 1990s and 2000s mark a significant shift in the global provision of economic goods.[5] After the Soviet Union's collapse in the 1990s, the United States held a de facto monopoly in this area. Political scientists Daniel Nexon and Alexander Cooley note that countries challenging US institutions and principles were often branded as "rogue states," complicating their international business dealings. With few alternatives, weaker nations had little choice but to conform to the institutions, laws, and agreements underpinning the liberal order.[6] However, the 2000s saw a change in this dynamic. Smaller countries found it increasingly possible to reduce their vulnerability to US hegemonic influence. The emergence of alternative economic partners offered these nations "exit options," diminishing pressure to adhere to democratization and neoliberal economic policies.

The theory presented here thus explains economic displacement by highlighting the provision of alternative goods from China in target states and the extent to which these goods address domestic development needs. When the US reduced its economic influence in LAC, it created a void that Chinese actors filled in some sectors. My empirical analysis suggests that sectors where this dynamic was more prominent are where we see countries with the most likelihood of experiencing displacement. The fact that the US withdrawal was not uniform across all countries or across time is what explains the variation in how China managed to penetrate different Latin American countries. Significant to this trend is the fact that Chinese actors made themselves instrumental for local policy to deliver results. In other words, they successfully tapped into a Latin American demand for goods offered by alternative actors (in this case, China).

Over time, the increase in China's economic influence has been explained with varying degrees of theoretical rigor. The following sections test existing explanations as well as my own hypothesis that China's growth is directly related to the contraction of the United States' influence in LAC. For this purpose, I developed various econometric models to test the validity of my hypothesis against rival arguments.

3.1 ALTERNATIVE EXPLANATIONS

There are two variables that have commonly been used by scholars and policymakers to explain China's growth in LAC: the commodity boom and the ideological affinity between left-wing governments and China. While I believe neither variable is sufficient to explain the unprecedented economic displacement we have witnessed in the last twenty years, it is useful to engage substantively with them to illuminate their limitations.

To test the alternative explanations for the growth of China's economic weight in LAC, I operationalized the commodity boom using the IMF's Net Commodity Export Price Index, which measures individual commodities weighted by the ratio of net exports to total commodity trade.[7] If the commodity boom could explain China's growth in the region, this variable would be positively related to our dependent variable. To measure the ideological affinity of left-wing governments with China, I used a dichotomous variable that takes a value of 1 to measure the ideology of the president if they are left-wing. These data come from the Inter-American Development Bank's Political Institutions Database, which codes party platforms.[8] The theoretical expectation, according to existing literature on these topics, is that when there is a left-wing government, the presence of Chinese actors offering substitute goods should increase. To empirically assess the economic voids left by the United States (the cornerstone of my hypothesis), I used the index of economic weight of the US as operationalized in Chapter 2 (Table 3.1). With these

TABLE 3.1 *Key arguments and their operationalization*

Explanation	Proxy (VARIABLE NAME)	Source	Expected effect
Commodity boom	Commodity Net Export Price Index (COMMODITIES)	IMF	+
Ideological affinity	Leftist presidents (LEFTIST)	IADB	+
US economic vacuums	US economic weight (USECOWEIGHT)	Own elaboration (Chapter 2)	–

Source: Elaborated by the author.

theoretical expectations established, the following sections turn to each explanatory hypothesis to explore the most likely cause for the growth of China's economic weight in LAC.

3.1.1 Economic Complementarity and the Commodity Boom in China–LAC Relations

The most recurrent variable in the existing literature on China–LAC economic relations is the phenomenon of the commodity boom. The assumption is that the strong complementarity between the economy of Chinese and Latin American commodity producers resulted in the exploitation of comparative advantages (referred to as "reprimarization").[9] The literature on the commodity boom shows that rising commodity prices between 2001 and 2011, as well the existence of a relative complementarity between China and LAC, played a crucial role in driving the relationship between the two. China's demand for natural resources provided a significant boost to Latin American economies, which in turn allowed them to invest in social policies, infrastructure, and other development projects. To sustain the booming trade, China then leveraged other tools of its financial economic diplomacy and provided LAC regions with billions of dollars in the form of development loans and FDI. These economic interactions, this theory posits, forged softer political and diplomatic ties between Latin American states and China.[10]

It is clear from this conventional argument that high commodity prices and, in general, the so-called commodity cycle resulting in booming trade became "a key driver" in the intensification of ties between China and Latin America.[11] For example, the price of copper increased

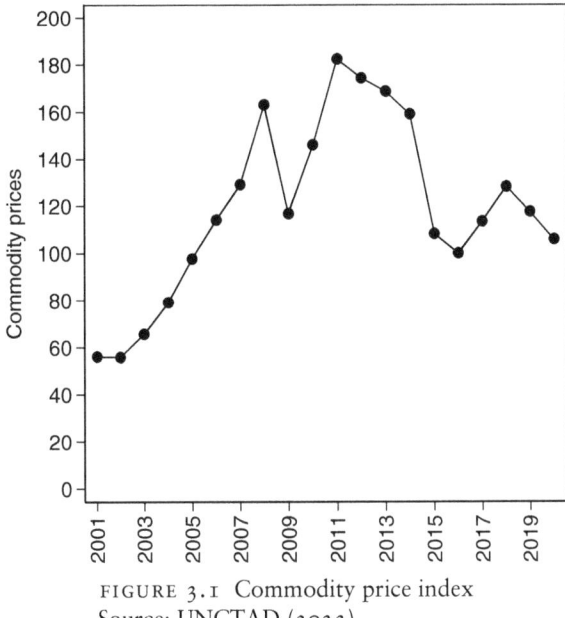

FIGURE 3.1 Commodity price index
Source: UNCTAD (2023).

from US$1,787/ton in 2001 to US$9,533/ton in 2011.[12] Similar trends occurred with oil[13] and soybeans.[14] As illustrated in Figure 3.1, the value of commodities tripled between 2001 and 2011.

Given its high economic growth, rapidly developing industrial sector, and growing middle class, China generated a strong demand for numerous natural resources to sustain its new development model and its growing industrial sector, as well as to feed its wealthier population.[15] The most in-demand commodities were copper, iron, oil, and numerous agricultural products, especially soybeans.[16] Furthermore, as a developing manufacturing powerhouse, the Chinese had to implement strategies aimed at finding new foreign markets to export their excess domestic capacity.[17] In other words, China had to internationalize its development strategy in the early 2000s, and LAC, due to its abundance in natural resources, was a natural partner. Chinese investments and infrastructure projects in LAC could enhance China's own energy security and food security.[18] Chinese economic growth thus represented increases in the main exports of Latin American raw materials, as well as a rise in their prices.[19] LAC exports to China increased from about US$10 billion in 2000 to more than US$200 billion in 2014. During this period, China surpassed the US as the main trading partner of several key economies in LAC, including Brazil, Chile, and Peru.[20] The importance of trade driven by the commodity cycle is also evident in the rapid proliferation of China's free trade agreements with Chile, Peru, Costa Rica, Ecuador, and Nicaragua (and soon with Honduras).[21]

This rapidly evolving relationship gave rise to a seemingly mutually complementary and beneficial interaction. For Beijing, its entry into LAC implied a solution to its resource needs and domestic overproduction. For LAC, China's boom helped countries quickly overcome the negative effects of the 2008–09 financial crisis.[22] The high prices during this commodities boom provided significant tailwinds for key sectors in Latin American exporting industries. It also built momentum for left-wing national governments during the so-called "Pink Tide" period,[23] as it helped them reduce economic inequality.[24]

Naturally, increased revenues enriched commodity exporters throughout the region.[25] For example, China's demand brought considerable gains to large copper companies in Chile, which, in 2009, were among the main Chilean companies trading with China.[26] At the same time, copper exports also significantly benefited Chile's national government because a large portion of profits from Codelco (Chile's state mining company) went to the state treasury. Similarly, private companies like Minera Escondida and Antofagasta Minerals paid high taxes and royalties to the Chilean state.[27] In Brazil, the state of Mato Grosso provides another illustrative example of the impact of Chinese demand on Latin American regional economies. Largely driven by China's growing demand for soybeans, Mato Grosso experienced a profound transformation that propelled the state from the eleventh position to the first in terms of per capita GDP within Brazil.[28]

The expansion of trade paved the way for new forms of Chinese economic engagement in the region. Initial investments and loans were trade driven, meaning they aimed to increase China's food or energy security at home. By the mid-2000s, however, Chinese commercial and policy banks began to provide financing to Latin American countries for numerous infrastructure and energy projects; a shift made mainly in service of sustaining the growing economic relationship.[29] Financing was predominantly done through loan provisions from institutions like the China Development Bank (CDB) and Exim Bank, and it was primarily targeted at resource-rich countries in South America such as Venezuela, Ecuador, Argentina, and Brazil.[30]

According to the literature, the commodity boom also had political effects. It provided resource-exporting countries access to significant new revenue streams, which were largely under the discretionary control of their governments.[31] This, in turn, weakened the disciplinary power exerted by Western international financial institutions and global capital markets, granting states a level of political autonomy. For the first time in a generation, recipient countries could deviate significantly from neoliberal economic orthodoxy; an argument further developed by Stephen Kaplan.[32] However, while Latin American exports to China have undeniably impacted domestic economies, this phenomenon has sparked diverse interpretations among scholars from institutionalist, dependency, and developmentalist perspectives. Carol Wise, for example, adopts an institutionalist perspective, arguing that a critical juncture like China's rise and the commodities boom could either strengthen or discourage political and economic institutions. China's role, she suggests, allowed Latin American policymakers considerable scope for agency and political innovation; a phenomenon that underscored the crucial importance of institutions, leadership, and sensible policy management.[33] Barbara Stallings, meanwhile, argues that the economic relationship with China during the boom replicated center-periphery patterns, revisiting dependency theories that once lay dormant in the 1970s in LAC.[34] Adopting a developmentalist view reminiscent of the school of thought espoused by the Economic Commission for Latin America and the Caribbean (ECLAC), Kevin Gallagher, Roberto Porzecanski, and Rhys Jenkins observe that LAC's exports to China are highly concentrated in a few countries and sectors, leaving most of LAC unable to significantly benefit from China as an export market. Furthermore, they note that China is increasingly competing with LAC in manufacturing exports both in global and regional markets, impeding industrialization.[35]

Clearly, it is indisputable that the commodity cycle and economic complementarity have played an essential role in intensifying bilateral relations between China and LAC. However, because China's influence has been variable across LAC, the explanatory power of this theory should be questioned on several fronts. While its main postulates are useful – even necessary – they do not offer sufficient cause to explain what has occurred across the region. If economic complementarity and the commodity cycle were indeed the main explanatory factors accounting for LAC's growing economic closeness with China, then one would expect variation within these explanatory variables (e.g., the existence and/or degree of economic complementarity) to lead to a variation in closeness between China and Latin America. But unfortunately, several empirical observations of current China–Latin America relations undermine the explanatory power of the commodity cycle postulates. For example, the golden age of the commodity cycle, which benefited many resource-rich countries in the Global South, came to an end around the year 2013.[36] If the commodity boom were really so central to China's economic and political engagement with LAC, we might expect a period of Beijing's withdrawal from the region as the cycle reversed. Yet empirical evidence presents a different picture. On the economic front, trade between China and LAC – particularly the region's exports to China – has been steadily increasing since 2015.[37] Then, regarding finance, China's economic engagement with Latin America evolved *after* the commodity boom ended. It expanded its foreign direct investment (FDI) to new countries, such as Chile and Colombia, while maintaining investments in traditional recipients such as Argentina and Brazil. China also diversified its investments across various economic sectors. Loan commitments from Chinese policy banks have declined since peaking in 2011 and remained static during the COVID-19 pandemic from 2020 to 2022,[38] yet Beijing has leveraged a new source of financial presence in the region, mainly through private commercial banks.[39] This suggests that China's engagement with LAC is not solely tied to commodity cycles; rather, it exhibits a degree of resilience and diversification.

In addition to the temporal comparison, geographical variation can be introduced to test if the commodity boom postulates hold. For example, it becomes evident that not all resource-rich countries in LAC, all of which were directly impacted by the commodity boom, developed the same form of economic interdependence with China. Take Chile, which has the highest degree of trade dependence on China in the region,[40] but it experienced a paradoxical situation. Until the late 2010s, despite its flourishing trade ties with China, it received only a small amount of FDI and no loans.[41] This differentiates Chile from Ecuador and Venezuela, also resource-rich countries, which received numerous loans from the CDB and Exim Bank. And yet, their degree of trade dependence on China is considerably lower. Relatedly, existing literature does not explain why countries that did not benefit from the commodity boom have recently started to follow policies aimed at getting closer to China and accommodating Chinese interests. Take, for example, the economies of Central American states, which are much less complementary than those located in South America. None of the Central American states developed as close ties with Beijing as did the Andean countries or Brazil. Moreover, their exports to China are considerably lower. Nevertheless, from 2019 to 2024 many Central American states changed their diplomatic alignment from Taipei to Beijing.

The logic of existing research on China's economic power and the One-China Policy would suggest that these countries changed their alignment mainly to attract investments from the China and other forms of economic cooperation. The commodity factor, therefore, remains irrelevant in this case.[42] Moreover, in the political realm, even after the end of the commodity cycle, the China–Community of Latin American and Caribbean States (CELAC) forum continued its activity. Furthermore, it was only after the commodity boom that China extended its BRI project to Latin America, and it was only at this point that some Latin American countries decided to join the AIIB. This mixed evidence suggests that there is no clearly observable pattern confirming that the absence of a commodity boom results in less economic interaction or political engagement between China and Latin American states. Thus, while I recognize the indisputable role of the commodity cycle in shaping relations between China and Latin America, both temporal and geographical variations in China–LAC relations cast much doubt on the sufficiency of this argument for contemporary trends in the relationship.

3.1.2 The Pink Tide and Ideological Affinities with China

A different perspective on China's varying economic influence in Latin America focuses on presidential ideology. This approach theorizes that left-leaning leaders are more inclined to bolster economic relations with China, either due to ideological alignment or anti-US sentiment. The argument centers on the Pink Tide era (2001–2010), when leaders such as Hugo Chávez, Nestor Kirchner, and Luiz Inacio Lula da Silva criticized US policies and the Washington Consensus. Proponents of this theory suggest that China offered an alternative model as a counterbalance to US-backed economic policies.[43]

The argument posits that a common goal among left-wing governments during this period was to increase state participation in the economy while contesting US influence in the region by establishing a more independent foreign and regional policy.[44] This ideology-based position readily intertwines with the previous economic perspective: scholars link them by proposing that the wealth generated by the commodity boom empowered left-wing governments to diverge from Washington Consensus principles. The increased economic autonomy afforded by China's demand for commodities allowed these governments to pursue alternative policies more aligned with their ideological leanings.[45] The shift in economic power dynamics facilitated the creation of regional projects like ALBA and UNASUR, which were less aligned with US interests.[46] Furthermore, some Latin American presidents maintained tense relations with Bretton Woods institutions, particularly the IMF and the World Bank. The more radical Pink Tide leaders, such as Venezuela's Chávez, Ecuador's Correa, and Bolivia's Morales, frequently engaged in public disputes with US officials, underscoring ideological conflicts with the hemisphere's dominant power.

The political landscape of Latin America in the early 2000s gave rise to an intuitive yet misleading expectation primarily seen in non-academic circles and the media. The presumption was that the ideological leanings of left-wing governments and their strained relations with the United States would naturally lead to closer economic ties with Beijing. It was thought that the Chinese Communist Party (CCP) would seize the opportunity to form an alternative coalition of ideologically aligned countries.[47] This perspective assumes, of course, that ideology was a key factor in China's economic and geopolitical entry into the region. Notably, it posits that less democratic or autocratic left-wing governments found an ally in China to reinforce their power. However, this argument oversimplifies the complex dynamics at play in China–Latin America relations.

The argument linking left-wing Latin American governments with increased Chinese influence has found more resonance in conservative policy circles than in academia. Washington DC policymakers have posited that Chinese capital erodes democracy, particularly in left-wing autocracies like Venezuela.[48] They have also suggested that anti-American sentiment in left-wing populism drives certain countries' affinity with China.[49] Ultimately, they argue that these phenomena have created a democracy–autocracy divide, with China contributing to the weakening of democratic foundations in the LAC region.[50] This perspective gained additional prominence as a result of the Trump administration's approach to China–Latin America relations despite lacking substantial empirical evidence. Indeed, it oversimplifies the complex dynamics of regional politics and international relations, presenting a reductive view of China's engagement in Latin America that doesn't fully capture the nuanced reality of these relationships.

A closer analysis of Latin American politics in the 2000s and current regional dynamics offers several important challenges to the argument linking ideology to China's engagement in LAC. First, the assumption that Beijing fully backed Latin American efforts to counter US influence lacks substantive evidence. There's no indication that China was prepared to unconditionally support all Latin American ambitions to create distance from the United States during this period. Such an approach would suggest a highly nuanced CCP foreign policy toward the region, which is not clearly demonstrated. In fact, Beijing often showed hesitancy to fully endorse anti-American sentiments, even with its allies. A notable example is China's reluctance to fully embrace Venezuela's anti-American rhetoric.[51] Additionally, in 2004, China declined Argentine President Kirchner's request for assistance in settling IMF debt, further illustrating the limits of ideological alignment in guiding China's regional approach.[52]

The ideology-based argument also falters when we consider post-2010 trends, after the Pink Tide subsided. If ideology were indeed crucial to China's economic dominance in Latin America, we would expect a decline in Beijing's commercial and financial presence as right-wing governments became more prevalent. However, the opposite occurred. The latter half of the 2010s saw continued growth in China–Latin America trade and new Chinese FDI agreements despite the region's rightward political shift. Paradoxically, Chinese policy banks have significantly reduced financing to Venezuela's left-wing autocratic government in recent years, focusing instead on loan recovery.[53] Notably, countries like Jamaica, Suriname, the Dominican Republic, and Trinidad and Tobago have all received more Chinese credit than communist Cuba. This pattern contradicts the notion that ideological alignment is driving China's economic engagement in the region.

Right-wing leaders who came to power after the Pink Tide era actively pursued closer economic ties with China, and China was clearly willing to reciprocate. Presidents such as Mauricio Macri in Argentina, Sebastián Piñera in Chile, and Luis Lacalle Pou in Uruguay all sought to increase Chinese foreign direct investment and expand export opportunities in the Chinese market through official visits to Beijing. Ecuador, illustratively, signed its Free Trade Agreement with China under a right-wing government. Furthermore, the majority of Latin American states joined China-led initiatives like the AIIB and BRI during the rightward political shift. These developments strongly suggest that economic pragmatism, rather than political ideology, more accurately explains the growing Chinese economic weight in Latin America.

3.2 FROM US MONOPOLY TO CHINESE OPTIONS: QUANTIFYING CHINA'S INFLUENCE IN LAC

This book began as an effort to explore two critical questions: (a) how and to what extent have geopolitical factors influenced China's economic rise in Latin America, particularly in assuming roles formerly monopolized by the US and becoming an alternative option for many countries in LAC; and (b) what are the long-term political effects of Beijing's economic presence in the region, especially in relation to US leadership? During this research, it became apparent that existing literature inadequately addresses issues of agency and intention. Despite two decades of prolific scholarship, conceptual clarity on China's global influence on international relations remains elusive.[54] Since the early 2000s, China has begun providing goods and services to LAC countries, offering an "exit option" – to use Albert Hirschman's term – as an alternative to US-dominated economic relationships.[55] This phenomenon, which I argue is not necessarily a result of intentional Chinese policy, has potentially eroded the ideological foundations of the American-led order in the Western Hemisphere between 2001 and 2021. As with the existing hypotheses on the growth of China's economic weight, current literature fails to fully explain this erosion of US influence.[56]

Traditional Latin Americanist scholarship, rooted in international development perspectives, has largely overlooked the geopolitical dimensions of China's economic rise in the region. This oversight becomes particularly glaring when we consider the transformative effects of China's engagement with Global South countries, including those in LAC.[57] Many Latin America experts have underestimated the potential for power shifts alongside China's challenge to US hegemony.[58] Some have even viewed China's presence as complementary rather than conflicting with US influence.[59] While the geopolitical aspect of their economic competition seemed negligible before the China–US trade war in 2018, it has since become a critical factor in global affairs, often overshadowing traditional developmentalist arguments. Notably, the geoeconomics and economic diplomacy literature does attempt to incorporate political dimensions into their work, particularly when analyzing China's global initiatives like the BRI. But there are significant shortcomings here as well. Geoeconomics suffers from conceptual ambiguity, with loose definitions making it difficult to operationalize for empirical research.[60] There is a lack of clear criteria for determining which state actions qualify as geoeconomic strategies.[61] Moreover, the direction of causality between economic and political factors remains ambiguous in this framework. Economic diplomacy literature, meanwhile, is useful for understanding China's Cold War strategies, but it faces its own challenges.[62] A primary issue is the problem of intentions: proving intentionality in positive economic diplomacy is particularly difficult. There's also an overemphasis on strategy, with an assumption that all economic actions have underlying geopolitical objectives. Additionally, the literature often displays a "great power bias," overestimating the ability of major powers to convert economic means into political benefits while underestimating the agency of target states.

In sum, development-focused literature neglects political dimensions, geoeconomics lacks conceptual clarity, and economic diplomacy struggles with issues of intentionality and state agency. A new approach is needed to fully grasp the complexities of China's engagement with the region, one that addresses these shortcomings and provides a more nuanced understanding of the interplay between economic and geopolitical factors in China's Latin American strategy.

To address the limitations of existing literature and quantify China's emergence as an alternative economic partner to the United States in Latin America, I developed a novel proxy variable (CHINESEACTORS). This metric measures the presence of Chinese economic entities in each country, offering a more objective approach to assessing China's economic influence. Specifically, CHINESEACTORS is a count variable that tallies the number of Chinese companies and banks maintaining a continuous presence in a given country. In this context, "continuous presence" is defined as having a physical address and conducting verifiable economic activities, such as making investments or providing loans. This approach allows for a more nuanced understanding of China's economic footprint in the region, moving beyond the conceptual ambiguities and intentionality debates that have hindered previous analyses.

To construct the CHINESEACTORS variable, I compiled data from an extensive original database containing over 4,800 news stories about Chinese investment, sourced from more than 800 newspapers and news portals covering the period from 2001 to 2020. Each news story was meticulously verified against investment data from authoritative sources, including fDi Markets, the China Global Investment Tracker, the China Foreign Direct Investment Observatory in LAC, and Mergr. This rigorous approach ensured the reliability of the data. The resulting variable reveals a striking trend across the thirty-three countries of Latin America and the Caribbean, as seen in Figure 3.2. On average, these nations had no Chinese economic actors present in their territories in 2001. This number grew to nearly five by 2011, and more than doubled to over eleven by 2020. However, this average conceals significant variations among countries, particularly among the region's largest economies. For instance, Brazil experienced a dramatic increase from zero Chinese actors

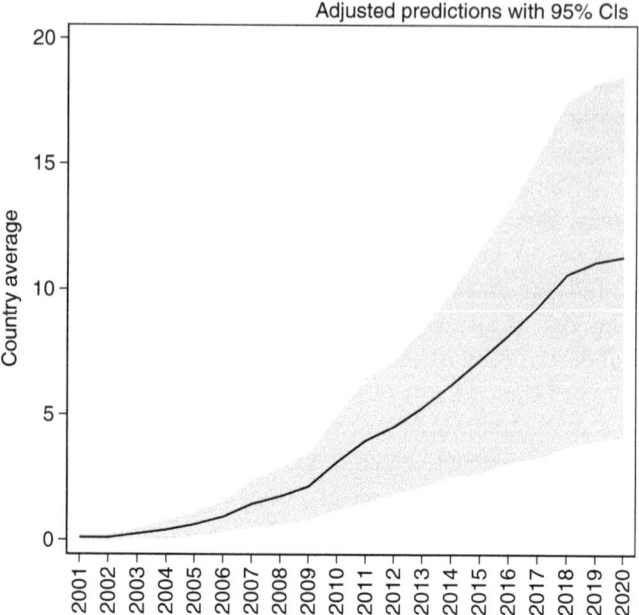

FIGURE 3.2 Average Chinese corporate and banking presence in Latin American countries

in 2001 to ninety-one in 2020. Similarly, Mexico saw a rise from two to seventy, while Argentina's presence of Chinese actors grew from zero to thirty over the same period.[63]

Although 238 Chinese companies invested in the region between 2001 and 2020, just thirty accounted for 81.4 percent of the total investment and leveraged credit from policy and commercial banks to be more competitive in public tenders. By the year 2020, the top ten Chinese companies with active presence in the region were: China Communications Construction Company (in twelve countries), Huawei (in ten countries), Power Construction Corporation of China (in nine countries), China Railway Construction (in seven countries), China National Machinery Industry Corporation (Sinomach) (in seven countries), China Three Gorges Corporation (in six countries), PetroChina (in six countries), Sinopec, Minmetals, and ZTE Corporation (in five countries each). The banks with the greatest presence in the region were ExIm Bank (seventeen countries), followed by ICBC (nine countries), and CDB and BOC (seven countries each).

If we examine the figure not by the amount invested, but by the number of projects each company and bank participated in, we observe an

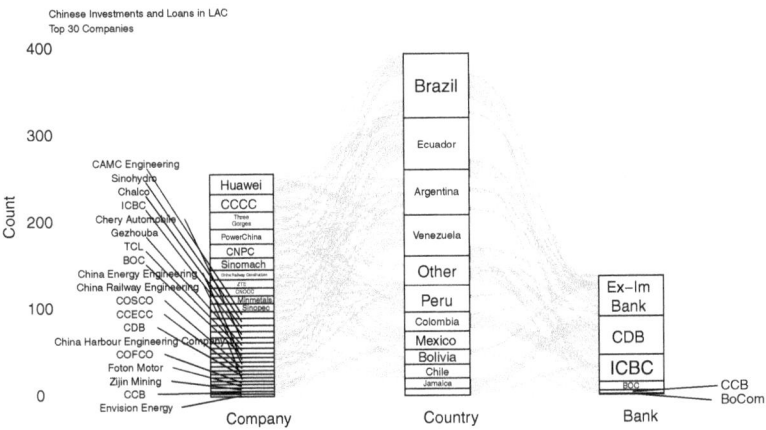

FIGURE 3.3 Top thirty leading Chinese investors and financiers by country, 2001–2020

image that clearly represents the idea of structural power: a complex network of independent Chinese actors managing to generate significant influence in each country (Figure 3.3).

3.2.1 Chinese Actors and the Provision of Alternative Goods

To estimate the effect of our four key variables on the active presence of Chinese actors (the presence of left-wing ideology, LEFTIST; the net commodity export price, COMMODITY; the GDP of the relevant country, GDP; and US economic weight, USECOWEIGHT), I used a panel data set from 2001 to 2020 for the thirty-three countries in LAC and defined a first-differences model with fixed effects by country. I included a lag of the dependent variable (CHINESEACTORS) to have an equilibrium correction mechanism and I used a lag of the independent variable USECOWEIGHT to capture both short-run dynamics and long-run equilibrium relationships. First, I estimated the effect of each variable separately. Then, in a fifth model, I estimated all the variables together. This fifth model is defined as follows:

$$\Delta \text{CHINESEACTORS}_{it} = \beta_{0it} + \beta_1 \text{CHINESEACTORS}_{it-1} + \beta_2 \Delta \text{USECOWEIGHT}_{it} \\ + \beta_3 \text{USECOWEIGHT}_{it-1} + \beta_4 \Delta \text{COMMODITY}_{it} + \beta_5 \Delta \text{LEFTIST}_{it} \\ + \beta_6 \Delta \text{GDP}_{it} + \omega_i$$

The results of the five models are presented in Table 3.2. Neither the variation in the ideology of governments nor the variation in the terms of

TABLE 3.2 *First difference regression models of Chinese goods provision*

	Model 1	Model 2	Model 3	Model 4	Model 5
CHINESEACTORS$_{t-1}$	−0.632***	−0.631***	−0.631***	−0.630***	−0.629***
	(0.0624)	(0.0615)	(0.0618)	(0.0686)	(0.0697)
ΔUSECOWEIGHT			−0.0676*		−0.0960+
			(0.0251)		(0.0491)
USECOWEIGHT$_{t-1}$					0.0336
					(0.0327)
ΔLEFTIST	−0.137				−0.141
	(0.190)				(0.198)
ΔCOMMODITY		−0.0028			−0.0024
		(0.0018)			(0.0017)
ΔGDP				0.00018	0.00021
				(0.00146)	(0.00150)
Constant	0.40***	0.41***	0.40***	0.40***	0.40***
	(0.038)	(0.038)	(0.040)	(0.047)	(0.051)
Country fixed effects	Yes	Yes	Yes	Yes	Yes
Observations	594	576	589	594	571
R²	0.32	0.32	0.32	0.32	0.32

Note: Robust standard errors in parentheses. $+P < 0.10$, $*P < 0.05$, $***P < 0.001$

trade for each country have a correlation with the increase in China's sustained presence in a country. Instead, the coefficient of USECOWEIGHT (the US's economic weight) is negatively associated with the number of Chinese actors – a finding that is in line with the hypothesis of this book. These results reveal a complex and dynamic relationship between US economic weight and the presence of Chinese economic actors in Latin American countries. The model, which incorporates both short-term changes and long-term levels, provides nuanced insights into this relationship. In the short term, we observe a displacement effect: increases in US economic weight are associated with decreases in the presence of Chinese actors. This suggests an immediate competitive dynamic between US and Chinese economic interests in the region, where gains in US influence may temporarily reduce opportunities for Chinese engagement. However, the long-term picture is less clear. While we initially observe a positive relationship between long-term US economic presence and the number of Chinese actors, this relationship is not statistically significant in our final model. This lack of significance suggests that the long-term US economic weight may not have a consistent, predictable impact on the presence of

Chinese actors across all countries in the region. Furthermore, our model reveals an equilibrium correction mechanism in the presence of Chinese actors. When their numbers deviate from an equilibrium level, there's a tendency for correction in subsequent periods.

My findings indicate that while short-term fluctuations reflect competitive dynamics, the long-term relationship between US and Chinese economic presence in Latin America is more complex and may vary considerably across different countries or contexts. This underscores the need for nuanced, country-specific analyses to fully understand the interplay between US and Chinese economic influences in the region. Significantly, the variables for government ideology and commodity price cycles, the two variables frequently cited in the literature as significant determinants of China's economic engagement in Latin America, seem not to affect the presence of Chinese actors. Moreover, across various model specifications, including those testing for both short-term and long-term equilibrium effects, these control variables consistently yielded statistically insignificant results. This lack of significance persisted regardless of how I specified the models or which combination of variables I included. These results suggest that the dynamics between US economic weight and Chinese economic presence in Latin America are more robust to these factors than previously thought.

3.2.2 Filling the Void

In this section, we turn to a critical question: in which sectors did Chinese actors fill voids left by the United States? Table 3.3 encapsulates data from four economic sectors: investments, trade, finance, and foreign aid. The columns show the total amounts for the United States and China in LAC from 2001 to 2020. The United States is measured both with and without Mexico, as it is crucial to recognize Mexico as a significant outlier in the economic weight of the United States in LAC. Many indicators vary notably depending on whether Mexico is included, reinforcing a conclusion from the previous chapter that LAC can be considered as two distinct regions: one where China has gained considerable economic influence (South America) and one where the United States has maintained its role as the main extra-regional economic partner (Central America, Mexico, and the Caribbean). The last column provides the ratio between the United States and China for each sector, with values equal to or less than 1 indicating those in which China has become more prominent and relevant.

TABLE 3.3 *Identifying sectors with emerging Chinese providers*

	US	US (excluding Mexico)	China	Ratio US: China (excluding Mexico)
Investments[a]				
Fossil fuels	33,100	27,100	27,375	0.99
Renewables	15,400	12,200	82,052	0.15
Metals & minerals	18,480	15,105	53,587	0.28
Total FDI flows	323,155	191,500	265,658	0.72
Jobs created through greenfield FDI[b]	1,018,181	498,146	210,927	2.36
Trade[a]				
Export of commodities	2,448,260	1,273,450	1,307,286	0.97
Total exports	7,447,364	2,043,691	1,451,000	1.41
Total imports	5,701,032	2,345,070	2,581,017	0.91
Total trade	13,148,396	4,388,761	4,032,017	1.09
Finance[a]				
Infrastructure financing	38,700	38,500	66,350	0.58
Total financing	1,650,000	1,330,000	138,000	9.64
Aid[a]				
Mask diplomacy[c]	0.293	0.282	0.278	1.01
Total aid	96,200	86,100	4,657	18.49

Sources: FDI from China and the US were elaborated upon using various sources, including fDi Markets and Mergr for the US. Finance in infrastructure for China is based on Kaplan, *Globalizing Patient Capital* and data from AIIB and NDB, while for the US it includes contributions from the World Bank (WB), the Inter-American Development Bank (IADB), and the Development Finance Corporation (DFC). Total Chinese finance is referenced from Ray and Myers, "Chinese Loans to Latin America and the Caribbean Database," with US finance also including the International Monetary Fund (IMF). Trade data for both countries were obtained from UN Comtrade. Aid information for China was sourced from CIDCA and AidData, for the US from USAID, and aid mask diplomacy was based on the author's own elaboration. In bold are highlighted the sectors where China has surpassed the US, or reached parity.
[a] Expressed in billions of US$.
[b] Based on fDi Markets.
[c] Counting the first two years of the COVID-19 pandemic.

This analysis prioritizes sectors where China's growth is more substantial, as these will be examined in the next chapter and are more illustrative of the change in economic influence. In investments, China has filled a void in energy, both in renewable energies and fossil fuels. It has also filled a void in the mining sector. Many Chinese investments in these sectors have been significant acquisitions, indicating that China did not create as many new jobs as US corporate investments during the period of analysis. In trade, China has become a critical market for the sale of commodities, often less limited by tariff and non-tariff barriers present in the United States. Additionally, China has become crucial for the import of manufactured products and intermediate goods. Financially, US-led actors maintain a significant predominance in credits to improve the balance of payments and credits to private actors. However, when it comes to financing infrastructure projects, Chinese policy and commercial banks have surpassed the combined efforts of the DFC, the World Bank, and the IADB. In terms of humanitarian aid, the United States still maintains (and is likely to continue to maintain for many years) a strong advantage over China. However, during the COVID-19 pandemic, China's aid was almost equivalent to that of the United States, which proved crucial for controlling the pandemic in some countries. Notably, despite Chinese growth in certain sectors, this evidence alone is not sufficient to illustrate the filling of an economic void (a topic addressed in greater depth in Chapter 4).

One of the central facets of the ascendance of China's economic weight is that its repercussions were palpably experienced on a local scale. Through the creation of employment opportunities and the enhancement of economic activity, politicians at both national and subnational levels endeavored to align themselves with Chinese entrepreneurs and officials whenever an investment was announced, a trade agreement was forged, or any economic pact was unveiled that promised benefits for the electorate of a given locality. For instance, from my database encompassing 4,894 news articles on Chinese investments covering 490 investment projects in LAC, 28 percent include statements from politicians. Only 10 percent of the articles feature declarations of investments pertaining to acquisitions or mergers, but a significant 39 percent of the news pieces on greenfield investments reference the viewpoints of relevant politicians. Joint announcements, speeches, and ribbon-cutting ceremonies have not been uncommon at the inauguration of greenfield investments.

One of the most authoritative estimates regarding the impact of China's economic rise on job creation in LAC was published by the International Labor Organization (ILO).[64] The estimate posits that Chinese investment and infrastructure projects in LAC generated over 600,000 jobs between 1995 and 2011, and that trade with China was responsible for creating 1.15 million jobs; a number that accounts for 2.15 percent of all new jobs generated in the region during this period. The ILO's estimations were grounded in a meticulous analysis of four countries – Argentina, Brazil, Chile, and Mexico – and extrapolated to the rest of the region. Notably, Mexico stands out as the sole country among the four where China's economic activities led to a net loss in employment rather than the creation of jobs.

3.2.3 Drivers of Economic Displacement: Analyzing the Pace and Prevalence of China's Economic Influence

Between 2000 and 2020, twelve countries in Latin America and the Caribbean (representing 60 percent of the population) experienced economic displacement of the United States by China. Having empirically demonstrated my assertion that Chinese actors filled voids when the economic weight of the United States diminished, I turn now to investigate why economic displacement happened earlier in some countries than others and why it didn't occur at all in some places. In this section, I test whether the time it takes for a country to experience displacement is due to the number and seniority of Chinese actors on the ground offering goods (ALTPROVIDERS), or if it is due to ideological affinities (LEFTIST), terms of trade (COMMODITIES), or development conditions (GDP). Following my overarching argument, I expect that the greater the supply of Chinese substitute goods, the faster the displacement will occur.

To test my hypothesis, I used a Cox survival model with a panel structure, where the dependent variable is the occurrence or non-occurrence of economic displacement. Through these models I wish to estimate how different variables influence the risk or rate of economic displacement occurring over time. The results confirm that, compared to alternative explanations, the occurrence of economic displacement is positively associated with the number of Chinese actors in the host country. The greater the presence of Chinese actors and the less developed the country, the faster the economic displacement occurs (Table 3.4). The first three models test each variable separately, and Model 4 includes them all together. Among the alternative explanations, the one with greater empirical support is ideological affinity, significant at the 10 percent level in Model 3. However, Model 4 emphatically emphasizes the importance of Chinese providers of alternative goods, as the coefficient remains significant and its magnitude increases compared to Model 1.

The hazard function in Model 4 provides a comprehensive visualization of how the risk of economic displacement by China changes over time, accounting for all key factors simultaneously, which helps identify

TABLE 3.4 *Cox survival model for the occurrence of economic displacement*

	Model 1	Model 2	Model 3	Model 4
ALTPROVIDERS	0.043**			0.13**
	(0.0134)			(0.047)
COMMODITIES		0.0002		0.0098
		(0.0143)		(0.0123)
LEFTIST			0.746+	0.622
			(0.0199)	(0.422)
GDP				−0.0027*
				(0.0011)
Observations	495	494	495	494

Note: Standard errors clustered by country in parentheses. +$P < 0.10$, *$P < 0.05$, **$P < 0.01$.

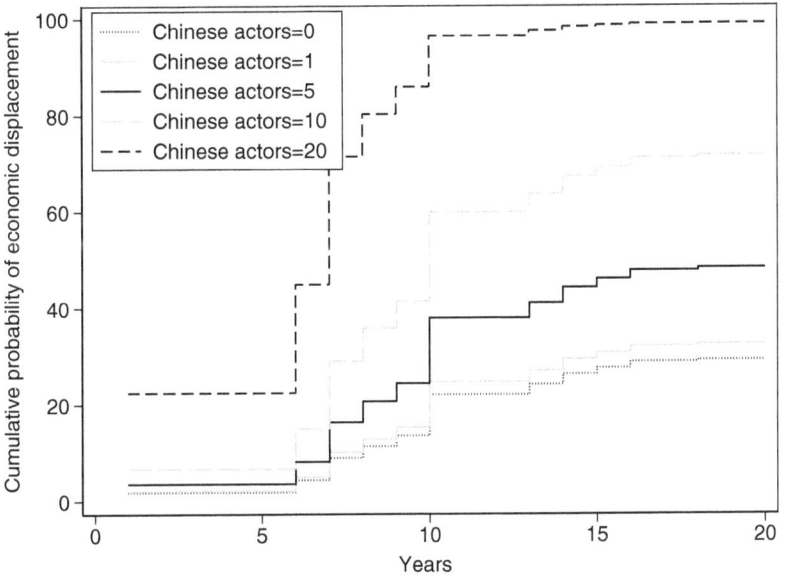

FIGURE 3.4 Chinese actor presence and economic displacement risk over time

critical periods of heightened risk and illustrates the combined impact of Chinese presence, ideological alignment, commodity dependence, and economic development on the likelihood of displacement occurring at any given moment (Figure 3.4). The presence of twenty Chinese actors for at least ten years almost perfectly predicts the occurrence of displacement. What we see is that, with ten or more Chinese actors, there is a greater likelihood than not that the country will experience displacement within a ten-year period.

3.3 TESTING THE UNIQUENESS OF CHINESE ECONOMIC ENGAGEMENT: A CONJOINT EXPERIMENT ON INVESTMENT PREFERENCES

There exists a possibility, at least theoretically, that the increasing economic weight of China in LAC is not attributable to China filling economic voids left by the US. It could be, for example, that the demand for alternative Chinese goods emerged due to their inherent attributes; because, say, they were superior. One could further imagine that Chinese investments are preferable because Latin Americans have a cultural affinity for China, or perhaps because the ethos of Chinese companies differs from that of Western companies. Alternatively, one might theorize that Chinese loans offer significantly lower interest rates than Western lenders, or generally more favorable terms.

Testing hypotheses of this nature entails a certain degree of complexity. For example: investments by Chinese companies are more frequent in certain economic sectors than in others, with the majority of investments coming from state-owned enterprises and in the form of mergers and acquisitions. Whether Chinese investment is more or less preferable over investment from another country might be due to something inherent to Chinese nationality or a preference for investment in sectors where Chinese companies are active, or even the manner in which they invest. Accessing the preferences of political decision-makers for goods provided by China is just as difficult, if not impossible, in large samples. At least here we can assume that the preferences of the public will not be vastly different from those of the decision-makers in representative democracies.[65]

One way to determine if there is anything special about the goods provided by China to LAC (such that it could explain China's economic displacement of the US by China) is through a conjoint experiment. In April 2021, I conducted an experiment designed to determine participant preferences toward foreign investment using a sample of 796 Chileans and following the standard methodology used in political science.[66] Survey respondents were presented with two pairs of investment projects where they randomly received variable attributes about the nationality of the investing company, the sector of investment, market concentration generated by the investment, and jobs created by the investment. The total sample consisted of N = 3,178 evaluated investments. When asked, for

TABLE 3.5 *Sample comparison of investment project pairs*

	Option A	Option B
Nationality	US	China
Sector	Copper	Hotels
Market concentration	5%	25%
Jobs created	500	100

example, "Which of these two investments do you think is more desirable for Chile?" the respondent was exposed to the following pair and had to choose one (Table 3.5):

The conjoint experiment, designed to assess Chilean preferences for foreign investments, revealed nuanced insights into the factors influencing public opinion. Participants evaluated hypothetical investment scenarios varying in investor nationality (US, China, Brazil, or Saudi Arabia), economic sector, market concentration, and potential for job creation. For a baseline, it used a US investment in electricity distribution with a 5 percent market share and 100 jobs. As Figure 3.5 suggests, Chileans were largely indifferent to the nationality of the investing company, including Chinese firms. Instead, the results showed that their preferences were primarily driven by economic impact factors. Investments that maintained lower market concentration and created more jobs were consistently favored. Interestingly, while most economic sectors elicited similar responses, the copper industry stood out as an exception, likely due to its status as a state-controlled, strategic resource in Chile. Otherwise, the sector of investment generally did not sway preferences significantly. These findings suggest that Chilean public opinion on foreign investment is more influenced by the potential economic benefits and market effects than by the origin of the investment, with particular sensitivity to strategic national interests in specific sectors.

This conjoint experiment suggests that the hypothesis tested and articulated in this book holds true: there is nothing particularly special about the goods offered by China. Rather, China economically displaced the US simply by filling the space left in sectors where the US had previously been a key player. As we will see in Chapter 4, local demand for Chinese goods was key to this process, though local actors often had few or no alternatives to the goods offered by Chinese actors, particularly in the sectors highlighted in Table 3.3. Nevertheless, there was a local demand, and Chinese actors met it.

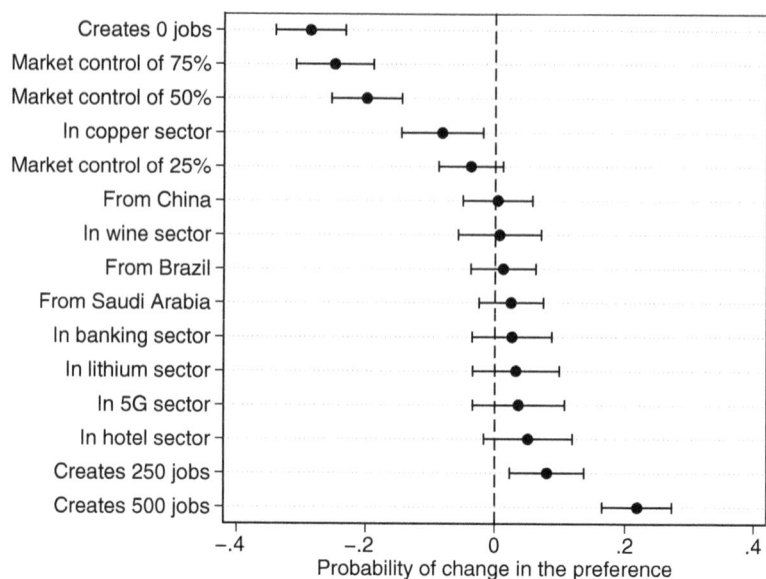

FIGURE 3.5 FDI preference: impact of investment attributes
Note: estimates are based on the regression estimators with clustered standard errors by respondent; bars represent 95 percent confidence intervals. In this figure, the baseline is an investment from the United States, with 5 percent market control in the energy sector, creating 100 jobs.

3.4 CONCLUSION

This dense, but fundamental, chapter has provided the empirical foundation for this book's core hypothesis by demonstrating the significant proposition that China economically displaced the US in LAC by filling voids left by the United States. This chapter has also raised a central question that leads us into Chapter 4: Was this displacement the result of a deliberate strategy by China or, rather, the result of Latin American agency? My argument is that it was the latter. Chapter 4 shows that Latin American actors actively turned to China in search of solutions to internal development needs in which Western actors were either unavailable or unwilling to engage. This demand came not only from nation-states, but also from subnational actors. By shifting the focus away from Chinese strategy – where China's increasing influence in LAC is often deemed the result of deliberate strategy – we are better able to perceive the active role of Latin American countries in shaping their own economic futures. This necessary reframing acknowledges that Latin American countries have agency in their international relations and are not merely passive recipients of foreign influence.

4

The Demand Side

Latin American Agency in Economic Displacement

A prevalent narrative in existing literature posits that China expands its global reach by exporting its development model and *imposing* it upon other nations.[1] This perspective overlooks the agency of developing countries. In this chapter, I show that China's influence grew through its engagement with a variety of local entities that actively sought what Chinese actors offered, and that these local entities thereby participated in China's rise through the consumption of Chinese alternative goods. According to my explanatory theory for why China has been able to expand its economic influence, a combination of access to alternative goods and specific development needs led political elites to turn to Chinese economic actors to deliver results to their constituents.

The active pursuit of Chinese goods and investments by Latin American countries is an understudied area. Most studies have focused on what China offers to LAC countries, rather than what LAC countries demand and how. An exception is literature on demand for credit from Chinese banks, with Jonas Bunte's book signifying a major contribution.[2] But based on empirical evidence from a burgeoning body of literature exploring local agency in Asia and Africa, we can propose that Latin American countries exercise agency in their dealings with China through two main mechanisms that reflect top-down and bottom-up approaches.[3] Delving into three case studies, this chapter illustrates the two ideal-type mechanisms through which national and subnational actors in LAC have exerted agency in demanding Chinese goods when Western alternatives were scarce or inexistent. The first mechanism I explore is the national–subnational relationship, in which agency originates with the national government and is expressed in a top-down dynamic. In these cases, national governments channel Chinese investments and credits to subnational actors, at times aiming to benefit political allies or address specific development needs in strategic localities. The second mechanism revolves around how national governments leverage the connections between subnational economic elites or subnational governments and China in a bottom-up dynamic. This mechanism is pivotal for illustrating the multitude of non-state channels that China has solidified over the past two decades, which represent its true structural power.

In Chapter 3, I presented instances of sectoral displacement where Chinese actors have clearly outperformed their US counterparts since 2001. These sectors include investment in energy projects, infrastructure financing, and, more recently, COVID-19 aid. I use these extreme cases of sectoral displacement to illustrate both mechanisms of goods consumption. Across the three illustrative case studies, there are several points of variation worth noting: temporal variation, as they span from 2010 to 2021; variation in national contexts, as they involve three different countries; and variation in the demand-side actor. In terms of the demand-side actor, I include one case in which agency is exerted by the national government (case 1), one case in which the agency is exerted by a company (case 2), and one case in which the agency is exerted by subnational governments (case 3).

The evidence shown in Chapter 3 suggested that the outcomes of China–Latin America interactions have resulted from a combination of China's offerings and Latin American countries' desires. This chapter builds on that argument, suggesting that the preferences of recipient countries play a particularly crucial role when engaging with Chinese public entities. In the sections to come, I will show that Latin American nations are not merely passive recipients of Chinese propositions, but active participants shaping agreements based on their own needs and priorities.

4.1 NATIONAL-LEVEL AGENCY: A TOP-DOWN MECHANISM

The top-down mechanism for demanding goods within the context of China–Latin America relations involves the national executive branch initiating engagement with Chinese actors. This can be through a ministry, the presidency, or a state agency acting on behalf of a private company or subnational government. In this scenario, the central government serves as a "broker." Depictions of this mechanism, which focuses on how national governments drive engagement with China, are prevalent in existing literature outside of LAC. Yuan Wang's research in Africa, for example, demonstrates that when projects are crucial to national leaders' political futures, these leaders become heavily involved. This "political championship" often outweighs Chinese influence in project realization.[4] Cross-country evidence in Kenya, Ethiopia, Laos, and Myanmar similarly shows that national leaders who viewed railway projects as vital to their political success ensured these projects progressed despite challenges.[5] Austin Strange has described these as "prestige-infrastructure projects" due to their symbolic value for national leaders.[6] Similar behavior has occurred in Latin America, with presidents and prime ministers personally championing certain Chinese-backed projects they believe would enhance their political standing. Other examples of top-down mechanisms for demanding Chinese goods include state involvement (primarily through foreign affairs and finance ministries) in joining Chinese multilateral banks – such as the AIIB and NDB (for Brazil) – or joining the BRI. Presidents in these cases have assumed the role of interacting with Chinese counterparts despite the fact that the ultimate beneficiaries of Chinese goods are often subnational actors. Thus, agency was exerted by the national government.

4.1.1 Case Study 1. Top-Down Dynamics in Energetic Infrastructure Projects: Fulfilling Subnational Energy Demands in Argentina through Chinese Lending

In the realm of energy infrastructure financing in LAC between 2001 and 2020, a significant contrast emerged between US-led institutions and Chinese entities. The World Bank and the Inter-American Development Bank (IADB) collectively lent US$32.3 billion. In contrast, Chinese institutions – namely the China Development Bank and the Export-Import Bank of China – extended a staggering US$57.6 billion in loans (Figure 4.1). This disparity highlights the growing influence of Chinese financing in the region's energy sector.

However, these aggregated figures mask significant heterogeneities between countries. Argentina stands out with one of the highest lending ratios in favor of China, receiving US$9.9 from Chinese banks for every dollar received from US-led banks. Venezuela tops the list with an impressive ratio of US$84.63 from Chinese banks for every dollar received from US-led banks, followed by Argentina, Brazil, and Ecuador. For countries where this ratio exceeds 1, Chinese actors have been crucial in financing energy projects, serving as an attractive alternative to Western loans, especially for subnational actors struggling to access international credit (Table 4.1).

TABLE 4.1 *Loans for energy infrastructure from 2001 to 2020 (in US$ millions)*

	Chinese banks	US-led banks	Ratio
Venezuela	19,516	231	84.63
Argentina	3,030	307	9.88
Brazil	26,781	4,796	5.58
Ecuador	5,335	1,258	4.24
Bolivia	1,000	551	1.81
Mexico	1,000	1,411	0.71
Guyana	39	588	0.06
Dominican Republic	600	0	–
Cuba	220	0	–
Colombia	0	459	–
Honduras	0	721	–
El Salvador	0	723	–
Peru	0	1,472	–
Chile	0	2,934	–
Jamaica	0	3,648	–

Source: Author's elaboration.

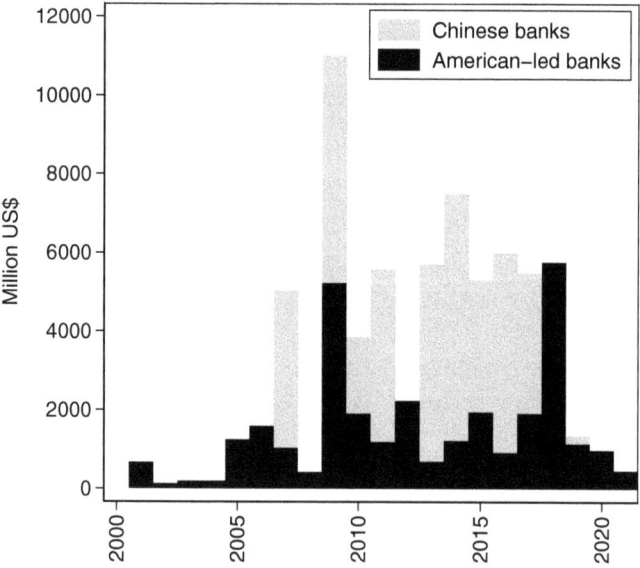

FIGURE 4.1 Loans for energy infrastructure in LAC, 2001–2020
Source: Author's elaboration. For Chinese loans, I used the database of Ray and Myers (2023); for the American-led banks, I used the repositories of the World Bank (WB) and the Inter-American Development Bank (IADB).

The case study presented here examines the Patagonian Dams project in Argentina, illustrating how Chinese financing was harnessed to meet both national energy demands and subnational aspirations. The analysis draws upon data from government documents, laws, speeches, and semi-structured interviews with public officials at both the national and provincial levels.[7]

4.1.1.1 Origins of the Patagonian Dams Project

The Santa Cruz River, a 385-km waterway in Argentine Patagonia, had long been considered for damming. Originating from the Argentino Lake and primarily fed by glacier meltwater from Los Glaciares National Park, the river's potential for hydroelectric power generation has been recognized since 1950.[8] However, the project remained in the evaluation phase for decades, overshadowed by more urgent developments along the Rio Negro and Rio Limay in northern Patagonia during the 1970s.[9]

The project's fortunes changed dramatically with the rise of Néstor Kirchner. His political journey from mayor of Río Gallegos (Santa Cruz's capital) to governor of Santa Cruz, and ultimately to president of Argentina, brought renewed focus to the dam project. Then, from 2007 onward, the initiative gained significant momentum under his wife and successor, President Cristina Kirchner. Initially dubbed the "Condor Cliff and Barrancosa" dams, the project was later renamed the "Néstor Kirchner and Jorge Cepernic" dams following Néstor Kirchner's sudden death in 2010. This renaming not only honored the late president but also symbolized the project's importance to the Kirchner political legacy. For clarity, however, we'll refer to them here as the "Patagonian Dams."

The project's revival coincided with Argentina's energy deficit between 2010 and 2019, which was hindering national growth. As shown in Figure 4.2, Argentina's energy balance (exports minus imports) was consistently negative during this period, reaching its lowest point in 2013 with a deficit of over US$6 billion. The Patagonian Dams emerged as arguably the most significant public infrastructure project in Argentina over the past two decades, as it promised to address this energy shortfall. However, its realization hinged on securing both financing and expertise in large-scale project management.

4.1.1.2 The Kirchner Legacy and Chinese Financing

The province of Santa Cruz's political landscape had been notably shaped by the Partido Justicialista (Peronism) since Argentina's return to democracy in 1983. Néstor Kirchner held the governorship of Santa Cruz for

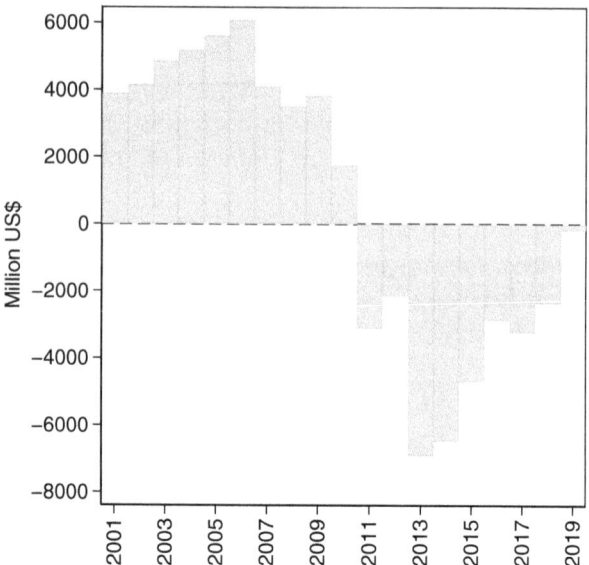

FIGURE 4.2 Argentina's energy trade balance (in US$ millions)
Source: Ministry of Economy of Argentina.

twelve years (1991–2003) before becoming president. After 2003, the provincial governorship remained under the influence of the Kirchner family, and successive governors remained firmly aligned with their political agenda, including Héctor Icazuriaga, Sergio Acevedo, Carlos Sancho, and Daniel Peralta. This continuity extended all the way to Alicia Kirchner, Néstor's sister, who assumed the governorship in 2016 and further cemented the Kirchner legacy in the province.

Despite sustained interest from Santa Cruz and from Kirchner himself, the Patagonia Dams project faced several setbacks before the Chinese became involved. In the summer of 2007, the first provincial tender was held, but it was scrapped due to the 2008 global financial crisis. Notably, no American company showed interest, and the greatest expectations were placed on major Brazilian construction firms such as Camargo Correa, Oderbrecht, and Andrade Gutierrez. A second tender in 2010 sought a consortium capable of constructing, financing, and operating the dams, as well as exploiting the natural resource through a concession. The winning consortium, composed of Impsa (owned by Argentine tycoon Enrique Pescarmona), Corporación América (owned by Argentine tycoon Eduardo Eurnekian), and the Brazilian group Camargo Correa, submitted a bid of AR$16.4 billion (about US$4.1 million). But despite approval from the Santa Cruz Legislature, the federal government refused to provide the necessary funds. José López, then-Secretary of Public Works, cited the winning consortium's failure to provide required financing as the reason.[10] However, political differences between Néstor Kirchner and Santa Cruz Governor Daniel Peralta, as well as China's growing interest in the project, were also cited as reasons for the cancellation.[11]

Following the two failed tenders, Argentina's national government (now under the leadership of Cristina Kircher) played a crucial role in enabling the Gezhouba Group, a state-owned enterprise from Wuhan, Hubei, to provide the necessary financial resources and technical expertise for the hydroelectric plants. Gezhouba was just beginning its operations in LAC, having recently started work on the Sopladora dam in Ecuador.[12] In an orchestrated collaboration, the Argentine national government was able to strategically harness Chinese financing to bridge the energy gap and meet the aspirations of its allied subnational province.

4.1.1.3 From Diplomatic Visits to Mega-projects

Cristina Kirchner's first diplomatic visit to Beijing in July 2010 marked a watershed moment in Sino–Argentine relations, resulting in agreements worth US$10 billion. Under the framework of the "Acuerdo de Cooperación en Materia de Infraestructura de Transporte" (Cooperation Agreement on Transport Infrastructure), both nations committed to significant Chinese lending in Argentina's railway sector. This included the repair and modernization of existing rail branches, as well as the procurement of wagons and engines from CNR, a Chinese company that later merged with CSR to form the China Railway Rolling Stock Corporation (CRRC). These initial agreements laid the groundwork for even more substantial collaboration. During subsequent visits, a Joint Declaration was formalized between the two governments, establishing a comprehensive framework for agreements across key sectors, including energy, mining, agriculture, and transportation.

Both Néstor and Cristina Kirchner's visits to China in 2004 and 2012, respectively, were instrumental in introducing political allies to Chinese business leaders. Néstor's 2004 delegation included Sergio Acevedo, then-governor of Santa Cruz, along with six other allied governors and approximately 200 Argentine business leaders.[13] This visit facilitated introductions to potential Chinese business partners and led to numerous subsequent agreements. Similarly, Cristina Kirchner's 2010 visit was accompanied by hundreds of business representatives.[14] And in 2012, the Patagonia Dams project moved forward with a new public bid.[15]

FIGURE 4.3 President Kirchner meets with Gezhouba Group and Electroingenieria executives, August 21, 2013
Source: Presidencia de Argentina (2013). Note: In this image, President Cristina Kirchner is sitting across the table from Jianguo Ren, the Vice President of Gezhouba Group Corporation. To her left is Julio De Vido, the Minister of Public Works. Gerardo Ferreyra, the CEO of Electroingenieria, sits to the right of Ren.

On January 10, 2013, tenders were officially reopened, with five consortiums submitting bids (although only four had their technical proposals approved). Two of the bidders featured Chinese companies.

The winning consortium included the Argentine firm Electroingeniería alongside Gezhouba, and the credit agreement was forged with three different Chinese banks: the China Development Bank Corporation (US$2.5 billion), the Industrial and Commercial Bank of China (US$1.41 billion), and the Bank of China (US$801 million). The terms of the loan included an interest rate of London Inter-Bank Offered Rate (LIBOR) plus 3.8 percent, which, at the time, amounted to 4.8 percent.[16] Additionally, credit insurance was provided by the China Export & Credit Insurance Corporation (Sinosure), incurring a cost equivalent to 7.1 percent of the total financing. The national government itself bore full responsibility for covering this insurance cost, which could be distributed across twenty installments (Figure 4.3).[17]

A milestone in the Sino–Argentine partnership occurred in July 2014 following Xi Jinping's first visit to Argentina. A "Framework Agreement of Cooperation in Economic and Investment Matters" was signed, with the Patagonian Dams and the Belgrano Cargas railway project emerging as flagship agreements. Both projects included cross-default clauses, meaning that non-compliance by one would have implications for the other. The path to executing these agreements was eased by the ratification of the Cooperation Framework Agreement by the Argentine National Congress in March 2015.[18] This legislative framework granted the national government authority to promote investment cooperation from Chinese companies, particularly in sectors with substantial export potential to the Chinese market. It also introduced the concept that acquisitions within the scope of Argentine public sector projects could be awarded through direct bidding, so long as they adhered to concessional financing criteria from the Chinese side and offered advantageous terms in both quality and price. The Patagonia Dams, with a budget of US$4.7 billion and a projected timeline of five years, were finally materializing as a historic project for the province.

4.1.1.4 *National Demand and the Structural Power of Chinese Capital*

The hydroelectric project promised significant benefits. It was expected to provide approximately 4 percent of Argentina's total energy consumption and increase hydroelectricity generation by an impressive 15 percent. The province of Santa Cruz itself stood to gain a significant share – 12 percent – of the royalties generated from electricity production. The construction phase alone promised substantial economic benefits, with the potential to employ around 5,000 individuals.[19]

One of the most notable aspects of the hydroelectric project was its financing arrangement, which broke new ground in Argentina. It not only covered the entirety of the project's cost, but also encompassed internal taxes, including VAT, amounting to a staggering 121 percent of the project's value. This level of comprehensive coverage surpassed the offerings of any other bidder in the tender process. The repayment period spanned fifteen years, featuring an initial grace period of sixty-six months – mirroring the construction phase – followed by an additional 9.5 years dedicated to repayment. Crucially, the Kirchner administration envisioned a self-sustaining credit repayment model. It hinged on the premise that the power generated by the dams would generate the necessary funds for loan repayment. Consequently, Argentina committed to commencing loan repayments to Chinese lenders only after the power plants had become operational. This "repayable with energy" arrangement was seen as a unique benefit that no Western lender would offer.

However, despite the fact that the Patagonian Dams benefited both the government of Santa Cruz and the national government, the construction of the dams was repeatedly paused. In the end, the project took more than ten years to complete. At the time of this writing, in fact, it remains uncompleted. Critics raised questions about the choice of Santa Cruz for this project, given that there are other rivers in Argentina with better water flow and closer proximity to major cities where electricity consumption is higher. Energy experts also questioned the efficiency of the project, noting that the dams could operate at full capacity for only a third of the year. The existing high-voltage power transmission lines were deemed insufficient, capable of accommodating just 45 percent of the energy generated by the dams. To address this issue, substantial additional investments would be required to build new transmission lines, further complicating the project's economic equation. It's also worth noting that in May 2015, the World Bank Group announced the disqualification of Gezhouba and its subsidiaries for a period of eighteen months due to their misconduct in three World Bank-financed projects in China.

Environmental concerns have also posed significant challenges. The project faced opposition from environmental organizations and national figures concerned about its impact on glaciers and native Patagonian fauna. The original plan involved flooding over 47,000 hectares of land to accommodate eleven turbines with a combined capacity of 1,740 MW. However, this plan was later reduced to mitigate environmental effects.[20] Then, in 2016, the Supreme Court of Argentina suspended the construction until a comprehensive environmental impact assessment process could be implemented.[21] The project's progress remained halted until the beginning of 2018 and stalled for over four years until October 2022 when bank payments were resumed to finance the project.

Notably, the transition of political power in Argentina has also created turmoil. President Macri's decision to suspend the project created a diplomatic crisis, as Chinese banks had already released initial funds. This abrupt policy shift strained relations between the two countries, with China issuing a stark ultimatum threatening to withdraw all loans to Argentina. A comparable situation arose during President Milei's first year in office in 2024.

China's formidable structural power in the relationship ultimately proved too substantial to allow for the project's termination. This power manifested in the intricate financial arrangements between the two nations, particularly in the payment facility agreements for the dams and the Belgrano Cargas railway project. These agreements included cross-default clauses, creating a situation where defaulting on one project would automatically trigger a default on the other.[22] This interconnected financial structure effectively bound the fates of these major infrastructure projects together, significantly raising the stakes for any potential project cancellation. Furthermore, the renewal of yuan currency swaps with the Bank of China was explicitly tied to the continued progress of the dam project. This financial mechanism, crucial for Argentina's monetary stability, added another layer of complexity to the relationship and further cemented China's influence over Argentina's economic decision-making.

4.1.1.5 Conclusion: Top-Down Agency in the Energy Sector

The case of the Patagonian Dams project in Argentina exemplifies the top-down mechanism of engagement with Chinese actors in which national-level agency plays a pivotal role. In this case, the Argentine national government, particularly under the Kirchner administrations, acted as a "broker" between Chinese financiers and the subnational interests of Santa Cruz province. Moreover, the project's trajectory aligns with infrastructure projects in other countries where national leaders became heavily involved in projects that were crucial to their political futures. The Kirchners' personal investment in the Patagonian Dams project, from its conception to its implementation, demonstrates how such "prestige-infrastructure projects" can become central to a leader's political legacy. This personal involvement proved instrumental in moving the project forward despite numerous challenges.

4.2 BOTTOM-UP MECHANISM: SUBNATIONAL AND NON-STATE AGENCY

The second mechanism through which national and subnational actors in LAC have exerted agency in demanding Chinese goods is a bottom-up dynamic characterized by governments capitalizing on connections between subnational economic elites and/or subnational governments and China. This mechanism is crucial in demonstrating the multitude of non-state channels that China has established over the past two decades, which represent its true structural power. For their part, states may share agency by leveraging initiatives started by subnational actors, orchestrate company agency to their benefit, or, in some cases, completely delegate agency in the demand for Chinese goods.

Evidence from Africa and Asia indicates that various levels of government control access to resources for Chinese investors, with local politics playing a significant role in attracting investment and aid.[23] This dynamic suggests that even countries perceived to have limited power actually wield considerable local influence.[24] In the Latin American context, this could mean that state or provincial governments significantly shape the implementation of Chinese investments or aid allocation in their regions. For example, a Brazilian state might develop its own policies or negotiations with Chinese entities, potentially competing to attract companies interested in local resources or infrastructure projects. Subnational governments may also utilize their own connections to China through province-to-province diplomacy[25] or party-to-party diplomacy,[26] particularly when national leaders are openly critical of China. In larger countries, local leaders often possess detailed knowledge about areas of Chinese investment interest that national authorities lack. These local officials can leverage their expertise and local knowledge to influence negotiations with Chinese entities.[27] For example, municipal leaders or regional experts may advocate for changes in Chinese project implementation to better align with local needs or conditions that outsiders might not fully comprehend.

Meanwhile, as part of their "Going Global" strategy, Chinese firms actively seek partnerships with local companies, particularly those with a proven track record in winning bids. Faced with the challenge of rapidly expanding into numerous international markets, these Chinese companies have recognized the need for swift adaptation and local expertise. In this context, several key factors make local companies attractive partners. For example, these firms have cultivated connections with both local and national leaders, indicating awareness that they provide valuable political capital. They also establish access to top-tier local law firms, which offer crucial insights into environmental regulations, labor laws, and other legal intricacies that could impact projects. Moreover, local firms possess an intimate understanding of the local business landscape, cultural nuances, and region-specific challenges. A proven ability to navigate local bidding processes successfully has been particularly valuable.

Overall, this partnership approach has allowed Chinese companies to leverage local expertise and connections while effectively mitigating risks as they navigate unfamiliar regulatory environments. It has represented a strategic adaptation to the challenges of rapid international expansion that has combined Chinese resources and ambition with local know-how and established networks.

4.2.1 Case Study 2. Bottom-Up Agency by Local Enterprises in Peru: The Chancay Multipurpose Port Project

The Chancay Port has emerged as one of the most ambitious infrastructure projects in Peru and Latin America in recent years. Located eighty kilometers north of Lima, this port development exemplifies a unique case of bottom-up agency in Peru–China infrastructure collaboration in which private actors took the lead in establishing ties with Chinese investors.[28] Since 2019, the construction of the Port of Chancay has been undertaken by the COSCO Shipping Ports Chancay Peru (CSPCP) consortium, a joint venture between the Peruvian mining company Volcan and COSCO Shipping Ports Limited. The latter is a subsidiary of China COSCO Shipping Corporation Limited, one of China's largest state-owned enterprises listed in the Forbes 500. COSCO's entry into Peru represents a significant milestone in the growing economic relationship between Peru and China, not only due to its substantial investment (estimated at US$3 billion) but also because it became the largest Chinese investment in Latin America's port sector.[29]

The formation of consortiums between Peruvian and Chinese companies is an increasingly frequent phenomenon in Peru, as is the expansion of investment in infrastructure-related sectors. The Port of Chancay project serves as a relevant case study to observe the role played by private companies in promoting mega investment projects and the relationship they establish with Chinese capital. While Peruvian national and local governments have closely monitored the project and publicly expressed the need to enhance their port infrastructure, it was the Peruvian private company Volcan that established direct contact with COSCO and facilitated access to Chinese capital. In this case, the private sector played a pivotal role in COSCO's entry into Peru.

4.2.1.1 *Peru's Strategic Pivot to China and the Birth of Chancay Port*

Peru's relationship with China as a buyer for its mineral exports has grown significantly since the early 2000s. The complementarity of both economies became evident during these years, leading to the negotiation of a Free Trade Agreement. Talks concluded in November 2008, and the agreement was officially ratified by both countries' governments on December 6, 2009. The shift in export patterns is striking: in 2001, 24 percent of Peru's mining exports went to the US, with only a small percentage going to China. By 2021, these figures had dramatically changed, with 8 percent of Peruvian mining exports going to the US and 40 percent to China (Figure 4.4).

With the boom in mineral exports to China, Peru quickly encountered a bottleneck in its port infrastructure. It became evident that substantial improvements would be necessary to increase exports to China. In response to this need, the Peruvian-owned company Chancay Port was

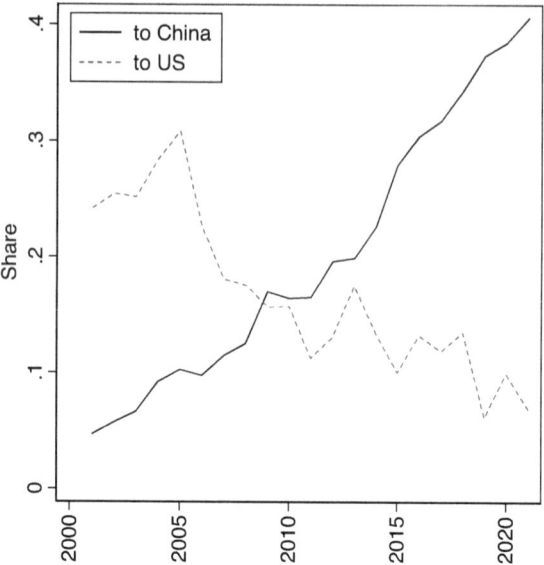

FIGURE 4.4 Share of Peruvian metal exports
Source: Author's elaboration based on data from UN Comtrade.

established in 2008 to assess the feasibility of constructing a port in the city of Chancay, then just a small fishing village. The company presented the project to the municipal government of Chancay that year, and, in 2009, the municipality designated the port as a strategic project for the district.[30]

The initiative for constructing the new port in Chancay took shape that same year (2009) when Chancay Port and Ferroviaria Central Andina expressed their interest to the Regional Government of Lima in investing in the construction of the Multipurpose Port in Chancay as well as the operation of a 112-kilometer railway line extending from Chancay to Huachipa. The latter would connect the Port with Lima. The Regional Government of Lima acknowledged the project's strategic significance and regional importance, seeing it as an upgrade to the Port of Callao with the potential to generate customs revenue for the Lima region.[31] With this approval, in 2010, the Chancay Port Company initiated the search for investors to commence construction.

4.2.1.2 *Volcan and the Search for a Strategic Partner*
Peruvian entrepreneurs recognized the economic opportunity but were aware that it would only be viable with a strong investor. In 2011, Volcan

Compañía Minera (Volcan), one of Peru's most important mining companies and a significant global producer of silver, lead, and zinc, acquired a 50 percent stake in the project. Volcan's involvement marked a crucial turning point, bringing substantial financial resources and industry expertise to the initiative. Operating since 1943, Volcan had numerous investments in the central highlands of Peru, mainly in Pasco and Junín, as well as investments in energy-generation projects, including the ownership of thirteen hydroelectric plants.[32]

Over the next few years, Volcan and Chancay Port focused on refining the original project to obtain approval from the Municipality of Chancay and to secure the necessary construction licenses. This process involved comprehensive environmental and social impact assessments to gain authorization from the National Port Authority.[33] But as the project's complexity and investment requirements grew, Chancay Port eventually withdrew from the consortium, leaving Volcan as the sole shareholder by 2016. That same year, Volcan began the construction of the port with a committed investment of only US$1.82 billion. In May 2016, in a public event attended by President Ollanta Humala, Volcan inaugurated the construction process, projecting completion by 2018.[34] At the event, both the president and the Minister of Transportation and Communications, José Gallardo Ku, emphasized the port's strategic importance for Peru's international projection, trade development, and connection with other Latin American countries. They indicated that Brazil, in particular, could use the port to export to Asia.

By supporting the project, the government hoped to attract foreign investors. And indeed, from the very beginning of the port's construction, Volcan had announced its intention to seek a partner who could offer "sector knowledge and financial resources" to continue with the project.[35] This quest was explicitly mentioned in the company's annual reports for 2017 and 2018, highlighting the progress made in construction but emphasizing the necessity of finding a suitable partner.[36] The partner selection process, overseen by French investment bank Lazard, involved evaluating at least thirteen interested firms from Europe, Asia, and the United States, all linked to the port sector as investors or pension funds.[37] A pivotal moment in this process came when China Harbour Engineering Company Ltd (CHEC), a subsidiary of China Communications Construction Company (CCCC), facilitated introductions between Volcan representatives and officials from COSCO Shipping during a visit to Shanghai and Beijing. CHEC, with substantial experience in the Latin American market, proactively offered to facilitate connections with COSCO, thus leveraging an existing contact in its dealings with Volcan.[38]

As the project gained prominence, it attracted increasing attention from the Peruvian government. During his inaugural overseas trip in September 2016, for example, President Pedro Pablo Kuczynski emphasized the need to modernize Peru's ports, including Chancay. The following year, he revealed that Chinese businesspeople had expressed interest in investing in the port. The transition of political power in Peru, with Martin Vizcarra assuming the presidency in 2018, did not diminish government support for the project. In July 2018, the vice minister of transport, Carlos Estremadoyro, announced COSCO Shipping's interest in acquiring Peruvian ports.[39] This announcement was followed by Chinese ambassador Jia Guide's disclosure of COSCO's plans to invest approximately US$2 billion in Peru as part of China's intended US$10 billion investment that year.[40]

The culmination of these efforts came in January 2019 at the World Economic Forum in Davos, where Volcan and COSCO publicly signed an agreement to jointly relaunch the construction of the port. The signing ceremony was attended by high-ranking officials from both Peru and China, including Vice President Mercedes Aráoz. At this event, it was announced that the Port would finally have an investment of US$3 billion dollars from COSCO.[41] The final contract was signed in Lima in May 2019, in a meeting with President Martín Vizcarra (Figure 4.5).[42] According to its terms, COSCO would become a 60 percent shareholder in the port of Chancay, leaving the other 40 percent in the hands of Volcan.

4.2.1.3 Project Significance and Expected Benefits

The agreement signed in 2019 marked COSCO's entry into the project through a private entity (Volcan) in need of a partner. However, the significance of the project was such that the government became actively involved and lent its symbolic support, even during times of political instability and presidential changes. Since the beginning of the project, various Peruvian leaders and authorities highlighted the benefits that the port would represent for the country. According to the Minister of Economy, Alex Contreras, Peru would not only become the new port hub of South America, but Peruvian exports to Asia would reach their destination in less time, strengthening the country's international competitiveness against its neighbors.[43]

One of the key features that makes the Port of Chancay unique and massive is its ability to accommodate vessels of 18,000 TEU (twenty-foot

The Demand Side

FIGURE 4.5 COSCO–Volcan contract signing in 2019 in Lima
Source: Presidencia de Peru (2019). Note: On the far-left stood José Ignacio de Romaña, who served as the Director of Volcan, accompanied by José Picasso, the Chairman of the Board of Volcan. Next to them was María Jara, who held the position of Minister of Transport and Communications of Peru. At the center of the image was Martín Vizcarra, the President of Peru, standing alongside Li Yun, who served as the Chargé d'Affaires of the Chinese Embassy in Peru. The group was completed by two COSCO Shipping executives: Xu Lirong, who was the Chairman of the company, and Zhang Wei, who held the position of Vice President and Director.

equivalent units), which are considered the world's largest container ships and that have not previously called at Latin American ports. This capability will allow companies to ship cargo directly between Peru and China rather than using smaller ships that must first stop in Mexico or California. The domestic effects are also expected to be considerable. The Chancay port would represent an economic shock with macroeconomic implications, contributing to better connectivity of routes for mineral exports and fostering public investment in infrastructure in the Chancay-Ancón-Callao axis.[44] Additionally, the government has considered the possibility of creating a Special Economic Zone around the port, with an industrial park that would contribute to local development.

For Volcan, as a private entity, the agreement with COSCO brings significant benefits. COSCO is the largest port business company in the world, with a presence in various port regions in China, Southeast Asia,

Europe, and the Mediterranean. COSCO's experience in building and operating major ports, including the Port of Piraeus in Greece (one of the top fifty ports in the world and the second largest in the Mediterranean), adds substantial value to the project. According to official documents, Volcan believes the construction of the Port of Chancay will position them as one of the most important companies in the country, now with a significant stake in the port industry in addition to their diversified presence in the mining and energy sectors.[45] The construction of the port has also enabled Volcan to drive and develop the Chancay Park Industrial Park project in the port's vicinity; an initiative under its complete control.

The contract with COSCO has been particularly convenient for Volcan, as it has facilitated access to international credit. In 2023, Volcan acquired a loan of US$975 million from a group of Chinese lenders led by Bank of China, including the Bank of Communications Co. and the China Minsheng Banking Corp. Shanghai Pilot Free Trade Zone Branch, among others. The company indicated that this loan would be aimed at developing the port.[46]

4.2.1.4 Conclusion: Bottom-up Agency in Infrastructure Development

The Chancay Multipurpose Port project serves as a compelling case study of bottom-up agency in infrastructure development by Chinese actors. Unlike many large-scale infrastructure projects, in which national governments often lead negotiations, the Chancay Port initiative was primarily driven by private sector actors. The Peruvian government played a supportive but secondary role. This bottom-up approach allowed for greater flexibility and efficiency in project development and partner selection. It also enabled Volcan to leverage its industry expertise and local knowledge while securing the technical and financial resources of a global leader like COSCO Shipping. The government's role in providing symbolic support and facilitating diplomatic connections further enhanced the project's viability and international significance.

As the Chancay Port project progresses, it will likely serve as a model for future infrastructure collaborations between Latin American countries and China. It demonstrates the potential for private sector initiative to drive large-scale development projects, with government support amplifying rather than directing these efforts. The success of this approach could influence how other countries in the region pursue infrastructure development and engage with international investors, particularly from China.

4.2.2 Case Study 3. Bottom-Up Agency by Subnational Governments: COVID-19 Mask Diplomacy in Brazil

The unexpected outbreak of the COVID-19 pandemic in 2020 presented a pressing challenge in global governance. Countries in the Global South were desperately searching for key health materials to mitigate its negative effects. Global leadership from the United States and other Western countries was expected, but many Western countries pursued what has been termed "Covid nationalism."[47] As a result, the international community experienced an evident "gap" in global leadership during the outbreak and subsequent stages of the global pandemic crisis.

No region of the world suffered as much from the COVID-19 pandemic as Latin America, both economically and in deaths per capita.[48] In this context, China provided several donations covering various much-needed items, including regular masks, N95 masks, COVID testing kits, ventilators, and other supplies like medical gowns, ambulances, thermometers, and so on. These actions have been dubbed "mask diplomacy."

In LAC, China played its role as a provider of substitute goods, both in the provision of aid and vaccines. But while the Chinese government encouraged donations, these largely came from companies. On the Latin American side, the demand was subnational and decentralized. This case study thus delves deep into the relationship between China and subnational actors in both countries, exploring how these actors sidestepped central governments to access medical equipment and supplies. This unique dynamic highlights the significant role Chinese enterprises played during the pandemic.[49]

4.2.2.1 *China's Aid to Latin America during the Pandemic*

China provided substantial aid to various Latin American countries during the first twelve months of the pandemic. Venezuela received the largest amount of aid at US$45.5 million, with 95 percent coming from the Chinese central government. Brazil followed with US$23.2 million. Interestingly, however, 97 percent of this aid came from Chinese enterprises rather than the government. Chile received US$10 million, with 87 percent from private enterprises. Other significant recipients included Cuba (US$9 million), Peru (US$6.8 million), and Argentina (US$5.6 million).

As Table 4.2 shows, the pattern of aid distribution varied significantly across countries. While some, like Venezuela and Colombia, received

TABLE 4.2 *Chinese donations by actor type and origin*

	Total aid (million US$)	Central Government	Provinces	Cities	Enterprises	Other
Venezuela	45.5	95%	0%	0%	5%	0%
Brazil	23.2	2%	0%	1%	97%	0%
Chile	10	1%	0%	1%	87%	11%
Cuba	9	73%	4%	0%	22%	0%
Peru	6.8	27%	0%	1%	50%	22%
Argentina	5.6	50%	2%	3%	7%	39%
Costa Rica	4.8	66%	5%	5%	5%	18%
Mexico	4.1	11%	1%	1%	2%	86%
Colombia	3	84%	0%	0%	11%	5%
Ecuador	3	10%	2%	3%	35%	50%

Note: Amounts and percentages reflect the first twelve months of the pandemic.
Source: Telias and Urdinez (2022). "Other" accounts for donations from foundations, universities, and the Chinese diaspora.

most of their aid from the Chinese central government, others like Brazil and Chile received the bulk of their assistance from Chinese enterprises. This diversity in aid sources highlights the complex nature of China's engagement with Latin America during the pandemic.

4.2.2.2 Brazilian Bottom-up Agency from Governors and Mayors

China was the primary trading partner of twenty of Brazil's twenty-seven states in 2018, the year Jair Bolsonaro was elected president. It was a period of economic boom that fostered strong ties between Brazilian and Chinese businesspeople as well as ties between the Chinese Communist Party and Brazil's major political groups. However, during his presidential campaign, Jair Bolsonaro accused China of "buying Brazil," using the acquisition of a niobium mine by a Chinese company as an emblem of his campaign.[50] Bolsonaro's "China threat" rhetoric regarding investments was a campaign tactic and, in some ways, a foreshadowing of his future foreign policy. Furthermore, during his campaign, Bolsonaro visited Taiwan, which violated the One-China principle and elicited a harsh diplomatic reaction from China.

Bolsonaro took office on January 1, 2019, with a clear dilemma: his spirit belonged to the United States and Trumpism, but his wallet belonged to China. He nominated openly sinophobic diplomat Ernesto Araujo as Foreign Minister, who claimed in 2020, for example, that the

The Demand Side

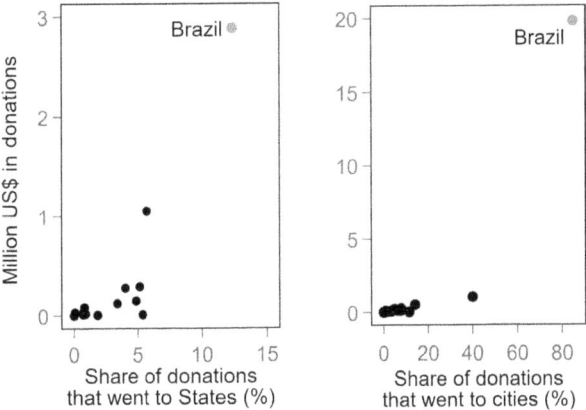

FIGURE 4.6 Chinese contributions received by Latin American governments and municipalities
Source: Author's elaboration.

COVID-19 pandemic was a global communist conspiracy headed by China to usher in a "New Global Order." This and other social media spats marked the de facto breakdown of any cordial relationship between the Brazilian federal government and the People's Republic of China as soon as the pandemic started. And although Brazil desperately needed masks, COVID tests, ventilators, and vaccines, the national government chose not to become dependent on China.

Nevertheless, China provided its second highest rate of pandemic assistance in LAC to Brazil, trailing only Venezuela. In light of existing animosity, the puzzle is why. The answer is that subnational governments exerted bottom-up agency to obtain Chinese donations. Brazil received 72 donations from Chinese actors (companies, provinces, municipalities, foundations, and colleges), with 58 going directly to states and municipalities. In fact, according to the data, Brazil was an outlier in LAC in terms of the amount of grants directed to subnational actors (Figure 4.6). The demand for assistance from Brazilian subnational governments coincided with the offer of assistance from Chinese businesses and labs, creating a unique situation in the region.

During the diplomatic crisis with China, the governors of the Federal District and São Paulo both sought assistance from the Chinese envoy to control the COVID-19 epidemic. Ibaneis Rocha, the governor of the Federal District, praised China's attempts to contain the virus and requested its help in slowing the infection rate in Brasilia, asking specifically for donations from Chinese companies. During a press

FIGURE 4.7 Governor Joao Doria and São Paulo officials meet Chinese businesspeople in Beijing, 2019
Source: GOVESP (2019). Note: In the photo, Governor Joao Doria stands with the delegation of Sao Paulo State officials and Chinese businesspeople who met in August 2019 in Beijing as part of the GRI China-Latam Infra Summit and Week 2019.

conference, São Paulo Governor Joao Doria asked for 500,000 masks from the Chinese ambassador. Doria had led a business mission to China months before the start of the pandemic to attract investments, and he gradually became the preferred interlocutor of the Chinese Embassy during the pandemic (Figure 4.7). Other politicians, including Senator Roberto Rocha and Bahia Governor Rui Costa, wrote to the envoy with similar requests for donations. Significantly, these efforts clearly intended to distinguish opposition politicians from the president's anti-China attitude.[51]

Despite tensions between the Brazilian government and China, several Chinese corporations made significant donations. China Molybdenum Company (CMOC) gave US$1.2 million to the city of Catalão, where it had purchased a niobium mine. Fosun, Three Gorges, State Grid, and Chery all gave significant donations of medical supplies and equipment to Brazilian states where they had investments. For its part, the Chinese Embassy in Brazil organized a US$800,000 donation of financial aid and supplies to the Amazonas government in January 2021. Ibrachina, a non-partisan institute promoting Brazilian–Chinese integration, also gave oxygen to Amazonas. Alibaba and TikTok provided the largest donation, giving the Federal District 100 ventilators worth an estimated US$4.5 million.

4.2.2.3 Vaccine Procurement and Production

During this time, the National Front of Mayors, a caucus that gathers mayors across the country, grew in importance as a channel to connect municipalities with Chinese donations. They solicited the Chinese Embassy's help to buy six million doses of COVID vaccines. The Chinese ambassador stated at the meeting that the embassy was similarly committed to being a "bridge between the Brazilian municipalities and China."[52] Meanwhile, the Northeast Consortium, a caucus that joins nine states of one of the most relegated regions of Brazil, wrote a public statement to the Embassy of China to be contacted directly to channel donations of health supplies. On a different occasion, they interceded when Chinese supplies to manufacture vaccines ceased to be delivered, possibly to punish Bolsonaro.[53]

The Northeast Consortium and the National Front of Mayors both worked directly with Chinese suppliers to guarantee vaccine availability because, despite the Bolsonaro administration's standoff with China, Brazil was forced to rely on Chinese suppliers to make COVID-19 vaccines. But faced with delays in vaccine production due to diplomatic frictions, governors and mayors played their own game to ensure the vaccination of their constituents. To begin with, the state of São Paulo led the initiative of the Butantan Institute, and the state of Rio de Janeiro led the initiative of the Fiocruz Institute to produce vaccines in the country.[54] The Butantan Institute and the Oswaldo Cruz Foundation (Fiocruz) are Brazil's two biggest scientific institutions for R&D in biological sciences, and they imported vaccine production inputs from Chinese labs to make more than 90 percent of the vaccines used in the country. The sending facilities included Sinovac and Wuxi Biologic facilities, as well as others like Jiangsu Hengrui Medicine, Zhenjiang Xuanju Pharmaceutical, and Cisen Pharmaceutical.[55]

The Butantan Institute and the municipality of Serrana, in São Paulo, also coordinated to carry out the so-called Project S. This project consisted of vaccinating 75 percent of the municipality's population with Sinovac vaccines at the beginning of 2021 to test the vaccine's efficacy in a controllable setting. This study was critical to the nation, as it was observed that, among Serrana citizens, mortality due to COVID-19 decreased by 95 percent and hospitalizations decreased by 86 percent. After this study, there was confidence that the vaccine would help control the virus in Brazil.[56] Within weeks, at least six states and 22 municipalities sent letters directly to the Butantan Institute to begin purchasing vaccines. By the end of 2021, six states had purchased vaccines from the Butantan Institute.

Co-led by the municipality of Serrana, the São Paulo state government, and the Butantan Institute, Project S was a non-federal collaboration that demonstrated the efficacy of the Chinese vaccines despite the fear-mongering coming from Bolsonaro at the federal level. Gradually, the governor of São Paulo, João Doria, emerged as one of the main opponents to Bolsonaro. Under his leadership, the state of São Paulo's Secretary of Health at times had more prominence than the national Ministry of Health in managing the pandemic.[57] For example, when the Brazilian National Regulatory Agency, ANVISA, approved a phase III clinical trial to test the efficacy and safety of the inactivated COVID-19 vaccine developed by Sinovac, it was the secretary of health in São Paulo who communicated that the Sinovac vaccine had efficacy "superior to the minimum recommended by the WHO."[58] Governor João Doria also proposed that the purchase of Chinese vaccines be made by the Governors' Forum instead of by the federal Ministry of Health.[59]

4.2.2.4 Conclusion: Bottom-Up Agency in Times of Crisis

This case study illustrates a unique form of bottom-up agency exercised by Brazilian subnational governments in their engagement with China during the COVID-19 pandemic. Despite tensions at the federal level, governors and mayors actively sought Chinese assistance, demonstrating the complex and multi-layered nature of international relations. This bottom-up agency demonstrates the evolving nature of international relations in the twenty-first century, with traditional state-to-state diplomacy increasingly being complemented (and sometimes challenged) by subnational and private-sector initiatives. As countries in Latin America and elsewhere continue to navigate their relationships with major powers like China and the United States, understanding and leveraging these multi-level dynamics will be crucial for effective policymaking and international cooperation.

4.3 CONCLUSION

The case studies of the Patagonian Dams in Argentina, the Chancay Port in Peru, and COVID-19 mask diplomacy in Brazil reveal significant agency exercised by LAC countries in their engagement with and demand for Chinese alternative goods. These cases demonstrate that LAC actors are not passive recipients but active and strategic consumers who leverage Chinese offerings to address specific domestic needs and development goals. Whether through top-down national initiatives, bottom-up subnational efforts, or private sector leadership, LAC countries have shown an ability to navigate complex diplomatic terrains and negotiate partnerships that align with their interests.

This agency manifests in diverse ways: strategically filling gaps left by traditional partners, balancing multiple international relationships, and even bypassing national policies to secure needed resources. However, it also presents challenges, including managing long-term economic implications and maintaining autonomy. As China's presence in the region grows, understanding and leveraging this agency will be crucial for LAC countries as they shape beneficial partnerships and for policymakers as they craft nuanced approaches to regional development and international cooperation.

PART II

THE POLITICAL CONSEQUENCES
OF ECONOMIC DISPLACEMENT

5

The Effects of Economic Displacement on Public Opinion and Political Elites

In this chapter, I begin by exploring the impact of economic displacement on the erosion of US soft power as reflected in public opinion. I contend that one of the channels through which displacement weakens US political leadership is in the way Latin American citizens perceive the United States. This chapter also analyzes the perspectives of Latin American legislators as a proxy for the opinions of the political elites in their respective countries. Legislators not only represent the sectoral interests of their constituents but also reflect the positions of their political parties. The underlying premise is that if the interests of these legislators are influenced by economic displacement, it is reasonable to expect that other political elites (such as mayors, ministers, diplomats, and even presidents) would also have modified their views on China as its economic influence in the region grew over time.[1] The outcome of analyzing both actors (everyday citizens and political elites) is to show that displacement not only affects perceptions of the US, it also affects domestic policymaking.[2]

For my investigation, I analyzed two distinct datasets: surveys spanning multiple countries that question the ability of China and the US to address Latin America's problems, as well as preferences in terms of country alignment. This was followed by an examination of a sample of over 2,500 legislators' opinions across fifteen countries and over more than ten years. These data sets collectively strengthen my argument that, as China's economic displacement intensifies, the image of the US as a provider suffers.

Finally, I analyzed the 2015 parliamentary debate in Argentina regarding the approval for the installation of a Chinese space monitoring station in Patagonia, an issue that sparked major controversy.[3] This is one of the few cases in which a country's relationship with China has been discussed in a parliament, aside from the approval of FTAs in Peru and Chile – which enjoyed large support – and the more recent action of the Peruvian Congress to approve a law that would allow COSCO Shipping Ports to maintain exclusivity of operation in Chancay. This analysis uses qualitative data to explore how legislators justified their votes for and against the project, framing their decisions in terms of China's growing economic importance for Argentina and the potential risks of confrontation with the United States. This case sheds light on the intricate balance lawmakers must strike between embracing economic opportunities and navigating complex geopolitical landscapes. It demonstrates that economic displacement not only influenced legislators' opinions about China but also shaped their legislative behavior.

5.1 THE EFFECT OF ECONOMIC DISPLACEMENT ON THE PUBLIC'S PERCEPTION OF THE US'S CAPACITY TO ADDRESS LATIN AMERICA'S PROBLEMS

In this section, I analyze data from two distinct periods to examine the effects of economic displacement on perceptions of the US and China in LAC. The first dataset comes from a Latinobarometer survey taken in 2015, a time when economic displacement was less prevalent than it is today. The survey, comprising seventeen countries and over 15,000 responses, provides a unique opportunity for comparative analysis.[4] Of the countries surveyed, eight had experienced economic displacement (Argentina, Bolivia, Brazil, Ecuador, Panama, Peru, Uruguay, and Venezuela), while nine had not (Chile, Colombia, Costa Rica, Dominican Republic, Guatemala, Mexico, Nicaragua, Paraguay, and El Salvador). This distribution allows us to compare perceptions across different economic contexts within Latin America.

Latinobarometer, renowned globally for its face-to-face public opinion surveys on political issues, included two key questions in its 2015 questionnaire that are particularly valuable for our study: "What is the capacity of the United States to address the problems of Latin America?" and "What is the capacity of China to address the problems of Latin America?". Respondents could answer these questions using an ordinal scale: 1. A lot; 2. Some; 3. Little; and 4. None. Moreover, in its rich dataset of over 15,000 responses, it included crucial demographic controls such as ideology, income, age, and city of residence. This wealth of data provides a robust foundation for analyzing how economic displacement

Public Opinion and Political Elites 109

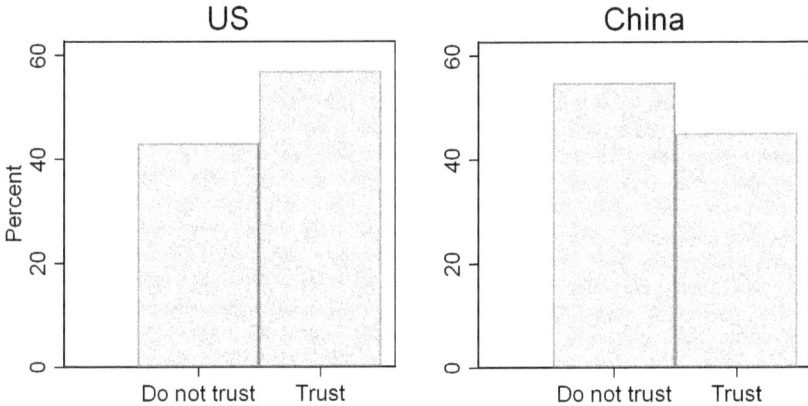

FIGURE 5.1 Comparing trust in US versus China for addressing Latin American issues
Note: N = 15,580, seventeen countries.

may influence perceptions of US and Chinese capabilities in addressing Latin American issues.

Initial analysis revealed a baseline for comparison: 57 percent of respondents expressed some or substantial trust in the US's ability to address Latin American problems. For China, this figure stands at 45 percent (Figure 5.1). This data establishes a starting point for examining how economic displacement may have influenced these perceptions over time, particularly in nations directly affected by the phenomenon.

To conduct our empirical test, we employed two logistic regression models. The dependent variables in these models assess whether individuals believe the US (first model) or China (second model) can effectively address Latin American problems. The key independent variable is whether the respondent's country has experienced economic displacement. Our regression includes a set of individual control variables and fixed effects at country level. The results, presented as marginal effects over probabilities in Figure 5.2, are striking. In the context of economic displacement, the probability of holding a positive view of China's problem-solving capacity for Latin America increases by 30 percent. Conversely, the probability of perceiving the US as capable of addressing these issues decreases by 21 percent in countries that have experienced displacement. These findings suggest a significant shift in perception favoring LAC American countries. While previous studies, such as political scientist Kerry Ratigan's research on Chinese investments in Peru, have shown mixed effects on China's soft power, our analysis specifically

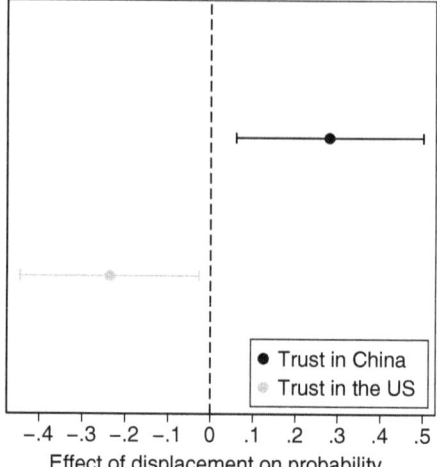

FIGURE 5.2 The impact of economic displacement on trust in US versus China for Latin American problem solving, 2015
Note: The coefficients are based on logistic regression with individual controls and fixed effects by country. N = 15,432, seventeen countries. Appendix Table E.1, models 1 and 2.

addresses the phenomenon of displacement and the trade-off between Chinese and US reputations in the region.[5]

Another way to analyze the trade-off in how displacement affects whether individuals view China or the US as more capable of providing solutions to LAC problems is by calculating the difference in the original response regarding China and the US. This results in an ordinal variable where the vast majority of the population (more than 50 percent) assigns the same level of confidence to both the US and China. The values to the right, the positive ones, denote those who have more confidence in China than in the US; to the left, in negative values, are the individuals who rated the US better than China (Figure 5.3). This ordinal variable, which ranges from −4 to 4, captures two extreme stances: at −3 are those who perceive the US as highly capable of solving problems and China as not at all capable. At 3, on the other hand, are those who see China as highly capable of addressing problems and the US as not capable at all.

Using this ordinal variable, I estimated an ordered logit regression using the same specification as in Figure 5.4, which displays the marginal effect of displacement on the probability of each response option. As the reader will notice, displacement produces a clear and consistent effect across the entire range of alternatives where China is viewed as more

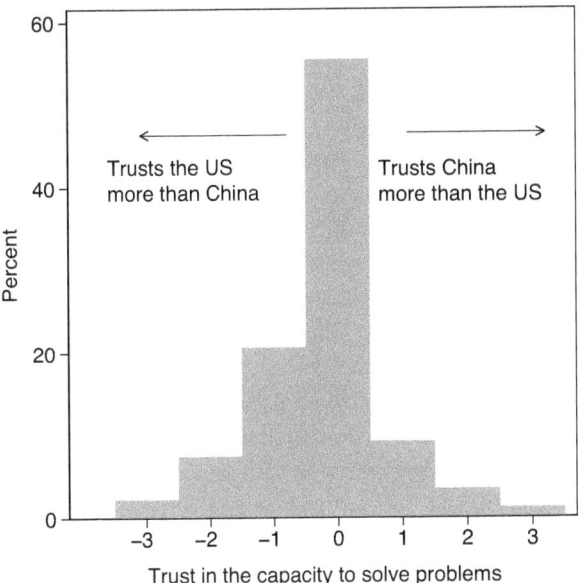

FIGURE 5.3 Perception of China versus US in addressing Latin American issues
Note: N = 15,580, seventeen countries.

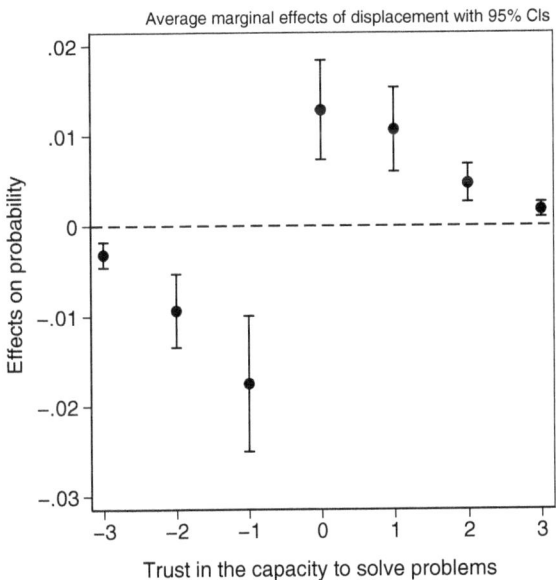

FIGURE 5.4 The effect of economic displacement on trust in China versus US for Latin American problem solving
Note: The coefficients are based on an ordered logistic regression with individual controls and fixed effects by country. N = 15,354, seventeen countries. Appendix Table E.1, model 3.

capable than the US in offering solutions in regions where it has economically displaced the United States.

To further strengthen the analysis and address potential concerns about the relevance of the 2015 data, I turned to the most recent Latinobarometer survey, which was conducted in 2023.[6] While this falls outside the primary temporal scope of our study period, it offers valuable insights into the persistence and potential intensification of the trends observed in 2015. The 2023 survey introduces a particularly pertinent question for our research: "Do you think your country should have a closer relationship with the United States or with China?" This direct comparison between the two global powers provides a clear indication of shifting allegiances in the region. The question garnered responses from 19,205 individuals across seventeen Latin American countries, offering a robust sample size for analysis. By examining this more recent data, we accomplished two key objectives: we validated the longevity of the trends identified in the 2015 survey and confirmed the hypothesis that the effects of economic displacement on perceptions of China and the US have not only persisted but potentially intensified in LAC over time. While the comparison would have been even better had the exact same question been asked, or if it were in a panel structure, the most interesting questions for our purposes unfortunately changed from year to year.

In 2023, nine of the countries analyzed had experienced economic displacement (Argentina, Bolivia, Brazil, Chile, Ecuador, Panama, Peru, Uruguay, and Venezuela), while eight had not (Colombia, Costa Rica, Dominican Republic, Guatemala, Mexico, Nicaragua, Paraguay, and El Salvador). Of the total respondents, a large majority, 58 percent, said they would prefer their country to have a closer relationship with the US; 27 percent said they would prefer their country to have a closer relationship with China; 9.2 percent said they would prefer their country to have a closer relationship with both; and 4 percent said they would not prefer their country to have a closer relationship with either global power. The remainder did not respond to the question. I estimated a multinomial logit model to establish the probability of respondents choosing each answer depending on whether their country had experienced displacement or not. The regression model includes a comprehensive set of individual control variables, along with fixed effects at the country and city levels for respondents.

The results are unequivocal: in countries that have experienced economic displacement, individuals are less likely to choose the US as their

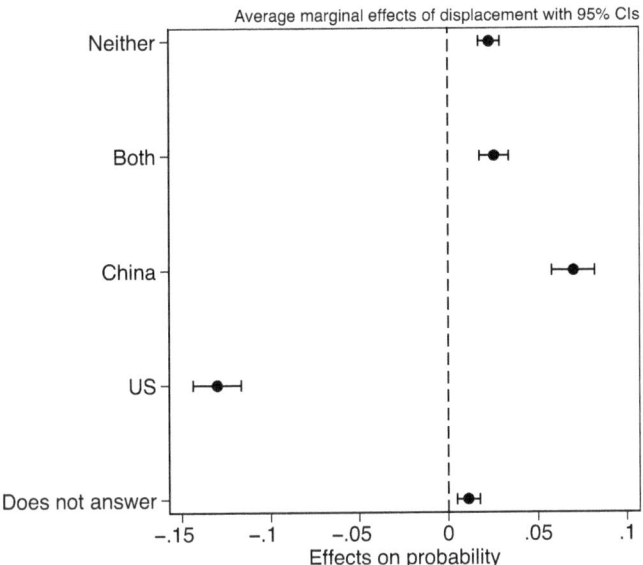

FIGURE 5.5 The impact of economic displacement on preference for US versus China relations, 2023
Note. N = 19,205. The coefficients are based on a multinomial logistic regression with individual controls and fixed effects by country. Appendix Table E.2.

priority for a closer relationship (13 percent less likely) and more likely to choose China (7 percent more likely) (Figure 5.5).

The evidence presented, based on data from 2015 and 2023, paints a clear picture of the changing dynamics in LAC over the past quarter-century. The erosion of US soft power in the region – a direct consequence of economic displacement – stands out as a defining trend of our times. From the shifting trade patterns to the evolving public sentiments captured in the Latinobarometer surveys, we see a region in flux. The statistical models, controlling for a myriad of factors, show that countries experiencing economic displacement are significantly more likely to pivot away from the United States and toward China.

The extent to which this finding applies to other regions of the world remains to be seen. However, a 2024 survey report by the ISEAS-Yusof Ishak Institute, a research institute in Singapore, provides an interesting case study.[7] For the first time since the survey's inception, respondents were asked, "If ASEAN were forced to align itself with one of the strategic rivals (i.e., the United States or China), which should it choose?" In previous years, the balance of regional opinion in Southeast Asia had been shifting steadily toward Washington, reaching a peak of 61.1 percent in the prior year's survey. However, the 2024 report revealed a sharp reversal of this trend. For the first time since 2020, Beijing established itself as the "preferred" choice among respondents. This shift suggests that China's influence in the ASEAN region may be growing, potentially reflecting broader global trends in economic and strategic alignments. Yet the agenda remains open in understanding how much economic displacement drives these trends outside LAC.

The erosion of US soft power in Latin America is not merely a footnote in the annals of inter-American relations; it is a transformative force shaping the geopolitical landscape of the Western Hemisphere. As policymakers, scholars, and citizens grapple with this new reality, one thing becomes abundantly clear: the next chapter in Latin American relations will be written not just in the halls of power, but in the shifting economic fortunes and evolving aspirations of its people.

5.2 SHIFTING ALLEGIANCES: ECONOMIC DISPLACEMENT AND LATIN AMERICAN POLITICAL ELITES' PERCEPTIONS OF CHINA AND THE US

So far, we know very little about what the political elites in LAC think about China.[8] One thing we do know is that they recognize China as a key economic player in the region.[9] We can also recognize their awareness that voters have preferences for greater or lesser economic integration with China depending on whether the effects of trade with China are a net creator or net destroyer of jobs in the locality.[10] But how economic displacement affects political elites' perception of China (and the US) has yet to be substantively explored.

This section is divided into several parts. First, it addresses the question of why the opinions of Latin American legislators about China should matter.[11] This is followed by an examination of data from the University of Salamanca's *Elites Latinoamericanas* project (PELA), which includes a sample of over 2,500 legislators across fifteen countries over a period of more than ten years.[12] Using this data, I explore statistically the effects of economic displacement on attitudes toward China. The results indicate that in response to economic displacement, legislators are less inclined to deepen trade relations with the United States and consider it a priority in foreign policy. Most interestingly, however, is an observable electoral divide in the valuation of a possible FTA with the US: ruling parties tend to value a hypothetical FTA with the US less when economic displacement has occurred. In contrast, opposition parties value it more, even in the face of displacement. This dynamic, in which the US and China are used instrumentally by both the government and the opposition for domestic political purposes, is analyzed in depth in one of the few cases of legislative voting on Chinese investment in Latin America.

5.2.1 Why Should We Care about What Legislators Think of China?

Understanding Latin American legislators' perspectives on China is crucial given the distinct role that legislative bodies play in foreign economic policy compared to their US counterparts.[13] Although Latin American legislatures may not be primary actors in shaping foreign economic policy, their influence and relevance in this domain should not be underestimated. This is especially pertinent in understanding their views on China, a major global economic player. It is important to recognize, for example, that national congresses, while not actively involved in the decision-making processes of foreign policy in Latin American countries, serve as significant gatekeepers. An illustrative case is the Brazilian Congress, which has exhibited this gatekeeping role by delaying the ratification of China's Market Economy Status within the WTO for over 14 years. This delay primarily stemmed from resistance by legislators representing regions that compete with Chinese imports. Entry into the AIIB was also delayed in some countries due to legislative resistance.[14] Free trade agreements, such as those in Chile and Peru, and investments that affect national sovereignty, must also pass through Congress, as we will see in the case of the space station in Argentina.

Legislators also frequently act as intermediaries between private firms and the executive branch. This broker role is instrumental in shaping how private sector interests align with and negotiate executive policies, particularly in international trade and economic relations. In countries where lobbying is regulated, such as in Chile, this is easier to observe. For example, when Tianqi Lithium bought a part of the Chilean mining company Sociedad Química y Minera de Chile (SQM), there were hearings with influential people including deputies and senators.[15] Legislators' views on global trading partners are certainly relevant to how these conversations unfold. Moreover, many legislators transition from Congress to more influential positions in the executive, where they have greater authority over spending and public visibility. This fluidity of career paths between the legislative and executive branches in Latin America further underscores the importance of legislators' views on China.[16] A congressman or congresswoman might be a governor today and cabinet member or even president tomorrow, where they might potentially play a pivotal role in negotiating contracts with Chinese entities.

The significance of legislators' perspectives is also highlighted by the strategic engagement of the Department of Latin American and Caribbean Affairs of the Ministry of Foreign Affairs of China. The Department's systematic organization of trips to China for newly elected congressmen is a testament to the value placed on these relationships.[17] These trips, aimed at fostering future collaboration and business opportunities, are a clear indication of the importance attributed to Latin American legislators by China. In addition, national congresses have become significant in China–LAC relations through the establishment of China Parliamentary Groups in various Latin American countries. A pivotal shift in international relations that signals a deepening of LAC political and economic ties with China, the emergence of these groups represent more than just a strategic shift in Latin America's foreign policy: they are a testament to China's growing influence in political and diplomatic spheres. By facilitating deeper bilateral relations, offering platforms for cultural and legislative exchange, and sometimes acting as conduits for addressing international and regional issues, these groups embody the multilayered nature of China–Latin America relations and indicate the significant role that legislators play in the relationship as the linchpin for deeper political relations.[18]

While Latin American legislatures may not traditionally wield direct influence over foreign economic policy, legislators' indirect role as gatekeepers, brokers, and future executive leaders make their views on China uniquely consequential. Understanding their perspectives, I argue, is key to comprehensively analyzing the region's foreign economic policy and its evolving relationship with China.

5.2.2 The Effect of Economic Displacement on Legislators' Views of China

In 2023, published results of a survey among Uruguayan legislators suggested that a majority of these political elites believed the country's main strategic ally was China.[19] According to my hypothesis, this is not surprising, considering that Uruguay experienced economic displacement in 2010. Nonetheless, it is a profound contrast to 2005, when it threatened to leave MERCOSUR in order to sign an FTA with the

United States following the failure of a regional FTA with all of Latin America.[20] This about-face begs the question: What effect does economic displacement have on how legislators position themselves vis-à-vis China and the US?

Despite legislators' notable, if indirect, effect on the country's foreign policy, there have been practically no studies on legislative opinion in matters of foreign policy to date.[21] The main limitation is the lack of data, as this type of survey is conducted in person and requires a lot of resources. It also requires patience to get busy legislators to respond to questions they see as non-urgent. The most ambitious project concerning the opinions of legislators was conducted by the University of Salamanca and is known by its Spanish acronym, PELA, standing for the Latin American Elites Project of the University of Salamanca.[22] To explore the question posed here, I have analyzed all seven waves of this project, which cover legislatures from 2000 to 2019. In total, there are over 8,700 survey responses from 18 countries. By filtering out questions on international themes, I developed a sample of 2,345 responses. This survey is not without challenges: the main problem being that ensuring the anonymity of the responses makes it impossible to identify the legislator with the province or department they represent; something that would allow me to better pinpoint the local effects of economic displacement. Nonetheless, it does identify the country, party affiliation, the year of election, legislative experience, political ideology, age, and a wide range of responses to various political questions.

My independent variable of interest was the economic displacement of the country each respondent was representing in the year of the survey. The hypothesis being that when economic displacement occurs, legislators will tend to view the US less favorably in light of China's consolidation as an alternative supplier of goods. As the dependent variable, I used three questions from the survey. The first one asks, "Of the following areas and countries, which one, in your opinion, should be the priority area for your country's government to design its foreign policy?" Because the alternative options exceeded ten, the responses were aggregated into three categories: "US," "China," and "others."[23] The second question I used as a dependent variable was similar: "Of the following potential trading partners, which one do you prefer for your country as a trading partner?" Again, to simplify the statistical analysis, I coded the options into three categories: "US," "China," and "others." A third question asked how legislators viewed a potential FTA with the US, with responses covering a ten-year span between 2007 and 2017. To analyze the effect of economic displacement on legislators' perceptions, I estimated multinomial logit models, including demographic controls, fixed effects by country, and a control for the ruling party.

For the first question, 24 percent of legislators responded that the first foreign policy priority of their country should be the US, 4.3 percent said China, and a majority of over 30 percent leaned toward other partners, such as "Latin American countries," the European Union, or Japan. To simplify the interpretation of the results, I have provided a figure showing the marginal effects of economic displacement on the probability of the legislator leaning toward each of the three options (Figure 5.6). The results show that, in the event of economic displacement, the probability of the legislator choosing China increases by 6.5 percentage points, and the choice of the US falls by 13 percentage points. The third option, "others," is not statistically significant. This effect is not large enough to reverse the order of preferences: even with economic displacement, the US remains the first choice of legislators. However, it confirms a core theoretical intuition: Economic displacement erodes the legitimacy that Latin American legislators grant to the US as an international leader. In this multinomial logit regression, no significant difference is observed in the opinion of legislators from the ruling party versus the opposition, so it has not been included in Figure 5.6.

Next, let's examine the second selected survey question to determine how economic displacement affects the way legislators view their countries' priorities in terms of trade partners. The majority of legislators (31.5 percent) chose the US as their preferred trading partner for their country, 5.5 percent chose China, and the remainder opted for other choices. Similar results to those in Figures 5.6 and 5.7 suggest that the probability of a legislator choosing China increases by 10 percentage points when there has been economic displacement, and their choice of the US decreases by 11 percentage points. The third option of "others" is not statistically significant. Once again, the effect is not large enough to reverse the order of preferences: even with economic displacement, the US remains the first choice among legislators. Yet we can see that economic displacement produces a shift in preferences that aligns with a phenomenon of alternative goods substitution.

The third selected question is of particular interest because it asks legislators, over a 10-year span, how they would evaluate a hypothetical FTA with the US. In 2005, a proposal for an FTA between Latin America and the US had been rejected at the Summit of the Americas in Mar del Plata due to a strong wave of anti-Americanism and critical

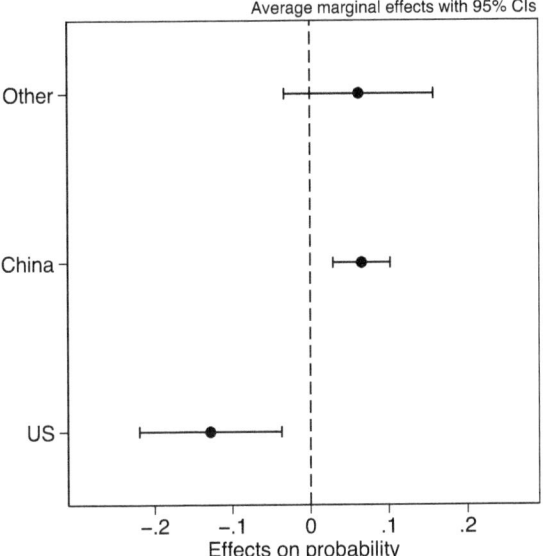

FIGURE 5.6 The influence of economic displacement on foreign policy priorities of legislators
Note: Probabilities estimated by multinomial logit, N=1,743. Appendix Table E.3, model 1.

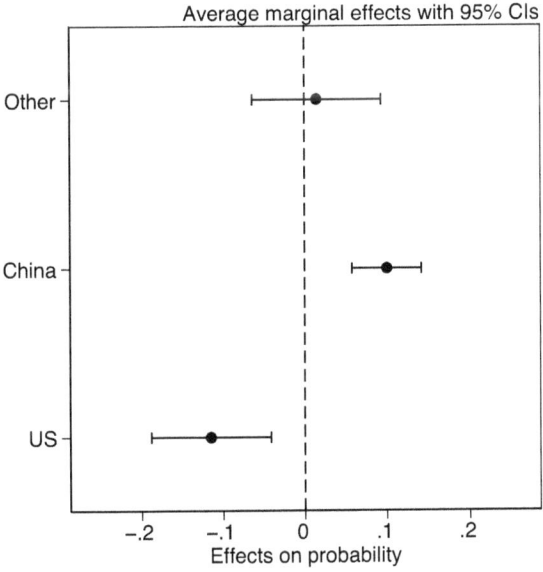

FIGURE 5.7 The impact of economic displacement on preferred trading partner preference
Note: Probabilities estimated by multinomial logit, N=2,566. Appendix Table E.3, model 2

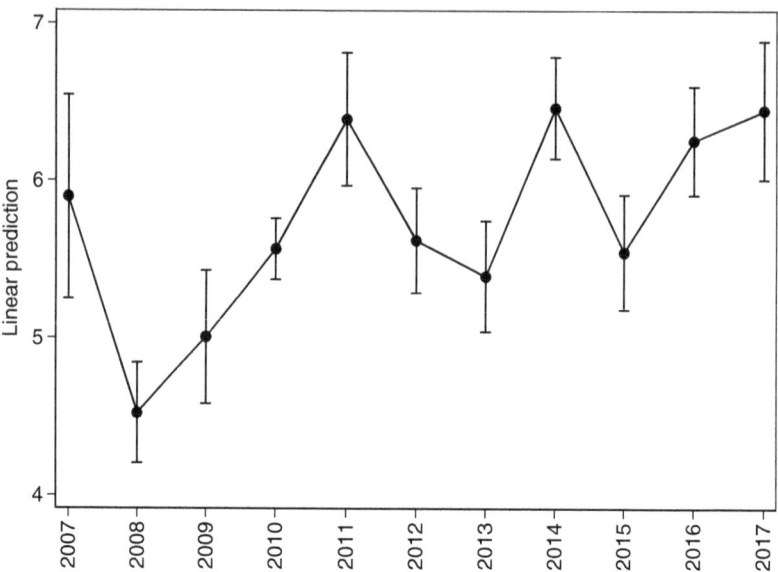

FIGURE 5.8 Perceived value of China–Latin America FTA
Note: N=3,587.

sentiment toward the Washington Consensus.[24] However, the fact that a question about a hypothetical FTA continued to be asked in survey form between 2007 and 2017 serves as an indicator of how important the issue remained. The question used for the dependent variable was, "How highly was a Latin America-US Free Trade Agreement valued?" with responses provided on an ordinal scale from 1 (very negative) to 10 (very positive). The average response was 5.6, and, as shown in Figure 5.8, the trend remained more or less constant in the decade between 2007 and 2017.

To estimate this impact of economic displacement on how highly legislators valued a hypothetical FTA between the US and Latin America, I estimated a linear regression where the independent variable was a dichotomous variable indicating whether the country had experienced economic displacement. I used another dichotomous variable to measure whether the legislator belonged to the ruling coalition or not. A third coefficient interacted with both independent variables, with the expectation that there would be heterogeneity in the value placed on increased trade with the US depending on whether the legislator benefitted from trade with China. For this third coefficient, the expectation was that ruling-party members would value an FTA with the US less than the opposition in places where

Public Opinion and Political Elites 121

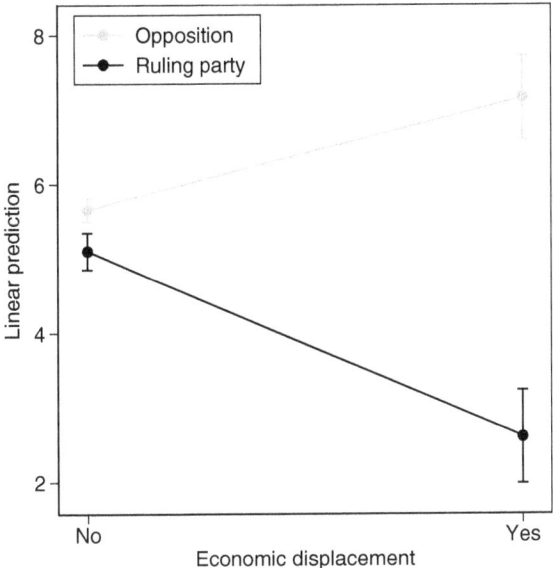

FIGURE 5.9 The impact of economic displacement on US–Latin America FTA support by party affiliation
Note: N=2,852. Appendix Table E.4.

economic displacement had occurred as a result of goods substitution. The regression also includes fixed effects by country and by year.

The results of this estimation are expressed in Figure 5.9, where we see that when economic displacement has not occurred, the value placed in a hypothetical FTA with the US is practically the same for both the ruling party and the opposition (around the average of 5.6). Interestingly, in the event of economic displacement, a heterogeneous effect is indeed observed between the opposition and the ruling party: for the government, the perceived value of an FTA with the US becomes less interesting, and the average perceived value falls to 2.5 points on a scale of 1 to 10. In contrast, for opposition governments, the option of an FTA with the US rises to almost seven points. This gap (more than four points) between opposition and ruling parties is particularly noteworthy because it is consistent with the theoretical expectation as well as the phenomena I have described in Chapters 4 and 5: as China becomes more economically influential, it is perceived by incumbent politicians as a country capable of offering economic solutions that serve to deliver to voters and win elections. An advantage for the ruling party; this is a disadvantage for the opposition.

5.3 ECONOMIC DISPLACEMENT AND LEGISLATIVE BEHAVIOR: DO OPINIONS TOWARD CHINA TRANSLATE INTO LEGISLATION?

The dynamic between government and opposition depicted just above can be explored in depth through one of the few legislative projects where the idea of proceeding with a Chinese investment was debated and voted on. This project was the installation of a Chinese space station in Neuquén, Argentina. The case offers a unique opportunity to understand how the government and the opposition voted in a country that, at the time, already had China as its main economic partner. Its dual nature (science meets high politics) renders it a particularly intriguing case for understanding apprehensions regarding the growing Chinese presence in Latin America.

What we see clearly from this case study is that the short answer to whether legislators' opinions toward China can translate into legislation is yes, they can. In the following analysis, I investigate the dynamics of legislative voting processes, including factors influencing legislative support or opposition to Chinese investments, in a country that has experienced economic displacement. Engaging substantively with this case study offers a nuanced understanding of legislative perceptions regarding the benefits and risks associated with Chinese investment initiatives.

5.3.1 The Neuquén Space Station: A Litmus Test for China–Argentina Relations

In December 2014, the Argentinean Senate approved a cooperation agreement with China for the "Construction, Establishment, and Operation of a Chinese Deep-Space Monitoring Station" in the Argentinean Province of Neuquén. Worth US$300 million, the proposed project was part of China's Moon Exploration Program and part of a broader framework of scientific cooperation between Argentina and China that began following the visit of Chinese President Hu Jintao in 2004.[25] This bilateral cooperation led to an agreement between Argentina's National Commission on Space Activities (CONAE) and China National Space Administration (CNSA), opening up opportunities for joint ventures in space exploration. The strategic decision to locate the base in the Patagonian region was a collaborative determination by these agencies. The agreement, however, sparked considerable debate and criticism from politicians, journalists, and academics. Concerns were raised about potential military use of the

FIGURE 5.10 Chinese space station in Neuquén: part of China's Deep Space Network
Source: Photo taken by Matias Subat, published by Diario Rio Negro (2024).

facilities, the extensive tax breaks granted to the Chinese, limited access for Argentine scientists, and the project's alleged secrecy.[26] Yet the project was approved, and the station was completed. It has been operational since October 2017 (Figure 5.10).

The legislative process and ensuing votes that greenlit this massive investment project reflect the complexities and nuances of Argentina's approach to engaging with China: a fine line of balancing economic opportunities with national security and sovereignty concerns. But the presence of the Chinese space-monitoring station in Patagonia was not an isolated case of a controversial Chinese investment in Argentina. A previous agreement in 2011 involving a land use agreement for soybean cultivation in the Patagonian province of Río Negro – made with a Chinese state-owned company, the Beidahuang Group, from Heilongjiang province – encountered such substantial opposition from the media, academia, and public opinion in general that it ultimately led to a repeal. Despite this history, the Chinese space monitoring station was the first to be debated at a congressional level. Situated in the remote subregion of Bajada Del Agrio in Patagonia, the project transcended its role as a substantial financial investment by China and evolved into a fulcrum of intense political debate and public scrutiny.

Undertaken by the China Harbour Engineering Company (CHEC) and CNSA, the space-monitoring station was replete with considerable controversy and extensive political discourse before it even made it to the legislature. Construction was, in fact, already underway when the project was presented to the National Congress for debate in July 2014, with subsequent discussions and the ratification of the provincial legislation formalizing the tax exemptions for CHEC and CNSA in November 2014. Notably, in the Argentine legislative process, Congress does not formally ratify treaties; instead, it approves or rejects the treaty text. This process typically involves preliminary discussions in commissions, with projects advancing to nominal voting only if consensus is not reached in the commissions. The space station initiative involved notable fiscal incentives provided by the province of Neuquén to CHEC, including extensive tax exemptions from VAT, customs duties, and internal taxes over a 50-year concession period. Additionally, the legal framework of the project granted Chinese employees in Neuquén the privilege of being subject to Chinese laws, a provision that also eased immigration regulations for Chinese officials involved in the initiative. These prerogatives exceeded the capacity of the province of Neuquén and necessitated congressional debate on the project.

5.3.2 Political Dynamics among Argentina's Political Elite

At the time of the congressional debate over the Chinese space-monitoring station, the governing president's faction of the Peronist Party held a substantial but not absolute majority in both the Chamber of Deputies and the Chamber of Senators. To secure the requisite majority for passing the bill, the government needed to maintain cohesion within the Peronist Party and garner unanimous support across its branches. Consequently, the primary cleavage within the National Congress tended to align with the government–opposition divide, highlighting a more strategic rather than ideological approach by Argentina's main political parties.[27]

Kirchnerismo, the Peronist faction led by the Kirchner family, utilized a noticeably anti-American rhetoric in its governance, though less intensively than other populist movements during the Pink Tide, such as Chavismo in Venezuela or Correismo in Ecuador. The Kirchners' foreign policy (under President Nestor Kirchner from 2003 to 2007 and President Cristina Kirchner from 2007 to 2015) was characterized by a marked opposition to the United States, distinguishing it from the previous administrations of Menem (1989–1999) and De la Rúa

(1999–2001), which were more closely aligned with US interests. This shift first became noticeably pronounced during the tenure of Duhalde (2002–2003), who, along with the Kirchners, pursued more autonomous policies with elements of anti-American sentiment. Their presidential terms signaled a significant reorientation in Argentina's foreign policy. However, as discussed in Chapter 3, ideological alignment alone has not been a sufficient reason to explain the increasing economic influence of China in the region.

The discourse within the Argentine legislature regarding the Chinese space station project epitomizes the intricate challenge that legislators faced: reconciling national interests with the potential benefits and risks inherent in strengthening ties with China. During the period it was being discussed, the national government was advancing negotiations with the province of Santa Cruz and Gezhouba for the construction of the dams analyzed in Chapter 4. Other infrastructure projects using Chinese investment, including the renovation of the Belgrano Cargas railway branch, were also being developed. Meanwhile, the Chinese company COFCO shook the Argentine agricultural market with the purchase of Nidera and Noble in 2014. Thus, China became not only a voracious buyer of raw materials and energy but also an important financier of public works and major strategic investor.

By linking the legislator's discourse with their final vote, I created and compared a text corpus of legislators in favor of and against the project.[28] For the analysis of the debate, I used Wordstat, a content analysis software, to identify and categorize thematic patterns in the speeches.[29] This tool facilitated the creation of various discursive categories, or "clusters," through its "theme extraction" function based on factor analysis. The method involved generating a document frequency matrix or, alternatively, dividing documents into smaller segments and creating a segment frequency matrix.

The congressional discussions lasted several hours. In total, thirty members of Congress expressed their views on the issue, making this source very rich in content. The project was first discussed in the Senate on December 17, 2014, where thirty-six legislators voted in favor, twenty-seven voted against, and none abstained.[30] Afterward, on February 25, 2015, the project was debated in the Chamber of Deputies, where 133 legislators voted in favor, 107 voted against, and none abstained.[31] The parliamentary discussions were obtained from the website of the Argentine Legal Information System (SAIJ), which is part of the Ministry of Justice.[32] Through another online platform, Decada Votada,[33] the vote of each of the legislators was identified, and I used this to classify each speech as either "in favor" of or "against" the investment.

The research directive for Wordstat was to organize the content of legislative speeches into five principal topic clusters. This categorization was based on the criterion that all words with a factor loading above 0.4 – the default threshold in the software – were included in the respective topic. Unlike hierarchical cluster analysis, where a word is confined to a single cluster, factor analysis allows for the possibility of a word being associated with multiple clusters. This approach more accurately captures the polysemous nature of language and the diverse contexts in which words are used.

5.3.3 Analyzing the Results

The government was the main proponent of the project. As seen in Chapter 4, Cristina Kirchner was a strong advocate for infrastructure projects financed with Chinese capital. Under Kirchnerismo, proponents of the project emphasized its potential economic and technological benefits for Argentina. They advocated for the project as a strategic opportunity to diversify Argentina's international relations, thereby reducing the country's historical dependency on the United States. This perspective represented a shift toward a more multipolar international engagement and reflected a desire to expand Argentina's diplomatic and economic horizons. Additionally, supporters highlighted the project's potential to enhance Argentina's standing in global space science, positing it as a significant step forward in the country's scientific advancement.

Among the arguments in favor was the idea that China presented an advantage as an alternative to the US and other historically significant countries as a supplier of goods. It was presented, for example, as an alternative to Argentina's excessive dependence on Brazil, whose government is said to have forgotten about Argentina. Deputy Roberto Feletti (Frente Para la Victoria, province of Buenos Aires) defended the deal because of China's economic strengths compared to those of all the country's historical partnerships. As he put it, "The truth is that when looking at the international integration with China, the European Union, Brazil, and the US, one will realize that the only dynamic country which grew strongly in these years was China, overcoming the 2008/2009 crisis. We are not so wrong to choose a bilateral agreement with China." This argument highlights China's short-term role as the "belle of the ball."[34]

Another example of how China was seen as a counterweight to the US due to its provision of capital and technology came from Alfredo Dato (Frente Para la Victoria, province of Tucuman):

I think there's an issue we must clarify and not get caught up in the clauses. We must clarify what a satisfactory role of foreign capital is in the national economy, i.e., if it contributes to the development of domestic productive forces or plays a role of despoiler of these forces [...], intended to widen the pockets of the owners of foreign capital. [...] [W]ith this agreement, will Argentina be a better nation? Is this agreement confined only to a financing process or also a process of economic and technological progress? Clearly, the possibility to access technology available today in China represents a quantum leap forward for our national economy.[35]

In stark contrast, legislators opposing the project – predominantly from the opposition to the government– raised serious concerns about sovereignty and national security implications. They questioned the transparency of the agreement and its terms, particularly highlighting the potential military applications of the space station and the long-term geopolitical consequences of allowing a substantial Chinese presence in Argentina. The opposition used this platform to criticize the governing party's foreign policy approach toward China at the time, framing it as a shift from a historical dependence on the United States to a new dependence on China.

Indeed, the shift from the US to China was brought up frequently among the arguments against the installation of the space-monitoring base, but legislators considered it to be a negative change, either because the US was a valuable ally or because the problems of economic dependence on the US would be accentuated in relation to China. Referring to these asymmetries, Oscar Aguad (UCR), deputy of the province of Cordoba, argued: "[Kirchner's] government rejected, perhaps with good reason, the agreement they wanted to do with the United States, the Free Trade Agreement of the Americas [...] What they said then was: 'we cannot associate with the US because that will consolidate a primary goods production matrix in Argentina.' Nevertheless, today we are doing the same with China." Deputy Fabián Rogel (UCR, province of Entre Rios) further highlighted the timing and strategic shortcomings of the government's approach to China. Criticizing the Peronist government for seeming to replace one form of regional hegemony with another due to a lack of long-term strategic planning toward China, he argued:

The agreements we are now considering are arriving late for a government that is ending soon, and it should have drawn up a strategic policy plan no less than two years ago. No one can bear the thought that, after twelve years in office, [the government] has finally achieved the replacement of both the old European model [of dependence] and that of domination by the United States with a new model of domination, that of an empire looming at least over Asia if not over Latin America: China.[36]

Representative Araceli Rossi (Unión por Cordoba, province of Cordoba) specifically voiced concern over the economic deficits in the agreements with China. "Argentina continues to sign agreements with China. The deficit in the trade balance has reached billions of dollars and is still growing. That is, some [the Chinese] get a lot and some [we] get very little." Similarly, Claudio Lozano (Unidad Popular, province of Buenos Aires) pointed out the trade imbalances: "96 percent of what we sell to China is of primary production, of which 85 percent is soybean, soybean oil, and crude oil, and what we receive from China are manufactured goods." These trade imbalances were also a point of contention in the space-monitoring station agreement, with Mario Negri (Unión por Cordoba, province of Cordoba) commenting, "The work is done with Chinese capital, Chinese companies, Chinese technology, and Chinese labor. And that obviously creates an imbalance."

Quantitative text analysis of the speeches reflects the trends captured in these illustrative quotations. It yielded distinct themes of argumentation and perspective articulated by legislators during the debate, each connected to a specific policy or project related to China. Each theme was then juxtaposed against reasons to support or oppose the policy or project, with the order of the themes in Wordstat going from the most to the least used. Theme 1 is the most important in terms of discursive structure, and theme 5 is the least important (Table 5.1). It's noteworthy that the central thesis of this book resonates quite a bit: China was seen, for better or worse, as an alternative supplier to the US by legislators.

The first theme highlighted a contrast between views on trade relations and infrastructure opportunities with China and the importance of economic relations with the United States. Legislators in favor of the project emphasized the potential benefits of improving trade relations and development opportunities with China. In contrast, those opposed underscored the importance of maintaining solid economic ties with the United States, suggesting a preference for maintaining long-established economic alliances. In the second theme, the debate focused on comparing the Chinese space station project with a parallel venture with the European Union. Proponents of the project drew parallels with the EU project to underline its legitimacy and feasibility. Detractors expressed concerns about the potential military applications of the Chinese space station, raising alarms about national security and the possible dual-use

TABLE 5.1 *Main themes highlighted by legislators who voted for and against the space station project*

Topic ranking	Topic content	Arguments of those who voted in favor (N = 133)	Arguments of those voted against (N = 107)
1	US replaced by China as goods provider	This agreement with China will bring future trade relations and infrastructure opportunities	Economic relations with the US could be hampered due to this project, causing more harm than good
2	Military threats and US–China rivalry	Through comparison with a similar EU space station installed in Mendoza, the concerns are not justified	Potential military usage of the space station in the future is a concern, as is uncertainty of what China will look like in fifty years
3	Is the US being displaced politically?	The relevance of the status of strategic relations in China–Argentina bilateral relations is an advantage that needs to be exploited	Political alignment with the US should be preserved, and this project signals that we do not care about the US
4	Chinese investments	A multipolar world order requires diversifying foreign relations and investments	The awarding of a direct contract by the national government to CHEC raises concerns; competitive bidding processes should be implemented to prevent corruption
5	Asymmetry of power and growth of economic weight	China's economic growth is good news for Argentina	Unbalanced "commodified" trade relations with China and increasing asymmetries are a concern

nature of the station. The third theme delved into the strategic implications of deepening relations with China as opposed to maintaining political alignment with the US. Supporters argued for the strategic value of establishing or improving a partnership with China, while opposition expressed apprehension about geopolitical realignment and a potential shift in political loyalty away from the US. In the fourth theme, discussions centered on embracing a multipolar world order versus expressing concern about the procedural aspects of the direct contract bidding process. Supporters of the project advocated for a diversified approach to international relations. Critics raised issues related to the transparency and fairness of the contract award process. Finally, the fifth theme presented a debate on the potential economic benefits of Chinese investment versus the existing trade deficit with China. Legislators supporting the project saw it as an opportunity to attract Chinese investment as a benefit to the economy. Opponents, however, highlighted the risks of exacerbating the trade deficit with China.

Overall, these main themes collectively represent a full spectrum of economic, political, and security considerations, illustrating the multifaceted nature of legislative decision-making in the context of foreign direct investment and international relations. The contrasting viewpoints within these clusters underline the complexity and intricacy of legislative decisions, where potential economic opportunities are weighed against strategic geopolitical considerations and national interests.

In light of this chapter's hypothesis about political elites, it is specifically worth noticing that, on the one hand, both the government and the opposition articulated justifications for Argentina's relationship with China. While I theorized that there would be marked government–opposition divide in the final vote (which there was), it is useful to see that both sides saw merit in China's significant role in the Argentinean economy. Both sides agreed that China was acting as an overweight substitute supplier of goods and that the deal was a concern for the US. This confirms, then, that Argentine legislators were fully aware of the nuanced geopolitical considerations in play regarding China's economic relationship with Argentina, and that their perspective on China's influence affected the way they defined their vote.

Thus, the legislative debate over the Chinese space station in Argentine Patagonia serves as a microcosm of the broader challenges and opportunities faced by South American countries in their interactions with China. The discussion reflects a reassessment of traditional alliances and dependencies in light of China's growing global influence. The case exemplifies that legislative views and decisions regarding China are not limited to specific projects but are integrally connected to broader considerations of national strategy, sovereignty, and the evolving geopolitical landscape.

5.4 CONCLUSION

The evidence presented in this chapter demonstrates that economic displacement negatively influences public and political elite opinions about the value of US strategic partnership. Based on significant empirical analysis, I have argued that in countries experiencing economic displacement, public opinion and the perspectives of political elites shift to view China as a reasonable provider of alternative goods. Historically, the US was the primary provider of both private and public goods. But the findings are unequivocal: in countries where economic displacement had already occurred by 2015, there was a higher likelihood of people viewing China as a capable substitute. As the second half of this chapter showed, this trend has played out in a deepening government–opposition divide among politicians regarding the value of approaching China and, in turn, distancing from the US. Now the question becomes: Is the same pattern occurring in voting within international organizations?

6

The Effects of Economic Displacement in International Organizations

This chapter delves into the effect of economic displacement on the ease or difficulty with which the US can secure the votes of Latin American countries in international organizations.[1] The theory presented here is rather straightforward: when a country's economic reliance on China surpasses its reliance on the US (economic displacement), the US is likely to encounter greater difficulties in garnering support from that country in voting resolutions within international bodies. This has direct implications on the structure of the liberal international order, which in this case we use as a synonym for the American-led order. Even if China does not manage to align countries' votes perfectly with its own, countries have more room to review aspects of the liberal international order with which they do not fully agree.

The chapter examines the alignment between LAC countries and the US in three international organizations of great significance, all of which are of utmost importance for US foreign policy:

(a) The United Nations General Assembly (UNGA): This forum stands as the most crucial global platform for deliberating on international matters.
(b) The United Nations Human Rights Council (UNHRC): As a key institution for the promotion and defense of human rights, it holds considerable influence.
(c) The Organization of American States (OAS): This hemispheric international organization has historically been a focal point for US diplomatic influence throughout much of the twentieth century.

The chapter is structured as follows: First, I provide an overview of the perspectives offered by the field of international relations on China's economic rise and its behavior in international forums. Subsequently, I analyze patterns in the three forums mentioned above, starting with the UNGA, followed by the UNHRC, and concluding with an examination of resolutions within the OAS. To conduct a thorough analysis of each case, considerable effort was invested in data coding, especially for the last two bodies.[2] Although each individual case may not provide irrefutable evidence by itself, and establishing causality can be challenging due to the possible endogeneity of economic displacement, I argue that the combined evidence from the three cases, all covering different years, countries, and types of votes, offers sufficiently compelling proof that economic displacement has negatively impacted the US's ability to persuade Latin American countries to align with its voting preferences.

6.1 CHINA'S EVOLVING DIPLOMATIC NARRATIVE: FROM CRITIQUE TO INFLUENCE WITHIN THE INTERNATIONAL ORDER (1965–2020)

The scholarly consensus suggests that China's stance toward the contemporary international order has been marked by a dynamic interplay of acceptance and critique.[3] Within this context, the discourse among Chinese elites has revolved around the extent of necessary alterations to the existing order and the optimal strategies for implementing them.[4] In "China, the UN, and Human Protection," political scientist Rosemary Foot underscores a noteworthy transformation in China's diplomatic narrative: in 1965, an editorial in the *People's Daily* (the official mouthpiece of the Chinese Communist Party) characterized the United Nations as a "dirty international political stock exchange in the grip of a few big powers." Four decades later, in 2005, an official communiqué portrayed the UN as a "universal" and "representative" entity, serving as the "preeminent platform for practicing multilateralism."[5] This marked shift in China's diplomatic discourse can be interpreted as a manifestation of China's ascendancy as a global power coupled with its growing inclination to shape the global landscape in a manner that safeguards its domestic interests and institutions.

China's heightened engagement in multilateral forums has been concomitant with a heightened receptiveness to its perspectives among developing countries, particularly in the context of ideas emanating from the Global South.[6] In tandem, there has been a reduced emphasis on the role of the United States in upholding the UN's multilateral framework. Against the backdrop of an international environment increasingly attuned to

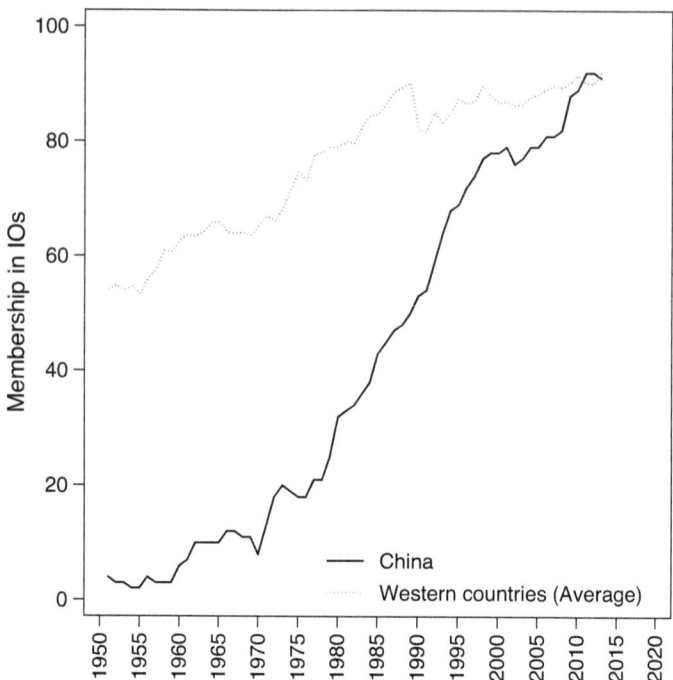

FIGURE 6.1 China's membership in international organizations: comparison with Western countries
Source: Data on IO membership was retrieved from Pevehouse et al. (2020).
Note: "Western countries" reflects the average participation of eighteen Western countries.

Chinese diplomatic overtures, it is reasonable to anticipate that Beijing would have cultivated an enhanced capacity to influence the normative discourse at the global level between 2001 and 2020. During this period, China completed its integration into the liberal international order established since the end of World War II. It's noteworthy that China achieved this integration by exerting influence from within existing organizations rather than by creating alternative entities. Throughout this process, China has actively participated in shaping the system according to its own interests, as depicted in Figure 6.1.[7]

While the concept that China is exerting influence on the international order "from within" gained prominence after the onset of the Trade War in 2017, empirical evidence suggests that China had been actively seeking to reshape discussions for at least a decade prior. Notably, an examination of China's approach within the UNHRC, the Security Council, and the General Assembly identified that China has played a pivotal role in reducing the emphasis Western countries place on human rights matters, effectively marginalizing human rights discussions within UN deliberations.[8] This trend was confirmed in an analysis of China's statements made during UN General Assembly sessions between 2000 and 2014. In essence, China consistently shielded developing countries from criticism for human rights abuses.[9] This was primarily motivated by concerns over the potential impact of such criticisms on the stability of the regimes in question.[10]

Some researchers have identified the creation of the AIIB as another attempt to influence the established order from within – in this case in relation to the multilateral lending system.[11] This effort is not surprising, as it makes more sense today for China to adjust the system in its favor than attempt to build a separate system from the outside. In the famous alternatives proposed by Albert Hirschman, "Exit, Voice, and Loyalty," China can threaten to exit to gain more voice.[12] But in the face of an active China within the system, how will China's economic influence affect the voting behavior of *third* countries? The literature suggests greater alignment with China, which is logical and has occurred with other major powers. However, do we know if greater alignment with China translates to less alignment with the United States?

There is abundant evidence regarding the influence of China's economic power in aligning other nations with its foreign policy, independently of its intentionality. This power is exerted through asymmetrical trade relationships, direct and indirect economic incentives, and strategic positioning within international organizations. While economic interdependence is a critical factor, the way in which this economic might is converted into political alignment is nuanced and varies based on specific issues and the nature of bilateral relationships. However, there remains a gap in understanding the effect of China's economic ascent in relation to the ability of the US to wield influence in votes within the United Nations and other regional organizations. The following three case studies shed light on this issue, particularly by focusing on the effects of economic displacement on the capacity of the US to influence the voting behaviors of other countries.

6.2 CASE 1: THE EFFECT OF ECONOMIC DISPLACEMENT ON VOTES IN THE UN GENERAL ASSEMBLY

The United Nations General Assembly (UNGA) stands as the principal deliberative organ of the UN, the world's preeminent international organization. Founded in 1945, the UNGA includes all 193 UN member states, each with equal voting rights, providing a unique forum for multilateral dialogue on a broad spectrum of international issues within the UN Charter's purview. The UNGA convenes annually in regular sessions, typically spanning from September to September of the following year. During these sessions, it fosters ongoing diplomatic interaction and decision-making. From 1946 to 2022, the Assembly passed an average of 125 resolutions annually on diverse topics, including international political cooperation, international law, human rights, and global collaboration in the economic, social, cultural, and health domains.

While UNGA resolutions are not legally binding, they carry significant symbolic weight in international relations. The frequency and breadth of voting by member states throughout the year thus offers valuable insights into countries' international preferences and ideological positions. IR scholar Erik Voeten, for example, has extensively utilized UNGA voting data to gauge countries' alignment with the international liberal order.[13] Today, voting convergence in the UNGA is widely accepted as a proxy for political affinity in international relations research, owing to its comprehensive temporal and geographical coverage. This analytical approach underscores the critical role of UNGA votes in illuminating patterns and trends in global state behavior and international relations dynamics.

6.2.1 The Effect of Chinese Influence within the UNGA

The literature on international relations focuses on the complex relationship between economic interdependence and international alignment. While China's uses of economic and diplomatic means to garner support within the United Nations and other international bodies has been extensively studied, how proximity to China may influence distancing from the United States is a dimension of these relationships that is less well understood. Drawing insights from the literature, this case study summarizes the mechanisms through which China's economic influence shapes alignment within UNGA voting.

Existing articles collectively provide a multifaceted perspective on the complex dynamics at play. Early studies on United Nations voting patterns, for example, reveal that asymmetrical economic interdependence, particularly in trade relationships, can confer political leverage to dominant partners.[14] Economically dependent nations often align their foreign policy with their major trade partners due to their vulnerability in these relationships. Since the 2000s, increased trade with China has correlated with foreign policy convergence, especially on issues like human rights, suggesting that stronger economic ties with China lead to greater alignment with its foreign policy interests.[15] In addition, research on Latin American countries' UN voting patterns has shown that as the power disparity between these nations and the United States decreases, their alignment with US positions in the UN General Assembly tends to diminish. This trend implies that as countries grow economically and narrow their power gap with the US, they may be more inclined to align with China's positions in international forums.[16]

Existing literature also explores the nuanced relationship between a country's trade dependence on China and its willingness to accommodate Chinese interests. Nations with extensive trade networks and shared memberships in intergovernmental organizations often develop foreign policy affinities due to overlapping interests.[17] While economic interdependence generally correlates with a greater willingness to accommodate China's interests, this relationship weakens in high-stakes political situations, indicating that the translation of economic ties into political alignment is not always straightforward.[18] Moreover, research suggests that foreign policy alignment is influenced not only by direct economic factors but also by shared regime characteristics between countries.[19]

While previous works argue that China's greater influence in international forums is a byproduct, or externality, of its greater economic influence, some authors have proposed that it reflects a deliberate Chinese strategy. As we delve deeper into China's economic influence on international alignment, it seems China may strategically approach countries to subtly alter international norms, especially within the UNGA.[20] Research on the topic suggests that China utilizes diplomatic and economic means to gradually reshape the normative framework over time, underscoring China's deliberate efforts to influence international organizations by aligning discourse and norms with its interests. However, as I discussed in Chapter 1, I am not concerned with demonstrating intent, as the classical economic statecraft literature has done.[21]

6.2.2 Quantitative Analysis: Leveraging UNGA Voting Records to Trace Changing International Alignments

To examine the voting patterns in the UNGA, I utilized the renowned database compiled by Voeten, Strezhnev, and Bailey.[22] This database has gained popularity for its use as a proxy to gauge the affinity between countries. My analysis began with a global sample of 186 countries

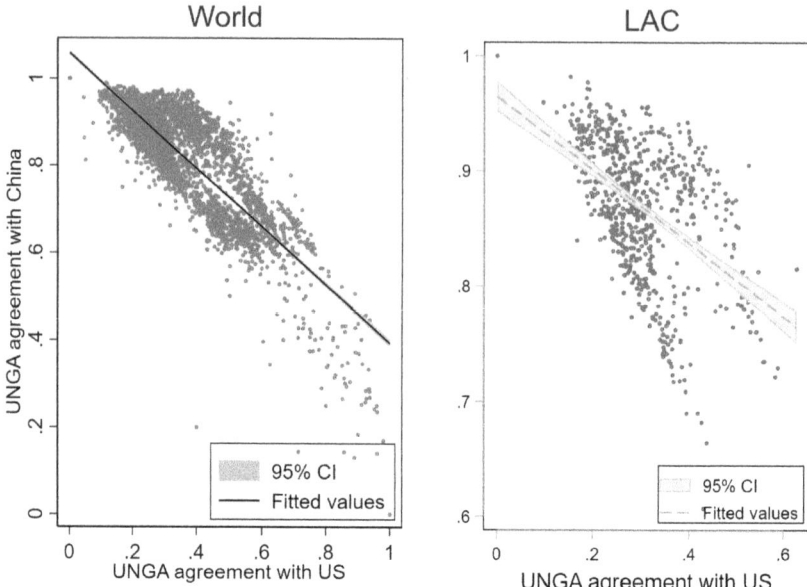

FIGURE 6.2 UNGA voting convergence: global and Latin American trends, 2001–2020

from 2001 to 2020. The key question I approached the data with is whether a greater ideological alignment with the US corresponds to lesser alignment with China, and vice versa. Generally, the data indicate this to be the case. Specifically, a one percentage point increase in annual vote convergence with China predicts a 0.6 percentage point decrease in annual convergence with the US.[23] Focusing exclusively on Latin America reveals a similar trend. Following the same logic, a one percentage point increase in annual vote convergence with China in this region predicts a 0.53 percentage point decrease in annual convergence with the US (Figure 6.2).[24] Just by looking at the negative correlations, the data from 2001 to 2020 suggest that it is highly improbable for a country to increase its alignment with China while simultaneously increasing its alignment with the US.

This pattern reflects significant shifts in international alignments and preferences, highlighting the evolving nature of global political dynamics. However, the literature makes an emphatic point regarding potential issues with using this vote convergence metric to infer ideological affinity. On the one hand, votes are highly vulnerable to changes in the UNGA agenda year after year. This not only makes them problematic for inferring ideological positions, but also means that intertemporal comparisons

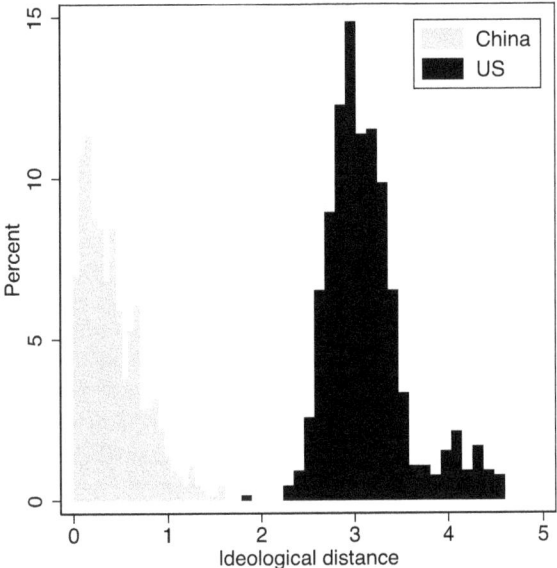

FIGURE 6.3 UNGA voting alignment: Latin American countries' proximity to China versus US

have limited external validity. Moreover, the dyadic vote agreement indicator cannot distinguish between changes in Country A's voting behavior and shifts in Country B's behavior.[25] To address this weakness, I used the ideal point estimation by Voeten et al. as a proxy for the ideological distance between the US and different LAC countries. This metric was created following in the footsteps of domestic politics scholars in estimating an empirical spatial model on a set of observed roll-call vote choices. These ideal points separate shifts in the UN's agenda from shifts in countries' ideological positions by holding as constant the roll-call parameters of identical resolutions. As shown in Figure 6.3, LAC countries had a greater distance from the US than with China: on average, the distance from China was 0.42 and the distance from the US was 3.12 in this ideal point metric.

For my analysis, I looked at each resolution and how Latin American countries voted, as well as whether the existence of economic displacement reduced voting convergence with the US. Analyzing resolution by resolution allowed me to disaggregate by theme and distinguish between all votes and the votes that the US State Department considers important.[26] In total, between 2001 and 2022, LAC countries voted on 2,028 different resolutions, of which 212 were on issues deemed important by the State

TABLE 6.1 *UNGA resolution types: voting distribution, 2001–2022*

Category	Number of resolutions
All resolutions	2,028
Important resolutions	212
HR	469
Palestine	378
Nuclear weapons	381
Arms control	471
Colonialism	273
Development	239

Department. This sample is large enough to complement the ideal point analysis above and discern which themes are most affected by the occurrence of displacement (Table 6.1).

6.2.3 Results: Assessing the Effect of Economic Displacement within the UNGA

As shown in Figure 6.4, the distance from China versus the US remained relatively constant over time. However, it can be seen that as the years pass, the distance grew somewhat between the US and countries where there was displacement. So, has economic displacement influenced the alignment of Latin American countries with the United States? To answer the question, I employed panel regressions in a sample of twenty-nine countries, each with an average of eighteen years of data. Besides fixed effects for both year and country, I included a range of controls that might determine the ideological proximity in United Nations voting with both China and the US.

I assumed that, apart from economic interdependence, ideological affinity between the presidents of a Global South country and China could contribute to voting proximity. Hence, I controlled for presidents with left-wing ideologies.[27] From the literature, we also know that more powerful countries have greater agency to distance themselves from the influence of major powers when voting in international bodies. To capture this effect, I controlled for each country's GDP.[28] Finally, democracies and autocracies are expected to vote differently on many resolutions involving human rights defense, individual freedoms, and election transparency. Thus, I controlled for a proxy, which is an index of checks and

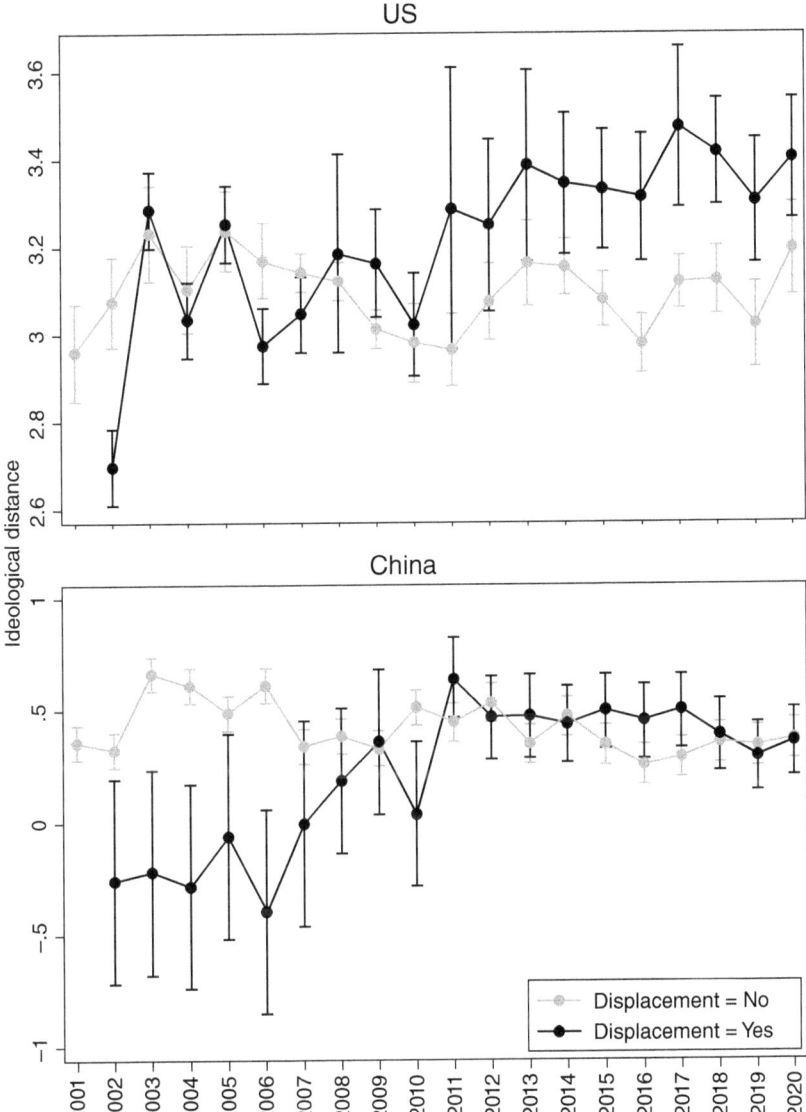

FIGURE 6.4 UNGA ideological alignment for LAC countries: US versus China, pre- and post-displacement

balances in the country.[29] As the dependent variable, I used the ideological distance of the Latin American country both from the US and from China. The greater the ideological distance, the less aligned two countries' votes would be on similar resolutions in the UNGA. I then defined

TABLE 6.2 *Effect of economic displacement on UNGA ideological distance*

	Ideological distance with US		Ideological distance with China	
	(1)	(2)	(3)	(4)
Lagged dependent variable	0.669***	0.657***	0.437***	0.429***
	(0.0748)	(0.0731)	(0.0666)	(0.0703)
China's economic displacement	0.0746*	0.0772*	0.000159	0.00655
	(0.0323)	(0.0343)	(0.0833)	(0.0890)
GDP		0.0000521		−0.000184***
		(0.0000311)		(0.0000402)
Leftist president		0.0581*		−0.00861
		(0.0276)		(0.0324)
Checks and balances		−0.0126		0.0144
		(0.0147)		(0.0166)
Constant	1.081***	1.087***	0.153***	0.232
	(0.231)	(0.224)	(0.0399)	(0.122)
Country Fixed Effects	Yes	Yes	Yes	Yes
Year Fixed Effects	Yes	Yes	Yes	Yes
N	627	544	627	544
R^2	0.55	0.58	0.32	0.34

Note: OLS estimates. Robust standard errors in parentheses. $*P < 0.05$, $***P < 0.001$.

four models, including one without controls and another with controls for the ideological distance with the US and China.

The results indicate that economic displacement leads to greater ideological distance with the US, although it does not have a statistically significant effect in reducing the distance with China (Table 6.2). This finding suggests that the process of substituting goods has not always translated into direct gains for China, but that it does negatively affect the position of the US. In the case of the UNGA, it impacts the US's ability to align regional votes.

The magnitude of the effect found is shown in Figure 6.5. On average, displacement leads to an increase in the distance with the US by about 0.07 units of ideological distance. To make this effect more intuitive, let's consider the effect when we use the percentage of votes as the dependent variable instead of the ideal point: on average, displacement leads to a divergence from US convergence by about one percentage point; a non-trivial effect considering the annual average vote convergence in our sample is 29 percent. As mentioned, however, this does not translate into greater ideological proximity to China.

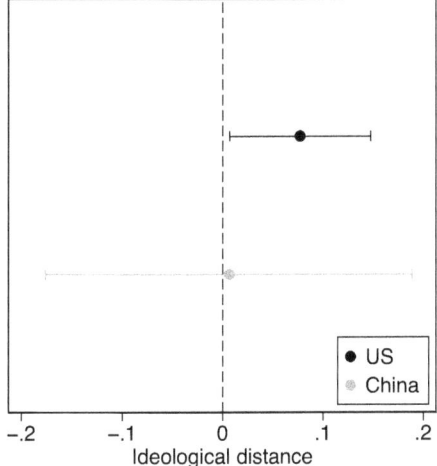

FIGURE 6.5 Impact of economic displacement on ideological distance from the US in UNGA voting

To gain a better understanding of the effect found, and to distinguish the effect by important themes, I conducted a difference-in-differences analysis of the effect of economic displacement on all resolutions, on resolutions important to the US State Department, and on thematic resolutions. The results, shown in Table 6.3, use a dichotomous dependent variable that assumes 1 if a Latin American country votes the same as the US, and assumes 0 if it does not. The regression includes fixed effects for year and country, as well as standard errors clustered at the resolution level. On average, displacement reduces the probability of voting like the US by 2.5 percent, but this effect increases to 7.1 percent when considering only important resolutions. When analyzing vote convergence by themes, we see that economic displacement negatively affects convergence in human rights votes – a sensitive issue for the US – by 3.6 percent. It also negatively affects convergence by 1.8 percent in relation to economic development themes. It does not affect other agendas.

Recent research aligns with the broader scholarly consensus on China's evolving stance on international human rights. Initially hesitant to engage with global human rights mechanisms, China has transformed into a key player in shaping these norms worldwide. This shift signifies a deliberate move to contest the prevailing liberal human rights paradigm, which traditionally emphasizes individual freedoms and political rights. China now champions an alternative interpretation of human rights that reflects its governance philosophy. It prioritizes state-driven development

TABLE 6.3 *Effect of economic displacement on UNGA resolution convergence*

	(1) All Votes	(2) Important votes	(3) HR	(4) Palestine	(5) Nuclear weapons	(6) Arms control	(7) Colonialism	(8) Development
Economic displacement	-0.0246***	-0.0715***	-0.0365***	-0.00856	-0.00421	-0.0146	0.00889	-0.0188*
	(0.00474)	(0.0174)	(0.0102)	(0.00597)	(0.00590)	(0.00743)	(0.00833)	(0.00899)
Constant	0.116***	0.00820	0.0542	0.0328	0.0981	0.144	0.0442	-0.0830***
	(0.0333)	(0.101)	(0.0540)	(0.0357)	(0.0711)	(0.0801)	(0.0677)	(0.0169)
Country Fixed Effects	Yes	Yes	Yes	Yes	Yes	Yes	Yes	Yes
Year Fixed Effects	Yes	Yes	Yes	Yes	Yes	Yes	Yes	Yes
N	53,640	6,060	12,870	9,960	10,020	12,630	6,780	6,060
R^2	0.047	0.103	0.050	0.040	0.145	0.082	0.084	0.148

Note: Clustered standard errors by resolution in parentheses. Statistical significance: *$P < 0.05$, **$P < 0.01$, ***$P < 0.001$.

and views individual civil and political liberties as potentially destabilizing factors. By advancing this perspective, China aims to reshape the global human rights discourse to better align with its national interests and governing principles.

The empirical evidence presented in Table 6.3 lends support to this observed shift in China's stance and its growing influence in shaping international human rights norms. Indeed, these findings underscore the broader implications of China's rising global influence, not just in economic terms, but also in the realm of international norms and governance. The case of the main international debate forum, the UNGA, thus confirms my hypothesis that economic displacement eroded US political leverage on international organizations.

6.3 CASE 2: THE EFFECT OF ECONOMIC DISPLACEMENT ON VOTES AT THE UN HUMAN RIGHTS COUNCIL

The UNHRC, established in 2006 as the successor to the United Nations Commission on Human Rights, represents a significant evolution in the international approach to human rights. As the principal intergovernmental body within the United Nations system focused on human rights, the UNHRC plays a vital role in addressing human rights issues across the globe. The Council is composed of forty-seven member states, reflecting a commitment to equitable geographical representation. This composition is crucial for ensuring that diverse perspectives from various regions are represented in discussions and decisions on human rights. The seats are allocated across different regional groups, ensuring representation from African, Asia-Pacific, Eastern European, LAC, Western European, and "Other" states.

Members of the UNHRC are elected by the UNGA through a direct and secret ballot, a process that underscores the importance of transparency and fairness in the selection of members. Each member serves for a period of three years, and, in a move designed to foster diversity and rotation in membership, they are not eligible for immediate re-election after serving two consecutive terms. This rule ensures that a variety of countries have the opportunity to contribute to and influence the Council's work over the years. The operational framework of the UNHRC reflects a structured approach to tackling human rights issues, with a focus on inclusivity and representation. The Council's activities, including addressing violations, making recommendations, and coordinating global efforts to promote and protect human rights, are thus informed by a wide range of international perspectives. This structure is indicative of the United Nations' broader commitment to universal human rights and the representation of its diverse member states in critical discussions and decision-making processes.[30]

The United States' relationship with the UNHRC has been marked by periods of engagement and withdrawal, reflecting broader shifts in its foreign policy and stance on international human rights mechanisms. Initially, the US was a member of the UNHRC during three separate periods: 2010–2012, 2013–2015, and 2017–2018. However, under the Trump administration, the US made a significant move by withdrawing from the Council in 2018. The rationale for this withdrawal, as articulated by then-US Ambassador to the UN, Nikki Haley, centered on criticisms of the Council's efficacy and impartiality. Haley contended that the UNHRC was, in her words, "a protector of human rights abusers, and a cesspool of political bias." A core issue underpinning this criticism was the membership of the Council, which included countries accused of grave human rights violations. This situation was perceived as undermining the Council's legitimacy and effectiveness in addressing global human rights issues.

However, the US stance toward the UNHRC shifted once again under the Biden administration. In 2021, the US rejoined the Council, marking a return to a more engaged approach to international human rights forums. In his statement regarding the US's rejoining, Secretary of State Anthony Blinken acknowledged the Council's imperfections, specifically citing the need for reforms in its agenda, membership, and focus. He highlighted concerns over what he described as the Council's "disproportionate focus on Israel." Despite these reservations, Blinken also recognized the potential value of the UNHRC, noting that, when functioning effectively, it could serve as a crucial platform for highlighting severe human rights abuses and providing a forum for those combating injustice and tyranny.[31] In 2022, the US was elected to the UNHRC for a three-year term, signaling a renewed commitment to participating in and potentially influencing the direction of the Council. This re-engagement reflects an acknowledgment of the UNHRC's role in the international human rights landscape and a desire to contribute to its evolution and reform.

6.3.1 What Do We Know about China's Behavior within the UNHCR?

China's approach to the Council and its broader engagement with the global human rights regime reveals a strategic and revisionist stance.

Unlike the United States, which has had periods of engagement and withdrawal, China has consistently sought to maintain its presence on the Council, successfully being elected each time it presented its candidacy. The relationship between China and the global governance of human rights has been characterized as "difficult, strained, and often contentious."[32] China has transitioned from being a reluctant adopter of international human rights norms to becoming an active shaper of these norms on the global stage.[33] This shift indicates a move toward challenging the established liberal human rights framework, which emphasizes individual and political freedoms, in favor of promoting the distinctly Chinese interpretation of human rights that prioritizes state-led development and stresses the potentially regime-destabilizing effects of individual civil and political rights. Experts have suggested that China aims to redefine the United Nations' foundational triad of development, peace and security, and human rights by proposing an alternative framework comprising development, a strong state, and social stability. This framework posits that the combination of these elements represents the most effective pathway to human protection, and it indicates Beijing's intent to reshape the United Nations and its approach to human rights from within.[34]

China's ambition to redefine global human rights norms is evident in its official statements and policy documents. At the 19th Party Congress in 2017, President Xi Jinping positioned China as offering a new model for countries seeking rapid development while maintaining independence. Similarly, a 2021 position paper by China's Ministry of Foreign Affairs outlined a human rights philosophy centered on the people, prioritizing rights to subsistence and development as fundamental.[35] This approach encompasses a comprehensive advancement of various rights, including economic, political, social, cultural, and environmental, aiming to promote overall human fairness, justice, and development. Further reinforcing this stance, China's State Council Information Office, in a white paper titled "Democracy that Works," asserted that living a contented life is the ultimate human right. This statement encapsulates China's effort to redefine human rights in terms that align with its governance model and developmental priorities. In doing so, it also poses a challenge to the conventional international human rights discourse.[36]

Scholarly analysis of China's approach to human rights reveals a nuanced and evolving stance in the global discourse. China's position is characterized by two distinct yet interconnected patterns that challenge the traditional Western-dominated narrative on human rights. First, China contests the Western-centric claim of universality in human rights, proposing instead a "dialogue among civilizations" pathway to achieving modernity in harmony and with social stability. Second, while acknowledging the existence of human rights violations, China questions the legitimacy and efficacy of interventionist approaches in addressing these issues. This viewpoint underpins China's advocacy for a reorientation of international human rights obligations, with a strong emphasis on state sovereignty, control over civil society, and the prioritization of economic development. Scholars have observed China's efforts to avoid country-specific monitoring mechanisms, particularly for developing nations, as it positions itself as a representative voice for the Global South in human rights discussions.[37]

China's strategy in influencing the human rights regime is multifaceted, leveraging both material and cultural resources to advance its objectives. Its approach is complemented by a growing willingness among other countries to embrace alternative leadership, which is often driven by grievances toward the current international order.[38] The interplay between China's proactive engagement and the receptiveness of other nations underscores the strategic nature of China's involvement in shaping the international human rights agenda. However, the extent to which China's preferences actually influence other countries' positions within the human rights regime remains an area ripe for further research. Given the multilateral nature of the international human rights framework, understanding how other countries respond to China's stance within these institutions is crucial for accurately assessing China's overall impact on the regime.[39]

6.3.2 Quantifying Shifts in UNHRC Voting: Economic Displacement and Latin America–US Alignment

This case study utilizes an original database comprising all votes at the Council from 2006 to 2020, as documented by Pauselli, Urdinez, and Merke (2023).[40] The data was sourced from the Geneva-based Human Rights Information and Documentation System (HURIDOCS), which includes records on 1,099 resolutions from 2006 to 2018. The dataset provides detailed information on each resolution's title, topic (from a list of 81 topics), agenda item, and states' voting patterns. For the years 2019 and 2020, where HURIDOCS data was unavailable, Pauselli et al. manually coded votes from the OHCHR repository. A resolution-state-year triadic dataset was then constructed, incorporating variables indicating China's participation in voting on a resolution and whether a given country "A" voted in alignment or opposition to China for each resolution-state-year. This approach is particularly insightful given that many resolutions are subject to votes in successive years, making China's presence in the council a variable of significant interest. On average, the Council passes about 121 resolutions annually, with roughly twenty-five of these decided by vote and the remainder by consensus. This empirical analysis focuses on those resolutions that went to a vote. In the Council's inaugural year, fewer than five resolutions were voted upon, but this number has since increased, stabilizing at around thirty resolutions per year.

The primary objective of this case study is to analyze resolutions favored by the US and to assess convergence with Latin American countries. The database records a total of 2,161 votes from fifteen different Latin American countries during periods of US membership in the Council (as presented in Table 6.4). Of these 2,161 votes, the US voted in favor 572 times, with Latin American countries aligning with the US with favorable votes 86 percent of the time. Intriguingly, 36 percent of these votes occurred in country-years where China's economic presence had displaced that of the US in the respective countries.

In total, the study encompasses 127 resolutions, many of which were subject to votes across multiple years. Table F.1 in the Appendix displays the twenty resolutions that received the most votes, all of which were

TABLE 6.4 *Latin American member countries of the UNHRC*

Country	Terms	Total votes
Argentina	2006–2007; 2009–2011; 2013–2015	241
Brazil	2006–2008; 2009–2011; 2013–2015; 2017–2019	341
Cuba	2006–2009; 2010–2012; 2014–2016; 2017–2019	117
Mexico	2006–2009; 2010–2012; 2014–2016; 2018–2020	194
Uruguay	2006–2009; 2010–2012	207
Ecuador	2006–2007; 2011–2013; 2016–2018	232
Guatemala	2006–2008; 2011–2013	132
Peru	2006–2008; 2012–2014; 2018–2020	241
Bolivia	2008–2010; 2015–2017	168
Nicaragua	2008–2010	177
Chile	2009–2011; 2018–2020	285
Venezuela	2013–2015; 2016–2018	245
El Salvador	2015–2017	114
Paraguay	2015–2017	113
Panama	2016–2018	113

Source: United Nations General Assembly Meetings, www.un.org/en/ga/meetings/.

voted on more than once. Among the most voted are "Right to development," "Human Rights in the Occupied Syrian Golan," and "Human Rights and International Solidarity," just to mention a few. It's also notable that some resolutions were only voted on once, generally in response to an unexpected crisis or an isolated event. Examples of these include "Protection of human rights and fundamental freedoms while countering terrorism" (2016) and "Migrants and asylum-seekers fleeing recent events in North Africa" (2011).

6.3.3 Results: Assessing the Effect of Economic Displacement on UNHRC Voting

The statistical analysis above only considers those resolutions that Latin American countries voted for in years when the US was a member. What we are interested in is whether countries are more likely to vote differently than the US after the US has been economically displaced by China. The model for our analysis here is defined as:

$$\Pr(\text{VoteAgainstResol})_{cit} = \beta_0 + \beta_1 \text{USSupport}_{it} + \beta_2 \text{EcoDisplacement}_{ct} + \beta_3 \text{USSupport} \times \text{EcoDispacement}_{cit} + \beta_{4.8} \text{Controls}_{ct} + \beta_{9.n} \text{CountryFixedEffects}_c + \epsilon$$

In this model, various factors that could influence the voting decisions of countries are controlled for. Recognizing that more powerful countries often have greater flexibility in their voting choices, the model includes the GDP of each country as a variable, similar to the approach taken in the analysis of voting behaviors in the UNGA. Additionally, the model considers the political structure and orientation of each country. The hypothesis was that a country's alignment with the US would likely be influenced by its democratic status and the political ideology of its president, particularly whether the president aligns with left-wing ideologies.

A crucial aspect of this model is the interactive term, which is central to testing the chapter's hypothesis. The regression coefficients for this term are displayed in Table 6.5 across two models: one incorporating these control variables and the other without them. Intriguingly, in both models, the interactive term's coefficient is positive, which stands in contrast to the negative coefficient of the variable "US supports the resolution." This finding suggests that economic displacement affects how countries face the cost of not aligning with the US, and it opens up new

TABLE 6.5 *Effect of economic displacement on vote convergence with the US in the UNHRC*

DV = Country votes against a resolution	(1)	(2)
US supports the resolution	−0.0657***	−0.0623***
	(0.0132)	(0.0127)
China's economic displacement	−0.0223	−0.0235
	(0.0150)	(0.0154)
US supports the resolution × China's economic displacement	0.335***	0.271***
	(0.0352)	(0.0298)
GDP		−0.00009*
		(0.0000447)
China is a member of UNHRC		0.000164
		(0.0139)
Country is a democracy		0.293
		(0.223)
President is of left ideology		−0.0248*
		(0.0108)
Constant	0.0275**	−0.202
	(0.00928)	(0.217)
Country Fixed Effects	Yes	Yes
N	2,161	2,011

Note: OLS estimate. Standard errors in parentheses, *$P < 0.05$, **$P < 0.01$, ***$P < 0.001$

avenues for understanding the dynamics of international voting behavior, particularly in the context of human rights resolutions and global governance.

To clarify the findings, Figure 6.6 illustrates the predicted probability of a country voting against a resolution under four different conditions: with and without economic displacement, and with and without US support for the resolution. The scenario where the US does not support a resolution reveals a consistent pattern among Latin American countries: the probability of them voting against the resolution is around 10 percent, regardless of whether they have undergone economic displacement. However, a stark contrast emerges when the US endorses a resolution. In this case, the voting behavior of countries that have not experienced economic displacement aligns closely with the US stance, showing opposition to the resolution only about 1.5 percent of the time. Conversely, for countries that have undergone economic displacement, the tendency to oppose a resolution supported by the US increases significantly, averaging 36.5 percent. This indicates that these countries are 300 times more likely to oppose a resolution favored by the US when they have

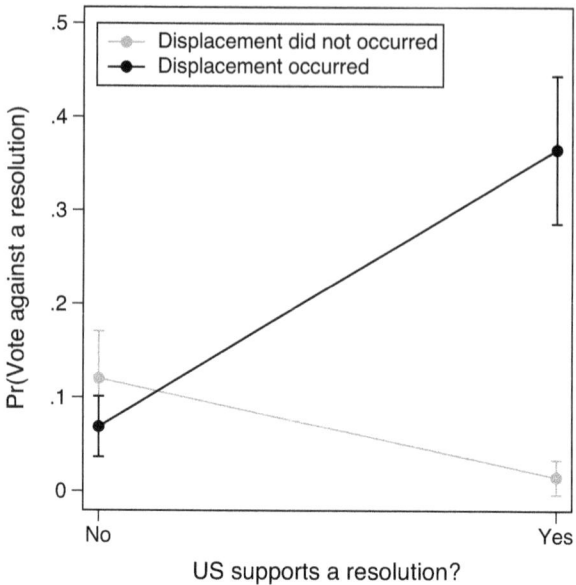

FIGURE 6.6 Probability of economic displacement in voting against a resolution in the UNHRC

experienced economic displacement. This variation underscores the substantial influence of economic factors on voting behavior in international forums, particularly in relation to alignment with US positions. This case confirms that economic displacement affects the way in which Latin American countries cease to support the US as frequently, in this instance within the UNHRC, in the facing of waning US influence.

6.4 CASE 3: THE EFFECT OF ECONOMIC DISPLACEMENT ON VOTES AT THE OAS

In contrast to the previous two cases, the Organization of American States presents a distinct scenario due to its nature as a regional international organization rather than a global one. Significantly, China is not a member of the OAS. This distinction provides a unique opportunity to explore whether economic displacement influences voting behaviors in an organization where China is absent. This case serves to show that displacement gives agency to other countries; specifically, that reduced economic dependence on the US grants greater agency to countries in their decision-making processes. Additionally, this case offers a lens to examine an international organization where the US has traditionally exerted significant control over the agenda and has been able to shape the preferences of other member countries.

The OAS is committed to strengthening democracy and fostering cooperation across the Americas. Established on April 30, 1948, the OAS is a pan-American international organization with a regional and continental scope. Its primary objective is to serve as a political forum for decision-making, multilateral dialogue, and the integration of the Americas. Its member states collaborate to promote human rights, defend common interests, and address major issues confronting the region. The OAS's major policies and goals are determined by its General Assembly, composed of foreign affairs ministers from countries across the Americas who convene annually. The ongoing activities and initiatives of the OAS are overseen by the Permanent Council, consisting of ambassadors appointed by the member states.

The OAS comprises thirty-five member states from North, Central, and South America, as well as the Caribbean. Historically, the OAS experienced a significant period of tension, most notably in relation to Cuba, which was excluded from participating in the organization from January 21, 1962 to June 3, 2009. The primary reason was that the Castro regime remained in conflict with the United States throughout the Cold War. Additionally, the OAS extends permanent observer status to states outside the Americas, with sixty-eight states and the European Union currently holding this status. Notably, the People's Republic of China was formally accepted as a permanent observer in 2004 following a request by its government.[41]

During history, the OAS has undergone two distinct phases. During the Cold War, it functioned as the primary organization through which the US sought to control the expansion of communism in the region. However, since the 1990s, the organization has reinvented itself with a focus on promoting democracy. Over time, however, it has gradually lost its vitality. Historian Robert Pastor argues that the OAS has been hindered throughout much of its existence by an "inherent contradiction between its two core principles, representative democracy and nonintervention."[42] He notes that almost every major crisis in the hemisphere – be it civil wars, fraudulent elections, or human rights abuses – has involved a clash of these principles. Consequently, the OAS has often found itself incapacitated, especially as these problems worsened or as the US intervened. Pastor's assessment is that the OAS's role in supporting US policy has led to a loss of credibility across the hemisphere, a view supported by other renowned historians.[43]

Scholarly assessments of the OAS generally concur that, throughout the Cold War era, the United States wielded considerable influence in shaping the organization's agenda and the voting outcomes of its Permanent Council. Former Guatemalan President Arevalo observed, for example, that the United States "always wins" in the OAS.[44] Similarly, Ecuadorian writer Benjamin Carrion critiqued the OAS as an entity that merely followed orders, giving the illusion of debate and voting privileges merely to satisfy the formalities of its powerful members.[45] This sentiment is encapsulated in a comment attributed to a Latin American delegate at an Inter-American Conference, as reported by the *New York Times* on March 8, 1954: "If the United States wanted to badly enough, it could have a resolution passed declaring two and two are five."[46]

Between 1950 and 1975, the OAS passed numerous resolutions aimed at destabilizing democratically elected governments amid fears of communism's spread in the region; a phenomenon that historians identify as an inherent contradiction within the organization. Indeed, the OAS was instrumentalized to such ends, with the United States exerting enormous influence over its voting processes. At an OAS meeting in Caracas in March 1954, for example, John Foster Dulles, then-United States Secretary of State under President Dwight D. Eisenhower, urged OAS delegates to support a resolution framing the control of any American state's political institutions by the international communist movement as a hemispheric threat. It necessitated, he claimed, "appropriate action" under existing treaties. As reported by historian Peter Smith, Dulles aimed to extend the Monroe Doctrine to include outlawing foreign ideologies in the American Republics. Of course, Latin American diplomats quickly recognized that this resolution was also a pretext for action against Guatemala. After two weeks of intense debate, the resolution was adopted with a vote of 17-1-2, with only Guatemala in opposition and Mexico and Argentina abstaining.[47]

As the Cold War drew to a close, the United States's ability to leverage the OAS as a foreign policy tool began to wane. This shift was starkly illustrated in the aftermath of the 1989 Panama invasion. The OAS's response was swift and largely critical, with President George H. W. Bush facing backlash for failing to consult Latin American leaders prior to the military action. The resulting OAS resolution, which expressed profound regret over the intervention and urged the withdrawal of American forces, garnered overwhelming support. Twenty nations voted in favor, seven abstained, and the United States stood alone in opposition.[48]

Indeed, the post-Cold War era saw a general transformation in US–Latin American relations, characterized by what many observers termed neglect and disinterest. This trend, which began during the Clinton administration and intensified under George W. Bush, resulted in an inconsistent and ambivalent US policy toward the region. While the US occasionally supported enhancements to the inter-American democratic framework, its approach often vacillated between passive disengagement and aggressive intervention, with actions frequently filtered through the prism of national interest.[49] Concurrently, the OAS underwent a process of power decentralization, moving away from its previous US-dominated structure.

A significant milestone in this evolution was the adoption of the Inter-American Democratic Charter (IADC) on September 11, 2001, which established democracy as a fundamental right to be upheld by governments. However, research spanning 2001 to 2020 indicates that while US support remained necessary for IADC enforcement, it was no longer sufficient. The US now required the backing of key regional powers, particularly Mexico and Brazil, to take action. And despite initial optimism surrounding the IADC, the OAS's responses to contentious political developments in Venezuela (2002), Haiti (2004), and Ecuador (2005) were widely perceived as inadequate.[50] This tepid reaction to challenges of constitutional order and democratic governance underscored the shifting power dynamics within the organization.[51]

6.4.1 Quantifying Shifts in OAS Voting: Economic Displacement and Hemispheric Alignment

The OAS's evolution during the post-Cold War era marked a significant departure from its earlier incarnation as a body heavily influenced by US interests. It was a shift reflecting broader changes in hemispheric relations and the diminishing capacity of the United States to unilaterally shape regional affairs. Yet there has been a dearth of quantitative research on the topic. The only existing research employing panel data analysis to comprehend voting patterns within the OAS was conducted by George Meek, himself a former General Secretariat at the OAS in the 1970s. In Meek's analysis, which covers the period from 1948 to 1974 (the phase of US dominance), the data indicates that the United States was in the minority, or on the losing side, in 25 percent of the 297 roll-call votes.[52] This illustrates that the United States wielded substantial influence over voting outcomes and possessed a significant ability to assert its agenda within the OAS during these years.

A significant challenge in analyzing more recent voting within the OAS, however, lies in the absence of systematically organized data by the organization itself. This has necessitated the laborious task of manually coding each voting record from transcripts of meeting minutes. Yet the merit of scrutinizing roll-call votes lies in their distinct presence in the official minutes of OAS meetings, assuming one meticulously scans each page. These votes are not excessively numerous, which helps us avoid undue complexity, and they offer a definitive record of the US position on each issue.

For my study, I downloaded and reviewed the minutes of the 147 resolutions passed between 2001 and 2021. These minutes provide verbatim accounts of discussions held during regular and special OAS sessions, indicating whether a resolution was adopted by consensus or subjected to a roll-call vote. My analysis of these minutes facilitated the identification of 22 resolutions that underwent roll-call voting, while the remainder were determined by consensus. Although the proportion of resolutions put to a vote is relatively low (14 percent), roll-call voting typically occurred when the resolution's subject matter was highly contentious, dividing member countries. This, I contend, more accurately reflects the foreign policy preferences of participating nations. The majority of consensus-approved resolutions pertained to scheduling events, reviewing past meeting minutes, minor procedural matters, and paying homage to former ambassadors and significant historical dates. Despite the smaller volume of votes compared to previous studies, I believe the data collected is adequate for statistical analysis, as the unit of analysis is the dyad US–country and assumes the value "1" if the country votes like the US in a given resolution, and "0" otherwise. Table 6.6 showcases the resolutions voted on by roll call, the total number of votes, and the percentage of alignment with the US stance.

In my approach to the data, my main independent variable (as in the two previous case studies) was a binary measure: I assigned a value of 1 to signify instances where China has economically displaced the United States within a specific nation during a designated year. The analysis included a range of control variables to mitigate the influence of potential confounding elements, using methodologies akin to those employed in the two preceding cases. These encompass the size of the country, the political ideology of its incumbent president, and the degree of democratic governance exercised within the country. This is the model I developed:

$$\Pr(\text{VoteLikeUS})_{cit} = \beta_0 + \beta_1 \text{EcoDisplacement}_{ct} + \beta_{4..8}\text{Controls}_{ct} + \beta_{9..n}\text{CountryFixedEffects}_c + \epsilon,$$

where c is the country, i is the resolution, and t is the year.

TABLE 6.6 *Resolutions adopted by the Permanent Council of the OAS by roll call vote on domestic political situations, 2001–2021*

Resolution	Title	Year	Votes	% voted like US
CP/RES. 953/09	Resolution on the Current Situation in Honduras	2009	32	100
CP/RES. 977/10 corr. 1	Situation in the Republic of Ecuador	2010	33	100
CP/RES. 978/10	Situation in the Border Area of Costa Rica and Nicaragua	2010	33	82
CP/RES. 986/11	Situation in Honduras	2011	33	97
CP/RES. 1017/13	Solidarity of the OAS member states with the President, Evo Morales Ayma, and the People of the Plurinational State of Bolivia	2013	32	0
CP/RES. 1078 (2108/17)	Resolution on Recent Events in Venezuela	2017	33	53
CP/RES. 1095 (2145/18)	Resolution on the Latest Developments in Venezuela	2018	33	53
CP/RES. 1108 (2172/18)	The Situation in Nicaragua	2018	32	60
CP/RES. 1110 (2182/18)	Recent Events in Nicaragua	2018	33	53
CP/RES. 1117/19	Resolution on the Situation in Venezuela	2019	33	53
CP/RES. 1123/19	Humanitarian Aid in Venezuela	2019	33	53
CP/RES. 1124/19 rev. 2	Resolution on the Situation in Venezuela	2019	33	50
CP/RES. 1127 (2228/19)	Violation of Parliamentary Immunity in Venezuela	2019	33	52
CP/RES. 1128 (2231/19)	The Situation in Nicaragua	2019	33	52
CP/RES. 1133 (2244/19)	Resolution on the Human Rights Situation in Venezuela	2019	33	55
CP/RES. 1135 (2244/19)	Resolution on the Appointment of a Commission on Nicaragua	2019	33	58
CP/RES. 1142/19 rev. 2	Rejecting Violence in Bolivia and Calling for Full Respect of the Rights of the Indigenous Peoples in the Plurinational State of Bolivia	2019	33	74
CP/RES. 1164/20 rev. 1	Rejection of the Parliamentary Elections Held on December 6 in Venezuela	2020	33	58

(*continued*)

TABLE 6.6 (continued)

Resolution	Title	Year	Votes	% voted like US
CP/RES. 1168 (2315/21)	The Situation in Haiti	2021	33	100
CP/RES. 1182 (2346/21)	The Situation in Nicaragua	2021	33	71
CP/RES. 1188 (2355/21)	Outcome of the Permanent Council's Deliberations of November 29, 2021, on the Situation in Nicaragua	2021	33	71

TABLE 6.7 *Comparative analysis of OAS voting alignments: impact of China's economic displacement on alignment with US*

DV = Country votes like the US	(1)	(2)
China's economic displacement	−0.173*	−0.258**
	(0.0752)	(0.0818)
Checks and balances		0.0809*
		(0.0401)
Executive electoral competitiveness		−0.0714*
		(0.0289)
Leftist president		−0.257**
		(0.0864)
GDP		−0.00072*
		(0.000335)
Constant	0.833***	1.018***
	(0.0906)	(0.203)
Country Fixed Effects	Yes	Yes
N	575	491
R^2	0.377	0.404

Note: OLS estimates. Standard errors in parentheses, $*P < 0.05$, $**P < 0.01$, $***P < 0.001$

The results of this analysis are detailed in Table 6.7, which delineates two distinct versions of the model: the first eschewing the inclusion of control variables, and the second including them. Across both models, the data shows a discernible negative correlation between China's economic displacement and a nation's likelihood to align its voting patterns with those of the United States. In both models, it is observed that economic

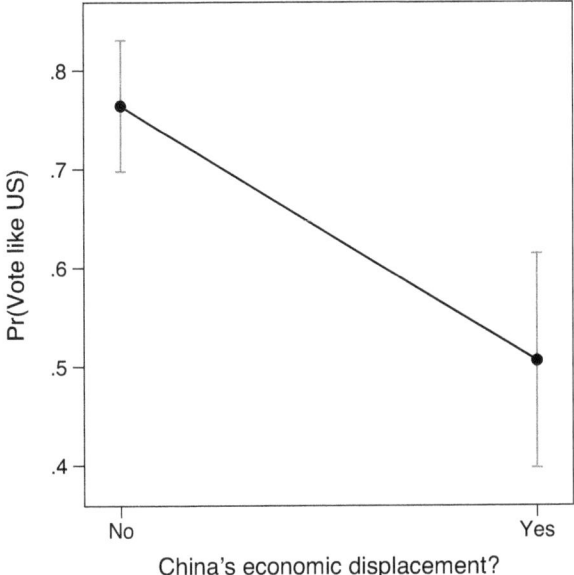

FIGURE 6.7 Effect of economic displacement on voting in the OAS

displacement by China decreases the probability of alignment in voting with the US in the OAS by 17 to 26 percentage points, depending on the model under consideration.

Figure 6.7 offers a succinct summation of the impact exerted by Chinese economic displacement on the OAS using the full model as a benchmark. The figure discloses a salient trend: on average, the probability of a country voting in alignment with the US decreases from approximately 75 to 50 percent when China has eclipsed the US in economic influence. This effect is undeniably large in magnitude. Such a statistic underscores the profound impact of China's economic footprint on the geopolitical landscape and voting dynamics of nations within its own hemisphere.

6.5 PROPOSING A TESTABLE HYPOTHESIS

In the three cases explored here, I confirm a similar pattern: economic displacement hinders the ability of the United States to secure aligned voting from other countries. The mechanism I believe accounts for this effect is the diminished efficacy of the US carrot and stick approach in the face of China's emergence as an alternative provider of goods. This implies

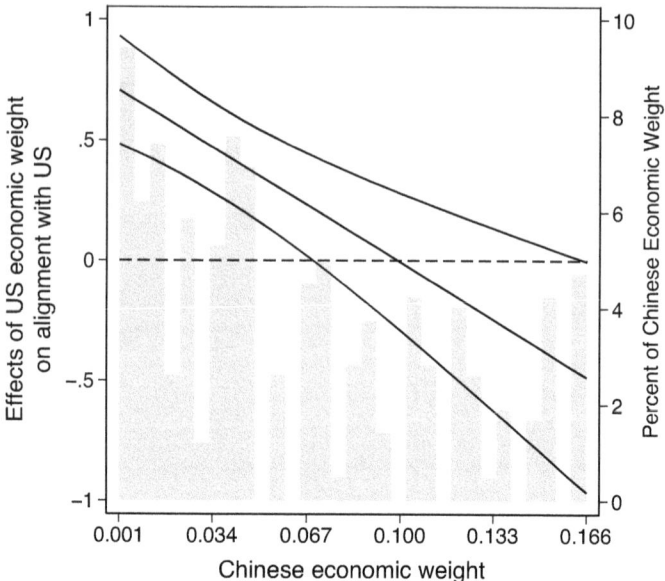

FIGURE 6.8 Marginal effect of US economic weight conditioned by China's economic weight on a country's vote alignment with the US in the UNHRC

that US economic statecraft loses traction in international organizations when it experiences economic displacement. To test this hypothesis, I have estimated an interactive model for voting in the UNHRC, capitalizing on it being the case with the highest number of observations.

The model's dependent variable is a dichotomous one, assigned 0 if a country votes differently from the US and 1 if it votes the same in a given resolution. Instead of using a binary independent variable for economic displacement, I employed the continuous variable of China's economic weight as defined in Chapter 2, and interacted it with the US economic weight variable, also defined in Chapter 2. The results are illustrated in Figure 6.8, with the model showing that the marginal effect of US economic weight decreases as China's economic weight increases. US economic means positively affect vote alignment in the UNHRC only in instances where China's economic weight is low (less than seven points of a country's GDP). Beyond this threshold, the sticks and carrots lose statistical significance.

While this analysis offers compelling insights, it is important to acknowledge its preliminary nature. A definitive conclusion that China's economic influence has nullified US agency in international forums would necessitate extensive qualitative research and in-depth interviews beyond the scope of this current study. Nevertheless, existing research provides valuable perspectives on the issue. A study by Pauselli et al, based on comprehensive interviews with UNHRC diplomats, sheds light on China's strategic approach to influencing votes.[53] Their findings reveal a sophisticated system of vote trading and reciprocal agreements among Council members. As one diplomat articulated, there exists an implicit understanding of mutual support: "you vote for us here, we'll vote for you there; you abstain for us here and we'll abstain for you there."[54] Furthermore, the research highlights China's nuanced strategy in cultivating support, particularly from developing nations. By positioning itself as an advocate for their interests and causes, China has built a network of allies within the Council. This approach is especially evident when these countries face scrutiny: China's consistent support in such instances reinforces a sense of solidarity and deepens diplomatic ties. These observations suggest a complex interplay of economic incentives, strategic diplomacy, and mutual interest alignment that characterizes China's growing influence in international forums. While not conclusive, these findings offer valuable insight into the evolving dynamics of global governance and the shifting balance of power in multilateral institutions.

6.6 CONCLUSION

The insights garnered from the three case studies examined in this chapter collectively shed light on the influence of China's economic ascendance on global voting patterns. They illuminate a complex and nuanced landscape of international relations, particularly in the context of shifting economic powers. First, it is crucial to note that the influence of the US's economic displacement by China does not necessarily translate into a direct alignment of countries with China. This is evident in forums like the OAS, where China is not even a member, yet its economic presence indirectly influences voting behaviors. Second, and more significantly, my findings suggest that China's economic rise serves to distance countries from the United States. This shift is not a straightforward realignment with China, but rather a divergence from US influence, indicating a more multipolar world where countries navigate between major powers.

The underlying mechanism of this effect remains a subject for further empirical exploration. My hypothesis posits that as China emerges as an economic alternative, particularly for Latin American countries, it endows these countries with enhanced agency in international forums. This increased autonomy manifests as a reduced susceptibility to US economic statecraft, which has traditionally leveraged economic incentives and penalties to align votes. The implication here is that China's economic footprint is altering the geopolitical fabric, loosening the ties that have historically bound countries to US policy directions. In essence, the three cases analyzed in this chapter reveal a transformative shift in international dynamics, where economic influence is increasingly becoming a crucial determinant of geopolitical alignments. As nations find alternative economic partners, their strategic and political decisions in international organizations evolve accordingly. The rise of China as a significant global economic player is not just reshaping trade and investment patterns, it is profoundly influencing the very nature of diplomatic and strategic alignments in the global arena. This evolving landscape underscores the need for continued scholarly attention to understand the full spectrum of implications arising from this shift in global power dynamics.

7

The New Cold War and the Future of China–US Rivalry in LAC

Look at the Americas today – democracy in every nation but one, a hemispheric free trade agreement on its way, and the triumph of open markets in the battle of ideas.
> Robert Zoelick, former US Trade Representative and former president of the World Bank, May 7, 2001.[1]

The crisis consists precisely in the fact that the old is dying and the new cannot be born; in this interregnum a great variety of morbid symptoms appear.
> Antonio Gramsci, *Quaderni del carcere*, 1929[2]

The debate over the costs of maintaining the liberal (i.e., American-led) international order has resurfaced with the rise of China. The United States often frames the US–China dichotomy as a moral choice between transparency, respect for human rights, and sustainability versus debt traps, corrosive capital, and extractivism. What is often overlooked in Washington is that LAC countries have sought Chinese goods, recognizing their imperfections, due to the lack of real alternatives – even as the United States promises otherwise.

This dynamic was exemplified during the COVID-19 pandemic, where despite US promises, many Latin American and Caribbean countries turned to Chinese vaccines due to their availability and accessibility. In Chile, during the first two years of the pandemic, most people were vaccinated with two doses of vaccines from the Chinese company Sinovac, making Chile one of the countries with the highest percentage of its population receiving Chinese vaccines. Yet, in November 2023, the Millennium Nucleus of China's Impacts in Latin America conducted a survey among 660 Chileans in which one of the questions was, "To what extent do you agree with the following statement? If they had been available, I would have preferred my first vaccines to be Pfizer or Moderna instead of Sinovac." Only 12 percent of respondents disagreed with this statement.[3]

I started this chapter with two historical quotes, as it's intriguing to see how perspectives can shift over time. The fact that Antonio Gramsci's quote from 1929 resonates more with contemporary times than Robert Zoelick's from 2001 is telling indeed. Let's take a moment to reflect on the stark contrast between the beginning of the twenty-first century and that of the twentieth century. Between 1897 and 1914, the United States's total investment abroad increased fivefold. A significant portion of these investments was directed toward the Global South, both through European companies involved in colonial exploitation and through direct investments in Mexico, Cuba, Central America, and, to a lesser extent, parts of South America. Having been a net importer of capital in the nineteenth century, the United States had become the world's largest exporter of capital by 1918. It maintained this vaunted position until 1981.[4]

It was in the 1920s that American corporations replaced their European competitors as the largest investors in LAC. Historian Ethan Kapstein shows that by 1930, American corporations had spent more in Latin America than in Western Europe: around US$5.3 billion compared to US$4.9 billion, with US$1 billion allocated solely to Cuba.[5] Then, after World War II, the exit of German companies from industries such as pharmaceuticals created new opportunities for American companies, while post-war demand for oil and minerals led companies to seek natural resources across the region. A parallel can be drawn between the first three decades of robust US investment in Latin America and the first two decades of Chinese investment in the region: both were driven by a desire to secure energy and food security, and both took advantage of buying assets at good prices from investors who were leaving the region. Between 1950 and 1953, oil-rich Venezuela was the main beneficiary of US investment – followed by Brazil and Cuba – with a focus on commodities like sugar, coffee, and iron.[6]

As the US's economic influence grew, local elites demanded a greater quantity and diversity of American goods and services. Latin American leaders argued that their support for the Allies during World War II should be compensated with a second Marshall Plan for the continent.[7] This pattern emerged multiple times throughout history, such as in 1948 during the Bogotá Conference. However, instead of materializing into full-fledged programs comparable to the original Marshall Plan, initiatives tended to evolve into different forms of assistance, often channeled through controlled international institutions like the World Bank and the Inter-American Development Bank (IADB), both of which became key players in promoting development in Latin America. Indeed, the IADB was established in response to the longstanding Latin American demand for a regional development bank.[8]

Latin American agency, which was instrumental in the IADB's creation, has similarly played a crucial role in the region's engagement with Chinese economic initiatives. This includes the expansion of China's BRI to LAC, the region's accession to the AIIB, the development of major infrastructure projects financed by the CDB and executed by national champions, and the signing of FTAs with China.

Importantly, the BRI in LAC should be viewed as a demand-driven process rather than an imperialist project imposed by China.[9] Since the launch of the BRI, several local politicians expressed their hopes for China to consider LAC as part of the project.[10] A pivotal moment came in 2018 at the China–Latin American and Caribbean States Community Forum (China–CELAC). There, Chinese Foreign Minister Wang Yi formally introduced the BRI to the region, describing Latin America as a "natural extension" of the twenty-first-century Maritime Silk Road. In recent years, US policymakers have tended to fall back on regional projects when discussing how to counter the BRI, championing proposals such as Build Back Better World (B3W), the Americas Partnership for Economic Prosperity, and others. However, rather than being well-planned and articulated proposals, these engagements have at times appeared to be mere reactions to the external threat posed by China's economic displacement of the US in recent years.

7.1 REACTIVE US FOREIGN POLICY IN LATIN AMERICA: FROM COLD WAR TO POST-SOVIET ERA

History shows that the United States has often been reactive rather than proactive in Latin America: the perception of the communist threat resulted in the maintenance of an expansive US strategy during the Cold War.[11] And after the collapse of the Soviet Union, US leaders continued to advocate for the moral necessity of maintaining this order. Without a significant power challenging the United States, the costs of maintaining it seemed manageable.

During the 1950s, the United States continued to be a prominent provider of capital to Latin America, to the extent that it even raised public concerns about American imperialism.[12] The sentiments of the Latin American Left regarding the role of American multinational corporations in the region were vividly reflected in the 1950 poem "The United Fruit Company," by Nobel Prize winner Pablo Neruda (published in his "Canto General"). The poem criticized the influence of companies like Coca-Cola, Anaconda Mining Company, Ford Motors, and the United Fruit Company.[13] By 1959, US FDI in Latin America had increased to US$8 billion, marking an increase of nearly 60 percent compared to the 1950 figures (after adjusting for inflation).[14]

Despite resistance to economic dependency on the United States, many Latin American presidents recognized the need for the US to continue providing public and private goods to help develop their nations and economies.[15] Scholar Tom Long, for example, highlights the demand-side of the equation in Latin America in the years leading up to the launch of the Alliance for Progress in 1960: Brazil's president, Juscelino Kubitschek, along with Argentine President Arturo Frondizi and Colombian President Alberto Lleras Camargo, advocated for improving economic relations between the US and LAC, pressing the Eisenhower administration for greater commitment and support.[16] The United States had a virtual monopoly in this area, as the USSR's capacity was limited and focused mainly on Cuba.

The Alliance for Progress, initiated during the Kennedy administration in 1961, perhaps represented the most comprehensive US strategy for providing economic public and private goods in Latin America. This program made the interconnection between US commercial and political objectives especially transparent.[17] Based on (mistaken) theories by Seymour Lipset and Walt Whitman Rostow about the relationship between modernization and democracy, the Alliance aimed to raise human development indices in Latin America, thus strengthening democratic governments in the region.[18] Quoting David E. Bell, head of the US Agency for International Development (USAID), historian Peter Smith aptly put it this way: "in the 1960s, there existed an 'overwhelmingly' positive historical relationship between economic growth and political democracy, a correlation that bore optimistic implications for the Third World." Bell himself continued, "While there is no guarantee that improved political institutions will follow in any automatic way, it seems clear that without economic progress the chances for strengthening democratic processes in the less developed countries would be greatly diminished."[19]

One of the key motives behind strengthening democracy was to counter the spread of communism, especially after the Cuban Revolution of 1959. In many ways, the Cuban Revolution acted as a catalyst for the United States to address Latin America's historical need for more capital. Not surprisingly, the most notable failure of the Alliance for Progress occurred in the area of promoting democracy. Instead of promoting and consolidating reformist civil government, the 1960s saw a proliferation of military coups across the region. Six coups occurred in 1962–1963 alone. Argentina, Brazil, Peru, Paraguay, and most of Central America were governed by dictators by the end of 1968; Bolivia and Ecuador were governed by the military; and Mexico remained under the rule of its unique authoritarian regime led by a civilian party that was nonetheless undeniably authoritarian.

The Alliance for Progress required Latin American nations to invest US$80 billion over a decade, while the United States committed US$20 billion over the same period.[20] But despite its political shortcomings, Smith notes that between 1962 and 1967, the United States ultimately provided nearly US$22.3 billion in aid, loans, and investments to Latin America, averaging nearly US$3.3 billion annually.[21] Considering the significance of China's initiatives in relation to its influence in the region during the early twenty-first century, it is notable that between 2001 and 2020, the annual flow of Chinese capital to the region matched the scale of the US's most ambitious effort in the twentieth century. Accounting for inflation, the yearly US$3.3 billion provided by the United States from 1962 to 1967 would be equivalent to about US$32.3 billion a year in 2022. According to my estimates, China's infrastructure investments and loans in Latin America averaged US$33 billion per year from 2001 to 2020.

7.2 FROM STATUS QUO TO STRATEGIC DEFICIT: AMERICA'S STRUGGLE TO COMPETE WITH CHINA IN LAC

Why was the United States displaced by China in Latin America? Did it neglect the material dimension in its foreign policy, or simply not have enough resources while focusing on other more priority regions? Did it delegate the provision of goods to China without considering the Asian superpower a threat? Was this a consequence of retrenchment? These questions remain open. However, this book has shown that China not only increased its economic weight in LAC, but the US reduced its own, and this caused an erosion of the US's political leverage. The book has argued that, although the United States has historically been a dominant economic force in the region, there was a lack of proactive strategies to encourage American companies to maintain or improve the US's economic weight in Latin America.

At a dinner with Indian leader Jawaharlal Nehru in 1951, during the early stages of the Cold War, Bobby Kennedy made a noteworthy observation in his notes: "We [Americans] only have the status quo to offer these people."[22] This statement reflects a sense of frustration that resonates with the narrative presented here. It raises another pertinent question: Why has the world's most powerful nation struggled to compete with the Chinese alternative in the Global South over the past two decades? While this question warrants an extensive study in its own right, my discussions with policymakers in Washington DC during my fellowship at the Wilson Center suggest that Kennedy's frustration continues to echo among current officials. The challenge of maintaining influence in the face of changing global dynamics remains a significant concern for American policymakers. In December 2022, for example, it was reported that China and Ecuador were close to finalizing an FTA. In an interview in January 2023, Ecuadorian President Guillermo Lasso was asked about the country's recent FTA with China and whether it was a result of the absence of the United States in the region. President Lasso replied: "We would like to reach a free trade agreement with the United States. According to President Biden, the current political climate in the United States is not favorable for a free trade agreement with Ecuador."[23] The FTA between China and Ecuador was signed virtually and simultaneously on May 10 in Quito and May 11, 2023 in Beijing, making Ecuador the fourth country in LAC to sign such an agreement with China in twenty years.

The greatest difficulty for the US in reversing Chinese displacement lies in the apparent (in)ability of the state to generate incentives for the private sector to "follow the flag;" that is, respond to the foreign policy interests of the United States. The second difficulty lies in the limitations of existing state tools such as the DFC, due to a reduced budget or impediments to investing in all countries. This intuition is shared by some authors who have suggested that China has a structural advantage in being able to mobilize surplus capital more easily than the United States; therefore, it is not a matter of *intentions* but of *capacity*.[24]

What's particularly intriguing is that China has managed to displace the United States without altering the prevailing institutional infrastructure in the region. Instead, China has skillfully leveraged existing structures to its advantage. The case of the IADB serves as perhaps the most compelling illustration of how Chinese firms, eager to expand their business, have increasingly outmaneuvered the US in recent years, all while playing by the established rules. China's strategic approach to the IADB began in 2009 when it joined the bank as a non-regional stakeholder. Initially, China's presence was minimal, acquiring just 184 shares, or 0.004 percent of the IADB's ordinary capital, which had become available following Yugoslavia's dissolution. This move marked China as the third East Asian member of the IADB, following South Korea and Japan, which had joined in 1976 and 2005, respectively. As part of its entry, China contributed US$350 million to the IADB group, funds that were subsequently used to finance various initiatives.

This seemingly modest membership granted Chinese companies a crucial advantage: the ability to bid on IADB-financed projects. This opened doors to new markets and procurement opportunities across Latin America and the Caribbean. The impact of this strategic positioning became evident in the years that followed. Between 2009 and 2022, Chinese businesses secured a staggering US$1.9 billion in procurement contracts from IADB-sponsored projects. In stark contrast, American businesses obtained only US$286 million during the same period. This disparity translates to a ratio where for every dollar awarded to American businesses, Chinese firms received US$6.6 (Figure 7.1).[25]

Some would argue that the phenomenon I have described in this book is nothing more than a symptom of something much larger: after seventy-five years of economic expansion to the west, the United States began to cede ground to China, which inevitably marked the end of the American empire.[26] I do not necessarily believe this to be the case, especially as the increase in China's economic weight is fraught with problems and may generate rejection in the coming decades.[27] In any case, the relevance of this book lies in showing the disruptive effects of China's economic rise in the United States's own backyard. For many, the COVID-19 pandemic only accelerated an early symptom of a decoupling that will lead to the end of economic globalization as we knew it, and to a bipolar world.[28]

Although this book focuses on LAC, I have also shown that the contraction of the United States's economic weight extends to other developing world regions. This phenomenon is evident in areas such as Western Africa and Central Asia, where it has created a marked contrast with the Cold War era. During the Cold War, the critical factor was not the importance of the Global South to the US economy, but rather the importance of the United States to most of the Global South's economies. Even more crucial than aspects such as mutual trade and foreign investments were the products and production patterns. For people in the Global

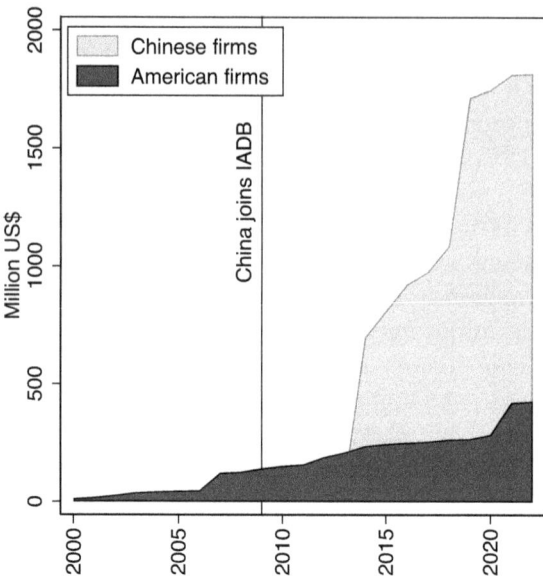

FIGURE 7.1 Cumulative IADB financing: Chinese versus American enterprise tenders (US$ millions)
Source: Author's elaboration based on IADB data.

South, the United States represented the source of advanced goods, a place where productive companies were based and where machinery had eliminated much of the tedium of production.[29] The trends of economic displacement suggest that we are moving toward increased competition for control of economic areas. As this competition intensifies, a crucial question emerges: Will the United States regain its economic lead in the Global South in the coming decades, particularly in emerging industries such as artificial intelligence (AI) and renewable energies? For the next two decades, I suspect this book will be useful to decision-makers and academics attempting to anticipate structural trends that will mark both the dynamics of rivalry between the US and China and their relationship with LAC and the Global South.

7.3 THREE POLICY IMPLICATIONS FOR THE COMING YEARS

Examining the evolution of the economic weights expressed by China and the United States over time and across different regions, I showed in Chapter 2 that, since 2000, China has increased its influence in LAC more than in any other region. Simultaneously, since the year 2000, and especially since the financial crisis of 2008, the United States has experienced a decline in its influence in Latin America.[30] This trend has important implications for US hegemony in the region. The analysis here lays the foundation for understanding when and where China has surpassed the United States and how China's displacement of the US has eroded its political preeminence. The growing economic weight of China in Latin America and the decreasing influence of the United States in the region should serve as a wake-up call for US policymakers. Without greater engagement in the region, the United States risks losing more market opportunities for American companies and eroding its influence when compared to China.[31]

From the findings of the book, we can draw at least three conclusions on how China's economic rise will affect US foreign policy toward Latin America and what we can expect to happen in the next two decades.

7.3.1 Policy Take #1

> The theoretical framework presented in this book highlights a critical yet overlooked aspect of developing nations: the forthcoming economic rivalry between China and the United States will center on their ability to offer competitive products and services, such as infrastructure in transportation and telecommunications, technology transfer, employment opportunities, and trade liberalization. We are moving toward a global scenario where economic activities are increasingly aligned with national interests, with China setting the pace and the United States playing catch-up.

Economist Arthur Kroeber describes a "gradual disillusionment" among American political and business elites regarding the benefits of China's rise. Historically, the United States has delegated the provision of economic goods in the Western Hemisphere to China, concentrating its attention on regions of higher strategic priority.[32] However, with the recognition that this strategy has failed, the need to offer competitive goods is now being recognized. Political scientist Evan Medeiros, along with other Western experts on China, agrees with the idea that the goods provided by China and the US will become increasingly competitive, a perspective that aligns with President Joe Biden's characterization of US–China interactions as "extreme competition" in February 2021, shortly after his inauguration. Medeiros contends that the competition between these global powers hinges on three critical conditions: the perception of contention between the parties, active efforts to gain mutual advantages, and the pursuit of scarce outcomes or goods, underscoring the strategic and high-stakes nature of this rivalry.[33]

The unanimity in Washington about the need to regain its lost influence in LAC dates back to the beginning of Donald Trump's administration in 2016. However, the development of US foreign economic policy demonstrated a persistent disinterest in the nations of LAC. This signaled what Cynthia Arnson refers to as a "mismatch between discourse and financial resources."[34] The Trump administration neglected to deploy "carrots" to maintain stability in its sphere of influence and focused mainly on "sticks." For example, it vehemently supported Taiwan's sovereignty claim, even threatening the nine Latin American nations that still recognize Taiwan not to change their diplomatic status.[35] Additionally, the US State Department seriously questioned nations that approached Huawei to deploy 5G technology.[36]

A concrete example of high-stakes competition between China and the US for providing in-demand goods is the so-called Humboldt Cable project in Chile. Between 2017 and 2021, Huawei Marine developed an underwater cabling project in southern Chile to provide fiber optics to the southern regions of the country. Then, during Sebastian Piñera's second government, Huawei was asked to evaluate the feasibility of a transoceanic cable that would connect Chile with China in order to generate the first submarine cable between Asia and LAC. The US State Department strongly opposed this project. It was suggested that Japanese companies could better develop the project, or that the cable could pass through Australia or New Zealand to guarantee control of the data transmitted by it. Finally, in 2023 it was announced that Google would be in charge of the project, an outcome strongly celebrated by the State Department.[37] Clearly, we are moving toward a world in which the lines between politics and economics will become even more blurred.

However, the United States faces serious challenges in mobilizing its private sector for political purposes in the same way that China does with its SOEs.[38] As former State Department official Roberta Jacobson noted, "Numerous government officials told us that we simply have no interest on the part of American companies. Especially in the smaller countries, even in Peru and Ecuador, but especially in the Caribbean and in Central America. Even when American companies are interested, they run the risk of being outbid by Chinese or foreign companies whose governments finance their operations."[39] The capacity of the US state to mobilize private capital, as it did in the early periods of the twentieth century, remains to be seen.

In 2019, the Trump administration launched the Growth in the Americas program, one of those "Marshall Plan reflexes" that Robert Pastor observed every time the US felt an external threat in the Western Hemisphere. According to an official press release at the time, the program was "an innovative whole-of-government approach to drive economic development in Latin America and the Caribbean by accelerating private sector investment in energy and other infrastructure projects."[40] Yet today, Latin American leaders, let alone US officials, have only a vague memory of the proposal.

The launch of the DFC in 2019 was probably the most concrete economic statecraft tool of recent years and is poised to gradually compete with the advancement of China's Belt and Road Initiative in the region.[41] However, neither the DFC nor the Inter-American Development Bank nor the US Trade Development Agency, which promotes the export of US goods and services, can interact with countries not classified as low or lower-middle income without a presidential waiver. This is limiting their actions in the region.[42] Of the thirty-three countries that make up Latin America and the Caribbean, only five are classified as low or lower-middle income (Bolivia, El Salvador, Nicaragua, Haiti, and Honduras). Moreover, there have been tensions facing the DFC between its development mandate and the desire of politicians and policymakers to use it as a tool for their foreign policy objectives.[43] In recent years, the foreign policy efforts of President Joe Biden, including initiatives such as the Build Back Better World (B3W) program and the Americas Partnership for Economic Prosperity (APEP) – presented at the 2022 Summit of the Americas – aimed to counter China's growing presence in the region with little or no concrete results at all.[44]

As to why the US took so long to realize that China was displacing it economically and that displacement would have an eroding effect on its political leadership the (rather stark) analogy is that of the boiling frog: a frog placed in boiling water will immediately jump out, but if placed in tepid water that is slowly heated, it will fail to perceive the danger until it's too late. Similarly, the United States was slow to recognize the full implications of China's rising economic power and its erosive effect on American political dominance. The incremental nature of this shift led the US to underestimate both its significance and urgency.

US foreign policy once understood that providing credit, infrastructure, and promoting free trade were key mechanisms for engaging countries in LAC. In his insightful book *Exporting Capitalism*, historian Ethan Kapstein offers innumerable examples of the role of private capital as a tool in US economic diplomacy throughout the twentieth century. The behavior of Chinese MNCs in Latin America resembles that of American MNCs between 1910 and 1940. American companies intervened to fill the gaps left by European capital, mainly British and German, which allowed the United States to exert political influence in this region of the world through its MNCs. Chinese companies are doing the same now. China has strategically emphasized its achievements in poverty reduction and quality of life improvements in its public diplomacy efforts, anticipating that this narrative will resonate strongly with many nations in the Global South. However, it's important to note that China has not yet presented a comprehensive ideological or moral alternative to the US-led global order, nor has it proposed a distinct "China Model" for global governance. The current competition between China and the United States primarily revolves around economic preeminence.

As China potentially surpasses the United States as the primary provider of goods in certain countries or industries, its growing economic influence could significantly challenge the US's ability to maintain the international leadership role it held in the postwar world. A bipolar order of open economic competition is taking place. This shift in economic dynamics is reshaping the global landscape, potentially altering long-standing alliances and partnerships, and necessitating a thorough reevaluation of geopolitical strategies and traditional relationships. The United States and its allies must adapt to this changing reality by developing new approaches to maintaining influence and promoting their values in a world where economic power is becoming increasingly diffuse. Other nations, meanwhile, particularly in the Global South, may find themselves navigating a more complex international environment, balancing relationships with both established and emerging powers. This situation underscores the need for nuanced diplomacy and innovative economic strategies from all global actors, as the competition for economic preeminence continues to shape the contours of international relations and global governance in the coming decades.

As we move forward, the dynamics of US–China competition in Latin America and the Caribbean are likely to intensify and evolve. The historical parallels between China's current economic strategies and those employed by the US in the early twentieth century provide valuable insights into the potential trajectory of this rivalry. However, the contemporary global landscape presents unique challenges and opportunities for both powers. The ability of the United States to mobilize its private sector for strategic purposes, as it once did, remains uncertain in the face of China's state-driven approach. Meanwhile, LAC nations find themselves at the crossroads of this competition, potentially benefiting from increased attention and investment while navigating the complexities of balancing relationships with both powers. This new era of competition will undoubtedly reshape the economic and political landscape of the region, demanding adaptability, strategic foresight, and nuanced diplomacy from all parties involved.

7.3.2 Policy Take #2

> In the economic competition between China and the US, LAC will be seen as two regions, not one. The deeper a country is economically intertwined with a leading superpower, the more its diplomatic and economic flexibility is restricted on the global stage. The economic displacement of the US by China in South America will result in difficulty regarding regional integration agendas. It will also mean that the United States will concentrate its efforts on solidifying its economic weight in Mexico and Central America.

Based on the analysis presented in Chapter 2, I have observed that, in South America, the United States has been economically displaced by China with the exceptions of Colombia and Paraguay. Now let's compare the regional change in economic weight between China and the United States in South America versus the rest of the region. To the right of the dotted line indicates economic displacement. The figure shows that in South America, the economic weight of the United States decreased to a half while that of China grew significantly (from almost 0 to 20 percent); in the rest of the region, including Mexico, Central America, and the Caribbean, the economic weight of both increased, but that of the United States did so more markedly (Figure 7.2).

Now let's examine the major economies of the region. From the analysis of economic weight, we can draw some interesting conclusions: If we look at the growth of the economic weight of the United States and China between 2001 and 2020, we can divide the figure

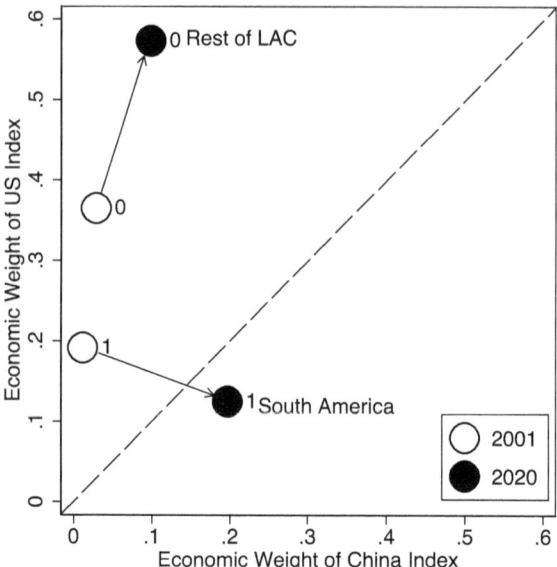

FIGURE 7.2 Difference in the trajectories of South America and the rest of Latin America and the Caribbean
Note: The diagonal line indicates economic displacement.

into two. Those countries to the right of the dotted line are those in which, by 2020, China had economically surpassed the United States. Colombia, Costa Rica, and Mexico are countries where the United States exerts more economic influence than China. In fact, Mexico is the only country in the figure where the influence of the United States increased. Interestingly, among the countries where displacement has occurred, there are two narratives to consider. One of these involves countries like Panama, Venezuela, and – to a lesser extent – Argentina, where the change is mainly due to a loss in the economic weight of the United States. Another group of countries, which includes Chile, Peru, Ecuador, and Brazil, experienced a change not so much due to a contraction of the United States, but rather to a substantial increase in the economic weight of China (Figure 7.3).

We can categorize LAC countries into three groups based on their evolving economic relationships with China and the US. The first group, including Mexico, Ecuador, and Colombia, managed to increase economic weight with both powers, moving upward and to the right on the graph. The second group, exemplified by Chile and Peru, significantly

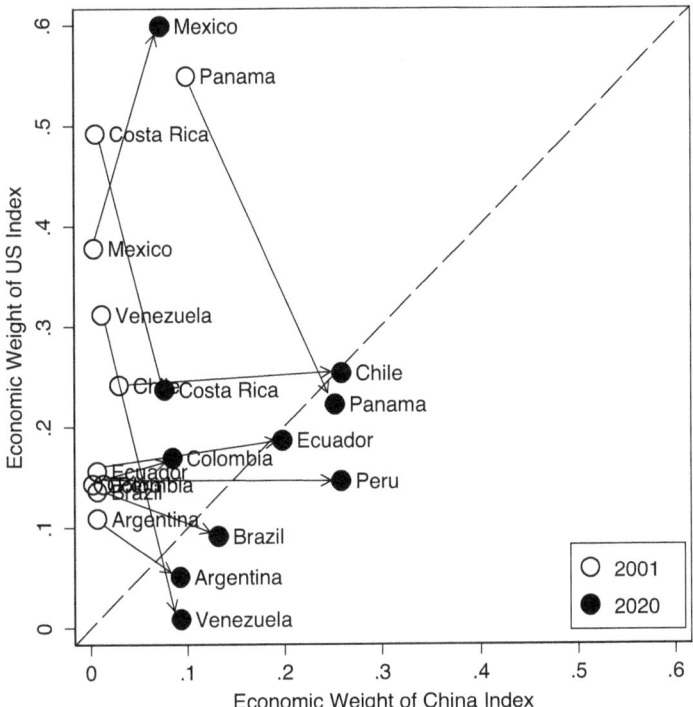

FIGURE 7.3 Trajectories of the largest economies in Latin America and the Caribbean
Note: The diagonal line indicates economic displacement.

increased China's economic weight without diminishing US influence. The third group, comprising Argentina, Brazil, Costa Rica, Panama, and Venezuela, saw increased Chinese economic weight come at the expense of US growth. This categorization illustrates the diverse strategies employed by LAC countries in navigating the changing dynamics between these two economic powers and highlights that China's rising influence hasn't followed a uniform pattern across the region. Some nations have successfully balanced relationships with both powers, while others have experienced a more pronounced shift toward China, often at the expense of US economic influence.

The further away a country moves from the dotted line, the more challenging it will be to maintain a policy of non-alignment. For example, looking at the figure, one can infer that Mexico has less margin to respond to negative economic maneuvers by the United States than does Peru, at least in theory. This indicates that the more economically aligned a country is with a particular superpower, the more limited its diplomatic and economic options will be in the context of global geopolitics. Countries that are strongly influenced or dominated by a great power may find it difficult to follow an independent or non-aligned foreign policy without facing economic or political repercussions. If indeed we are moving toward a scenario of increased economic competition between China and the United States, what I have described in this book would be the beginning of a bipolar economic landscape. On the one hand, there will be South America, which will become increasingly politically and economically misaligned from the United States; a trend that will solidify over time. On the other hand, there will be Central America, Mexico, and the Caribbean, where the United States will regain influence.[45]

The Biden Administration has contemplated the idea of withdrawing investments from China and relocating factories to countries in LAC that are more aligned with the interests of the United States, a strategy known as "friend-shoring." Meanwhile, China is expected to leverage its influence in the Western Hemisphere to strengthen its position in Southeast Asia. As competition between China and the US increases, it is likely that China will try to advance in what is traditionally seen as the natural area of US influence to demonstrate the importance of controlling the South China Sea. Thomas Shannon, former Under Secretary of State for Political Affairs (2016–2018) and, briefly, Acting Secretary of State in the early days of the Trump administration, suggested in an article in *Time Magazine* that China could show the United States that "we can play in your neighborhood just as you play in ours."[46]

Look, for example, to Taiwan recognition. The 2019 Taiwan Allies International Protection and Enhancement Initiative Act (TAIPEI), which requires the State Department to report annually to Congress on efforts to strengthen Taiwan's diplomatic relations and global partnerships, reflects US efforts to prevent China from convincing the six countries in Central America and the Caribbean that still maintain diplomatic relations with Taiwan (out of a total of thirteen worldwide) to change allegiance. As Berg and Ziemers note, five countries have changed their diplomatic recognition from Taiwan to China since 2017, more than in the previous two decades.[47] Furthermore, the United States is likely to intensify its efforts through retaliation and economic incentives in these countries. China is most certainly playing in the US's "neighborhood."

7.3.3 Policy Take #3

> It will be difficult to maintain good terms with both the US and China, as the rivalry between them will penetrate domestic politics. A more assertive economic statecraft by the US will force geopolitical loyalties, reducing the agency of Global South countries to consume substitute goods. Countries will gradually have to choose a side and abandon hedging strategies. Countries significantly influenced or dominated by a major power may find it challenging to adopt an independent or neutral stance in their foreign policies without facing potential economic or political fallout.

The more assertive policy initiated by Trump and maintained by Biden to increase pressures to contain China generated more rejection than acceptance among Latin American leaders. During his first day in Bangkok, where he traveled to participate in the 2023 Asia-Pacific Economic Cooperation Forum (APEC), Chilean President Gabriel Boric warned that he had been privately pressured to support one of the two powers, China or the US. In response, the Chilean president reflected that "as a sovereign country we have the autonomy to have relations with everyone and we want to increase our relations with both."[48] Peruvian President Francisco Sagasti likewise stated in an interview that the United States should "get out of the outdated Cold War mentality" and that "both the United States and China are important to Peru, for different reasons."[49] Argentina's President, Alberto Fernández, meanwhile, expressed in 2023 that China had a "state-backed financial capacity that gives it a competitive advantage over other cases, such as the United States, but it is not Argentina's purpose to favor China at the expense of the United States, there is no such thing." He continued, "China has supported us a lot in recent years with public works, also financially, but if help came from Europe or the United States, it would also be welcome, as would Chinese investment."[50] These are just a few select examples.

In the recent Latin American IR debate, it has been argued that Latin American countries should follow a policy of "active non-alignment" in the face of an emerging "new Cold War," thus reviving the non-alignment movement of the Bandung Conference in 1955.[51] IR authors analyzing Southeast Asia, such as Cheng-Chwee Kuik, Kai He, and Huiyun Feng, have employed the concept of "hedging" in a similar manner. They define hedging as an insurance-seeking behavior adopted by states in situations characterized by high uncertainty and high stakes. In this context, a rational state avoids explicitly aligning with any particular side and instead pursues a balanced approach toward competing powers to maintain a fallback position.[52]

However, there are two main obstacles, or limitations, I see arising from these sorts of policies.

7.3.3.1 *Limitation #1: Countries Will Be Forced to Choose*

The first is that, historically, US foreign policy forces countries in the region to choose, placing them in a position where equidistance becomes impossible.[53] In political and normative terms, there is no doubt that an equidistant stance should be adopted with respect to the economic rivalry between the United States and China. But this will likely become harder, as the alliance policy deployed by both powers could become more rigid, therefore limiting the possibility of building positive agendas with both powers simultaneously.[54] In the near future, I expect the US to instrumentalize rules of origin and compliance with environmental standards to control key value chains through the concept of "environmental clubs."[55] This could involve requiring companies manufacturing lithium batteries to use lithium sourced from countries that meet certain requirements, which could effectively prevent Chinese companies from entering the market. It is also anticipated that the US will promote investment screening laws with clauses that make it difficult for Chinese companies to invest, such as requirements for information transparency. Countries will have to choose between complying with American-backed standards or maintaining relationships with Chinese actors.

To the extent that the foreign policy of the United States becomes Manichean in its use of economic incentives, there will be less room for agency for Latin American countries. There are recent cases, in fact, in which the United States conditioned the agency of the countries of the region toward China. When renegotiating the free trade agreement with Mexico and Canada, for example, the United States prohibited these countries from signing with China and threatened countries allowing Huawei to deploy 5G infrastructure. Similarly, the US pressured Brazil to refrain from selling Avibras, a defense and aerospace company known for producing military equipment including rocket systems, to Norinco (China North Industries Corporation), a Chinese state-owned defense corporation.

The book's analysis of economic weight trajectories for China and the US in various countries from 2001 to 2020 reveals a noteworthy pattern.

As illustrated in Figure 7.3, in the 2000s, the US still maintained unquestioned economic leadership. However, by 2020, economic displacement had occurred in a significant part of the region. Beyond the displacement threshold lies a "displacement zone": once a country enters this zone, it becomes increasingly difficult to exit due to growing economic dependencies on China. The US is likely to attempt to reverse the current trend, aiming to move countries out of the displacement zone (shown in Figure 7.3 as the area below the dotted line). The most effective strategy for this would be to simultaneously increase US economic weight while reducing China's influence. However, it's important to note that if a country in the displacement zone experiences growth in economic weight for both China and the US, it will likely remain within the displacement zone. While this is a simple conceptual model, it serves to highlight a crucial point: doctrines advocating for active non-alignment or hedging may be overlooking the power of assertive economic and trade policies that will come. Just as it did during the Cold War, an aggressive economic approach from the US could make non-alignment extremely challenging – if not impossible – for many countries.

7.3.3.2 Limitation #2: Domestic Tensions

The second obstacle to an active non-alignment policy is that the dispute between the United States and China will increasingly move to domestic politics and generate tensions among domestic audiences, something that has been widely discussed among neoclassical realists. Evidence of this already taking place was shown in Chapter 5 in relation to the installation of a Chinese space-monitoring base in Argentina. During the period covered by this book (2001–2021), we have observed that LAC countries consumed economic goods from China for lack of alternatives, even when the ideologies of their governments were openly anti-China at times. Indeed, as we saw in Chapter 3, China's economic influence transcends ideological barriers, and there are two recent examples that illustrate this point. Jair Bolsonaro, who became president of Brazil in 2018, initially criticized China. However, between 2019 and 2021, Brazil's trade with China increased by 40 percent, and Chinese investments in Brazil reached US$11.5 billion. While this amount is significant, it's actually less than the US$28 billion invested between 2014 and 2018.[56] Similarly, Javier Milei, elected president of Argentina in 2023, was skeptical about China during his campaign. However, on his first day in office, he not only sent a letter of apology to Xi Jinping but also met with Qiu Xiaoqi, the Chinese Government's Special Representative for Latin American

Affairs. His goal to reestablish a US$6 billion currency swap agreement previously established with the Chinese central bank was a crucial step toward urgently settling IMF debts.[57]

Scholars acknowledge that diplomatic elites in LAC may be acutely aware that maintaining a hedging strategy between the United States and China is a delicate and challenging task. This balanced approach requires considerable skill and nuance in diplomacy, as well as a deep understanding of the complex dynamics at play.[58] If the rivalry between China and the United States becomes politicized to levels where it becomes an electoral issue, as was the case during the presidency of Jair Bolsonaro in Brazil,[59] it is expected that increasingly political and economic elites will take sides toward one country or another and interest groups explicitly favorable to one country or another will emerge.

The lack of cohesion among elites will then further block Latin America's regional cohesion, which will likely result in the region being perceived as two distinct groups rather than a unified entity, as explained earlier in Policy Take #2. Latin America's stagnation in deepening regional integration and its failure to operate with a cohesive regional logic necessitates a broader debate on strengthening regionalism in the face of resurgent great power politics.[60] In a region divided into two blocs, collective agency becomes severely limited. While some scholars argue that small states can maximize their influence with great powers by finding mutual benefits,[61] the scenario where some countries align with the United States and others with China makes generating consensus among LAC nations increasingly challenging. This division not only weakens the region's bargaining power globally, it makes it more susceptible to external influences, which could potentially exacerbate existing economic and political disparities within the region.[62] Addressing these challenges may require Latin American countries to reassess their approach to regional cooperation, possibly developing more flexible frameworks for collaboration that can accommodate varying alignments while still promoting shared regional interests.

7.4 A NOD TO THE FUTURE

As we look to the future, the dynamics of US–China competition in Latin America and the Caribbean are set to intensify and evolve in complex ways. I hope that this book has illuminated the significant shifts in economic influence and political alignments that have occurred in the region over the past two decades. The rise of China as an alternative provider of goods and the relative decline of US economic weight have reshaped the geopolitical landscape, challenging long-standing assumptions about hemispheric relations. Moving forward, LAC nations will face the delicate task of navigating between these two superpowers, balancing economic opportunities with political pressures. The potential division of the region into two distinct spheres of influence, coupled with a more assertive US, suggests a future marked by strategic dilemmas and shifting loyalties.

As the global order continues to transform, the ability of countries in the region to maintain agency, foster regional cooperation, and leverage their position in this new bipolar context will be crucial. The coming decades will undoubtedly test the adaptability, diplomatic skill, and strategic foresight of all actors involved, as the Western Hemisphere becomes an increasingly important theater in the broader narrative of global power competition.

Appendices

CHAPTER I APPENDIX

The replication file for the book can be accessed at Harvard Dataverse: https://dataverse.harvard.edu/dataverse/furdinez. There you will find a script to reproduce tables and figures in Stata and R, organized chapter by chapter.

To develop the typology of demand for Chinese alternative goods presented in Chapter 4 and the policy implications discussed in Chapter 7, I conducted an exploratory analysis using fifty-six semi-structured interviews with experts and key stakeholders. Given the sensitive nature of the topic, I have chosen not to systematically analyze these interviews or directly quote any participants. The research was approved by the PUC Chile ethics committee under protocol numbers 220622027 (China's economic rise, asset substitution and the erosion of US hegemony in Latin America and the Caribbean) and 180528012 (The International Politics of China's Rising Role in Financing Infrastructure). The interviews that informed both chapters included a diverse range of participants, including the President of Chile's National Telecommunications Association, former ministers and undersecretaries from multiple countries, public health officials at national and local levels, diplomats from various embassies (including Chinese diplomatic representatives), health commission presidents, municipal health secretaries, immunization directors, and business leaders. Notable participants included former presidents, ministers of foreign affairs, finance, and public works, as well as representatives from international organizations like the Inter-American Development Bank, USAID, and the Organization of American States. The private sector was represented through interviews with managers from companies like COFCO Latin America, grain exporters, and 99Taxi, while civil society perspectives came from environmental activists and NGO representatives. The interviews were conducted between 2018 and 2023 through various means, primarily via videoconferencing platforms (Zoom and Skype), with some taking place in person. The geographical scope covered key Latin American nations including Chile, Uruguay, Brazil, Peru, Paraguay, Mexico, and Argentina, as well as perspectives from US officials and international development institutions based in Washington, DC.

Here are all the interviews organized chronologically:

2018:
1. Secretariat for Strategic Affairs, Presidency of Brazil (20 November, Skype)
2. Undersecretary General for Economic and Financial Affairs, Brazilian Ministry of Foreign Affairs (26 November, Skype)
3. Secretary of International Affairs, Brazilian Ministry of Economics (26 November, Skype)
4. Head of Financial Policy Division, Brazilian Ministry of Foreign Affairs (28 November, Skype)
5. Secretary for International Affairs, Brazilian Ministry of Planning (24 November, Skype)

2019:
6. Minister, Ministry of Foreign Affairs, Chile (2 June, in person)
7. Minister, Ministry of Finance, Chile (13 June, in person)
8. Ambassador, Chilean Embassy in China (14 June, in person)
9. Senior Official, Department of Commerce (DIRECON), Chile (5 July, in person)
10. Diplomat, Chilean Embassy in China (6 July, in person)

2020:
11. Chief of Staff of the Undersecretary of International Economic Relations, Ministry of Foreign Affairs, Chile (6 October, Skype)
12. Diplomat, Chinese Embassy in Santiago (20 October, Skype)
13. Counsel to the Directorate of Multilateral Policy, Ministry of Foreign Affairs, Chile (30 September, Skype)

Appendices

14. Diplomat, Chilean Embassy in Beijing (25 October, Skype)
15. Official, Confederation of Production and Commerce of Chile (30 September, Skype)
16. Official, Ministry of Health of Chile (26 October, Skype)
17. Diplomat, US Embassy in Chile (28 October, Skype)
18. Diplomat, US Embassy in Argentina (26 October, Skype)

2022:
19. President, Chilean National Telecommunications Association (5 April, Zoom)
20. Former Undersecretary, Ministry of Industry, Energy and Mining, Uruguay (10 April, Zoom)
21. Researcher, Pontifical Catholic University in Chile (12 April, Zoom)
22. Official, Chinese Embassy in Chile (30 March, in person)
23. Undersecretary of Public Health, Ministry of Health, Uruguay (30 March, Zoom)
24. President of Health Commission, Senate, Uruguay (30 March, Zoom)
25. Health Secretary, São Paulo Prefecture, Brazil (18 March, Zoom)
26. Health Secretary, Espiritu Santo Government, Brazil (1 April, Zoom)
27. Health Secretary, Roraima Government, Brazil (3 April, Zoom)
28. Former Immunization Director, Ministry of Health, Brazil (5 May, Zoom)
29. Former Undersecretary, Ministry of Foreign Affairs, Uruguay (10 April, Zoom)
30. Diplomat, Ministry of Foreign Affairs, Peru (9 April, Zoom)
31. Former Minister, Ministry of Foreign Affairs, Peru (19 April, Zoom)
32. Advisor, Ministry of Foreign Affairs, Peru (20 April, Zoom)
33. Public Health Director, Ministry of Public Health and Social Welfare, Paraguay (2 May, Zoom)
34. Sinovac Cooperation Representative, Butantan Institute, Brazil (2 May, Zoom)
35. Manager, CTR, Chile (6 May, Zoom)
36. Ambassador to China, Ministry of Foreign Affairs, Uruguay (6 May, Zoom)
37. Director, Brazil-China Chamber of Commerce and Industry (15 May, Zoom)

38. Former Paraguay Representative, Organization of American States (15 May, Zoom)
39. Manager, COFCO Latin America, Brazil (11 May, Zoom)
40. Manager, GuaranFeeder, Paraguay (9 May, Zoom)
41. Manager, Tecnomyl, Paraguay (19 May, Zoom)
42. Public Policy Manager, 99Taxi, Brazil (15 May, Zoom)
43. Director General for Global Investment, Ministry of Foreign Affairs, Mexico (15 June, Zoom)
44. Former Official, Ministry of Public Works, Argentina (5 August, Zoom)
45. Lawyer, Chinese Construction Company in Argentina (5 August, Zoom)
46. Official, Chinese Businesspeople Chamber in Argentina (12 August, Zoom)
47. Environmental Activist, NGO concerned about Santa Cruz dams (12 August, Zoom)
48. Former Senior Executive for Latin America, US State Department (15 November, Zoom)
49. Former Senior Executive, Inter-American Development Bank (1 December, in person)

2023:
50. Latin America Specialist, USAID, US (6 March, in person)
51. Former Diplomat to Colombia, US State Department, US (4 March, in person)
52. Former President, Presidency of Peru (4 February, Zoom)
53. Minister, Ministry of Foreign Affairs of Peru (24 February, Zoom)
54. Former Employee, Ministry of Energy and Mining, Peru (2 October, Zoom)
55. Former Consultant, Ministry of Transportation and Communications, Peru (10 October, Zoom)
56. Public Works Bidding System Expert, Ministry of Public Works, Argentina (30 March, in person)

TABLE A.1 *List of Chinese companies in Forbes 500 ranking*

Company name	Ownership	SASAC oversight	2020	2010	2000
China Petrochemical Corporation (Sinopec)	SOE	Yes	2	7	58
State Grid	SOE	Yes	3	8	83
State Power Corporation of China	SOE	Yes	–	–	83*
China National Petroleum Corporation	SOE	Yes	4	10	–
China State Construction Engineering Corporation	SOE	Yes	18	187	–
Ping An Insurance	POE	No	21	383	–
Industrial and Commercial Bank of China	SOE	No	24	87	208
China Construction Bank	SOE	No	30	116	364
Agricultural Bank of China	SOE	No	35	141	341
Bank of China	SOE	No	43	143	255
China Life Insurance	SOE	Yes	45	118	–
Huawei	POE	No	49	397	–
China Railway Engineering Group	SOE	Yes	50	137	–
SAIC Motor	SOE	Yes (Shanghai SASAC)	52	–	–
China Railway Construction	SOE	Yes	54	133	–
China National Offshore Oil Corporation	SOE	Yes	64	252	–
China Mobile Communications	SOE	Yes	65	77	–
Pacific Construction Group	POE	No	75	–	–
China Communications Construction Company	SOE	Yes	78	224	–
China Resources	SOE	Yes	79	395	–
China FAW Group	SOE	Yes	89	258	–

* The State Power Corporation of China was established in 1996 as a state-owned enterprise responsible for managing China's electrical power operations. The corporation existed for approximately six years before being restructured between 2002 and 2003, when it was divided into multiple separate entities as part of China's power sector reforms.

Source: Fortune 500 (2021) and SASAC (2023).

Continuous Measurement of Economic Displacement

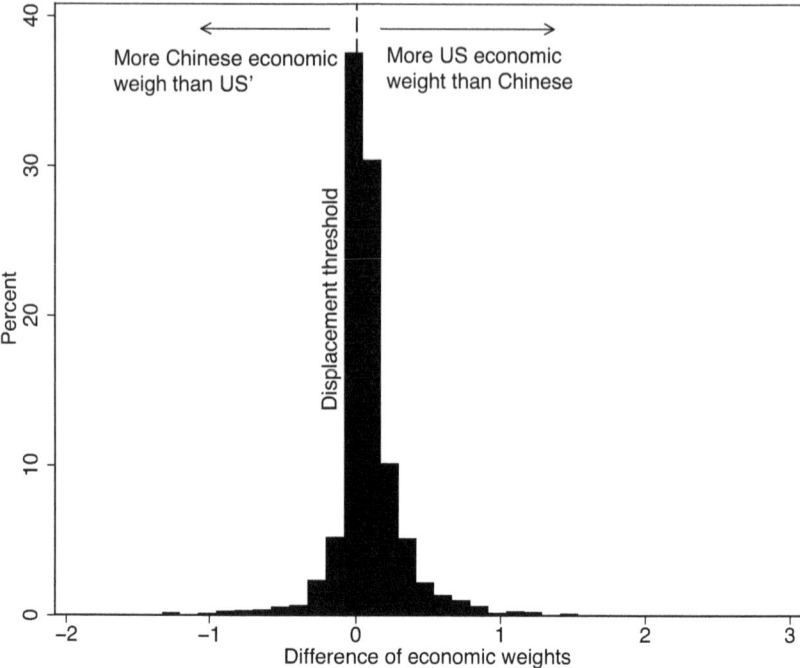

FIGURE A.1 Difference between the economic weight of China and the US by country in a global sample, 2001–2020

CHAPTER 2 APPENDIX

Variable Definitions and Sources

Links to the Sources of Data Used to Create Economic Weight Indices
Replication data for the book: https://dataverse.harvard.edu/dataverse/furdinez

Trade:
Exports to China and the US
- United Nations Comtrade (2022). Retrieved from: https://comtradeplus.un.org/.

Aid:
Chinese
- Axel Dreher, Andreas Fuchs, Bradley Parks, Austin Strange, and Michael J. Tierney, *Banking on Beijing: The Aims and*

Impacts of China's Overseas Development Program (Cambridge University Press, 2022). Retrieved from: www.aiddata.org/data/aiddatas-global-chinese-development-finance-dataset-version-3-0.
- Diego Telias and Francisco Urdinez, "China's Foreign Aid Political Drivers: Lessons from a Novel Dataset of Mask Diplomacy in Latin America During the COVID-19 Pandemic," *Journal of Current Chinese Affairs* 51, no. 1 (2022): 108–36. Retrieved from: https://doi.org/10.7910/DVN/EIAXSE, Harvard Dataverse, V1, UNF:6:NDQSJFdgm8GhlSBMZxcFoA== [fileUNF].
- China International Development Cooperation Agency (CIDCA). Retrieved from: www.cidca.gov.cn/20240604/fc031ffe9b92482b9fb33f8494f9b504/c.html.

American
- United States Agency for International Development (USAID) and the Department of State. Retrieved from: https://foreignassistance.gov/ and www.usaid.gov/developer/greenbookapi.

FDI:
Chinese
- Derek Scissors, China Global Investment Tracker (AEI, 2011). Retrieved from: www.aei.org/china-global-investment-tracker/
- Enrique Dussel Peters, Monitor de la OFDI china en América Latina y el Caribe 2020 (Red ALC-China, 2020). Retrieved from: www.redalc-china.org/monitor/.
- MOFCOM, Statistical Bulletin of the PRC (2020). Retrieved from: https://fdi.mofcom.gov.cn/resource/pdf/2020/.
- Mergr: M&A and Private Equity Database. *Paid subscription*. Retrieved from: https://mergr.com.
- fDi Markets Database, *Financial Times*. *Paid subscription*. Retrieved from: www.fdimarkets.com/.
- Urdinez, Francisco, and Margaret Myers. "Regional Repository of Chinese Investments in Latin America." edited by ICLAC and Inter-American Dialogue, 2024. https://china-latam-iclac.netlify.app https://iclac.cl/mapa-repositorio-regional-de-inversiones-chinas.

American
- Bureau of Economic Analysis (2023). Foreign Direct Investment in the US: Balance of Payments and Direct Investment Position Data. Retrieved from: www.bea.gov/international/di1fdibal.

- Mergr: M&A and Private Equity Database. *Paid subscription*. Retrieved from: https://mergr.com.
- fDi Markets Database, *Financial Times*. *Paid subscription*. Retrieved from: www.fdimarkets.com/.

Loans:
Chinese
- R. Ray and M. Myers "Chinese Loans to Latin America and the Caribbean Database," (Inter-American Dialogue and Boston University Global Development Policy Center, 2024). Retrieved from: www.thedialogue.org/map_list/.
- B. Steil, B. Della Rocca and D. Walker. Central Bank Currency Swaps Tracker. (Council of Foreign Relations, 2023). Retrieved from: www.cfr.org/article/central-bank-currency-swaps-tracker.
- Dreher, Axel, Andreas Fuchs, Bradley Parks, Austin Strange, and Michael J. Tierney. *Banking on Beijing: The Aims and Impacts of China's Overseas Development Program*. (Cambridge University Press, 2022). Retrieved from: www.aiddata.org/data/aiddatas-global-chinese-development-finance-dataset-version-3-0.
- Asian Infrastructure Investment Bank (AIIB). (2022). Retrieved from: www.aiib.org/en/projects/list/index.html?status=Approved.
- New Development Bank (NDB). Retrieved from: www.ndb.int/projects/all-projects/.
- Boston University Global Development Policy Center. (China's Overseas Development Finance Database, 2023). Retrieved from www.bu.edu/gdp/chinas-overseas-development-finance/.

American
- World Bank (2023). Projects & Operations. Retrieved from: https://projects.worldbank.org/en/projects-operations/project-country.
- IMF (2023). IMF Members' Financial Data by Country. Retrieved from: www.imf.org/external/np/fin/tad/exfin1.aspx.
- US International Development Finance Corporation. (2023). Active Projects. Retrieved from: www.dfc.gov/our-impact/all-active-projects
- https://mydata.iadb.org/.

Size of the economy:
- World Bank (2021). Data: Gross Domestic Product (GDP current US$). Retrieved from: https://data.worldbank.org/indicator/NY.GDP.MKTP.CD.

Deflator:
- Bureau of Economic Analysis (2023). GDP Price Deflator. Retrieved from: www.bea.gov/data/prices-inflation/gdp-price-deflator.

TABLE B.1 *Descriptive statistics of variables used to create the Chinese Economic Weight Index*

Variable	N	Mean	SD	Min	Max
Exports to China (million US$)	3,787	3,140	10,200	0	164,000
Official Development Assistance (million US$)	3,787	30.4	276	0	10,600
Chinese investment stock (million US$)	3,787	379	1,23	0	22,100
Loans by Chinese policy and multilateral banks, and swaps by w/ BOC (million US$)	3,787	271	2,05	0	84,000
GDP (million US$)	3,409	189,000	481,000	28.1	42,200,000

TABLE B.2 *Chinese investment stock to LAC (in US$ millions), 2001–2020*

Own elaboration	fDi Markets plus Mergr[a]	Scissors (2021)[b]	Statistical Bulletin of the PRC[c]
265,590	140,200	190,010	629,810

Sources:
[a] www.fdimarkets.com and https://mergr.com/.
[b] www.aei.org/china-global-investment-tracker/.
[c] https://fdi.mofcom.gov.cn/resource/pdf/2020/12/09/048b1af24cde4c1995f2245c2a735109.pdf.

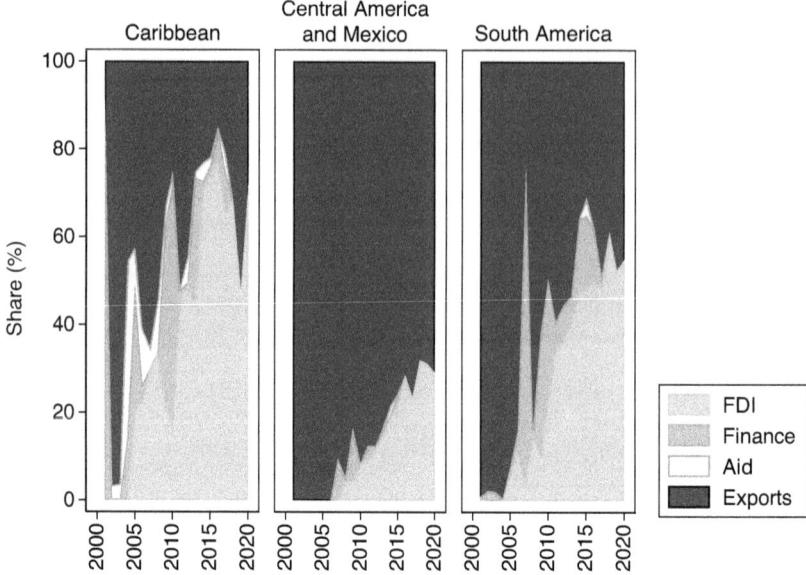

FIGURE B.1 Weight of each component of the index for each LAC subregion
Source: Author's elaboration.

TABLE B.3 *Descriptive statistics of variables used to create the US Economic Weight Index*

Variable	N	Mean	SD	Min	Max
Exports to the US (million US$)	5,031	4,100	10,400	0	96,500
Official Development Assistance (million US$)	6,041	275	1,250	−2	28,500
US investment stock (million US$)	7,331	10,700	59,000	−2	1,010,000
Loans by DFC, IADB, IMF, and WB	7,331	1,440	4,200	0	62,900
GDP (million US$)	6,762	157,000	481,000	44	6,270,000

Source: Author's elaboration.

Appendices

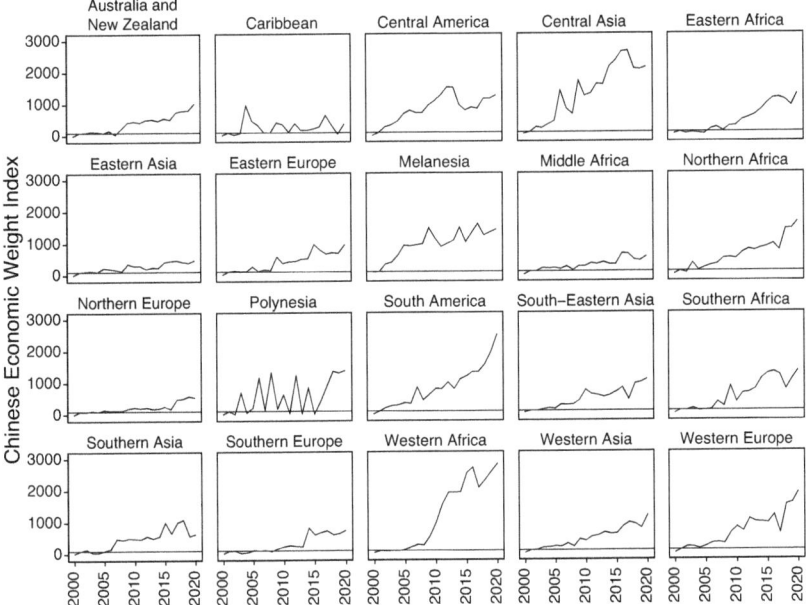

FIGURE B.2 Chinese Economic Weight Index by subregion (2001 = 100)
Source: Author's elaboration.

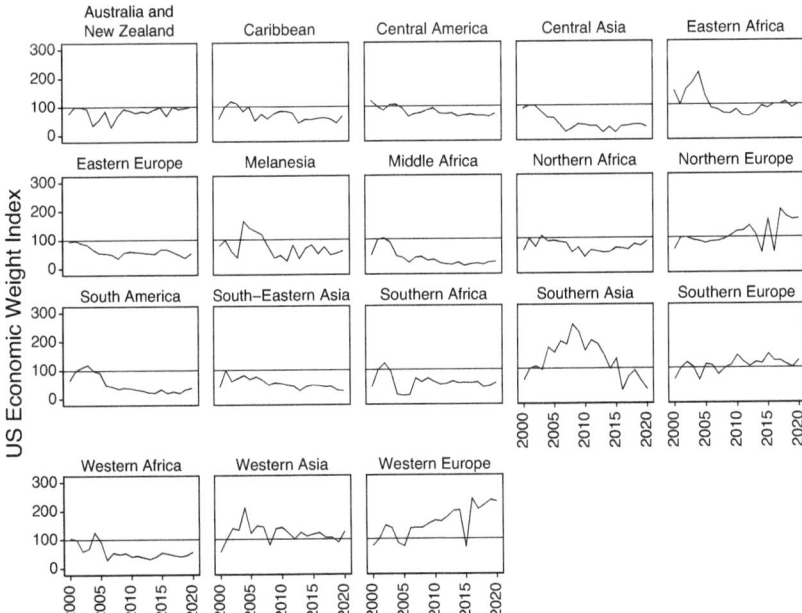

FIGURE B.3 US Economic Weight Index by subregion (2001 = 100)
Source: Author's elaboration.

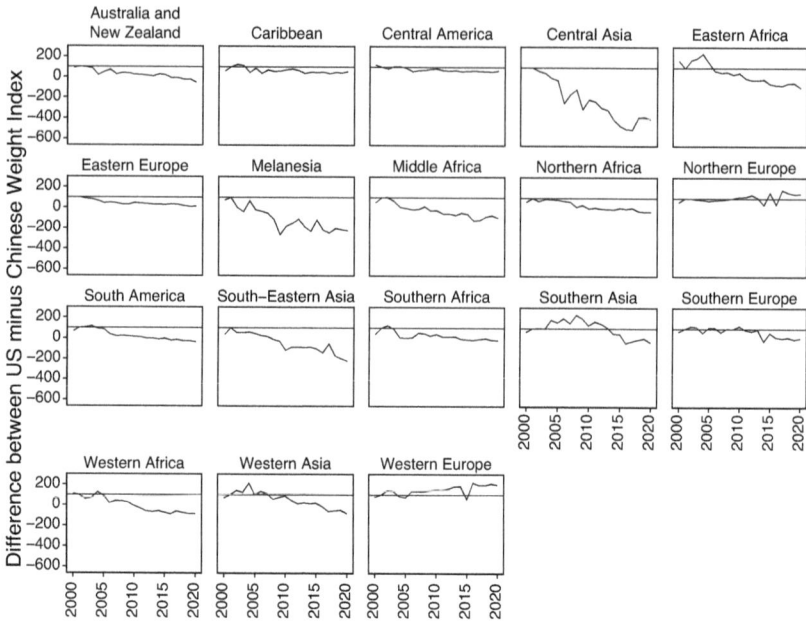

FIGURE B.4 Continuous measurement of economic displacement by subregion
Source: Author's elaboration.
Note: values below the horizontal line denote greater economic weight of China.

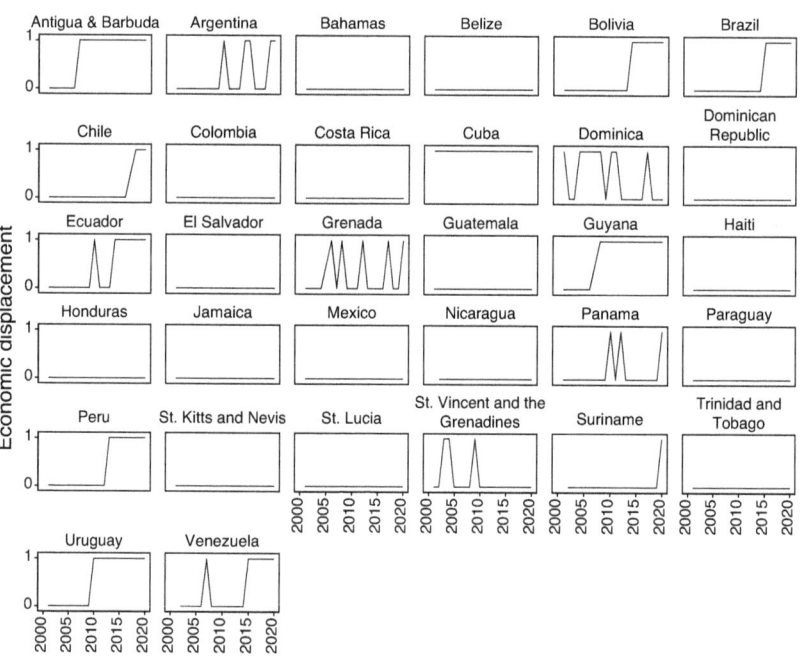

FIGURE B.5 Dichotomous version of economic displacement by country in Latin America and the Caribbean
Source: Author's elaboration.

CHAPTER 3 APPENDIX

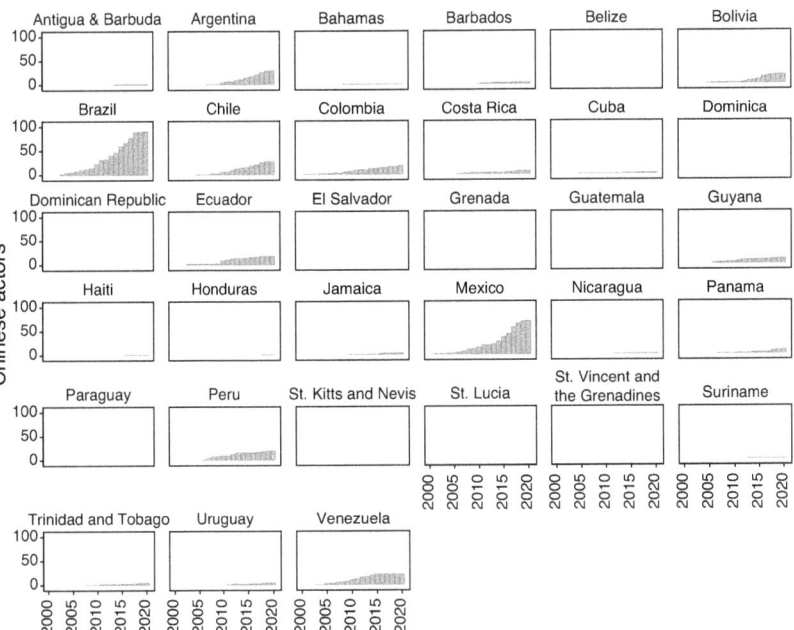

FIGURE C.1 Number of Chinese actors by country in Latin America and the Caribbean
Source: Author's elaboration.

CHAPTER 5 APPENDIX

TABLE E.1 *Effect of economic displacement on Latin American public opinion*

	(1)	(2)	(3)
Dependent variable	Trust in China	Trust in the US	US vs China continuum
Economic displacement	1.323*	0.790	1.581***
	(0.149)	(0.084)	(0.147)
Age	0.998*	0.999	0.998*
	(0.0010)	(0.0010)	(0.0010)
Ideology	1.011**	1.034***	0.978***
	(0.0034)	(0.0033)	(0.0031)
Income	0.919***	0.950**	0.964*
	(0.016)	(0.016)	(0.016)
Country fixed effects	Yes	Yes	Yes
N	15,432	16,580	15,354
Pseudo R^2	0.020	0.034	0.016

Note: Logit (1, 2) and ordered logit models (3). Coefficients expressed as odds ratios. Standard errors in parentheses. *$P < 0.05$, **$P < 0.01$, ***$P < 0.001$.

TABLE E.2 *Preferred country for a closer relationship in public opinion*

	RRR	SE	P-value	95%CI
Does not answer				
Economic displacement	0.2809	0.0586	0.000	0.186; 0.422
Age	1.011	0.00238	0.000	1.00635; 1.0157
Income	0.9044	0.02749	0.001	0.8521; 0.9600
Ideology	1.0042	0.00125	0.001	1.00182; 1.00674
China				
Economic displacement	0.2033	0.0358	0.000	0.14395; 0.28734
Age	0.9872	0.00174	0.000	0.9837; 0.9906
Income	1.0687	0.258	0.006	1.0191; 1.12207
Ideology	0.9933	0.0010	0.000	0.9914; 0.9955
United States				
Economic displacement	0.1600	0.0265	0.000	0.1156; 0.2216
Age	0.9922	0.00161	0.000	0.9890; 00.9954
Income	1.0250	0.2257	0.261	0.9817; 1.0702
Ideology	0.9963	0.000	0.000	0.9945; 0.9981
Neither				
Economic displacement	0.9470	0.2288	0.8322	0.5891; 1.5206
Age	1.0041	0.0026	0.111	0.999; 1.0093
Income	1.0232	0.0374	0.530	1.0030; 1.0082
Ideology	1.0056	0.0013	0.000	1.0030; 1.0082
Country Fixed Effects	Yes			
N	19,205			
Pseudo R^2	0.07			

Note: "Both" is the base category. Multinomial logit coefficients expressed as relative risk ratios. *$P < 0.05$, **$P < 0.01$, ***$P < 0.001$.

TABLE E.3 *The influence of economic displacement on legislators' preferences*

Dependent variable	(1) Foreign policy priorities			(2) Preferred trading partner preference		
	RRR	SE	95%CI	RRR	SE	95%CI
China						
Economic displacement	43.287	42.614	6.286; 298.08	12.35	6.539	4.379; 34.86
Incumbent party	1.332	0.526	0.613; 2.891	1.147	0.251	0.747; 1.761
Ideology	1.215	0.114	1.010; 1.461	1.124	0.060	1.011; 1.249
US						
Economic displacement	0.360	0.176	0.138; 0.941	0.37	0.137	0.1793; 0.765
Incumbent party	1.253	0.234	0.868; 1.809	0.984	0.144	0.739; 1.310
Ideology	1.21	0.048	1.119; 1.309	1.272	0.041	1.195; 1.355
Country Fixed Effects	Yes			Yes		
N	1,675			2,475		
Pseudo R2	0.10			0.11		

Note: "Other" is the base category. Multinomial logit coefficients expressed as relative risk ratios. $^*P < 0.05$, $^{**}P < 0.01$, $^{***}P < 0.001$.

TABLE E.4 *Legislative support for an FTA with the US*

Dependent variable	(1) Support for US–Latin America FTA
Economic displacement	1.122***
	(0.304)
Incumbent party	−0.284*
	(0.137)
Economic displacement × Incumbent party	−2.608***
	(0.319)
Ideology	0.544***
	(0.60)
Country fixed effects	Yes
Year fixed effects	Yes
N	2,852
R²	0.38

Note: OLS estimates. Standard errors in parentheses. $^*P < 0.05$, $^{**}P < 0.01$, $^{***}P < 0.001$.

CHAPTER 6 APPENDIX

TABLE F.1 *Resolutions with the most votes in the UNHRC*

Name	LAC Votes	Times voted	Years voted
Israeli settlement	100	14	2007, 2008, 2009, 2010, 2011, 2012, 2013, 2014, 2015, 2016, 2017, 2018, 2019, 2020
Human rights in the occupied Syrian Golan	99	14	2007, 2008, 2009, 2010, 2011, 2012, 2013, 2014, 2015, 2016, 2017, 2018, 2019, 2020
Human rights and international solidarity	124	12	2007, 2008, 2009, 2010, 2011, 2012, 2013, 2015, 2016, 2017, 2018, 2019
Right to development	112	12	2009, 2010, 2011, 2012, 2013, 2014, 2015, 2016, 2017, 2018, 2019, 2020
Human rights and unilateral coercive measures	87	12	2007, 2008, 2009, 2010, 2011, 2012, 2013, 2015, 2016, 2017, 2018, 2020
Human rights situation in Occupied Palestinian Territory, including East Jerusalem	84	11	2007, 2011, 2012, 2013, 2014, 2015, 2016, 2017, 2018, 2019, 2020
The use of mercenaries as a means of violating human rights and impeding the exercise of the right of peoples to self-determination	79	11	2009, 2010, 2011, 2012, 2013, 2014, 2015, 2016, 2017, 2018, 2019
Situation of human rights in Belarus	92	10	2011, 2012, 2013, 2014, 2015, 2016, 2017, 2018, 2019, 2020
Promotion of the right to peace	72	10	2008, 2009, 2010, 2011, 2012, 2013, 2014, 2015, 2017, 2019
Right of the Palestinian people to self-determination	71	10	2010, 2011, 2012, 2013, 2014, 2015, 2017, 2018, 2019, 2020

Situation of human rights in the Islamic Republic of Iran	71	10	2011, 2012, 2013, 2014, 2015, 2016, 2017, 2018, 2019, 2020
The effects of foreign debt and other related international financial obligations of states on the full enjoyment of all human rights, particularly economic, social and cultural rights	84	9	2009, 2010, 2011, 2012, 2013, 2015, 2016, 2018, 2019
Composition of staff of the Office of the United Nations High Commissioner for Human Rights	57	9	2009, 2010, 2011, 2012, 2013, 2015, 2016, 2017, 2019
The negative impact of the non-repatriation of funds of illicit origin to the countries of origin on the enjoyment of human rights, and the importance of improving international cooperation	70	8	2011, 2012, 2013, 2014, 2015, 2016, 2017, 2018
Promotion of a democratic and equitable international order	55	8	2008, 2011, 2012, 2014, 2015, 2016, 2018, 2019
From rhetoric to reality: a global call for concrete action against racism, racial discrimination, xenophobia and related intolerance	45	6	2007, 2011, 2012, 2013, 2015, 2017
Situation of human rights in the Democratic People's Republic of Korea	41	6	2008, 2009, 2010, 2011, 2014, 2015
The human rights situation in the Syrian Arab Republic	254	5	2011, 2016, 2017, 2019
Promotion and protection of the human rights of peasants and other people working in rural areas	54	4	2012, 2014, 2015, 2017
The continuing grave deterioration of the human rights and humanitarian situation in the Syrian Arab Republic	45	3	2013, 2014, 2015

Notes

1 ECONOMIC WEIGHT AND DISPLACEMENT

1. For a compelling interpretation of this phenomenon in which the Chinese economy causally and inevitably marks the end of the American empire, see Stuart Rollo, *Terminus: Westward Expansion, China, and the End of American Empire* (John Hopkins University Press, 2023).
2. By 2024, when this book was finalized, the trend had intensified further, with China's representation among the world's 500 largest companies continuing to grow and solidifying its lead over the United States and other major economies.
3. "Fortune 500," 2021, https://fortune.com/fortune500/.
4. "The 15 Largest Banks in the US," 2023, www.bankrate.com/banking/biggest-banks-in-america/.
5. Zhuan Xie and Xiaobo Zhang, "The Patterns of Patents in China," *China Economic Journal* 8, no. 2 (2015): 122–42.
6. Min Ye, *The Belt Road and Beyond: State-Mobilized Globalization in China: 1998–2018* (Cambridge University Press, 2020).
7. The State-Owned Assets Supervision and Administration Commission of the State Council (SASAC) played a significant role in China's "Going Global" policy, supervising and managing the largest SOEs in China and approving large foreign direct investment (FDI). See Table A.1 in the Appendix. For a reference, see Wendy Leutert, "Firm Control: Governing the State-owned Economy under Xi Jinping," *China Perspectives* 2018, no. 2018/1-2 (2018): 27–36.
8. Ilias Alami, Adam D. Dixon, Ruben Gonzalez-Vicente et al., "Geopolitics and the 'New' State Capitalism," *Geopolitics* 27, no. 3 (2022); Milan Babić, *The Rise of State Capital: Transforming Markets and International Politics* (Agenda Publishing, 2023), 2.
9. For examples of this approach, see: Dawn C Murphy, *China's Rise in the Global South: The Middle East, Africa, and Beijing's Alternative World*

Order (Stanford University Press, 2022); Rhys Jenkins, *How China Is Reshaping the Global Economy: Development Impacts in Africa and Latin America* (Oxford University Press, 2022).

10. See Rory Miller, *Britain and Latin America in the 19th and 20th Centuries* (Routledge, 2014); Matthew Brown, *Informal Empire in Latin America: Culture, Commerce and Capital* (John Wiley & Sons, 2009).

11. For example, in 2024, China possessed only 10 percent of the nuclear warheads that the United States had (Hans Kristensen, Matt Korda, Eliana Johns, Mackenzie Knight, and Kate Kohn, *Status of World Nuclear Forces*, Federation of American Scientists [March 29, 2024], https://fas.org/initiative/status-world-nuclear-forces/). Regarding military budgets, China also trails behind the US significantly. In 2023, the United States and China maintained their positions as the world's top two military spenders, with both countries increasing their expenditures compared to 2022. The US spent $916 billion on its military, while China's estimated spending was $296 billion (Nan Tian, Diego Lopes da Silva, Xiao Liang, and Lorenzo Scarazzato, *Trends in World Military Expenditure, 2023*, Stockholm International Peace Research Institute [Stockholm, April 2024], www.sipri.org/sites/default/files/2024-04/2404_fs_milex_2023.pdf).

12. The assertion that China does not offer an ideological or moral alternative to the US has been increasingly contested by various observers, including some within China itself, in the last few years. Contrary to this view, certain analysts argue that China's alternative lies precisely in its more pragmatic, nonideological approach to global affairs. This perspective suggests that China's model emphasizes practical cooperation and mutual benefit over the promotion of a specific ideological framework, presenting a distinct contrast to the US's more values-driven foreign policy. See, for example, the proposal for a Community of Common Destiny (The State Council Information Office of the People's Republic of China, 'A Global Community of Shared Future: China's Proposals and Actions' [White Paper of the Ministry of Foreign Affairs of the People's Republic of China, September 2023]).

13. See Francisco Urdinez, "Undermining US Reputation: Chinese Vaccines and Aid and the Alternative Provision of Public Goods during COVID-19," *The Review of International Organizations* 19, no. 2 (2024): 243–68.

14. Jan Knoerich and Francisco Urdinez, "Contesting Contested Multilateralism: Why the West Joined the Rest in Founding the Asian Infrastructure Investment Bank," *The Chinese Journal of International Politics* 12, no. 3 (2019): 333–70, https://doi.org/10.1093/cjip/poz007.

15. See Benn Steil, *The Marshall Plan: Dawn of the Cold War* (Oxford University Press, 2018).

16. Alvin Camba, "The Sino-centric Capital Export Regime: State-Backed and Flexible Capital in the Philippines," *Development and Change* 51, no. 4 (2020): 970–97.

17. Matthew C. Klein and Michael Pettis, *Trade Wars Are Class Wars: How Rising Inequality Distorts the Global Economy and Threatens International Peace* (Yale University Press, 2020), 19.

18. Odd Arne Westad, *The Global Cold War: Third World Interventions and the Making of Our Times* (Cambridge University Press, 2005), 29.
19. See Michael R Adamson, "'Must We Overlook All Impairment of Our Interests?' Debating the Foreign Aid Role of the Export-Import Bank, 1934–41," *Diplomatic History* 29, no. 4 (2005): 589–623; Gonzalo Sebastián Paz, "China, United States and Hegemonic Challenge in Latin America: An Overview and Some Lessons from Previous Instances of Hegemonic Challenge in the Region," *The China Quarterly* 209 (2012): 18–34.
20. Urdinez, "Undermining US Reputation."
21. For a classic approach to economic statecraft, see, for example, David A. Baldwin, *Economic Statecraft: New Edition* (Princeton University Press, 2020). On China, see: William J. Norris, *Chinese Economic Statecraft: Commercial Actors, Grand Strategy, and State Control* (Cornell University Press, 2016); James Reilly, *Orchestration: China's Economic Statecraft across Asia and Europe* (Oxford University Press, 2021). In an article on Beijing's economic statecraft in Sri Lanka, Lim and Mukherjee describe economic statecraft as the "*deliberate Manipulation* [my emphasis] of economic interactions to advance its broader strategic aims" (Darren J. Lim and Rohan Mukherjee, "What Money Can't Buy: The Security Externalities of Chinese Economic Statecraft in Post-War Sri Lanka." *Asian Security* 15, no. 2 (2019): 73–92, 73).
22. Andreas Grimmel and Viktor Eszterhai, "The Belt and Road Initiative and the Development of China's Economic Statecraft: European Attitudes and Responses," *International Studies* 57, no. 3 (2020): 223–39; William C. Wohlforth, 'The Challenge of Evaluating Grand Strategy', in *The Oxford Handbook of Grand Strategy*, edited by Thierry Balzacq and Ronald R. Krebs, 575–89. Oxford Academic, 2021. For instance, in her study on Japan's economic statecraft, Suzuki (2022) argues that the apparent overestimation of security/geopolitical elements in work on economic statecraft is problematic given that strategic and commercial motives are typically intertwined. Suzuki suggests that it is nearly impossible to separate these motives and determine the true objective. Suzuki, Shogo. "Economic Statecraft, Interdependence, and Sino-Japanese 'Rivalry'." *The Pacific Review* 35, no. 5 (2022): 971–94.
23. Muyang Chen, *The Latecomer's Rise: Policy Banks and the Globalization of China's Development Finance* (Cornell University Press, 2024).
24. For example, Ramon Pacheco Pardo, "Europe's Financial Security and Chinese Economic Statecraft: The Case of the Belt and Road Initiative," *Asia Europe Journal* 16 (2018): 237–50. In their comparative examination of Korean and American approaches to economic statecraft, Weiss and Thurbon (2021) share these perspectives. The authors conclude by proposing a typology in which the Korean exercise of economic statecraft strives to achieve commercial objectives overseas – notably maintaining and growing the competitiveness of Korean enterprises – whereas the American approach concentrates on security and geopolitical considerations. Lastly, they suggest a third hybrid type, which is represented by contemporary China, where economic and geopolitical objectives play a key role in Beijing's economic statecraft. This third category, suggested by Weiss and Thurbon (2021), simply

highlights the difficulties of analyzing the true aims of China's overseas economic engagement. Linda Weiss and Elizabeth Thurbon, "Developmental State or Economic Statecraft? Where, Why and How the Difference Matters." *New Political Economy* 26, no. 3 (2021): 472–89.

25. In his book on China's conduct of economic statecraft, William Norris mentions the possibility of security externalities, representing "the security consequences arising as a by-product of economic interactions" (Norris *Chinese Economic Statecraft:* 13). Similarly, in discussing China's economic effects, Lim and Mukherjee consider that "an externality can be thought of as an indirect impact of one domain of activity on another typically unrelated domain" ("What Money Can't Buy": 73).
26. Francisco Urdinez, Fernando Mouron, Luis L. Schenoni, and Amâncio J. de Oliveira, "Chinese Economic Statecraft and US Hegemony in Latin America: An Empirical Analysis, 2003–2014," *Latin American Politics and Society* 58, no. 4 (2016): 3–30; Jing-Lin Duanmu and Francisco Urdinez, "The Dissuasive Effect of US Political Influence on Chinese FDI During the "Going Global" policy era," *Business and Politics* 20, no. 1 (2018): 38–69.
27. Tim Nicholas Rühlig, *China's Foreign Policy Contradictions: Lessons from China's R2P, Hong Kong, and WTO Policy* (Oxford University Press, 2021).
28. Reilly, *Orchestration*.
29. The Carnegie Endowment for International Peace published a series of articles in a series called "China Local/Global" on adaptive Chinese strategies that work within local realities of target countries. The articles show that Chinese actors engaging with Latin American, African, and Asian countries, often for the first time, face evident processes of learning, imitation, and unforced errors. See https://carnegieendowment.org/projects/china-localglobal?lang=en.
30. As Hirschman noted, political influence grows with dependency: "from the fact that the trade undertaken between country A, on the one hand, and countries B, C, D, etc., on the other side, is worth something." See Albert O Hirschman, *National Power and the Structure of Foreign Trade*, vol. 105 (University of California Press, 1980), 17.
31. Reilly, *Orchestration, 10–12, 31–36*.
32. Hugo Meijer, *Awakening to China's Rise: European Foreign and Security Policies toward the People's Republic of China* (Oxford University Press, 2022); Zenobia T Chan and Sophie Meunier, "Behind the Screen: Understanding National Support for a Foreign Investment Screening Mechanism in the European Union," *The Review of International Organizations* 17, no. 3 (2022): 513–41.
33. J. W. Davis (2003) and Randall Everest Newnham (2002) analyzed how Germany employed various forms of positive economic statecraft to achieve foreign policy objectives vis-à-vis Poland and Russia, respectively, ten years prior. In both instances, the bias favoring the sender is considerable, leaving the replies of the recipient virtually unexamined. Similarly, when Tim Summers (2021) analyzed Beijing's economic strategy in its relationship with Hong Kong and when Lee and Maher (2022) provided a thorough assessment of how great powers (i.e., senders) deploy economic statecraft,

none of these authors discussed the response of states on the receiving end (James Lee and Richard Maher, "US Economic Statecraft and Great Power Competition." *Business and Politics* 24, no. 4 (2022): 332–47).

34. Tom Long and Francisco Urdinez, "Status at the Margins: Why Paraguay Recognizes Taiwan and Shuns China," *Foreign Policy Analysis* 17, no. 1 (2021): oraa002.
35. See Kristi Govella, "The Adaptation of Japanese Economic Statecraft: Trade, Aid, and Technology," *World Trade Review* 20, no. 2 (2021): 186–202. Special mention should be made of a seminal book by Blanchard and Ripsman (2013), who also reverse the predominant trend in the academic literature by focusing on specific domestic conditions in the target state and illustrating how these factors affect the sender's economic statecraft effectiveness: Jean-Marc F. Blanchard and Norrin M. Ripsman, *Economic Statecraft and Foreign Policy: Sanctions, Incentives, and Target State Calculations* (Routledge, 2013).
36. Robert A Dahl, "The Concept of Power," *Behavioral Science* 2, no. 3 (1957): 201–15.
37. Susan Strange, *States and Markets* (Bloomsbury Publishing, [1988] 2015), 24.
38. Alexandre Debs and Nuno P Monteiro, "Known Unknowns: Power Shifts, Uncertainty, and War," *International Organization* 68, no. 1 (2014): 1–31.
39. Beckley (2018) is also a good example of a non-dyadic power proposition. See Michael Beckley, *Unrivaled: Why America Will Remain the World's Sole Superpower* (Cornell University Press, 2018).
40. Pepper D Culpepper, "Structural Power and Political Science in the Post-Crisis Era," *Business and Politics* 17, no. 3 (2015): 391; Susan Strange, *States and Markets*, 396–98.
41. Lee Jones and Shahar Hameiri, *Fractured China* (Cambridge University Press, 2021).
42. In recent years, the concept of structural power is slowly being revisited for its usefulness in the analysis of China–US competition. On the one hand, there is the argument that China is eroding US structural power (Anton Malkin, "Challenging the Liberal International Order by Chipping Away at Us Structural Power: China's State-Guided Investment in Technology and Finance in Russia," *Cambridge Review of International Affairs* 33, no. 1 (2020): 81–104); on the other hand, interactions between three forms of capital – state, private, and foreign – have produced development dynamics that limit China's ability to assume the position of global economic hegemon (Mingtang Liu and Kellee S. Tsai, "Structural Power, Hegemony, and State Capitalism: Limits to China's Global Economic Power." *Politics & Society* 49, no. 2 (2021): 235–67). Some authors have questioned whether US economic power has declined in recent years (Jan Fichtner, "Perpetual Decline or Persistent Dominance? Uncovering Anglo-America's True Structural Power in Global Finance." *Review of International Studies* 43, no. 1 (2017): 3–28). By operationalizing economic weight in this book, however, I conclude that the economic weight of the US has depreciated to China – at least in LAC – in both absolute terms (comparing 2001 to 2020, for example) and in relative terms.

43. Although my operationalization of economic displacement does not capture it, at the time of writing, the dominance of the US dollar as the currency of exchange in international banking is a great source of structural power for the US, and China has had little success in globalizing the use of the yuan. See Patrick Emmenegger, "The Long Arm of Justice: US Structural Power and International Banking," *Business and Politics* 17, no. 3 (2015): 473–93.
44. Although the gap has narrowed at this point and Chinese universities have improved their international rankings, disparities persist. For example, according to *Times Higher Education*, there were twenty-eight US universities among the top 100 in the world in 2023 (www.timeshighereducation.com/world-university-rankings/2023/world-ranking), including most of the top ten. China, by contrast, had six, ranking fourth behind the UK and Australia. This is just one example; others could include the number of Nobel Prizes, annual science budgets, and the yearly quantity of articles published in high-impact scientific journals.
45. See Randall L Schweller and Xiaoyu Pu, "After Unipolarity: China's Visions of International Order in an Era of US Decline," *International Security* 36, no. 1 (2011): 41–72; Michael Mastanduno, "System Maker and Privilege Taker: US Power and the International Political Economy," *World Politics* 61, no. 1 (2009): 121–54.
46. See Amitav Acharya, "After Liberal Hegemony: The Advent of a Multiplex World Order," *Ethics & International Affairs* 31, no. 3 (2017): 271–85; Kai He and Huiyun Feng, "If Not Soft Balancing, Then What? Reconsidering Soft Balancing and US Policy Toward China," *Security Studies* 17, no. 2 (2008): 363–95; Jürgen Rüland, "The Rise of 'Diminished Multilateralism': East Asian and European Forum Shopping in Global Governance," *Asia Europe Journal* 9, no. 2–4 (2012): 255–70; David Shambaugh, "Containment or Engagement of China?: Calculating Beijing's Responses," *International Security* 21, no. 2 (1996): 180–209.
47. For a discussion on dyadic measurements see Paul Poast, "Dyads are Dead, Long Live Dyads! The Limits of Dyadic Designs in International Relations Research," *International Studies Quarterly* 60, no. 2 (2016): 369–74.
48. See Figure A.1 in the Appendix.
49. For example, see Francisco Urdinez and Margaret Myers, "Regional Repository of Chinese Investments in Latin America," edited by ICLAC and Inter-American Dialogue (2024). https://china-latam-iclac.netlify.app https://iclac.cl/mapa-repositorio-regional-de-inversiones-chinas/; Diego Telias and Francisco Urdinez, "China's Foreign Aid Political Drivers: Lessons from a Novel Dataset of Mask Diplomacy in Latin America During the COVID-19 Pandemic," *Journal of Current Chinese Affairs* 51, no. 1 (2022): 108–36; Long and Urdinez, "Status at the Margins."
50. See Urdinez, "Chinese Economic Statecraft and US Hegemony in Latin America."
51. Sean Starrs, "American Economic Power Hasn't Declined – It Globalized! Summoning the Data and Taking Globalization Seriously," *International Studies Quarterly* 57, no. 4 (2013): 817–30.

52. For a recent discussion see Patricio Yamin and Julieta Zelicovich, "Carrots or Sticks? Analyzing the Application of US Economic Statecraft Towards Latin American Engagement with China," *Latin American Engagement with China. Latin American Politics and Society*, 1–20; e-ISSN: 1548–2456 (2024).

2 CHINA'S ECONOMIC DISPLACEMENT OF THE US IN LATIN AMERICA

1. See United Nations, Department of Economic and Social Affairs, Population Division. (n.d.). 'Definition of regions.' World Population Prospects. https://population.un.org/wpp/definition-of-regions/.
2. For a look at subregions, see Figure B.2 in the Appendix.
3. Among others, for example: Carol Wise, *Dragonomics* (Yale University Press, 2020); Matt Ferchen, "China–Latin America relations: long-term boon or short-term boom?," *The Chinese Journal of International Politics* 4, no. 1 (2011): 55–86; Ariel C. Armony and Julia C. Strauss, "From Going Out (Zou Chuqu) to Arriving In (Desembarco): Constructing a New Field of Inquiry in China–Latin America Interactions," *The China Quarterly* 209 (2012): 1–17; Barbara Stallings, *Dependency in the Twenty-first Century?: The Political Economy of China–Latin America Relations* (Cambridge University Press, 2020).
4. Raúl Bernal-Meza and Li Xing, eds., *China–Latin America Relations in the 21st Century: The Dual Complexities of Opportunities and Challenges*, International Political Economy Series (Palgrave Macmillan, 2020).
5. Stephen B Kaplan, *Globalizing Patient Capital: The Political Economy of Chinese Finance in the Americas* (Cambridge University Press, 2021).
6. Juliana González Jáuregui, "How Argentina pushed Chinese investors to help revitalize its energy grid," *China Local/Global* (2021), https://carnegieendowment.org/research/2021/12/how-argentina-pushed-chinese-investors-to-help-revitalize-its-energy-grid?lang=en.
7. Zhongshu Li, Kevin Gallagher, Xu Chen, Jiahai Yuan, and Denise L. Mauzerall, "Pushing Out or Pulling In? The Determinants of Chinese Energy Finance in Developing Countries," *Energy Research & Social Science* 86 (2022): 102441.
8. See Table B.1 in the Appendix for descriptive statistics.
9. For a distinction of Chinese economic weight by component, see Figure B.1 in the Appendix.
10. See Long and Urdinez, "Status at the Margins."
11. Ministry of Commerce of the People's Republic of China (MOFCOM), *Statistical Bulletin of China's Outward Foreign Direct Investment 2021* (Beijing 2022).
12. For example, recently released data reveals that half of the Chinese loans in Sub-Saharan Africa are missing from sovereign debt records. See Kathleen J. Brown, "Why Hide? Africa's Unreported Debt to China," *The Review of International Organizations* 20 (2025): 1–32.
13. See Table B.3 in the Appendix for descriptive statistics.
14. For a look at differences across subregions, see Figure B.3 in the Appendix.

15. Figure B.3 in the methodological Appendix shows that Europe's growth is mainly concentrated in Western Europe.
16. As defined by Paul K. MacDonald and Joseph M. Parent, *Twilight of the Titans: Great Power Decline and Retrenchment* (Cornell University Press, 2018).
17. See Thomas J. Wright, *All Measures Short of War: The Contest for the Twenty-first Century and the Future of American Power* (Yale University Press, 2017).
18. I chose to include IMF and WB credits in the index due to the substantial influence that the US exerts over both entities. The evidence is extensive, but see, in particular: Axel Dreher and Nathan M. Jensen, "Independent Actor or Agent? An Empirical Analysis of the Impact of US Interests on International Monetary Fund Conditions," *The Journal of Law and Economics* 50, no. 1 (2007): 105–24; Jonas Gamso and Anna Dimitrova, "Rewarding a Friend: Does the World Bank Direct Non-commercial Risk Insurance to Countries that Support US Foreign Policy Interests?," *New Political Economy* 29, no. 1 (2023): 159–72.
19. Ronen Palan, Richard Murphy, and Christian Chavagneux, *Tax Havens: How Globalization Really Works* (Cornell University Press, 2010).
20. Jonas B. Bunte, *Raise the Debt: How Developing Countries Choose Their Creditors* (Oxford University Press, 2019).
21. Noel Maurer, *The Empire Trap: The Rise and Fall of US Intervention to Protect American Property Overseas, 1893–2013* (Princeton University Press, 2013).
22. For example, as scholar Hal Brands put it: "IMF officials generally took the lead in negotiating these reforms, because of their technical competence, and because this approach allowed the Fund – rather than the United States – to absorb the lion's share of the criticism that often resulted. 'We all hid behind the IMF,' one State Department Latin America hand recalled. In numerous ways, however, the administration used its own influence to encourage adjustment. Washington used PL-480 food assistance and Export-Import Bank credits to reward leaders who undertook major reforms, while strongly urging the recalcitrant to cooperate. To reinforce these messages, USAID tied assistance programs such as its Economic Support Fund to the implementation of liberalizing measures." In Hal Brands, *Making the Unipolar Moment: US Foreign Policy and the Rise of the Post-Cold War Order*. Cornell University Press, 2016, 205.
23. Andrew Cooper and Thomas Legler, *Intervention Without Intervening?: The OAS Defense and Promotion of Democracy in the Americas*. Springer, 2006, 55.
24. Stephen D. Krasner, "Power Structures and Regional Development Banks," *International Organization* 35, no. 2 (1981): 305, https://doi.org/10.1017/S0020818300032458.
25. For an excellent example see Bunte, *Raise the Debt*.
26. Starrs, "American Economic Power Hasn't Declined – It Globalized!"
27. Klein and Pettis note, related to this point, that "gadgets assembled in China (or, nowadays, Vietnam) and shipped to North America or Europe are filled

with imported components, including components made in the United States, just as German cars are built with Eastern European parts and American trucks are filled with Mexican content. Yet the statistics produced by customs offices attribute all of the value of the imported inputs to whichever country happens to ship the finished product." In Klein and Pettis, *Trade Wars Are Class Wars*, 29.
28. Robert A. Pastor, "Exiting the Whirlpool, US Foreign Policy Toward Latin America and the Caribbean," 2nd ed. (Westview Press, 2001).
29. Peter H. Smith, *Talons of the Eagle: Dynamics of US-Latin American Relations* (New York: Oxford University Press, 1996), 126; Ethan B. Kapstein, *Exporting Capitalism: Private Enterprise and US Foreign Policy* (Harvard University Press, 2022).
30. Samuel P. Huntington, "The Lonely Superpower." *Foreign Affairs* 78, no. 2 (1999) 35–49.
31. These figures were taken from Thomas F. O'Brien, *Making the Americas: The United States and Latin America from the Age of Revolutions to the Era of Globalization* (University of New Mexico Press, 2007).
32. O'Brien, *Making the Americas*.
33. As reported by the United Nations Conference on Trade and Development (UNCTAD) 'Latin America and the Caribbean attract largest share of foreign direct investment in the developing world in 1999.' https://unctad.org/press-material/latin-america-and-caribbean-attract-largest-share-foreign-direct-investment.
34. A perspective discussed by Peter Hakim in "Is Washington Losing Latin America?," *Foreign Affairs* 85, no. 1 (2006) 39–53. For a very insightful project that offers data on the magnificent economic cost of the US war on terror, see the Costs of War Project: https://watson.brown.edu/costsofwar/.
35. David R. Mares and Arie M. Kacowicz, *Routledge Handbook of Latin American Security* (Routledge, 2015), 254–65; Steve Ellner, "Pink-Tide Governments: Pragmatic and Populist Responses to Challenges from the Right" (Sage Publications, 2019). This trend was observed and analyzed by various scholars, including Néstor Castaneda, "New Dependency?: Economic Links between China and Latin America," *Issues & Studies* 53, no. 01 (2017): 1740001; Ferchen, "China–Latin America relations"; Andrés Malamud and Luis L. Schenoni, "Neoliberal Institutionalism and Neofunctionalism in Latin American Security Studies," in *Routledge Handbook of Latin American Security* (Routledge, 2015).
36. See Francisco Panizza, "Nuevas izquierdas y democracia en América Latina," *Revista CIDOB d'afers internacionals* 85/86 (2009): 75–88; Sebastián L. Mazzuca, "The Rise of Rentier Populism," *Journal of Democracy* 24 (2013): 108; Daniela Campello, *The Politics of Market Discipline in Latin America: Globalization and Democracy* (Cambridge University Press, 2015).
37. As noted by a report of the Congressional Research Service. See Ricardo Barrios and Karla I. Rio, *China's Engagement with Latin America and the Caribbean* (Congressional Research Service, 2023), https://crsreports.congress.gov/product/pdf/IF/IF10982.

38. See Daniel W. Drezner, "Does Obama Have a Grand Strategy? Why We Need Doctrines in Uncertain Times," *Foreign Affairs* 90, no. 4 (2011): 57–68; Colin Dueck, *The Obama Doctrine: American Grand Strategy Today* (Oxford University Press, 2015).
39. As noted by David Shambaugh, "Assessing the US "Pivot" to Asia," *Strategic Studies Quarterly* 7, no. 2 (2013): 10–19.
40. For an insightful article published in 2022 in *Politico* comparing Chinese and US influence in Latin America, see: Nahal Toosi, "'Frustrated and Powerless': In Fight with China for Global Influence, Diplomacy is America's Biggest Weakness," *Politico*, October 23, 2022, www.politico.com/news/2022/10/23/china-diplomacy-panama-00062828. I thank Cindy Arnson for sharing thoughts on this article in December 2022.
41. Kapstein, *Exporting Capitalism*.
42. Westad, *The Global Cold War*, 28.
43. For a good discussion of this point, see Paz, "China, United States and Hegemonic Challenge in Latin America."
44. MacDonald and Parent, *Twilight of the Titans*, 6.
45. For a look at differences across subregions see Figure B.4 in the Appendix.
46. For details on a country-to-country basis, see Figure B.5 in the Appendix.
47. For those interested in the trajectory of other LAC countries during the same period, see Figures 7.2 and 7.3 in Chapter 7.

3 FILLING THE VOID

1. An exception would be Urdinez et al., "Chinese Economic Statecraft and US Hegemony in Latin America."
2. Christopher Layne, "This Time It's Real: The End of Unipolarity and the Pax Americana," *International Studies Quarterly* 56, no. 1 (2012): 203–13; Alexander Cooley and Daniel Nexon, *Exit from Hegemony: The Unraveling of the American Global Order* (Oxford University Press, 2020).
3. See Morten Skumsrud Andersen, Alexander Cooley, and Daniel H. Nexon, *Undermining American Hegemony: Goods Substitution in World Politics* (Cambridge University Press, 2021).
4. See Kevin P Gallagher, *The China Triangle: Latin America's China Boom and the Fate of the Washington Consensus* (Oxford University Press, 2016); and Urdinez et al., "Chinese Economic Statecraft and US Hegemony in Latin America."
5. Huntington, "The Lonely Superpower."
6. Cooley and Nexon, *Exit from Hegemony*, 161–63.
7. The advantage of this index over others like the UNCTAD Commodity Price Index is that the one we use varies over time and also between countries. See Daniela Campello and Cesar Zucco, *The Volatility Curse: Exogenous Shocks and Representation in Resource-rich Democracies* (Cambridge University Press, 2020).
8. Carlos Scartascini, Cesi Cruz, and Philip Keefer, "The Database of Political Institutions 2020 (DPI2020)," (Washington: Inter-American Development Bank, 2021).

9. This argument, with some variations, has been backed by Matt Ferchen and Rhys Jenkins, and by ECLAC in its reports. Matt Ferchen. "China–Latin America Relations: Long-Term Boon or Short-Term Boom?". *The Chinese Journal of International Politics* 4, no. 1 (2011): 55–86; Rhys Jenkins. "Is Chinese Competition Causing Deindustrialization in Brazil?" *Latin American Perspectives* 42, no. 6 (2015): 42–63.
10. See Gustavo A. Flores-Macías and Sarah E. Kreps, "The Foreign Policy Consequences of Trade: China's Commercial Relations with Africa and Latin America, 1992–2006," *The Journal of Politics* 75, no. 2 (2013): 357–71.
11. Jorge Domínguez, "China's Relations with Latin America: Shared Gains, Asymmetric Hopes," *Inter-American Dialogue* (2006): 10. https://projects.iq.harvard.edu/files/wcfia/files/dominguez_chinas.pdf.
12. Market Index, "Copper Price & Charts" (December 29, 2023), www.marketindex.com.au/copper.
13. Department of Energy Office of Energy Efficiency & Renewable Energy, "Timeline: A Brief History of Oil Prices and Vehicle Technologies," (December 29, 2023), www.energy.gov/eere/timeline-brief-history-oil-prices-and-vehicle-technologies.
14. MacroTrends, "Soybean Prices – Historical Chart Data," (December 29, 2023). www.macrotrends.net/2531/soybean-prices-historical-chart-data.
15. Ferchen, "China–Latin America Relations"; Rhys Jenkins, "China's Global Expansion and Latin America," *Journal of Latin American Studies* 42, no. 4 (2010): 809–37; Carol Wise and Victoria Chonn Ching, "Conceptualizing China–Latin America Relations in the Twenty-first Century: The Boom, the Bust, and the Aftermath," *The Pacific Review* 31, no. 5 (2018): 553–72.
16. Jonathan R. Barton and Johannes Rehner, "Neostructuralism Through Strategic Transaction: The Geopolinomics of China's Dragon Doctrine for Latin America," *Political Geography* 65 (2018): 77–87; Gallagher, *The China Triangle*.
17. Ferchen, "China–Latin America relations"; Jenkins, *How China is Reshaping the Global Economy*.
18. Armony and Strauss, "From Going Out (Zou Chuqu) to Arriving in (Desembarco)"; William Ratliff, "In Search of a Balanced Relationship: China, Latin America, and the United States," *Asian Politics & Policy* 1, no. 1 (2009): 1–30; Wise, *Dragonomics*.
19. Kevin P. Gallagher, Juan Carlos Moreno-Brid, and Roberto Porzecanski, "The Dynamism of Mexican Exports: Lost in (Chinese) Translation?," *World Development* 36, no. 8 (2008): 1365–80; Kevin Gallagher and Roberto Porzecanski, *The Dragon in the Room: China and the Future of Latin American Industrialization* (Stanford University Press, 2010).
20. United Nations, "Comtrade Database" (15 November 2023). https://comtrade.un.org/.
21. Ministry of Commerce of the People's Republic of China (MOFCOM), "China FTA Network" (December 12, 2023), http://fta.mofcom.gov.cn/english/index.shtml; Margaret Myers and Carol Wise, *The Political Economy of China-Latin America Relations in the New Millennium: Brave New World* (Taylor & Francis, 2016); an advancement of the agreement was signed on July 2, 2024: 'Early Harvest Arrangement of The Free Trade

Agreement Between The Government of The People's Republic of China and The Government of The Republic of Honduras,' http://fta.mofcom.gov.cn/honduras/xieyi/hdls_zqsh_en.pdf.
22. Gallagher, *The China Triangle*.
23. Barbara Hogenboom, "Depoliticized and Repoliticized Minerals in Latin America," *Journal of Developing Societies* 28, no. 2 (2012): 133–58; Steven Levitsky and Kenneth M Roberts, *The Resurgence of the Latin American Left* (Johns Hopkins University Press, 2011).
24. Gallagher, *The China Triangle*.
25. Armony and Strauss, "From Going Out (Zou Chuqu) to Arriving in (Desembarco)."
26. Juan Carlos Gachúz, "Chile's Economic and Political Relationship with China," *Journal of Current Chinese Affairs* 41, no. 1 (2012): 133–54.
27. Jenkins, *How China is Reshaping the Global Economy*.
28. Valor Soja, "Mato Grosso es Grosso: El mayor estado agrícola de Brasil es también el que tiene el mayor PIB per cápita," *Bichos de Campo*, December 19, 2023, https://bichosdecampo.com/mato-grosso-es-grosso-el-mayor-estado-agricola-de-brasil-es-tambien-el-que-tiene-el-mayor-pib-per-capita/.
29. Deborah Bräutigam and Kevin P. Gallagher, "Bartering Globalization: China's Commodity-backed Finance in Africa and Latin America," *Global Policy* 5, no. 3 (2014): 346–52; Kevin P. Gallagher and Amos Irwin, "China's Economic Statecraft in Latin America: Evidence from China's Policy Banks," *Pacific Affairs* 88, no. 1 (2015): 99–121.
30. R. Ray and M. Myers, "Chinese Loans to Latin America and the Caribbean Database," (Washington: Inter-American Dialogue, 2023). www.thedialogue.org/MapLists/#/Policy/List/amount.
31. See Nicholas Jepson, *In China's Wake: How the Commodity Boom Transformed Development Strategies in the Global South* (Columbia University Press, 2019).
32. Kaplan, *Globalizing Patient Capital*.
33. Wise, *Dragonomics*.
34. Stallings, *Dependency in the Twenty-first Century?*.
35. Gallagher and Porzecanski, *The Dragon in the Room*; Jenkins, *How China is Reshaping the Global Economy*.
36. Bertrand Gruss, *After the Boom: Commodity Prices and Economic Growth in Latin America and the Caribbean* (International Monetary Fund, 2014).
37. United Nations, "Comtrade Database."
38. Ray and Myers, "Chinese Loans to Latin America and the Caribbean Database."
39. Kaplan, *Globalizing Patient Capital*.
40. In 2022, China bought 39 percent of Chilean exports and represented 26 percent of all Chile's imports.
41. Jorge Heine, "The Chile–China Paradox: Burgeoning Trade, Little Investment," *Asian Perspective* 40, no. 4 (2016): 653–73.
42. Long and Urdinez, "Status at the Margins."
43. Thomas Ambrosio, "The Rise of the 'China Model' and 'Beijing Consensus': Evidence of Authoritarian Diffusion?," *Contemporary Politics* 18, no. 4 (2012):

381–99; Giovanni Arrighi and Lu Zhang, "Beyond the Washington Consensus: a New Bandung?," In *Globalization and Beyond: New Examinations of Global Power and its Alternatives*, edited by Jon Shefner and María Patricia Fernández-Kelly, 25–57. Penn State Press, 2011; Suisheng Zhao, "The China Model: Can it Replace the Western Model of Modernization?," *Journal of Contemporary China* 19, no. 65 (2010): 419–36.

44. Alex E. Fernández Jilberto and Barbara Hogenboom, *Latin America Facing China: South-south Relations Beyond the Washington Consensus*, vol. 98 (Berghahn Books, 2010); Andrés Serbín and Andrei Serbin Pont, "The Foreign Policy of the Bolivarian Republic of Venezuela: The Role and Legacy of Hugo Chávez," *Latin American Policy* 8, no. 2 (2017): 232–48.
45. See Jepson, *In China's Wake*. This argument has also been suggested by Chinese scholars such as Shuangsheng He. *China-Latin America Relations*. Paths International Limited, 2012.
46. Rut Diamint, "Regionalismo y posicionamiento suramericano: UNASUR y ALBA/Regionalism and South American orientation: UNASUR and ALBA," *Revista CIDOB d'Afers Internacionals* 101 (2013): 55–79.
47. Jörn Dosch and David S. G. Goodman, "China and Latin America: Complementarity, Competition, and Globalisation," *Journal of Current Chinese Affairs* 41, no. 1 (2012): 3–19; Ivo Ganchev, "China Pushed the Pink Tide and the Pink Tide Pulled China: Intertwining Economic Interests and Ideology in Ecuador and Bolivia (2005–2014)," *World Affairs* 183, no. 4 (2020): 359–88.
48. Anthony B. Kim and Alexander Jelloian, *How Chinese "Corrosive Capital" Influences Foreign Governments*, (The Heritage Foundation, July 26, 2021), www.heritage.org/asia/commentary/how-chinese-corrosive-capital-influences-foreign-governments; Leopoldo Lopez, *Challenging Autocracy From the Front Lines*, (Wilson Center, July 2023), www.wilsoncenter.org/sites/default/files/media/uploads/documents/Challenging%20Autocracy%20From%20the%20Front%20Lines.pdf.
49. Evan R. Ellis, "The Impact of the Turn to the Left on the Advance of the People's Republic of China in Latin America," *Journal of Indo-Pacific Affairs* (October 5, 2023), www.airuniversity.af.edu/JIPA/Display/Article/3540672/the-impact-of-the-turn-to-the-left-on-the-advance-of-the-peoples-republic-of-ch/.
50. Jonathan Bissell, "The Rise of Leftist Populism: A Challenge to Democracy?," *Military Review*, no. January–February (2016), www.armyupress.army.mil/Portals/7/military-review/Archives/English/MilitaryReview_20160228_art014.pdf.
51. Bissell, "The Rise of Leftist Populism."
52. Paz, "China, United States and Hegemonic Challenge in Latin America."
53. In fact, Venezuela has not received a new loan from Chinese policy banks since 2015. See Ray and Myers, "Chinese Loans to Latin America and the Caribbean Database."
54. Scott Kastner and Margaret Pearson offer a sharp diagnosis of our current understanding of China's international influence: "without thoughtful conceptualization of key assumptions and creation of research designs that allow

identification of mechanisms of potential influence, we cannot gain an accurate understanding of Chinese influence. How can we assess Beijing's intentions? Through what mechanisms – both intended and unintended – might influence arise, and under what conditions is influence most likely to occur? To what degree are Chinese companies agents of the state and therefore tools of economic statecraft? What factors condition how host countries react to economic ties with China?" See "Exploring the Parameters of China's Economic Influence," *Studies in Comparative International Development* 56 (2021): 18.

55. K. Dowding, P. John, T. Mergoupis, and M. Van Vugt "Exit, Voice and Loyalty: Analytic and Empirical Developments." *European Journal of Political Research* 37 no. 4 (2000): 469–95. https://doi.org/10.1023/A:1007134730724
56. Urdinez et al., "Chinese Economic Statecraft and US Hegemony in Latin America."
57. While not the focus of this book, I observe similar trends in the literature exploring Africa–China relations. See Lina Benabdallah, *Shaping the Future of Power: Knowledge Production and Network-Building in China–Africa Relations* (University of Michigan Press, 2020); Xiaoyang Tang, *Coevolutionary Pragmatism: Approaches and Impacts of China-Africa Economic Cooperation* (Cambridge University Press, 2021).
58. Such views have been posed Rhys Jenkins, who claimed that "China has neither the desire nor the capacity to challenge US hegemony" in Jenkins, "China's Global Expansion and Latin America," 835.
59. In words of Carol Wise, "a confrontation between China and the US over hegemony in the Western Hemisphere is still a very remote possibility." Wise, *Dragonomics*, 15.
60. For a good discussion on the conceptual shortcoming of the concept geoeconomics, see Dong Jung Kim, "Making Geoeconomics an IR Research Program," *International Studies Perspectives* 22, no. 3 (2021): 321–39.
61. Some use a definition of geoeconomics that states the concept denotes "the geostrategic use of economic power." This broad definition has been shared by numerous contemporary scholars who assert that geoeconomics is the "application of economic means of power by states to achieve strategic objectives." In a widely read and cited work on geoeconomics, Blackwill and Harris conceptualize geoeconomics as the process of "applying economic instruments to advance geopolitical ends." In light of these definitions, it can be argued that under the geoeconomic spectrum, states employ economic means to achieve non-economic ends. See Mark Beeson, "Geoeconomics with Chinese Characteristics: The BRI and China's Evolving Grand Strategy," *Economic and Political Studies* 6, no. 3 (2018)" 240–56; Mark Beeson and Corey Crawford, "Putting the BRI in Perspective: History, Hegemony and Geoeconomics," *Chinese Political Science Review* 8, no. 1 (2023): 45–62; Mingjiang Li, "The Belt and Road Initiative: Geo-economics and Indo-Pacific Security Competition," *International Affairs* 96, no. 1 (2020): 169–87. Similarly, Cai enters the debate in the geoeconomics research programme by explaining how different domestic economic considerations can explain China's decision to launch the One Belt One Road (OBOR) project and

381–99; Giovanni Arrighi and Lu Zhang, "Beyond the Washington Consensus: a New Bandung?," In *Globalization and Beyond: New Examinations of Global Power and its Alternatives*, edited by Jon Shefner and María Patricia Fernández-Kelly, 25–57. Penn State Press, 2011; Suisheng Zhao, "The China Model: Can it Replace the Western Model of Modernization?," *Journal of Contemporary China* 19, no. 65 (2010): 419–36.
44. Alex E. Fernández Jilberto and Barbara Hogenboom, *Latin America Facing China: South-south Relations Beyond the Washington Consensus*, vol. 98 (Berghahn Books, 2010); Andrés Serbín and Andrei Serbin Pont, "The Foreign Policy of the Bolivarian Republic of Venezuela: The Role and Legacy of Hugo Chávez," *Latin American Policy* 8, no. 2 (2017): 232–48.
45. See Jepson, *In China's Wake*. This argument has also been suggested by Chinese scholars such as Shuangsheng He. *China-Latin America Relations*. Paths International Limited, 2012.
46. Rut Diamint, "Regionalismo y posicionamiento suramericano: UNASUR y ALBA/Regionalism and South American orientation: UNASUR and ALBA," *Revista CIDOB d'Afers Internacionals* 101 (2013): 55–79.
47. Jörn Dosch and David S. G. Goodman, "China and Latin America: Complementarity, Competition, and Globalisation," *Journal of Current Chinese Affairs* 41, no. 1 (2012): 3–19; Ivo Ganchev, "China Pushed the Pink Tide and the Pink Tide Pulled China: Intertwining Economic Interests and Ideology in Ecuador and Bolivia (2005–2014)," *World Affairs* 183, no. 4 (2020): 359–88.
48. Anthony B. Kim and Alexander Jelloian, *How Chinese "Corrosive Capital" Influences Foreign Governments*, (The Heritage Foundation, July 26, 2021), www.heritage.org/asia/commentary/how-chinese-corrosive-capital-influences-foreign-governments; Leopoldo Lopez, *Challenging Autocracy From the Front Lines*, (Wilson Center, July 2023), www.wilsoncenter.org/sites/default/files/media/uploads/documents/Challenging%20Autocracy%20From%20the%20Front%20Lines.pdf.
49. Evan R. Ellis, "The Impact of the Turn to the Left on the Advance of the People's Republic of China in Latin America," *Journal of Indo-Pacific Affairs* (October 5, 2023), www.airuniversity.af.edu/JIPA/Display/Article/3540672/the-impact-of-the-turn-to-the-left-on-the-advance-of-the-peoples-republic-of-ch/.
50. Jonathan Bissell, "The Rise of Leftist Populism: A Challenge to Democracy?," *Military Review*, no. January–February (2016), www.armyupress.army.mil/Portals/7/military-review/Archives/English/MilitaryReview_20160228_art014.pdf.
51. Bissell, "The Rise of Leftist Populism."
52. Paz, "China, United States and Hegemonic Challenge in Latin America."
53. In fact, Venezuela has not received a new loan from Chinese policy banks since 2015. See Ray and Myers, "Chinese Loans to Latin America and the Caribbean Database."
54. Scott Kastner and Margaret Pearson offer a sharp diagnosis of our current understanding of China's international influence: "without thoughtful conceptualization of key assumptions and creation of research designs that allow

identification of mechanisms of potential influence, we cannot gain an accurate understanding of Chinese influence. How can we assess Beijing's intentions? Through what mechanisms – both intended and unintended – might influence arise, and under what conditions is influence most likely to occur? To what degree are Chinese companies agents of the state and therefore tools of economic statecraft? What factors condition how host countries react to economic ties with China?" See "Exploring the Parameters of China's Economic Influence," *Studies in Comparative International Development* 56 (2021): 18.

55. K. Dowding, P. John, T. Mergoupis, and M. Van Vugt "Exit, Voice and Loyalty: Analytic and Empirical Developments." *European Journal of Political Research* 37 no. 4 (2000): 469–95. https://doi.org/10.1023/A:1007134730724
56. Urdinez et al., "Chinese Economic Statecraft and US Hegemony in Latin America."
57. While not the focus of this book, I observe similar trends in the literature exploring Africa–China relations. See Lina Benabdallah, *Shaping the Future of Power: Knowledge Production and Network-Building in China–Africa Relations* (University of Michigan Press, 2020); Xiaoyang Tang, *Coevolutionary Pragmatism: Approaches and Impacts of China-Africa Economic Cooperation* (Cambridge University Press, 2021).
58. Such views have been posed Rhys Jenkins, who claimed that "China has neither the desire nor the capacity to challenge US hegemony" in Jenkins, "China's Global Expansion and Latin America," 835.
59. In words of Carol Wise, "a confrontation between China and the US over hegemony in the Western Hemisphere is still a very remote possibility." Wise, *Dragonomics*, 15.
60. For a good discussion on the conceptual shortcoming of the concept geoeconomics, see Dong Jung Kim, "Making Geoeconomics an IR Research Program," *International Studies Perspectives* 22, no. 3 (2021): 321–39.
61. Some use a definition of geoeconomics that states the concept denotes "the geostrategic use of economic power." This broad definition has been shared by numerous contemporary scholars who assert that geoeconomics is the "application of economic means of power by states to achieve strategic objectives." In a widely read and cited work on geoeconomics, Blackwill and Harris conceptualize geoeconomics as the process of "applying economic instruments to advance geopolitical ends." In light of these definitions, it can be argued that under the geoeconomic spectrum, states employ economic means to achieve non-economic ends. See Mark Beeson, "Geoeconomics with Chinese Characteristics: The BRI and China's Evolving Grand Strategy," *Economic and Political Studies* 6, no. 3 (2018)" 240–56; Mark Beeson and Corey Crawford, "Putting the BRI in Perspective: History, Hegemony and Geoeconomics," *Chinese Political Science Review* 8, no. 1 (2023): 45–62; Mingjiang Li, "The Belt and Road Initiative: Geo-economics and Indo-Pacific Security Competition," *International Affairs* 96, no. 1 (2020): 169–87. Similarly, Cai enters the debate in the geoeconomics research programme by explaining how different domestic economic considerations can explain China's decision to launch the One Belt One Road (OBOR) project and

establish the AIIB; Kevin G. Cai "The One Belt One Road and the Asian Infrastructure Investment Bank: Beijing's New Strategy of Geoeconomics and Geopolitics." *Journal of Contemporary China* 27, no. 114 (November 2, 2018): 831–47; Robert D. Blackwill and Jennifer M. Harris. *War by Other Means: Geoeconomics and Statecraft.* Harvard University Press, 2016, 23–26.

62. See Shu Guang Zhang, *Economic Cold War: America's Embargo against China and the Sino-Soviet Alliance, 1949–1963* (Stanford University Press, 2001); Shu Guang Zhang, *Beijing's Economic Statecraft During the Cold War, 1949–1991* (Johns Hopkins University Press, 2014).
63. For a look at Chinese economic actors per country, see Figure C.1 in the Appendix.
64. Enrique Dussel Peters and Ariel C Armony, *Effects of China on the Quantity and Quality of Jobs in Latin America and the Caribbean*, ILO Technical Reports 6 (Lima: International Labor Organization, 2017).
65. See Christopher Wlezien, "Public Opinion and Policy Representation: On Conceptualization, Measurement, and Interpretation," *Policy Studies Journal* 45, no. 4 (2017): 561–82; Christopher Wlezien, "Patterns of Representation: Dynamics of Public Preferences and Policy," *The Journal of Politics* 66, no. 1 (2004): 1–24; Alan S. Blinder and Alan B. Krueger, "What Does the Public Know About Economic Policy, and How Does It Know It?" (Cambridge, MA: National Bureau of Economic Research Cambridge, 2004).
66. See Jens Hainmueller, Daniel J. Hopkins, and Teppei Yamamoto, "Causal Inference in Conjoint Analysis: Understanding Multidimensional Choices Via Stated Preference Experiments," *Political Analysis* 22, no. 1 (2014): 1–30.

4 THE DEMAND SIDE

1. See Stefan Halper, *The Beijing Consensus: How China's Authoritarian Model Will Dominate the Twenty-first Century*, vol. 16 (ReadHowYouWant. com, 2010).
2. Bunte, *Raise the Debt*. Also see Francisco Urdinez, "The Accession of Latin American Countries to the Asian Infrastructure Investment Bank: Lessons from Brazil and Chile," *Asian Education and Development Studies* 10, no. 3 (2021): 374–85.
3. See, for example: Folashadé Soulé, "'Africa+ 1' Summit Diplomacy and the 'New Scramble' Narrative: Recentering African Agency," *African Affairs* 119, no. 477 (2020): 633–46; Benabdallah, *Shaping the Future of Power*; Linda Calabrese and Yue Cao, "Managing the Belt and Road: Agency and Development in Cambodia and Myanmar," *World Development* 141 (2021): 105297; Juliet Lu, "For Profit or Patriotism? Balancing the Interests of the Chinese State, Host Country and Firm in the Lao Rubber Sector," *The China Quarterly* 250 (2022): 332–55.
4. Yuan Wang, "Executive Agency and State Capacity in Development: Comparing Sino-African Railways in Kenya and Ethiopia," *Comparative Politics* 54, no. 2 (2022): 349–77.

5. David M Lampton, Selina Ho, and Cheng-Chwee Kuik, *Rivers of Iron: Railroads and Chinese Power in Southeast Asia* (University of California Press, 2020); Keren Zhu, Ben Mwangi, and Lynn Hu, "Socio-economic Impact of China's Infrastructure-led Growth Model in Africa: A Case Study of the Kenyan Standard Gauge Railway," *Journal of International Development* 35, no. 4 (2023): 614–38.
6. Austin Strange, *Chinese Global Infrastructure*, Elements in Global China (Cambridge University Press, 2024).
7. The list of interviewees includes a former official from the Ministry of Public Works of Argentina, a lawyer responsible for representing a Chinese construction company in Argentina, an official from a chamber of Chinese businesspeople in Argentina, an environmental activist, and an expert in the public works bidding system in Argentina.
8. See República Argentina, Agua y Energía Eléctrica Sociedad del Estado (AyE) (2023). Available at: https://mepriv.mecon.gob.ar/Agua_y_Energia/ResHist-Agua.htm.
9. See República Argentina, Decreto 1381/2001: Infraestructura hídrica. Tasa. Constitución del fideicomiso (2001), available at: www.argentina.gob.ar/normativa/nacional/decreto-1381-2001-69652; República Argentina, Aprovechamientos Hidroeléctricos del Río Santa Cruz – Adjudicación (2013), available at: www.boletinoficial.gob.ar/detalleAviso/primera/93505/20130821.
10. Interview with an expert from the Legal and Technical Secretariat of the Presidency, and J. De Vido and F. Bernal, *Néstor y Cristina Kirchner: Planificación y federalismo en acción* (Planeta, 2015).
11. See Adrián Ventura, "Malestar en la Corte con el kirchnerismo," *La Nación*, September 16, 2010, www.lanacion.com.ar/politica/malestar-en-la-corte-con-el-kirchnerismo-nid1305142/.
12. See Presidencia, *Inauguración Del Proyecto Hidroeléctrico Sopladora* (Quito: República del Ecuador, 2016).
13. See Comercio Internacional y Culto Ministerio de Relaciones Exteriores, "Viaje Presidencial a China," news release, June 17, 2004, www.cancilleria.gob.ar/es/actualidad/comunicados/viaje-presidencial-china.
14. Comercio Internacional y Culto Ministerio de Relaciones Exteriores, "Visita de Estado a China de la Presidenta Cristina Fernández de Kirchner," news release, July 17, 2010, https://cancilleria.gob.ar/es/actualidad/comunicados/visita-de-estado-china-de-la-presidenta-cristina-fernandez-de-kirchner.
15. Government of the People's Republic of China & Government of the Argentine Republic, Declaración conjunta entre el Gobierno de la República Popular China y el Gobierno de la República Argentina (2012). Available at: www.fmprc.gov.cn/esp/wjdt/gongbao/201007/t20100719_910945.html.
16. República Argentina, Resolución 760/2013: Acuerdo de Crédito. Aprobación (2013).
17. República Argentina, Decreto 269/2022 [Decree 269/2022] (2022); Alberto Jaramillo, "Cristina presidió el acto de adjudicación para la construcción

de las represas 'Néstor Kirchner' y 'Jorge Cepernic'," *Telam* (Buenos Aires), August 21, 2013, www.telam.com.ar/notas/201308/29602-cristina-presidioel-acto-de-adjudicacion-para-la-construccion-de-las-represas-nestor-kirchner-y-jorge-cepernic.html. The decree number 269/2022 from the Argentine government, sanctioned on May 25, 2022, and published in the National Bulletin on May 26, 2022, approved the amendment and reinstatement agreement model for the credit line. The agreement involved the China Development Bank, the Industrial and Commercial Bank of China Limited, and the Bank of China Limited, and it included nine sections and four annexes in both English and Spanish.
18. República Argentina, Framework Agreement on Economic Cooperation and Investments, Law 27.122 (2015).
19. Mariano Musso, Communication Director of Electroingeniería, underscored that a noteworthy 92 percent of the contracted workers hailed from Santa Cruz, selected through collaboration between the construction union (UOCRA) and local municipalities. See Jaramillo, "Cristina presidió el acto de adjudicación para la construcción de las represas 'Néstor Kirchner' y 'Jorge Cepernic'."
20. In 2016, the power capacity of Cóndor Cliff was reduced from 1140 MW with six turbines of 190 MW each to 950 MW with five turbines of 190 MW each. Similarly, the power capacity of La Barrancosa was reduced from 600 MW with five turbines of 120 MW each to 360 MW with three turbines of 120 MW each. The reason cited for this reduction was the insufficient flow of the river to support the operation of so many turbines. The current project for the dam has an installed capacity of 1310 MW. See EBISA, Aprovechamientos Hidroeléctricos del Río Santa Cruz: Estudio de Impacto Ambiental, Capítulo 3 – Descripción del Proyecto (2017).
21. See Ministerio de Energía y Minería & Ministerio de Ambiente y Desarrollo Sustentable, "Resolución Conjunta 3-E/2017" (2017).
22. Please refer to clause (b) of Article 21.4 in the contract. See República Argentina, Decreto 269/2022: Apruébase el modelo de acuerdo de enmienda y restablecimiento al contrato de línea de crédito con relación al Programa Nacional de Obras Hidroeléctricas (2022).
23. Juliet Lu, "Strategic Resources and Chinese State Capital: A View from Laos," *Made in China Journal* 5, no. 1 (2020): 154–59.
24. Zhu, Mwangi, and Hu, "Socio-economic Impact of China's Infrastructure-led Growth Model in Africa."
25. Margaret Myers, *Going Local: An Assessment of China's Administrative-Level Activity in Latin American and the Caribbean*, Inter-American Dialogue (December 2020), www.thedialogue.org/wp-content/uploads/2020/12/Going-Local-Chinas-Administrative-Level-Activity-in-LAC.pdf.
26. Lina Benabdallah, "Power or Influence? Making Sense of China's Evolving Party-to-Party Diplomacy in Africa," *African Studies Quarterly* 19, no. 3 & 4 (2020): 95–114.
27. Folashadé Soulé-Kohndou, "Bureaucratic Agency and Power Asymmetry in Benin–China Relations," in Chris Alden and Daniel Large (eds) *New Directions in Africa–China Studies* (Routledge, 2018): 189–204.

28. The list of interviewees for this case includes a former president of Peru, a former Minister of Foreign Affairs of Peru, a diplomat from the Ministry of Foreign Affairs, a consultant in the mining sector, and a former consultant for the Ministry of Transportation and Communications of Peru.
29. See Omar Narrea, *Sharing Chinese and Peruvian Visions about the Future Chancay Port: Exploring Opportunities under the Belt and Road*, Universidad del Pacífico (2022), https://cechap.up.edu.pe/wp-content/uploads/Working-Paper-Nro3-Omar-Narrea.pdf.
30. Ministerio de Vivienda Construcción y Saneamiento, "Plan de Desarrollo Urbano del Distrito de Chancay 2008–2018" (2009).
31. Asociación Peruana de Agentes Marítimos, "Volcan adquiere empresa Terminales Portuarios Chancay y busca socio," news release, May 18, 2016, https://apam-peru.com/web/volcan-adquiere-empresa-terminales-portuarios-chancay-y-busca-socio/.
32. Volcan, "Operaciones en Energía," news release, 2021, www.volcan.com.pe/operaciones/energia/. Volcan, however, is not without controversy. According to different journalistic reports, Volcan is the Peruvian company with the most fines for environmental violations throughout the country, mainly for its mining activities in Cerro de Pasco. The level of political influence of the company also generated media attention, given that the company's owners – the Letts family – have been linked numerous times to authoritarian Fujimorismo and have supported Keiko Fujimori's presidential candidacy since 2011. See Gabriel Arriarán, "La operación secreta de la minera más infractora del Perú," *Portal Convoca*, May 16, 2016, https://panamapapers.convoca.pe/historias/la_operacion_secreta_de_la_minera_mas_infractora_del_peru; Arcasi Mariño Walter Gonzalo, "Volcan donó más de US$ 200 mil a Confiep para campaña publicitaria en 2011," *Gestión*, November 21, 2019, https://gestion.pe/peru/politica/confiep-volcan-dono-us-200-mil-a-confiep-para-campana-publicitaria-en-2011-noticia/#google_vignette.
33. MacroInvest, "Informe sobre la razonabilidad económica del proyecto de escisión del negocio portuario," 2023, www.volcan.com.pe/wp-content/uploads/2023/07/230824-RB_051_2023-Acuerdo-JGA-24082023-Anexo-2.pdf.
34. TV Perú Noticias, "Pdte. Ollanta Humala encabezó puesta en marcha de terminal portuario de Chancay," May 26, 2016, www.tvperu.gob.pe/noticias/politica/pdte-ollanta-humala-encabezo-puesta-en-marcha-de-terminal-portuario-de-chancay.
35. MacroInvest. "Informe sobre la razonabilidad económica del proyecto de escisión del negocio portuario," May 2023, www.volcan.com.pe/wp-content/uploads/2023/07/230824-RB_051_2023-Acuerdo-JGA-24082023-Anexo-2.pdf.
36. Reuters, "China's COSCO to build $2 billion shipping port in Peru: ambassador," news release, June 1, 2018, www.reuters.com/article/us-peru-china-idUSKCN1IX5WW.

37. Wilfredo Huanachín, "En junio iniciamos la construcción del puerto de Chancay y durará 30 meses," *Diario Gestión*, July 2, 2017, https://plataforma.ipnoticias.com/Landing?cac=23YVAmTK3vAF%2BtWvpBAPSw%3D%3D&i=8rjVc38Q1fmQN9n3eazhjw%3D%3D&pm=1HUfQzPjQy3fRQ4WkUAmEQ%3D%3D&c=YEqkd0XasT53w7cz4ukg8aCeF7R2EsJxney4fx9cD04%3D.
38. Helthon Fuentes, "José Ignacio de Romaña: una carrera dedicada al Perú," *Diario El Chaski*, August 27, 2023, https://chaski.pe/detalle/jose-ignacio-de-romana-una-carrera-dedicada-al-peru.
39. Asociación Peruana de Agentes Marítimos, "Cosco Shipping de China con un pie en puertos peruanos," news release, July 5, 2018, https://apam-peru.com/web/cosco-shipping-de-china-con-un-pie-en-puertos-peruanos/.
40. Reuters, "China's COSCO to build $2 billion shipping port in Peru."
41. Andina Agencia Peruana de Noticias, "Empresa peruana Volcan y la china Cosco Shipping Ports Limited firman acuerdo para la construcción de terminal portuario en Chancay," January 23, 2019.
42. Volcan, "Volcan firma convenio con Cosco Shipping Ports Limited para construcción del Terminal Portuario de Chancay," news release, May 14, 2019, www.volcan.com.pe/volcan-firma-convenio-con-cosco-shipping-ports-limited/.
43. Ministerio de Economía y Finanzas, "Ministro Contreras: el mega puerto de Chancay convertirá al Perú en un polo de crecimiento y desarrollo en la región," news release, September 6, 2023, www.mef.gob.pe/es/?option=com_content&view=article&id=7940&Itemid=102627.
44. Agencia Peruana de Noticias Andina, "Gobierno creará zona económica especial Chancay-Ancón-Callao," July 20, 2023, https://andina.pe/agencia/noticia-gobierno-creara-zona-economica-especial-chancayanconcallao-948213.aspx.
45. Volcan, "Memoria Anual 2021," news release, 2021, www.volcan.com.pe/wp-content/uploads/2021/03/Memoria-Anual-2021-vJOA.pdf.
46. Volcan, "Hechos de importancia," news release, March 28, 2023, www.moneycontroller.es/noticias-de-la-bolsa-espa%C3%B1ola/volcan-compania-minera-saa/otros-hechos-de-importancia-1242383.
47. See Javier Hernandez, "Trump Slammed the W.H.O. Over Coronavirus. He's Not Alone," *The New York Times*, April 8, 2020, www.nytimes.com/2020/04/08/world/asia/trump-who-coronavirus-china.html.
48. Eduardo Cavallo and Andrew Powell, "Opportunities for Stronger and Sustainable Postpandemic Growth," *IDB: 2021 Latin American and Caribbean Macroeconomic Report* (2021).
49. The data for this report stems from a two-year project that analyzed Chinese mask and vaccine diplomacy in Latin America. See Telias and Urdinez, "China's foreign aid political drivers." This case specifically relies on data from official sources, corroborated with press information and interviews. The study also delves into the pandemic's peak months, examining twenty letters exchanged between Brazilian politicians and the Chinese ambassador.

50. Francisco Urdinez, "'They Own Our Country!' Voter Reaction to Anti-China Rhetoric: The Case of the Presidential Election in Brazil in 2018," *Electoral Studies* 86 (2023): 102708.
51. Marina Lang, "Gobernadores de Brasil abren sus propios canales con China," *Diálogo Chino*, August 13, 2020, https://dialogochino.net/es/comercio-y-inversiones-es/36888-por-la-inercia-de-bolsonaro-gobernadores-brasil-abren-sus-propios-canales-con-china/.
52. Jorge Fernando Rodrigues, "Frente Nacional dos Prefeitos: Não disputamos com o governo a compra de vacinas," *CNN Brasil*, March 2, 2021, www.cnnbrasil.com.br/saude/frente-nacional-dos-prefeitos-nao-disputamos-com-o-governo-a-compra-de-vacinas. Also see Frente Nacional de Prefeitos [National Front of Mayors] https://fnp.org.br/.
53. Partido dos Trabalhadores (PT), "Com embaixador da China, Consórcio NE apela por insumos e vacina," news release, May 19, 2021, https://pt.org.br/com-embaixador-da-china-consorcio-ne-apela-por-insumos-e-vacina/.
54. Instituto Butantan, "Butantan e Governo de SP vão testar e produzir vacina inédita contra coronavírus," news release, June 11, 2020, https://butantan.gov.br/noticias/butantan-e-governo-de-sp-vao-testar-e-produzir-vacina-inedita-contra-coronavirus.
55. EFE, "Suspenden producción de vacuna de la Sinovac en Brasil por falta de insumos," *swissinfo.ch*, May 14, 2021, www.swissinfo.ch/spa/coronavirus-brasil_suspenden-producci%C3%B3n-de-vacuna-de-la-sinovac-en-brasil-por-falta-de-insumos/46619842.
56. Florencia Trucco, "Instituto Butantan en Brasil dice que vacuna de Sinovac tiene eficacia 'superior al mínimo recomendado por la OMS'," *CNN*, December 24, 2020, https://cnnespanol.cnn.com/2020/12/24/instituto-butantan-en-brasil-dice-que-vacuna-de-sinovac-tiene-eficacia-superior-al-minimo-recomendado-por-la-oms; Elaine Cruz, "Butantan inicia producción de vacuna contra la covid-19," *AgênciaBrasil*, April 28, 2021, https://agenciabrasil.ebc.com.br/es/saude/noticia/2021-04/butantan-inicia-produccion-de-vacuna-contra-la-covid-19.
57. The Government of São Paulo issued a press release in 2021: Leonardo Martins, Rafael Bragança, and Allan Brito, "Government Asks Chinese Ambassador for Help to Expedite Delivery of IFA for IB Vaccine" (available at: https://noticias.uol.com.br/saude/ultimas-noticias/redacao/2021/01/20/doria-escritorio-de-sp-na-china-negocia-liberacao-de-insumos-da-vacina.htm). The release discusses the São Paulo government's request to the Chinese ambassador for assistance in accelerating the delivery of the Active Pharmaceutical Ingredient (IFA) needed for the production of the Butantan Institute's COVID-19 vaccine.
58. Trucco, "Instituto Butantan en Brasil dice que vacuna de Sinovac tiene eficacia 'superior al mínimo recomendado por la OMS'."
59. Portal do Governo de São Paulo, "Governo pede a embaixador Chinês ajuda para agilizar entrega da IFA da vacina do IB," news release, 2021, www.saopaulo.sp.gov.br/noticias-coronavirus/governo-pede-a-embaixador-chines-ajuda-para-agilizar-entrega-da-ifa-da-vacina-do-ib/.

5 THE EFFECTS OF ECONOMIC DISPLACEMENT ON PUBLIC OPINION AND POLITICAL ELITES

1. Naná De Graaff and Bastiaan Van Apeldoorn, "US–China relations and the liberal world order: contending elites, colliding visions?," *International Affairs* 94, no. 1 (2018): 113–31; Benjamin Toettoe and Richard Turcsanyi, "National Dependence and Public Perceptions: Understanding the Economic Determinants of Foreign Policy Preferences Toward China," *International Interactions* 50, no. 6 (2024): 941–74.
2. One of the few existing works to date comparing public opinion and legislative elite attitudes toward China in LAC are Asbel Bohigues, Shoujun Cui, and Scott Morgenstern, "Party Cohesion, Congruence, and Foreign Powers: Latin American Views About China and the United States," *Journal of Politics in Latin America* 16, no. 3 (2024): 380–404; and Daniela Campello and Francisco Urdinez, "Voter and Legislator Responses to Localized Trade Shocks from China in Brazil," *Comparative Political Studies* 54, no. 7 (2021): 1131–62.
3. This case is based, albeit with substantial differences, on the work by Francisco Urdinez, Jan Knoerich, and Pedro Feliú Ribeiro, "Don't Cry for me "Argenchina": Unraveling Political Views of China through Legislative Debates in Argentina," *Journal of Chinese Political Science* 23, no. 2 (2018): 235–56.
4. Latinobarómetro (2015). *Data*. Retrieved from www.latinobarometro.org/lat.jsp.
5. In an illuminating study, Kerry Ratigan shows that the exposure of Peruvians to Chinese investments has mixed effects on its soft power. On one hand, they have a positive opinion of the country; on the other, they do not value China as a development model. However, this study does not address the phenomenon of displacement nor the trade-off between Chinese and American reputation. See Kerry Ratigan, "Are Peruvians enticed by the "China Model"? Chinese investment and public opinion in Peru," *Studies in Comparative International Development* 56 (2021): 87–111.
6. Latinobarómetro. (2023). *Data*. Retrieved from www.latinobarometro.org/lat.jsp.
7. Sharon Seah, Joanne Lin, Melinda Martinus et al., *The State of Southeast Asia: 2024 Survey Report*, ISEAS – Yusof Ishak Institute (Singapore, 2024), www.iseas.edu.sg/wp-content/uploads/2024/03/The-State-of-SEA-2024.pdf.
8. While the literature on political elites' positioning in regard to China is sparse, a notable contribution is Daniel Novotny, *Torn between America and China: Elite Perceptions and Indonesian Foreign Policy* (Institute of Southeast Asian Studies, 2010).
9. Andres Borquez, Felipe Muñoz, and Diego Leiva, "The Growing Chinese Economic Presence in Chile," *China Review* 23, no. 3 (2023): 131–54.
10. See Campello and Urdinez, "Voter and Legislator Responses to Localized Trade Shocks from China in Brazil."
11. See Benedicte Bull and Antulio Rosales, "Elite Dynamics and China's Influence in Latin America," *Development and Change* 55 (2024): 1206–29.
12. Retrieved from https://oir.org.es/pela/.

13. Helen V. Milner and Dustin H. Tingley, "The Political Economy of US Foreign Aid: American Legislators and the Domestic Politics of Aid," *Economics & Politics* 22, no. 2 (2010): 200–32.
14. Monitor Mercantil, "Projeto ratifica participação do Brasil no BAII," January 29, 2019, https://monitormercantil.com.br/projeto-ratifica-participa-o-do-brasil-no-baii/.
15. See Meeting with Congressman Mario Desbordes for the Presentation of Tianqi Lithium Corporation on October 9, 2018. Retrieved from www.infolobby.cl/Ficha/Audiencia/nr006ar105001 and Hearing for the Formal Presentation of the representative who will work in Chile on behalf of Tianqi firm with Senator Manuel José Ossandón Irarrázabal on November 29, 2014. Retrieved from: www.infolobby.cl/Ficha/Audiencia/nr00569841.
16. As in David Samuels, *Ambition, Federalism, and Legislative Politics in Brazil* (Cambridge University Press, 2003).
17. See, for example, Parlatino, "China estrecha lazos con parlamentos de América Latina y el Caribe," January 9, 2019, https://parlatino.org/news/china-estrecha-lazos-con-parlamentos-de-america-latina-y-el-caribe/; Aarón Sequeira, Natasha Cambronero, and Esteban Oviedo, "Gobierno de China es el que más financia viajes de diputados," *Nacion*, October 9, 2023, www.nacion.com/el-pais/politica/gobierno-de-china-es-el-que-mas-financia-viajes-de/RN6Q5YY2LVCLFARNSCT7WUFFEY/story/; International Department Central Committee of CPC, "Wang Yajun Holds Working Talks with Multiparty Study Group of Brazilian Parliament Members," news release, September 17, 2019, www.idcpc.org.cn/english2023/lldt/201909/t20190921_160794.html.
18. For instance, in 2020, Julio César Quiñones, the coordinator of the Friendship Group in Ecuador, questioned China's refusal to allow three Ecuadorian white shrimp companies access to the Chinese market on sanitary grounds. The group deemed this action unjustified, challenging China's decision and requesting their Chinese counterparts (the China-Ecuador Friendship Group in China) and the Chinese Minister of Production to reconsider their stance. See El Telégrafo, "Legisladores se pronuncian a favor de los exportadores de camarón," July 16, 2020, www.eltelegrafo.com.ec/noticias/economia/1/legisladores-exportadores-camaron. In Argentina in 2023, Hector Tito Stefani, the representative of the Friendship Group for the province of Tierra del Fuego, raised concerns about the Shaanxi Chemical Industry Group, a Chinese company planning to construct a multipurpose port in the province, due to lack of information. See Alejandro Villalobos, "Argentina rechazó el proyecto chino en Tierra del Fuego," *Loginews*, June 26, 2023.
19. See La Diaria Política, "La mayoría de los legisladores uruguayos piensa que el principal "aliado estratégico" del país es China," May 27, 2023, https://ladiaria.com.uy/politica/articulo/2023/5/la-mayoria-de-los-legisladores-uruguayos-piensa-que-el-principal-aliado-estrategico-del-pais-es-china/.
20. See Roberto Porzecanski, "¿Por qué Uruguay no firmó un TLC con Estados Unidos?," *Letras Internacionales*, no. 95-4 (2010). On November 20, 2003,

the United States and Uruguay announced plans to negotiate a bilateral investment treaty during the Miami Ministerial Meeting of the Free Trade Area of the Americas. Negotiations began on May 11, 2004, and concluded on September 7, 2004, leading only to the signing of a Bilateral Investment Treaty on October 25, 2004. See www.sice.oas.org/tpd/ury_usa/ury_usa_s.asp.

21. For the few exceptions, see: Francisco Urdinez, Camilo López Burian, and Amâncio Jorge de Oliveira, "Mercosur and the Brazilian Leadership Challenge in the Era of Chinese Growth: a Uruguayan Foreign Policy Perspective," *New Global Studies* 10, no. 1 (2016): 1–25; Campello and Zucco, *The Volatility Curse*. There are also few studies that use voting to derive preferences; a good example is Pedro Feliú Ribeiro, "Partidos políticos y política exterior en América Latina," *Revista Mexicana de Ciencias Políticas y Sociales* 64, no. 235 (2019): 353–93.
22. The website for the project is https://oir.org.es/pela/.
23. "Others" includes "Latin American countries," "neighbors," "the European Union," "Japan," etc.
24. Christopher M. Bruner, "Hemispheric Integration and the Politics of Regionalism: The Free Trade Area of the Americas (FTAA)," *U. Miami Inter-Am. L. Rev.* 33 (2002): 1.
25. See Ministry of Foreign Affairs of the People's Republic of China, "Conversación entre el Presidente Hu Jintao y el Presidente Argentino Kirchner," news release, June 30, 2004, www.mfa.gov.cn/esp/zxxx/200406/t20040630_734891.html.
26. Ministry of Foreign Affairs International Trade and Worship of Argentina, "Argentina and China Reaffirm Peaceful Use of Space Facility in Neuquén," news release, September 16, 2016, https://cancilleria.gob.ar/en/news/releases/argentina-and-china-reaffirm-peaceful-use-space-facility-neuquen.
27. This observation aligns with the findings in legislative studies such as in Mark P Jones, Wonjae Hwang, and Juan Pablo Micozzi, "Government and Opposition in the Argentine Congress, 1989–2007: Understanding Interparty Dynamics through Roll Call Vote Analysis," *Journal of Politics in Latin America* 1, no. 1 (2009): 67–96. These scholars assert that the Argentine Congress, while more reactive than proactive, remains a crucial actor in policy formation. They note that during the 1989–2007 period, the majority party exercised dominant control over the legislative agenda, relegating the opposition to a largely reactive role.
28. The debates were manually downloaded from the Ministry of Justice website (www.infoleg.gob.ar/). The Decada Votada site (www.decadavotada.com.ar/) provides information on each nominal vote for both chambers, detailing how each legislator voted.
29. See John Wilkerson and Andreu Casas, "Large-scale Computerized Text Analysis in Political Science: Opportunities and Challenges," *Annual Review of Political Science* 20 (2017): 529–44.
30. Argentina, Honorable Senado de la Nación. "Versión Taquigráfica de la 22° Sesión." December 17, 2014. www.senado.gob.ar/parlamentario/sesiones/17-12-2014/22/downloadTac.

31. Argentina, Honorable Cámara de Diputados de la Nación. "Versión Taquigráfica de la 27° Reunión, Período 132." 2014. www.hcdn.gob.ar/sesiones/sesion.html?id=947&numVid=0&reunion=27&periodo=132 video available at: https://videos.hcdn.gob.ar/video/evento/e/1105.
32. Accessible at www.infojus.gob.ar.
33. Accessible at www.decadavotada.com.ar/.
34. Argentina, Honorable Cámara de Diputados de la Nación. "Versión Taquigráfica de la 27° Reunión, Período 132."
35. Argentina, Honorable Cámara de Diputados de la Nación. "Versión Taquigráfica de la 27° Reunión, Período 132."
36. Argentina, Honorable Cámara de Diputados de la Nación. "Versión Taquigráfica de la 27° Reunión, Período 132."

6 THE EFFECTS OF ECONOMIC DISPLACEMENT IN INTERNATIONAL ORGANIZATIONS

1. I follow the definition of Erik Voeten of international institutions, describing them as "widely recognized formal and informal rules that dictate how actors should collaborate and compete within the international system." This chapter focuses on international organizations, (commonly also known as intergovernmental organizations). These organizations are formed through agreements between two or more countries, as established by treaties. See Erik Voeten, *Ideology and International Institutions* (Princeton University Press, 2021), 18.
2. I also rely on data from Erik Voeten, Anton Strezhnev, and Michael Bailey, "United Nations General Assembly Voting Data," edited by Erik Voeten, volume 18 (Harvard Dataverse, 2009), https://doi.org/10.7910/DVN/LEJUQZ; and Gino Pauselli, Francisco Urdínez, and Federico Merke, "Shaping the Liberal International Order from the Inside: A Natural Experiment on China's Influence in the UN Human Rights Council," *Research & Politics* 10, no. 3 (2023): 20531680231193513.
3. Yongjin Zhang, "China and Liberal Hierarchies in Global International Society: Power and Negotiation for Normative Change," *International Affairs* 92, no. 4 (2016): 795–816; Alastair Iain Johnston, "China in a World of Orders: Rethinking Compliance and Challenge in Beijing's International Relations," *International Security* 44, no. 2 (2019): 9–60; Rana Mitter, "The World China Wants: How Power Will – and Won't – Reshape Chinese Ambitions," *Foreign Aff.* 100 (2021): 161.
4. Shiping Tang, "China and the Future International Order(s)," *Ethics & International Affairs* 32, no. 1 (2018): 31–43.
5. Rosemary Foot, *China, the UN, and Human Protection: Beliefs, Power, Image* (Oxford University Press, 2020), 1.
6. Xiaoyu Pu, *Rebranding China: Contested Status Signaling in the Changing Global Order* (Stanford University Press, 2019).
7. Jon CW Pevehouse, Timothy Nordstrom, Roseanne W. McManus, and Anne Spencer Jamison, "Tracking Organizations in the World: The Correlates of War IGO Version 3.0 Datasets," *Journal of Peace Research* 57, no. 3 (2020): 492–503.

8. Michael Fullilove, "China and the United Nations: The Stakeholder Spectrum," *The Washington Quarterly* 34, no. 3 (2011): 63.
9. Christopher B. Primiano, "China's Human Rights Statements in the United Nations: What are the Future Implications?," *China: An International Journal* 16, no. 4 (2018): 183–98.
10. Livio Di Lonardo, Jessica S. Sun, and Scott A. Tyson, "Autocratic Stability in the Shadow of Foreign Threats," *American Political Science Review* 114, no. 4 (2020): 1247–65.
11. Knoerich and Urdinez, "Contesting Contested Multilateralism."
12. Albert O Hirschman, *Exit, Voice, and Loyalty: Responses to Decline in Firms, Organizations, and States* (Harvard University Press, 1972).
13. Voeten, Strezhnev, and Bailey, "United Nations General Assembly Voting Data."
14. Neil R. Richardson, Charles W. Kegley, and Ann C. Agnew, "Symmetry and Reciprocity in Dyadic Foreign Policy Behavior," *Social Science Quarterly* 62, no. 1 (1981): 128.
15. Flores-Macías and Kreps, "The Foreign Policy Consequences of Trade."
16. Fernando Mourón and Francisco Urdinez, "A Comparative Analysis of Brazil's Foreign Policy Drivers Towards the USA: Comment on Amorim Neto (2011)," *Brazilian Political Science Review* 8 (2014): 94–115.
17. Xun Pang, Lida Liu, and Stephanie Ma, "China's Network Strategy for Seeking Great Power Status," *The Chinese Journal of International Politics* 10, no. 1 (2017): 1–29.
18. Scott L Kastner, "Buying Influence? Assessing the Political Effects of China's International Trade," *Journal of Conflict Resolution* 60, no. 6 (2016): 980–1007.
19. Georg Strüver, "What Friends are Made of: Bilateral Linkages and Domestic Drivers of Foreign Policy Alignment with China," *Foreign Policy Analysis* 12, no. 2 (2016): 170–91.
20. Samuel Brazys and Alexander Dukalskis, "Rising Powers and Grassroots Image Management: Confucius Institutes and China in the Media," *The Chinese Journal of International Politics* 12, no. 4 (2019): 557–84.
21. Randall W Stone, Yu Wang, and Shu Yu, "Chinese Power and the State-owned Enterprise," *International Organization* 76, no. 1 (2022): 229–50.
22. Voeten, Strezhnev, and Bailey, "United Nations General Assembly Voting Data."
23. In a linear regression with fixed effects by country and the inclusion of the lagged dependent variable as a control. $R^2 = 0.78$.
24. In a linear regression with fixed effects by country and the inclusion of the lagged dependent variable as a control. $R^2 = 0.39$.
25. Voeten, *Ideology and International Institutions*, 31–32.
26. Erik Voeten, "Resisting the Lonely Superpower: Responses of States in the United Nations to US Dominance," *The Journal of Politics* 66, no. 3 (2004): 730.
27. Octavio Amorim Neto and Andrés Malamud, "What Determines Foreign Policy in Latin America? Systemic Versus Domestic Factors in Argentina, Brazil, and Mexico, 1946–2008," *Latin American Politics and Society* 57, no. 4 (2015): 1–27.

28. Mourón and Urdinez, "A Comparative Analysis of Brazil's Foreign Policy Drivers towards the USA."
29. David B. Carter and Randall W. Stone, "Democracy and Multilateralism: The Case of Vote Buying in the UN General Assembly," *International Organization* 69, no. 1 (2015): 1–33.
30. See United Nations (2023). "Human Rights Council." Retrieved from www.un.org/en/ga/about/hrcelectfaq.shtml.
31. See R. Roth and M. Vazquez (October 14, 2021) "US Officially Rejoins Controversial UN Human Rights Council." CNN. Retrieved from: www.cnn.com/2021/10/14/politics/us-united-nations-human-rights-council/index.html.
32. Yongjin Zhang and Barry Buzan, "China and the Global Reach of Human Rights," *The China Quarterly* 241 (2020): 169.
33. Malin Oud, "Powers of Persuasion? China's Struggle for Human Rights Discourse Power at the UN," *Global Policy* 15 (2024): 85–96.
34. Foot, *China, the UN, and Human Protection: Beliefs, Power, Image.*
35. China's State Council Information Office (2021). http://english.scio.gov.cn/whitepapers/2023-09/26/content_116710660_5.htm.
36. State Council Information Office of the People's Republic of China (December 4, 2021). "China: Democracy That Works." Retrieved from http://english.scio.gov.cn/whitepapers/2021-12/04/content_77908921.htm.
37. Jessica Chen Weiss and Jeremy L. Wallace, "Domestic Politics, China's Rise, and the Future of the Liberal International Order," *International Organization* 75, no. 2 (2021): 635–64; Sonya Sceats and Shaun Breslin, *China and the International Human Rights System* (Chatham House, 2012); Primiano, "China's Human Rights Statements in the United Nations."
38. As noted by J. Lawrence Broz, Zhiwen Zhang, and Gaoyang Wang, "Explaining Foreign Support for China's Global Economic Leadership," *International Organization* 74, no. 3 (2020): 417–52.
39. China's human rights stance can be described as more aligned with the Westphalian principles of sovereignty and non-intervention rather than being aggressive or interventionist. As Foot articulates in *China, the UN, and Human Protection*, China defends the post-1945 Westphalian order while rejecting the post-Cold War order that endorses interventionism and regime change. This perspective is echoed by Tang in "China and the Future International Order," who notes China's defense of the Westphalian order.
40. In the study conducted by Pauselli, Urdinez, and Merke ("Shaping the Liberal International Order from the Inside"), the focus is on China's influential role within the Human Rights Council. Their research illuminates how China's presence in the Council can sway the voting behavior of other states, aligning them with Chinese interests. This phenomenon is indicative of China's ability to exert deliberate influence on the voting patterns of third countries. Such findings are emblematic of China's strategic proficiency in international bodies, leveraging its membership to further its foreign policy agendas. The case study herein builds upon the foundational insights of this pioneering research.
41. See "People's Republic of China is Newest Permanent Observer to OAS," May 26, 2004, retrieved from: www.oas.org/en/media_center/press_release.asp?scodigo=e-087/04.

42. Pastor, "Exiting the Whirlpool, US Foreign Policy Toward Latin America and the Caribbean," 311.
43. See Smith, Peter H. *Talons of the Eagle: Dynamics of US-Latin American Relations*. Oxford University Press, 1996, 171.
44. Originally published in 1961, see Juan José Arévalo, *The Shark and the Sardines* (Pickle Partners Publishing, 2017), 126.
45. Benjamin Carrion, "Oración fúnebre por la OEA," *Cuadernos Americanos* 141, no. 4 (1965): 29.
46. Taken from George Meek, "US Influence in the Organization of American States," *Journal of Interamerican Studies and World Affairs* 17, no. 3 (1975): 311–25.
47. See Smith, *Talons of the Eagle*, 136.
48. The UNGA passed an even stronger resolution condemning the intervention.
49. See Cooper and Legler, *Intervention without Intervening?*, 13–16.
50. See Stefano Palestini and Erica Martinelli, "Enforcing Peoples' Right to Democracy: Transnational Activism and Regional Powers in Contemporary Inter-American Relations," *European Journal of International Relations* 29, no. 3 (2023): 780–805.
51. Mikulas Fabry, "The Inter-American Democratic Charter and Governmental Legitimacy in the International Relations of the Western Hemisphere," *Diplomacy & Statecraft* 20, no. 1 (2009): 107–35.
52. Meek, "US influence in the Organization of American States," 312.
53. Pauselli et al., "Shaping the Liberal International Order from the Inside."
54. G. Pauselli, F. Urdínez, and F. Merke. "Shaping the Liberal International Order from the Inside: A Natural Experiment on China's Influence in the UN Human Rights Council." *Research & Politics*, 10, no. 3 (2023): 7.

7 THE NEW COLD WAR AND THE FUTURE OF CHINA–US RIVALRY IN LAC

1. R. B. Zoelick, "Free Trade and the Hemispheric Hope," Remarks at the Council of the Americas (May 7, 2001). https://ustr.gov/archive/assets/Document_Library/USTR_Speeches/2001/asset_upload_file236_4283.pdf.
2. Antonio Gramsci. *Quaderni del carcere*, edited by Valentino Gerratana. Einaudi, 1975, 18.
3. See Nicole Jenne, Claudia Labarca, María Montt, and Francisco Urdinez, *Monitor De Opinión Pública 2023: ¿qué Piensan Los Chilenos Sobre China?*, ICLAC (July 9, 2024).
4. Westad, *The Global Cold War*, 29.
5. Kapstein, *Exporting Capitalism*, 70.
6. Kapstein, *Exporting Capitalism*, 71–74.
7. This sentiment is well reflected in a document titled "Charge in Argentina (Ray) to the Secretary of State, August 1, 1947," in which Argentine officials suggested that the Marshall Plan should be expanded to include Latin America. See Stephen G Rabe, "The Elusive Conference United States Economic Relations with Latin America, 1945-1952," *Diplomatic History* 2, no. 3 (1978): 279–94.

8. Thomas Stephen Long, *Latin America Confronts the United States: Asymmetry and Influence* (Cambridge University Press, 2015), 58.
9. Scholars Margaret Myers and Gustavo Oliveira, similarly, argue that LAC's incorporation into the BRI was largely driven by growing interest among Latin American political and economic elites. See Gustavo de LT Oliveira and Margaret Myers, "The Tenuous Co-production of China's Belt and Road Initiative in Brazil and Latin America," *Journal of Contemporary China* 30, no. 129 (2021): 481–99.
10. See Margaret Myers, "China's Belt and Road Initiative: What Role for Latin America?," *Journal of Latin American Geography* 17, no. 2 (2018): 239–43.
11. As stated by Pastor in Pastor, "Exiting the Whirlpool, US Foreign Policy Toward Latin America and the Caribbean."
12. A. McPherson, *Yankee No!: Anti-Americanism in US–Latin American Relations*. (Harvard University Press, 2003).
13. The novel *Harsh Times* (2019) by Nobel Prize winner Mario Vargas Llosa, in a similar vein, tells the story of Chiquita's involvement in Guatemalan tumultuous politics in the 1950s.
14. Kapstein, *Exporting Capitalism*, 82.
15. As discussed in Evans's 1979 (updated 2018) work in Peter B Evans, *Dependent Development: The Alliance of Multinational, State, and Local Capital in Brazil* (Princeton University Press, 1979).
16. Long, *Latin America Confronts the United States*, 62–69.
17. Ronald Cox, *Power and Profits: US Policy in Central America* (University Press of Kentucky, 2014).
18. Seymour Martin Lipset, "Some Social Requisites of Democracy: Economic Development and Political Legitimacy," *American Political Science Review* 53, no. 1 (1959): 69–105.
19. In Smith, *Talons of the Eagle*, 199.
20. Office of the Historian, US Department of State (n.d.). 'Alliance for Progress (1961–1968)'. Retrieved January 11, 2024, from https://history.state.gov/milestones/1961-1968/alliance-for-progress.
21. Smith, *Talons of the Eagle*, 150–53.
22. In Richard D Mahoney, *The Kennedy Brothers: The Rise and Fall of Jack and Bobby* (Skyhorse Publishing Inc., 2011).
23. Lally Weymouth, "Ecuador's President is Bucking the Latin American Trend," *The Washington Post*, January 25, 2023, www.washingtonpost.com/opinions/2023/01/25/ecuador-president-lasso-economic-reform/.
24. Shahar Hameiri and Lee Jones, "Why the West's Alternative to China's International Infrastructure Financing is Failing," *European Journal of International Relations* (2023): 13540661231218573.
25. See Inter-American Development Bank (n.d.). 'Awarded Contracts.' Retrieved October 2023, from https://projectprocurement.iadb.org/en/awarded-contracts.
26. See Rollo, *Terminus*.
27. See Urdinez, "'They Own Our Country!';" Luke Patey, *How China Loses: The Pushback Against Chinese Global Ambitions* (Oxford University Press, 2021).

28. See Peter Zeihan and Peter Zeihan, *The End of the World is Just the Beginning: Mapping the Collapse of Globalization*, vol. 14 (Harper Business, 2022); Esteban Actis and Nicolas Creus, *La disputa por el poder global: China contra Estados Unidos en la crisis de la pandemia* (Capital Intelectual, 2021).
29. Westad, *The Global Cold War*, 29; Emily Rosenberg, *Spreading the American Dream: American Economic and Cultural Expansion, 1890–1945* (Hill and Wang, 1982).
30. Toosi, "'Frustrated and powerless'."
31. Cynthia J. Arnson and Jeffrey Davidow, eds., *China, Latin America, and the United States: The New Triangle* (Washington, DC: Wilson Center 2011).
32. See Arthur R. Kroeber, "The Economic Origins of US-China Strategic Competition," in *Cold Rivals: The New Era of US-China Strategic Competition*, edited by Evan Medeiros (Georgetown University Press, 2023), 172–75.
33. Evan Medeiros, ed., *Cold Rivals: The New Era of US-China Strategic Competition* (Georgetown University Press, 2023).
34. Cynthia Arnson, "U.S. Leadership in the Western Hemisphere," in *U.S. Leadership in a World in Conflict* (Cartagena, Colombia: Aspen Institute, 2023).
35. Ryan Hass, *Stronger: Adapting America's China Strategy in an Age of Competitive Interdependence* (Yale University Press, 2021).
36. Michael R. Pompeo, "The United States Protects National Security and the Integrity of 5G Networks," news release, May 15, 2020, www.state.gov/the-united-states-protects-national-security-and-the-integrity-of-5g-networks/.
37. See Google Cloud (2023, August 28). 'Announcing Humboldt: The First Cable Route between South America and Asia Pacific.' Google Cloud Blog, https://cloud.google.com/blog/products/infrastructure/announcing-humboldt-the-first-cable-route-between-south-america-and-asia-pacific.
38. See Wendy Leutert and Sarah Eaton, "Deepening not Departure: Xi Jinping's Governance of China's State-owned Economy," *The China Quarterly* 248, no. S1 (2021): 200–21.
39. Toosi, "'Frustrated and powerless'."
40. State Department, "Growth in the Americas," news release, 2019, https://2017-2021.state.gov/growth-in-the-americas/.
41. Shayerah I. Akhtar and Nick M. Brown, *U.S. International Development Finance Corporation: Overview and Issues*, Congressional Research Service (Washington DC, January 10, 2022), https://crsreports.congress.gov/product/pdf/R/R47006.
42. Adva Saldinger, "What is DFC's mandate? Debate over a bill turns up many answers," *Devex*, July 27, 2021, www.devex.com/news/what-is-dfc-s-mandate-debate-over-a-bill-turns-up-many-answers-100460.
43. For example, the initial version of the Ensuring American Global Leadership and Engagement Act, or EAGLE Act, included a section that would have allowed the DFC to invest in high-income countries.
44. Arnson, "U.S. Leadership in the Western Hemisphere"; The White House, "Fact sheet: President Biden and G7 Leaders Launch Build Back Better

World (B3W) Partnership," news release, June 12, 2021, www.whitehouse.gov/briefing-room/statements-releases/2021/06/12/fact-sheet-president-biden-and-g7-leaders-launch-build-back-better-world-b3w-partnership/.

45. Jorge Castañeda, who was the Secretary of Foreign Affairs of Mexico from 2000 to 2003 during the administration of Vicente Fox Quesada, argues something similar in Jorge Castañeda, "América Latina y el No Alineamiento Activo," in *El No Alineamiento Activo y América Latina: Una Doctrina para el Nuevo Siglo*, edited by Carlos Fortin, Jorge Heine, and Carlos Ominami (Catalonia, 2021).

46. Ciara Nugent and Charlie Campell, "The U.S. and China Are Battling for Influence in Latin America, and the Pandemic Has Raised the Stakes," *Time*, February 4, 2021, https://time.com/5936037/us-china-latin-america-influence/.

47. Ryan C. Berg and Henry Ziemer, *The Outcompete World: Revisiting U.S. Economic Priorities for Competition with China in Latin America and the Caribbean*, (Center for Strategic & International Studies, 2023), www.csis.org/analysis/outcompete-world-revisiting-us-economic-priorities-competition-china-latin-america-and.

48. Isabel Caro, "Presidente Boric sobre guerra comercial China-Estados Unidos: 'Hemos recibido presiones para decir de qué lado estamos'," *La Tercera* (Santiago), November 17, 2022, www.latercera.com/politica/noticia/presidente-boric-sobre-guerra-comercial-china-estados-unidos-hemos-recibido-presiones-para-decir-de-que-lado-estamos/B6I5T3W6BJBXNCBIT6USZ5JX2U/.

49. Francisco Sagasti, "A Conversation with President Francisco Sagasti of Peru," interview by Benjamin Gedan and Cynthia Arnson, *Latin American Program*, February 18, 2021, www.wilsoncenter.org/event/conversation-president-francisco-sagasti-peru.

50. Telam, "Fernández afirmó que 'no quiere un mundo bipolar' y que son 'bienvenidas' todas las inversiones," December 7, 2022, www.telam.com.ar/notas/202212/613549-fernandez-inversiones-china-estados-unidos.html.

51. Carlos Fortin, Jorge Heine, and Carlos Ominami, *Latin American Foreign Policies in the New World Order: The Active Non-Alignment Option* (Anthem Press, 2023).

52. Kai He and Huiyun Feng, *After Hedging: Hard Choices for the Indo-Pacific States between the US and China*. Cambridge University Press, 2023; Cheng-Chwee Kuik, "Getting Hedging Right: A Small-state Perspective," *China International Strategy Review* 3, no. 2 (2021): 300–15. Also see Sheena Chestnut Greitens and Isaac Kardon, "Playing Both Sides of the U.S.-Chinese Rivalry," *Foreign Affairs*, March 15, 2024, www.foreignaffairs.com/united-states/playing-both-sides-us-chinese-rivalry.

53. In the words of Juan Gabriel Tokatlian, "Estados Unidos-América Latina: por una diplomacia de equidistancia," in *El No Alineamiento Activo y América Latina: Una Doctrina para el Nuevo Siglo*, edited by Carlos Fortin, Jorge Heine, and Carlos Ominami (Catalonia, 2021).

54. For a historical point of view, see Aleksandar Životić and Jovan Čavoški, "On the Road to Belgrade: Yugoslavia, Third World Neutrals, and the Evolution

of Global Non-Alignment, 1954–1961," *Journal of Cold War Studies* 18, no. 4 (2016): 79–97. For a reflection on its applicability to LAC see: Esteban Actis and Nicolás Creus, "La competencia EEUU-China y su impacto en América Latina en el mundo post pandemia," in *El No Alineamiento Activo y América Latina: Una Doctrina para el Nuevo Siglo*, edited by Carlos Fortin, Jorge Heine, and Carlos Ominami (Catalonia, 2021).

55. Lukas Hermwille, Stefan Lechtenböhmer, Max Åhman, et al., "A Climate Club to Decarbonize the Global Steel Industry," *Nature Climate Change* 12, no. 6 (2022): 494–96.

56. See China Power Team, "Does China Dominate Global Investment?" ChinaPower (January 28, 2021; retrieved January 11, 2024), https://chinapower.csis.org/china-foreign-direct-investment/.

57. N. Galarraga Gortázar and G. Abril, "China avisa al argentino Milei que romper relaciones sería 'un grave error'." El País Argentina (November 22, 2023; retrieved January 11, 2024), https://elpais.com/argentina/2023-11-22/china-avisa-al-argentino-milei-que-romper-relaciones-seria-un-grave-error.html.

58. Oliver Stuenkel, "América Latina en el mundo post-occidental," in *El No Alineamiento Activo y América Latina: Una Doctrina para el Nuevo Siglo*, edited by Carlos Fortin, Jorge Heine, and Carlos Ominami (Catalonia, 2021). Tokatlian, "Estados Unidos-América Latina."

59. Urdinez, "'They Own Our Country!'."

60. As discussed by Andrés Malamud, Pía Riggirozzi, or Cintia Quiliconi, to mention just three among many.

61. Tom Long, *A Small State's Guide to Influence in World Politics* (Oxford University Press), 71.

62. See Mark Petersen and Carsten-Andreas Schulz, "Setting the Regional Agenda: A Critique of Posthegemonic Regionalism," *Latin American Politics and Society* 60, no. 1 (2018): 102–27.

Bibliography

Acharya, Amitav. "After Liberal Hegemony: The Advent of a Multiplex World Order." *Ethics & International Affairs* 31, no. 3 (2017): 271–85.

Actis, Esteban and Nicolás Creus. "La competencia EE.UU.-China y su impacto en América Latina en el mundo post pandemia." In *El No Alineamiento Activo Y América Latina: Una Doctrina Para El Nuevo Siglo*, edited by Carlos Fortin, Jorge Heine, and Carlos Ominami, 100–14. Catalonia, 2021.

Actis, Esteban and Nicolas Creus. *La disputa por el poder global: China contra Estados Unidos en la crisis de la pandemia*. Capital Intelectual, 2021.

Adamson, Michael R. "'Must We Overlook All Impairment of Our Interests?' Debating the Foreign Aid Role of the Export-Import Bank, 1934–41." *Diplomatic History* 29, no. 4 (2005): 589–623.

Adrián, Ventura. "Malestar en la corte con el kirchnerismo." *La Nación*, September 16, 2010. www.lanacion.com.ar/politica/malestar-en-la-corte-con-el-kirchnerismo-nid1305142/.

Akhtar, Shayerah I. and Nick M. Brown. *U.S. International Development Finance Corporation: Overview and Issues*. Congressional Research Service, 2022. https://crsreports.congress.gov/product/pdf/R/R47006.

Alami, Ilias, Adam D. Dixon, Ruben Gonzalez-Vicente, et al. "Geopolitics and the 'New' State Capitalism." *Geopolitics* 27, no. 3 (2022): 995–1023.

Ambrosio, Thomas. "The Rise of the 'China Model' and 'Beijing Consensus': Evidence of Authoritarian Diffusion?" *Contemporary Politics* 18, no. 4 (2012): 381–99.

Andersen, Morten Skumsrud, Alexander Cooley, and Daniel H. Nexon. *Undermining American Hegemony: Goods Substitution in World Politics*. Cambridge University Press, 2021.

Andina, Agencia Peruana de Noticias. "Gobierno creará zona económica especial Chancay-Ancón-Callao." July 20, 2023. https://andina.pe/agencia/noticia-gobierno-creara-zona-economica-especial-chancayanconcallao-948213.aspx.

Arévalo, Juan José. *The Shark and the Sardines*. Pickle Partners Publishing, 2017.

Argentina, Honorable Senado de la Nación. "Versión Taquigráfica de la 22° Sesión." December 17, 2014. www.senado.gob.ar/parlamentario/sesiones/17-12-2014/22/downloadTac.

Argentina, Honorable Cámara de Diputados de la Nación. "Versión Taquigráfica de la 27° Reunión, Período 132." 2014. www.hcdn.gob.ar/sesiones/sesion.htm l?id=947&numVid=0&reunion=27&periodo=132 video available at: https://videos.hcdn.gob.ar/video/evento/e/1105.

Armony, Ariel C. and Julia C. Strauss. "From Going Out (Zou Chuqu) to Arriving in (Desembarco): Constructing a New Field of Inquiry in China–Latin America Interactions." *The China Quarterly* 209 (2012): 1–17.

Arnson, Cynthia. "U.S. Leadership in the Western Hemisphere." In *U.S. Leadership in a World in Conflict*. Aspen Institute, 2023. www.aspeninstitute.org/wp-content/uploads/2023/03/Cartagena2023_Report.pdf.

Arnson, Cynthia J. and Jeffrey Davidow, eds. *China, Latin America, and the United States: The New Triangle*. Wilson Center, 2011.

Arriarán, Gabriel. "La operación secreta de la minera más infractora del Perú." *Portal Convoca*, May 16, 2016. www.idl-reporteros.pe/la-operacion-secreta-de-la-minera-mas-infractora-del-peru/.

Arrighi, Giovanni and Lu Zhang. "Beyond the Washington Consensus: A New Bandung?" In *Globalization and Beyond: New Examinations of Global Power and Its Alternatives*, edited by Jon Shefner and María Patricia Fernández-Kelly, 25–57. Penn State Press, 2011.

Asociación Peruana de Agentes Marítimos. "Cosco shipping de China con un pie en puertos peruanos." News release, July 5, 2018. https://apam-peru.com/web/cosco-shipping-de-china-con-un-pie-en-puertos-peruanos/.

Asociación Peruana de Agentes Marítimos. "Volcan adquiere empresa Terminales Portuarios Chancay y busca socio." News release, May 18, 2016. https://apam-peru.com/web/volcan-adquiere-empresa-terminales-portuarios-chancay-y-busca-socio/.

Babić, Milan. *The Rise of State Capital: Transforming Markets and International Politics*. Agenda Publishing Limited, 2023.

Baldwin, David A. *Economic Statecraft: New Edition*. Princeton University Press, 2020.

Bankrate. "The 15 Largest Banks in the US." 2023, accessed June 27, 2023, www.bankrate.com/banking/biggest-banks-in-america/.

Barrios, Ricardo and Karla I. Rio. "China's Engagement with Latin America and the Caribbean." Congressional Research Service, 2023. https://crsreports.congress.gov/product/pdf/IF/IF10982.

Barton, Jonathan R. and Johannes Rehner. "Neostructuralism through Strategic Transaction: The Geopolinomics of China's Dragon Doctrine for Latin America." *Political Geography* 65 (2018): 77–87.

Beckley, Michael. *Unrivaled: Why America Will Remain the World's Sole Superpower*. Cornell University Press, 2018.

Beeson, Mark. "Geoeconomics with Chinese Characteristics: The Bri and China's Evolving Grand Strategy." *Economic and Political Studies* 6, no. 3 (2018): 240–56.

Beeson, Mark and Corey Crawford. "Putting the Bri in Perspective: History, Hegemony and Geoeconomics." *Chinese Political Science Review* 8, no. 1 (2023): 45–62.
Benabdallah, Lina. "Power or Influence? Making Sense of China's Evolving Party-to-Party Diplomacy in Africa." *African Studies Quarterly* 19, no. 3 & 4 (2020): 95–114.
Benabdallah, Lina. *Shaping the Future of Power: Knowledge Production and Network-Building in China-Africa Relations.* University of Michigan Press, 2020.
Berg, Ryan C. and Henry Ziemer. "The Outcompete World: Revisiting U.S. Economic Priorities for Competition with China in Latin America and the Caribbean." Center for Strategic & International Studies, 2023. www.csis.org/analysis/outcompete-world-revisiting-us-economic-priorities-competition-china-latin-america-and.
Bernal-Meza, Raúl and Li Xing, eds. *China–Latin America Relations in the 21st Century: The Dual Complexities of Opportunities and Challenges.* International Political Economy Series. Palgrave Macmillan, 2020.
Bissell, Jonathan. "The Rise of Leftist Populism – A Challenge to Democracy?". *Military Review*, no. January–February (2016): 77–87. www.armyupress.army.mil/Portals/7/military-review/Archives/English/MilitaryReview_20160228_art014.pdf.
Blackwill, Robert D. and Jennifer M. Harris. *War by Other Means: Geoeconomics and Statecraft.* Harvard University Press, 2016.
Blanchard, Jean-Marc F. and Norrin M. Ripsman. *Economic Statecraft and Foreign Policy: Sanctions, Incentives, and Target State Calculations.* Routledge, 2013.
Blinder, Alan S. and Alan B. Krueger. "What Does the Public Know about Economic Policy, and How Does It Know It?", National Bureau of Economic Research Cambridge, 2004.
Bohigues, Asbel, Shoujun Cui, and Scott Morgenstern. "Party Cohesion, Congruence, and Foreign Powers: Latin American Views about China and the United States." *Journal of Politics in Latin America* 16, no. 3 (2024): 380–404.
Bolt, Jutta, and Jan Luiten Van Zanden. "The Maddison Project: Collaborative Research on Historical National Accounts." *The Economic History Review* 67, no. 3 (2014): 627–51.
Borquez, Andres, Felipe Muñoz, and Diego Leiva. "The Growing Chinese Economic Presence in Chile." *China Review* 23, no. 3 (2023): 131–54.
Brands, Hal. *Making the Unipolar Moment: US Foreign Policy and the Rise of the Post-Cold War Order.* Cornell University Press, 2016.
Bräutigam, Deborah, and Kevin P. Gallagher. "Bartering Globalization: China's Commodity-Backed Finance in Africa and Latin America." *Global Policy* 5, no. 3 (2014): 346–52.
Brazys, Samuel, and Alexander Dukalskis. "Rising Powers and Grassroots Image Management: Confucius Institutes and China in the Media." *The Chinese Journal of International Politics* 12, no. 4 (2019): 557–84.
Brown, Kathleen J. "Why Hide? Africa's Unreported Debt to China." *The Review of International Organizations* 20 (2025): 1–32.

Brown, Matthew. *Informal Empire in Latin America: Culture, Commerce and Capital*. John Wiley & Sons, 2009.

Broz, J. Lawrence, Zhiwen Zhang, and Gaoyang Wang. "Explaining Foreign Support for China's Global Economic Leadership." *International Organization* 74, no. 3 (2020): 417–52.

Bruner, Christopher M. "Hemispheric Integration and the Politics of Regionalism: The Free Trade Area of the Americas (Ftaa)." *University of Miami Inter-American Law Review* 33 (2002): 1.

Bull, Benedicte and Antulio Rosales. "Elite Dynamics and China's Influence in Latin America." *Development and Change* 55 (2024): 1206–29.

Bunte, Jonas B. *Raise the Debt: How Developing Countries Choose Their Creditors*. Oxford University Press, 2019.

Cai, Kevin G. "The One Belt One Road and the Asian Infrastructure Investment Bank: Beijing's New Strategy of Geoeconomics and Geopolitics." *Journal of Contemporary China* 27, no. 114 (2018): 831–47. https://doi.org/10.1080/10670564.2018.1488101.

Calabrese, Linda and Yue Cao. "Managing the Belt and Road: Agency and Development in Cambodia and Myanmar." *World Development* 141 (2021): 105297.

Camba, Alvin. "The Sino-Centric Capital Export Regime: State-Backed and Flexible Capital in the Philippines." *Development and Change* 51, no. 4 (2020): 970–97.

Campello, Daniela. *The Politics of Market Discipline in Latin America: Globalization and Democracy*. Cambridge University Press, 2015.

Campello, Daniela and Francisco Urdinez. "Voter and Legislator Responses to Localized Trade Shocks from China in Brazil." *Comparative Political Studies* 54, no. 7 (2021): 1131–62.

Campello, Daniela and Cesar Zucco. *The Volatility Curse: Exogenous Shocks and Representation in Resource-Rich Democracies*. Cambridge University Press, 2020.

Caro, Isabel. "Presidente Boric sobre guerra comercial China-Estados Unidos: 'hemos recibido presiones para decir de qué lado estamos'." *La Tercera (Santiago)*, November 17, 2022. www.latercera.com/politica/noticia/presidente-boric-sobre-guerra-comercial-china-estados-unidos-hemos-recibido-presiones-para-decir-de-que-lado-estamos/B6I5T3W6BJBXNCBIT6USZ5JX2U/.

Carrion, Benjamin. "Oración fúnebre por la Oea." *Cuadernos Americanos* 141, no. 4 (1965): 19–35.

Carter, David B. and Randall W. Stone. "Democracy and Multilateralism: The Case of Vote Buying in the Un General Assembly." *International Organization* 69, no. 1 (2015): 1–33.

Casarosada. "'El crecimiento económico demanda cada vez más energía', dijo la presidenta en Santa Cruz." Casa Rosada, 2013, accessed January 5, 2024, www.casarosada.gob.ar/informacion/archivo/26662-la-presidenta-encabezo-acto-de-adjudicacion-de-obras-para-la-construccion-de-represas-en-santa-cruz.

Castañeda, Jorge. "América Latina y el no alineamiento activo." In *El No Alineamiento Activo Y América Latina: Una Doctrina Para El Nuevo Siglo*, edited by Carlos Fortin, Jorge Heine, and Carlos Ominami, 193–203. Catalonia, 2021.

Castaneda, Néstor. "New Dependency?: Economic Links between China and Latin America." *Issues & Studies* 53, no. 01 (2017): 1740001.
Cavallo, Eduardo and Andrew Powell. "Opportunities for Stronger and Sustainable Postpandemic Growth." *IDB: 2021 Latin American and Caribbean Macroeconomic Report* (2021). http://dx.doi.org/10.18235/0003107.
Chan, Zenobia T. and Sophie Meunier. "Behind the Screen: Understanding National Support for a Foreign Investment Screening Mechanism in the European Union." *The Review of International Organizations* 17, no. 3 (2022): 513–41.
Charlip, Julie A. "Latin America in World History." In *The Cambridge World History: Volume 7: Production, Destruction and Connection, 1750-Present*, edited by J. R. McNeill and Kenneth Pomeranz, 526–55. Cambridge University Press, 2015.
Chen, Muyang. *The Latecomer's Rise: Policy Banks and the Globalization of China's Development Finance*. Cornell University Press, 2024.
China, The State Council Information Office of the People's Republic of. *A Global Community of Shared Future: China's Proposals and Actions*, Ministry of Foreign Affairs of the People's Republic of China, 2023. http://english.scio.gov.cn/whitepapers/2023-09/26/content_116710660_5.htm.
Cooley, Alexander and Daniel Nexon. *Exit from Hegemony: The Unraveling of the American Global Order*. Oxford University Press, 2020.
Cooper, Andrew and Thomas Legler. *Intervention without Intervening?: The OAS Defense and Promotion of Democracy in the Americas*. Springer, 2006.
Cox, Ronald. *Power and Profits: US Policy in Central America*. University Press of Kentucky, 2014.
Cristina Fernandez de Kirchner. "Gezhuoba Group Corporation, Electroingeniería E Hidrocuyo construirán las represas en Santa Cruz," news release, August 22, 2013. www.cfkargentina.com/represas-nestor-kirchner-jorge-cepernic-santa-cruz/.
Cruz, Elaine. "Butantan inicia producción de vacuna contra la Covid-19." *Agência Brasil*, April 28, 2021. https://agenciabrasil.ebc.com.br/es/saude/noticia/2021-04/butantan-inicia-produccion-de-vacuna-contra-la-covid-19.
Culpepper, Pepper D. "Structural Power and Political Science in the Post-Crisis Era." *Business and Politics* 17, no. 3 (2015): 391–409.
Dahl, Robert A. "The Concept of Power." *Behavioral Science* 2, no. 3 (1957): 201–15.
Davis, J. W. *Threats and Promises: The Pursuit of International Influence*. John Hopkins University Press, 2003.
De Graaff, Naná and Bastiaan Van Apeldoorn. "US–China Relations and the Liberal World Order: Contending Elites, Colliding Visions?". *International Affairs* 94, no. 1 (2018): 113–31.
De Vido, J. and F. Bernal. *Néstor Y Cristina Kirchner: planificación y federalismo en acción*. Planeta, 2015.
Debs, Alexandre and Nuno P. Monteiro. "Known Unknowns: Power Shifts, Uncertainty, and War." *International Organization* 68, no. 1 (2014): 1–31.

Di Lonardo, Livio, Jessica S. Sun, and Scott A. Tyson. "Autocratic Stability in the Shadow of Foreign Threats." *American Political Science Review* 114, no. 4 (2020): 1247–65.

Diamint, Rut. "Regionalismo y posicionamiento suramericano: Unasur Y Alba [Regionalism and South American Orientation: Unasur and Alba]." *Revista CIDOB d'afers internacionals* 101 (2013): 55–79.

Diario Rio Negro. "Así empezaba y así está ahora la estación China en Neuquén: un recorrido en 10 fotos." April 6, 2024. www.rionegro.com.ar/fotogalerias/asi-empezaba-y-asi-esta-ahora-la-estacion-china-en-neuquen-un-recorrido-en-10-fotos-3507002/.

Domínguez, Jorge. "China's Relations with Latin America: Shared Gains, Asymmetric Hopes." *Inter-American Dialogue* (2006). https://projects.iq.harvard.edu/files/wcfia/files/dominguez_chinas.pdf.

Dosch, Jörn and David S. G. Goodman. "China and Latin America: Complementarity, Competition, and Globalisation." *Journal of Current Chinese Affairs* 41, no. 1 (2012): 3–19.

Dowding, K., P. John, T. Mergoupis, and M. Van Vugt. "Exit, Voice and Loyalty: Analytic and Empirical Developments." *European Journal of Political Research* 37, no. 4 (2000): 469–95.

Dreher, Axel and Nathan M. Jensen. "Independent Actor or Agent? An Empirical Analysis of the Impact of Us Interests on International Monetary Fund Conditions." *The Journal of Law and Economics* 50, no. 1 (2007): 105–24.

Dreher, Axel, Andreas Fuchs, Bradley Parks, Austin Strange, and Michael J. Tierney. *Banking on Beijing: The Aims and Impacts of China's Overseas Development Program*. Cambridge University Press, 2022.

Drezner, Daniel W. "Does Obama Have a Grand Strategy? Why We Need Doctrines in Uncertain Times." *Foreign Affairs* 90, no. 4 (2011): 57–68.

Duanmu, Jing-Lin and Francisco Urdinez. "The Dissuasive Effect of US Political Influence on Chinese FDI during the 'Going Global' Policy Era." *Business and Politics* 20, no. 1 (2018): 38–69.

Dueck, Colin. *The Obama Doctrine: American Grand Strategy Today*. Oxford University Press, 2015.

Dussel Peters, Enrique. "Monitor de la OFDI China en América Latina y el Caribe," edited by Red ALC-China, 2020. www.redalc-china.org/monitor/.

Dussel Peters, Enrique and Ariel C. Armony. "Effects of China on the Quantity and Quality of Jobs in Latin America and the Caribbean." Ilo Technical Reports 6. International Labor Organization, 2017.

EBISA. *Aprovechamientos hidroeléctricos del río Santa Cruz: estudio de impacto ambiental, capítulo 3 – descripción del proyecto*, 2017. https://saludsantacruz.gob.ar/secretariadeambiente/wp-content/uploads/2017/11/CAP%C3%8DTULO-3-%E2%80%93-DESCRIPCION-DEL-PROYECTO.pdf.

EFE. "Suspenden producción de vacuna de la Sinovac en Brasil por falta de insumos." *swissinfo.ch*, May 14, 2021. www.swissinfo.ch/spa/coronavirus-brasil_suspenden-producci%C3%B3n-de-vacuna-de-la-sinovac-en-brasil-por-falta-de-insumos/46619842.

El Telégrafo. "Legisladores se pronuncian a favor de los exportadores de camarón." July 16, 2020. www.eltelegrafo.com.ec/noticias/economia/1/legisladores-exportadores-camaron.

Ellis, Evan R. "The Impact of the Turn to the Left on the Advance of the People's Republic of China in Latin America." *Journal of Indo-Pacific Affairs* 6, no. 7 (October 5, 2023): 9. www.airuniversity.af.edu/JIPA/Display/Article/3540672/the-impact-of-the-turn-to-the-left-on-the-advance-of-the-peoples-republic-of-ch/.

Ellner, Steve. "Pink-Tide Governments: Pragmatic and Populist Responses to Challenges from the Right." *Latin American Perspectives* 46, no. 1 (2019): 4–22.

Emmenegger, Patrick. "The Long Arm of Justice: US Structural Power and International Banking." *Business and Politics* 17, no. 3 (2015): 473–93.

Evans, Peter B. *Dependent Development: The Alliance of Multinational, State, and Local Capital in Brazil*. Princeton University Press, 1979.

Fabry, Mikulas. "The Inter-American Democratic Charter and Governmental Legitimacy in the International Relations of the Western Hemisphere." *Diplomacy & Statecraft* 20, no. 1 (2009): 107–35.

Feliú Ribeiro, Pedro. "Partidos políticos y política exterior en América Latina." *Revista Mexicana de CienciasPpolíticas y Sociales* 64, no. 235 (2019): 353–93.

Ferchen, Matt. "China–Latin America Relations: Long-Term Boon or Short-Term Boom?". *The Chinese Journal of International Politics* 4, no. 1 (2011): 55–86.

Fichtner, Jan. "Perpetual Decline or Persistent Dominance? Uncovering Anglo-America's True Structural Power in Global Finance." *Review of International Studies* 43, no. 1 (2017): 3–28.

Flores-Macías, Gustavo A. and Sarah E. Kreps. "The Foreign Policy Consequences of Trade: China's Commercial Relations with Africa and Latin America, 1992–2006." *The Journal of Politics* 75, no. 2 (2013): 357–71.

Foot, Rosemary. *China, the Un, and Human Protection: Beliefs, Power, Image*. Oxford University Press, 2020.

Fortin, Carlos, Jorge Heine, and Carlos Ominami. *Latin American Foreign Policies in the New World Order: The Active Non-Alignment Option*. Anthem Press, 2023.

Fortune. "Fortune 500," 2021. https://fortune.com/fortune500/.

Fuentes, Helthon. "José Ignacio De Romaña: Una carrera dedicada al Perú." *Diario El Chaski*, August 27, 2023. https://chaski.pe/detalle/jose-ignacio-de-romana-una-carrera-dedicada-al-peru.

Fullilove, Michael. "China and the United Nations: The Stakeholder Spectrum." *The Washington Quarterly* 34, no. 3 (2011): 63–85.

Gachúz, Juan Carlos. "Chile's Economic and Political Relationship with China." *Journal of Current Chinese Affairs* 41, no. 1 (2012): 133–54.

Gallagher, Kevin P. *The China Triangle: Latin America's China Boom and the Fate of the Washington Consensus*. Oxford University Press, 2016.

Gallagher, Kevin P. and Amos Irwin. "China's Economic Statecraft in Latin America: Evidence from China's Policy Banks." *Pacific Affairs* 88, no. 1 (2015): 99–121.

Gallagher, Kevin P. and Roberto Porzecanski. *The Dragon in the Room: China and the Future of Latin American Industrialization*. Stanford University Press, 2010.

Gallagher, Kevin P., Juan Carlos Moreno-Brid, and Roberto Porzecanski. "The Dynamism of Mexican Exports: Lost in (Chinese) Translation?". *World Development* 36, no. 8 (2008): 1365–80.
Gamso, Jonas and Anna Dimitrova. "Rewarding a Friend: Does the World Bank Direct Non-Commercial Risk Insurance to Countries That Support US Foreign Policy Interests?". *New Political Economy* 29, no. 1 (2023): 159–72.
Ganchev, Ivo. "China Pushed the Pink Tide and the Pink Tide Pulled China: Intertwining Economic Interests and Ideology in Ecuador and Bolivia (2005–2014)." *World Affairs* 183, no. 4 (2020): 359–88.
Gonzalo, Walter and Arcasi Mariño. "Volcan donó más de US$ 200 mil a Confiep para campaña publicitaria en 2011." *Gestión*, November 21, 2019. https://gestion.pe/peru/politica/confiep-volcan-dono-us-200-mil-a-confiep-para-campana-publicitaria-en-2011-noticia/#google_vignette.
Govella, Kristi. "The Adaptation of Japanese Economic Statecraft: Trade, Aid, and Technology." *World Trade Review* 20, no. 2 (2021): 186–202.
Government of the People's Republic of China & Government of the Argentine Republic. *Declaración conjunta entre el gobierno de la República Popular China y el gobierno de la República Argentina*, 2012. www.fmprc.gov.cn/esp/wjdt/gongbao/201007/t20100719_910945.html.
GOVESP. "Chineses mostram interesse no trem intercidades," News release, 2019, www.saopaulo.sp.gov.br/spnoticias/ultimas-noticias/chineses-mostram-interesse-no-trem-intercidades-2/.
Gramsci, Antonio. "Quaderni Del Carcere," edited by Valentino Gerratana. Einaudi, 1975.
Greitens, Sheena Chestnut and Isaac Kardon. "Playing Both Sides of the U.S.-Chinese Rivalry." *Foreign Affairs*, March 15, 2024. www.foreignaffairs.com/united-states/playing-both-sides-us-chinese-rivalry.
Grimmel, Andreas and Viktor Eszterhai. "The Belt and Road Initiative and the Development of China's Economic Statecraft: European Attitudes and Responses." *International Studies* 57, no. 3 (2020): 223–39.
Gruss, Bertrand. *After the Boom: Commodity Prices and Economic Growth in Latin America and the Caribbean.* International Monetary Fund, 2014.
Hainmueller, Jens, Daniel J. Hopkins, and Teppei Yamamoto. "Causal Inference in Conjoint Analysis: Understanding Multidimensional Choices via Stated Preference Experiments." *Political Analysis* 22, no. 1 (2014): 1–30.
Hakim, Peter. "Is Washington Losing Latin America?" *Foreign Affairs* 85, no. 1 (2006): 39–53.
Halper, Stefan. *The Beijing Consensus: How China's Authoritarian Model Will Dominate the Twenty-First Century*, vol. 16. ReadHowYouWant.com, 2010.
Hameiri, Shahar and Lee Jones. "Why the West's Alternative to China's International Infrastructure Financing Is Failing." *European Journal of International Relations* 30, no. 3 (2023): 697–724.
Hass, Ryan. *Stronger: Adapting America's China Strategy in an Age of Competitive Interdependence.* Yale University Press, 2021.
He, Shuangsheng. *China-Latin America Relations.* Paths International, 2012.
He, Kai and Huiyun Feng. *After Hedging: Hard Choices for the Indo-Pacific States between the US and China.* Cambridge University Press, 2023.

He, Kai and Huiyun Feng. "If Not Soft Balancing, Then What? Reconsidering Soft Balancing and US Policy toward China." *Security Studies* 17, no. 2 (2008): 363–95.
Heine, Jorge. "The Chile–China Paradox: Burgeoning Trade, Little Investment." *Asian Perspective* 40, no. 4 (2016): 653–73.
Hermwille, Lukas, Stefan Lechtenböhmer, Max Åhman, et al. "A Climate Club to Decarbonize the Global Steel Industry." *Nature Climate Change* 12, no. 6 (2022): 494–96.
Hernandez, Javier. "Trump Slammed the W.H.O. Over Coronavirus. He's Not Alone." *The New York Times*, April 8, 2020. www.nytimes.com/2020/04/08/world/asia/trump-who-coronavirus-china.html.
Hirschman, Albert O. *Exit, Voice, and Loyalty: Responses to Decline in Firms, Organizations, and States*. Harvard University Press, 1972.
Hirschman, Albert O. *National Power and the Structure of Foreign Trade*, vol. 105. University of California Press, 1980.
Hogenboom, Barbara. "Depoliticized and Repoliticized Minerals in Latin America." *Journal of Developing Societies* 28, no. 2 (2012): 133–58.
House, The White. "Fact Sheet: President Biden and G7 Leaders Launch Build Back Better World (B3W) Partnership," news release, June 12, 2021, www.whitehouse.gov/briefing-room/statements-releases/2021/06/12/fact-sheet-president-biden-and-g7-leaders-launch-build-back-better-world-b3w-partnership/.
Huanachín, Wilfredo. "En junio iniciamos la construcción del puerto de Chancay y durará 30 meses." *Diario Gestión*, July 2, 2017. https://plataforma.ipnoticias.com/Landing?cac=23YVAmTK3vAF%2BtWvpBAPSw%3D%3D&i=8rjVc38Q1fmQN9n3eazhjw%3D%3D&pm=1HUfQzPjQy3fRQ4WkUAmEQ%3D%3D&c=YEqkd0XasT53w7cz4ukg8aCeF7R2EsJxney4fx9cD04%3D.
Huntington, Samuel P. "The Lonely Superpower." *Foreign Affairs* 78, no. 2 (1999): 35–49.
Instituto Butantan. "Butantan E Governo De Sp Vão Testar E Produzir Vacina Inédita Contra Coronavírus," news release, June 11, 2020, https://butantan.gov.br/noticias/butantan-e-governo-de-sp-vao-testar-e-produzir-vacina-inedita-contra-coronavirus.
International Department Central Committee of CPC. "Wang Yajun Holds Working Talks with Multi-Party Study Group of Brazilian Parliament Members," news release, September 17, 2019, www.idcpc.org.cn/english2023/lldt/201909/t20190921_160794.html.
Jaramillo, Alberto. "Cristina presidió el acto de adjudicación para la construcción de las represas 'Néstor Kirchner' y 'Jorge Cepernic'." *Telam* (Buenos Aires), August 21, 2013. www.telam.com.ar/notas/201308/29602-cristina-presidioel-acto-de-adjudicacion-para-la-construccion-de-las-represas-nestor-kirchner-y-jorge-cepernic.html.
Jáuregui, Juliana González. "How Argentina Pushed Chinese Investors to Help Revitalize Its Energy Grid." *China Local/Global*. (2021). https://carnegieendowment.org/research/2021/12/how-argentina-pushed-chinese-investors-to-help-revitalize-its-energy-grid?lang=en.

Jenkins, Rhys. "China's Global Expansion and Latin America." *Journal of Latin American Studies* 42, no. 4 (2010): 809–37.

Jenkins, Rhys. *How China Is Reshaping the Global Economy: Development Impacts in Africa and Latin America.* Oxford University Press, 2019.

Jenkins, Rhys. *How China Is Reshaping the Global Economy: Development Impacts in Africa and Latin America.* Oxford University Press, 2022.

Jenkins, Rhys. "Is Chinese Competition Causing Deindustrialization in Brazil?" *Latin American Perspectives* 42, no. 6 (2015): 42–63.

Jenne, Nicole, Claudia Labarca, María Montt, and Francisco Urdinez. "Monitor de opinión pública 2023: ¿qué piensan los chilenos sobre China?" ICLAC (July 9, 2024). https://zenodo.org/records/12700686.

Jepson, Nicholas. *In China's Wake: How the Commodity Boom Transformed Development Strategies in the Global South.* Columbia University Press, 2019.

Johnston, Alastair Iain. "China in a World of Orders: Rethinking Compliance and Challenge in Beijing's International Relations." *International Security* 44, no. 2 (2019): 9–60.

Jones, Lee and Shahar Hameiri. *Fractured China.* Cambridge University Press, 2021.

Jones, Mark P., Wonjae Hwang, and Juan Pablo Micozzi. "Government and Opposition in the Argentine Congress, 1989–2007: Understanding Inter-Party Dynamics through Roll Call Vote Analysis." *Journal of Politics in Latin America* 1, no. 1 (2009): 67–96.

Kaplan, Stephen B. *Globalizing Patient Capital: The Political Economy of Chinese Finance in the Americas.* Cambridge University Press, 2021.

Kapstein, Ethan B. *Exporting Capitalism: Private Enterprise and US Foreign Policy.* Harvard University Press, 2022.

Kastner, Scott L. "Buying Influence? Assessing the Political Effects of China's International Trade." *Journal of Conflict Resolution* 60, no. 6 (2016): 980–1007.

Kastner, Scott L. and Margaret M. Pearson. "Exploring the Parameters of China's Economic Influence." *Studies in Comparative International Development* 56 (2021): 18–44.

Kim, Dong Jung. "Making Geoeconomics an IR Research Program." *International Studies Perspectives* 22, no. 3 (2021): 321–39.

Kim, Anthony B. and Alexander Jelloian. *How Chinese "Corrosive Capital" Influences Foreign Governments.* The Heritage Foundation, 2021. www.heritage.org/asia/commentary/how-chinese-corrosive-capital-influences-foreign-governments.

Klein, Matthew C. and Michael Pettis. *Trade Wars Are Class Wars: How Rising Inequality Distorts the Global Economy and Threatens International Peace.* Yale University Press, 2020.

Knoerich, Jan and Francisco Urdinez. "Contesting Contested Multilateralism: Why the West Joined the Rest in Founding the Asian Infrastructure Investment Bank." *The Chinese Journal of International Politics* 12, no. 3 (2019): 333–70.

Krasner, Stephen D. "Power Structures and Regional Development Banks." *International Organization* 35, no. 2 (1981): 303–28. https://doi.org/10.1017/S0020818300032458.

Kristensen, Hans, Matt Korda, Eliana Johns, Mackenzie Knight, and Kate Kohn. *Status of World Nuclear Forces*. Federation of American Scientists, 2024. https://fas.org/initiative/status-world-nuclear-forces/.

Kroeber, Arthur R. "The Economic Origins of US–China Strategic Competition." In *Cold Rivals: The New Era of Us-China Strategic Competition*, edited by Evan Medeiros, 172–204. Georgetown University Press, 2023.

Kuik, Cheng-Chwee. "Getting Hedging Right: A Small-State Perspective." *China International Strategy Review* 3, no. 2 (2021): 300–15.

La Diaria Política. "La mayoría de los legisladores uruguayos piensa que el principal 'aliado estratégico' del país es China." May 27, 2023. https://ladiaria.com.uy/politica/articulo/2023/5/la-mayoria-de-los-legisladores-uruguayos-piensa-que-el-principal-aliado-estrategico-del-pais-es-china/.

Lampton, David M., Selina Ho, and Cheng-Chwee Kuik. *Rivers of Iron: Railroads and Chinese Power in Southeast Asia*. University of California Press, 2020.

Lang, Marina. "Gobernadores de Brasil abren sus propios canales con China." *Diálogo Chino*, August 13, 2020. https://dialogochino.net/es/comercio-y-inversiones-es/36888-por-la-inercia-de-bolsonaro-gobernadores-brasil-abren-sus-propios-canales-con-china/.

Layne, Christopher. "This Time It's Real: The End of Unipolarity and the Pax Americana." *International Studies Quarterly* 56, no. 1 (2012): 203–13.

Lee, James, and Richard Maher. "US Economic Statecraft and Great Power Competition." *Business and Politics* 24, no. 4 (2022): 332–47.

Leutert, Wendy. "Firm Control: Governing the State-Owned Economy under Xi Jinping." *China Perspectives* 2018, no. 2018/1–2 (2018): 27–36.

Leutert, Wendy and Sarah Eaton. "Deepening Not Departure: Xi Jinping's Governance of China's State-Owned Economy." *The China Quarterly* 248, no. S1 (2021): 200–21.

Levitsky, Steven and Kenneth M. Roberts. *The Resurgence of the Latin American Left*. Johns Hopkins University Press, 2011.

Li, Mingjiang. "The Belt and Road Initiative: Geo-Economics and Indo-Pacific Security Competition." *International Affairs* 96, no. 1 (2020): 169–87.

Li, Zhongshu, Kevin Gallagher, Xu Chen, Jiahai Yuan, and Denise L. Mauzerall. "Pushing Out or Pulling In? The Determinants of Chinese Energy Finance in Developing Countries." *Energy Research & Social Science* 86 (2022): 102441.

Lim, Darren J. and Rohan Mukherjee. "What Money Can't Buy: The Security Externalities of Chinese Economic Statecraft in Post-War Sri Lanka." *Asian Security* 15, no. 2 (2019): 73–92.

Lipset, Seymour Martin. "Some Social Requisites of Democracy: Economic Development and Political Legitimacy." *American Political Science Review* 53, no. 1 (1959): 69–105.

Liu, Mingtang, and Kellee S. Tsai. "Structural Power, Hegemony, and State Capitalism: Limits to China's Global Economic Power." *Politics & Society* 49, no. 2 (2021): 235–67.

Long, Thomas Stephen. *Latin America Confronts the United States: Asymmetry and Influence*. Cambridge University Press, 2015.

Long, Tom. *A Small State's Guide to Influence in World Politics*. Oxford University Press, 2022.

Long, Tom and Francisco Urdinez. "Status at the Margins: Why Paraguay Recognizes Taiwan and Shuns China." *Foreign Policy Analysis* 17, no. 1 (2021): oraa002.
Lopez, Leopoldo. *Challenging Autocracy from the Front Lines*. Wilson Center, 2023. www.wilsoncenter.org/sites/default/files/media/uploads/documents/Challenging%20Autocracy%20From%20the%20Front%20Lines.pdf.
Lu, Juliet. "For Profit or Patriotism? Balancing the Interests of the Chinese State, Host Country and Firm in the Lao Rubber Sector." *The China Quarterly* 250 (2022): 332–55.
Lu, Juliet. "Strategic Resources and Chinese State Capital: A View from Laos." *Made in China Journal* 5, no. 1 (2020): 154–59.
MacDonald, Paul K. and Joseph M. Parent. *Twilight of the Titans: Great Power Decline and Retrenchment*. Cornell University Press, 2018.
MacroInvest. "Informe sobre la razonabilidad económica del proyecto de escisión del negocio portuario." 2023. www.volcan.com.pe/wp-content/uploads/2023/07/230824-RB_051_2023-Acuerdo-JGA-24082023-Anexo-2.pdf.
MacroTrends. "Soybean Prices – Historical Chart Data." December 29, 2023. www.macrotrends.net/2531/soybean-prices-historical-chart-data.
Mahoney, Richard D. *The Kennedy Brothers: The Rise and Fall of Jack and Bobby*. Skyhorse Publishing Inc., 2011.
Malamud, Andrés and Luis L. Schenoni. "Neoliberal Institutionalism and Neofunctionalism in Latin American Security Studies." In *Routledge Handbook of Latin American Security*, edited by David R. Mares and Arie M. Kacowicz, 44–55. Routledge, 2015.
Malkin, Anton. "Challenging the Liberal International Order by Chipping Away at US Structural Power: China's State-Guided Investment in Technology and Finance in Russia." *Cambridge Review of International Affairs* 33, no. 1 (2020): 81–104.
Mares, David R. and Arie M. Kacowicz. *Routledge Handbook of Latin American Security*. Routledge, 2015.
Market Index. "Copper Price & Charts." December 29, 2023. www.marketindex.com.au/copper.
Martins, Leonardo, Rafael Bragança, and Allan Brito. "Doria: Escritório de SP na China negocia liberação de insumos da vacina." UOL Notícias. January 20, 2021. https://noticias.uol.com.br/saude/ultimas-noticias/redacao/2021/01/20/doria-escritorio-de-sp-na-china-negocia-liberacao-de-insumos-da-vacina.htm.
Mastanduno, Michael. "System Maker and Privilege Taker: US Power and the International Political Economy." *World Politics* 61, no. 1 (2009): 121–54.
Maurer, Noel. *The Empire Trap: The Rise and Fall of US Intervention to Protect American Property Overseas, 1893-2013*. Princeton University Press, 2013.
Mazzuca, Sebastián L. "The Rise of Rentier Populism." *Journal of Democracy* 24 (2013): 108.
McPherson, A. *Yankee No!: Anti-Americanism in US–Latin American Relations*. Harvard University Press, 2003.
Medeiros, Evan, ed. *Cold Rivals: The New Era of US-China Strategic Competition*. Georgetown University Press, 2023.

Meek, George. "US Influence in the Organization of American States." *Journal of Interamerican Studies and World Affairs* 17, no. 3 (1975): 311–25.
Meijer, Hugo. *Awakening to China's Rise: European Foreign and Security Policies toward the People's Republic of China*. Oxford University Press, 2022.
Miller, Rory. *Britain and Latin America in the 19th and 20th Centuries*. Routledge, 2014.
Milner, Helen V. and Dustin H. Tingley. "The Political Economy of Us Foreign Aid: American Legislators and the Domestic Politics of Aid." *Economics & Politics* 22, no. 2 (2010): 200–32.
Ministerio de Economía y Finanzas. "Ministro Contreras: el mega puerto de Chancay convertirá al Perú en un polo de crecimiento y desarrollo en la región," news release, September 6, 2023, www.mef.gob.pe/es/?option=com_content&view=article&id=7940&Itemid=102627.
Ministerio de Energía y Minería & Ministerio de Ambiente y Desarrollo Sustentable. "Resolución Conjunta 3-E/2017." (2017), www.argentina.gob.ar/normativa/nacional/resoluci%C3%B3n-3-2017-278621/texto.
Ministerio de Relaciones Exteriores, Comercio Internacional y Culto. "Viaje Presidencial a China," News release, June 17, 2004, www.cancilleria.gob.ar/es/actualidad/comunicados/viaje-presidencial-china.
Ministerio de Relaciones Exteriores, Comercio Internacional y Culto. "Visita de estado a China de la presidenta Cristina Fernández de Kirchner," News release, July 17, 2010, https://cancilleria.gob.ar/es/actualidad/comunicados/visita-de-estado-china-de-la-presidenta-cristina-fernandez-de-kirchner.
Ministerio de Vivienda Construcción y Saneamiento. *Plan De Desarrollo Urbano Del Distrito De Chancay 2008–2018*, 2009, https://issuu.com/parlamentochancay2016/docs/plan_de_desarrollo_urbano_chancay_2/74.
Ministry of Commerce of the People's Republic of China (MOFCOM). "China FTA Network." December 12, 2023. http://fta.mofcom.gov.cn/english/index.shtml.
Ministry of Commerce of the People's Republic of China (MOFCOM). *Statistical Bulletin of China's Outward Foreign Direct Investment 2021*. Beijing, 2022, https://fdi.mofcom.gov.cn/EN/come-datatongji-con.html?id=15932.
Ministry of Foreign Affairs International Trade and Worship of Argentina. "Argentina and China Reaffirm Peaceful Use of Space Facility in Neuquén," news release, September 16, 2016, https://cancilleria.gob.ar/en/news/releases/argentina-and-china-reaffirm-peaceful-use-space-facility-neuquen.
Ministry of Foreign Affairs of the People's Republic of China. "Conversación entre el presidente Hu Jintao y el presidente argentino Kirchner," news release, June 30, 2004, www.mfa.gov.cn/esp/zxxx/200406/t20040630_734891.html.
Mitter, Rana. "The World China Wants: How Power Will-and Won't-Reshape Chinese Ambitions." *Foreign Affairs* 100 (2021): 161.
Monitor Mercantil. "Projeto ratifica participação do Brasil no Baii." January 29, 2019. https://monitormercantil.com.br/projeto-ratifica-participa-o-do-brasil-no-baii/.
Mourón, Fernando and Francisco Urdinez. "A Comparative Analysis of Brazil's Foreign Policy Drivers Towards the USA: Comment on Amorim Neto (2011)." *Brazilian Political Science Review* 8 (2014): 94–115.

Murphy, Dawn C. *China's Rise in the Global South: The Middle East, Africa, and Beijing's Alternative World Order.* Stanford University Press, 2022.

Myers, Margaret. "China's Belt and Road Initiative: What Role for Latin America?". *Journal of Latin American Geography* 17, no. 2 (2018): 239–43.

Myers, Margaret. *Going Local: An Assessment of China's Administrative-Level Activity in Latin American and the Caribbean.* Inter-American Dialogue (December 2020). www.thedialogue.org/wp-content/uploads/2020/12/Going-Local-Chinas-Administrative-Level-Activity-in-LAC.pdf.

Myers, Margaret and Carol Wise. *The Political Economy of China-Latin America Relations in the New Millennium: Brave New World.* Taylor & Francis, 2016.

Narrea, Omar. *Sharing Chinese and Peruvian Visions about the Future Chancay Port: Exploring Opportunities under the Belt and Road.* Universidad del Pacífico (2022). https://cechap.up.edu.pe/wp-content/uploads/Working-Paper-Nr03-Omar-Narrea.pdf.

Neto, Octavio Amorim and Andrés Malamud. "What Determines Foreign Policy in Latin America? Systemic versus Domestic Factors in Argentina, Brazil, and Mexico, 1946–2008." *Latin American Politics and Society* 57, no. 4 (2015): 1–27.

Newnham, Randall E. *Deutsche Mark Diplomacy: Positive Economic Sanctions in German-Russian Relations.* Penn State Press, 2002.

Newnham, Randall E. "More Flies with Honey: Positive Economic Linkage in German Ostpolitik from Bismarck to Kohl." *International Studies Quarterly* 44, no. 1 (2000): 73–96.

Norris, William J. *Chinese Economic Statecraft: Commercial Actors, Grand Strategy, and State Control.* Cornell University Press, 2016.

Noticias, Andina Agencia Peruana de. "Empresa peruana Volcan y la china Cosco Shipping Ports Limited firman acuerdo para la construcción de terminal portuario en Chancay." January 23, 2019, https://andina.pe/agencia/galeria-empresa-peruana-volcan-y-china-cosco-shipping-ports-limited-firman-acuerdo-para-construccion-terminal-portuario-chancay-5412.aspx.

Noticias, TV Perú. "Pdte. Ollanta Humala encabezó puesta en marcha de terminal portuario de Chancay." (May 26, 2016). www.tvperu.gob.pe/noticias/politica/pdte-ollanta-humala-encabezo-puesta-en-marcha-de-terminal-portuario-de-chancay.

Novotny, Daniel. *Torn between America and China: Elite Perceptions and Indonesian Foreign Policy.* Institute of Southeast Asian Studies, 2010.

Nugent, Ciara and Charlie Campell. "The U.S. And China Are Battling for Influence in Latin America, and the Pandemic Has Raised the Stakes." *Time*, February 4, 2021. https://time.com/5936037/us-china-latin-america-influence/.

O'Brien, Thomas F. *Making the Americas: The United States and Latin America from the Age of Revolutions to the Era of Globalization.* University of New Mexico Press, 2007.

Office of Energy Efficiency & Renewable Energy, Department of Energy. "Timeline: A Brief History of Oil Prices and Vehicle Technologies." December 29, 2023. www.energy.gov/eere/timeline-brief-history-oil-prices-and-vehicle-technologies.

Oliveira, Gustavo de L. T. and Margaret Myers. "The Tenuous Co-Production of China's Belt and Road Initiative in Brazil and Latin America." *Journal of Contemporary China* 30, no. 129 (2021): 481–99.

Oud, Malin. "Powers of Persuasion? China's Struggle for Human Rights Discourse Power at the Un." *Global Policy* 15 (2024): 85–96.

Pacheco Pardo, Ramon. "Europe's Financial Security and Chinese Economic Statecraft: The Case of the Belt and Road Initiative." *Asia Europe Journal* 16 (2018): 237–50.

Palan, Ronen, Richard Murphy, and Christian Chavagneux. *Tax Havens: How Globalization Really Works*. Cornell University Press, 2010.

Palestini, Stefano and Erica Martinelli. "Enforcing Peoples' Right to Democracy: Transnational Activism and Regional Powers in Contemporary Inter-American Relations." *European Journal of International Relations* 29, no. 3 (2023): 780–805.

Pang, Xun, Lida Liu, and Stephanie Ma. "China's Network Strategy for Seeking Great Power Status." *The Chinese Journal of International Politics* 10, no. 1 (2017): 1–29.

Panizza, Francisco. "Nuevas izquierdas y democracia en América Latina." *Revista CIDOB d'afers internacionals* 85/86 (2009): 75–88.

Parlatino. "China estrecha lazos con parlamentos de América Latina y el Caribe." January 9, 2019. https://parlatino.org/news/china-estrecha-lazos-con-parlamentos-de-america-latina-y-el-caribe/.

Partido dos Trabalhadores (PT). "Com embaixador da China, consórcio Ne apela por insumos e vacina." News release, May 19, 2021, https://pt.org.br/com-embaixador-da-china-consorcio-ne-apela-por-insumos-e-vacina/.

Pastor, Robert A. *Exiting the Whirlpool, US Foreign Policy toward Latin America and the Caribbean*, 2nd ed. Westview Press, 2001.

Patey, Luke. *How China Loses: The Pushback against Chinese Global Ambitions*. Oxford University Press, 2021.

Pauselli, Gino, Francisco Urdínez, and Federico Merke. "Shaping the Liberal International Order from the Inside: A Natural Experiment on China's Influence in the UN Human Rights Council." *Research & Politics* 10, no. 3 (2023): 20531680231193513.

Paz, Gonzalo Sebastián. "China, United States and Hegemonic Challenge in Latin America: An Overview and Some Lessons from Previous Instances of Hegemonic Challenge in the Region." *The China Quarterly* 209 (2012): 18–34.

Petersen, Mark and Carsten-Andreas Schulz. "Setting the Regional Agenda: A Critique of Posthegemonic Regionalism." *Latin American Politics and Society* 60, no. 1 (2018): 102–27.

Pevehouse, Jon C. W., Timothy Nordstrom, Roseanne W. McManus, and Anne Spencer Jamison. "Tracking Organizations in the World: The Correlates of War Igo Version 3.0 Datasets." *Journal of Peace Research* 57, no. 3 (2020): 492–503.

Poast, Paul. "Dyads Are Dead, Long Live Dyads! The Limits of Dyadic Designs in International Relations Research." *International Studies Quarterly* 60, no. 2 (2016): 369–74.

Pompeo, Michael R. "The United States Protects National Security and the Integrity of 5G Networks," News release, May 15, 2020, www.state.gov/the-united-states-protects-national-security-and-the-integrity-of-5g-networks/.

Population. "Definition of Regions." 2023, https://population.un.org/wpp/DefinitionOfRegions/.

Portal do Governo de São Paulo. "Governo pede a embaixador chinês ajuda para agilizar entrega da IFA da vacina do IB," News release, 2021, www.saopaulo.sp.gov.br/noticias-coronavirus/governo-pede-a-embaixador-chines-ajuda-para-agilizar-entrega-da-ifa-da-vacina-do-ib/.

Porzecanski, Roberto. "¿Por qué Uruguay no firmó un TLC con Estados Unidos?". *Letras Internacionales*, no. 95-4 (2010).

Presidencia. *Inauguración del proyecto hidroeléctricto Sopladora*. República del Ecuador, 2016.

Primiano, Christopher B. "China's Human Rights Statements in the United Nations: What Are the Future Implications?" *China: An International Journal* 16, no. 4 (2018): 183–98.

Pu, Xiaoyu. *Rebranding China: Contested Status Signaling in the Changing Global Order*. Stanford University Press, 2019.

Rabe, Stephen G. "The Elusive Conference United States Economic Relations with Latin America, 1945–1952." *Diplomatic History* 2, no. 3 (1978): 279–94.

Ratigan, Kerry. "Are Peruvians Enticed by the 'China Model'? Chinese Investment and Public Opinion in Peru." *Studies in Comparative International Development* 56 (2021): 87–111.

Ratliff, William. "In Search of a Balanced Relationship: China, Latin America, and the United States." *Asian Politics & Policy* 1, no. 1 (2009): 1–30.

Ray, R. and M. Myers. "Chinese Loans to Latin America and the Caribbean Database." *Inter-American Dialogue* (2023). www.thedialogue.org/MapLists/#/Policy/List/amount.

Reilly, James. *Orchestration: China's Economic Statecraft across Asia and Europe*. Oxford University Press, 2021.

República Argentina. Agua y energía eléctrica sociedad del estado (AyE), 2023. https://mepriv.mecon.gob.ar/Agua_y_Energia/ResHist-Agua.htm.

República Argentina. Aprovechamientos hidroeléctricos del río Santa Cruz – adjudicación, 2013. www.boletinoficial.gob.ar/detalleAviso/primera/93505/20130821.

República Argentina. Decreto 269/2022 [Decree 269/2022], 2022. www.argentina.gob.ar/normativa/nacional/decreto-269-2022-365305.

República Argentina. Decreto 269/2022: Apruébase el modelo de acuerdo de enmienda y restablecimiento al contrato de línea de crédito con relación al programa nacional de obras hidroeléctricas, 2022. www.argentina.gob.ar/normativa/nacional/decreto-269-2022-365305.

República Argentina. Decreto 1381/2001: infraestructura hídrica. Tasa. Constitución del fideicomiso, 2001. www.argentina.gob.ar/normativa/nacional/decreto-1381-2001-69652.

República Argentina. Framework Agreement on Economic Cooperation and Investments. Law 27.122, 2015. www.senado.gob.ar/parlamentario/parlamentaria/31828/LEY%20%20%28Texto%20Sancionado%29%20-%2027122/descargarPdfParla.

República Argentina. Resolución 760/2013: acuerdo de crédito. Aprobación, 2013. www.argentina.gob.ar/normativa/nacional/resoluci%C3%B3n-760-2013-218673.
Reuters. "China's Cosco to Build $2 Billion Shipping Port in Peru: Ambassador." News release, June 1, 2018, www.reuters.com/article/us-peru-china-idUSKCN1IX5WW.
Richardson, Neil R., Charles W. Kegley, and Ann C. Agnew. "Symmetry and Reciprocity in Dyadic Foreign Policy Behavior." *Social Science Quarterly* 62, no. 1 (1981): 128.
Rodrigues, Jorge Fernando. "Frente Nacional dos Prefeitos: não disputamos com o governo a compra de vacinas." *CNN Brasil*, March 2, 2021. www.cnnbrasil.com.br/saude/frente-nacional-dos-prefeitos-nao-disputamos-com-o-governo-a-compra-de-vacinas.
Rollo, Stuart. *Terminus: Westward Expansion, China, and the End of American Empire*. John Hopkins University Press, 2023.
Rosenberg, Emily. *Spreading the American Dream: American Economic and Cultural Expansion, 1890-1945*. Hill and Wang, 1982.
Rühlig, Tim Nicholas. *China's Foreign Policy Contradictions: Lessons from China's R2P, Hong Kong, and WTO Policy*. Oxford University Press, 2021.
Rüland, Jürgen. "The Rise of 'Diminished Multilateralism': East Asian and European Forum Shopping in Global Governance." *Asia Europe Journal* 9, no. 2–4 (2012): 255–70.
Sagasti, Francisco. "A Conversation with President Francisco Sagasti of Peru." Interview by Benjamin Gedan and Cynthia Arnson. *Latin American Program*. Wilson Center. February 18, 2021. www.wilsoncenter.org/event/conversation-president-francisco-sagasti-peru.
Saldinger, Adva. "What Is Dfc's Mandate? Debate over a Bill Turns Up Many Answers." *Devex*, July 27, 2021. www.devex.com/news/what-is-dfc-s-mandate-debate-over-a-bill-turns-up-many-answers-100460.
Samuels, David. *Ambition, Federalism, and Legislative Politics in Brazil*. Cambridge University Press, 2003.
SASAC. "Directory." 2023, http://en.sasac.gov.cn/n_688_4.htm.
Scartascini, Carlos, Cesi Cruz, and Philip Keefer. "The Database of Political Institutions 2020 (Dpi2020)." Inter-American Development Bank, 2021. https://publications.iadb.org/en/database-political-institutions-2020-dpi2020.
Sceats, Sonya and Shaun Breslin. *China and the International Human Rights System*. Chatham house, 2012.
Schweller, Randall L. and Xiaoyu Pu. "After Unipolarity: China's Visions of International Order in an Era of Us Decline." *International Security* 36, no. 1 (2011): 41–72.
Scissors, Derek. *China Global Investment Tracker*. Washington, DC: The Heritage Foundation, 2011. www.aei.org/china-global-investment-tracker/
Seah, Sharon, Joanne Lin, Melinda Martinus, et al. *The State of Southeast Asia: 2024 Survey Report*. ISEAS – Yusof Ishak Institute, 2024. www.iseas.edu.sg/wp-content/uploads/2024/03/The-State-of-SEA-2024.pdf.
Sequeira, Aarón, Natasha Cambronero, and Esteban Oviedo. "Gobierno de China es el que más financia viajes de diputados." *Nacion*, October 9, 2023.

www.nacion.com/el-pais/politica/gobierno-de-china-es-el-que-mas-financia-viajes-de/RN6Q5YY2LVCLFARNSCT7WUFFEY/story/.

Serbín, Andrés and Andrei Serbin Pont. "The Foreign Policy of the Bolivarian Republic of Venezuela: The Role and Legacy of Hugo Chávez." *Latin American Policy* 8, no. 2 (2017): 232–48.

Shambaugh, David. "Assessing the US 'Pivot' to Asia." *Strategic Studies Quarterly* 7, no. 2 (2013): 10–19.

Shambaugh, David. "Containment or Engagement of China?: Calculating Beijing's Responses." *International Security* 21, no. 2 (1996): 180–209.

Smith, Peter H. *Talons of the Eagle: Dynamics of US-Latin American Relations*. Oxford University Press, 1996.

Soulé, Folashadé. "'Africa+ 1' Summit Diplomacy and the 'New Scramble' Narrative: Recentering African Agency." *African Affairs* 119, no. 477 (2020): 633–46.

Soulé-Kohndou, Folashadé. "Bureaucratic Agency and Power Asymmetry in Benin–China Relations." In *New Directions in Africa–China Studies*, edited by Chris Alden and Daniel Large, 189–204. Routledge, 2018.

Stallings, Barbara. *Dependency in the Twenty-First Century?: The Political Economy of China-Latin America Relations*. Cambridge University Press, 2020.

Starrs, Sean. "American Economic Power Hasn't Declined – It Globalized! Summoning the Data and Taking Globalization Seriously." *International Studies Quarterly* 57, no. 4 (2013): 817–30.

State Department. "Growth in the Americas." News release, 2019, https://2017-2021.state.gov/growth-in-the-americas/.

Steil, Benn. *The Marshall Plan: Dawn of the Cold War*. Oxford University Press, 2018.

Stone, Randall W., Yu Wang, and Shu Yu. "Chinese Power and the State-Owned Enterprise." *International Organization* 76, no. 1 (2022): 229–50.

Strange, Austin. *Chinese Global Infrastructure: Elements in Global China*. Cambridge University Press, 2024.

Strange, Susan. *States and Markets*. Bloomsbury Publishing, [1988] 2015.

Strüver, Georg. "What Friends Are Made Of: Bilateral Linkages and Domestic Drivers of Foreign Policy Alignment with China." *Foreign Policy Analysis* 12, no. 2 (2016): 170–91.

Stuenkel, Oliver. "América Latina en el mundo post-occidental." In *El no alineamiento activo y América Latina: una doctrina para el nuevo siglo*, edited by Carlos Fortin, Jorge Heine and Carlos Ominami, 180. Catalonia, 2021.

Summers, Tim. "China's 'New Silk Roads': Sub-National Regions and Networks of Global Political Economy." *Third World Quarterly* 37, no. 9 (September 1, 2016): 1628–43.

Summers, Tim. "Carrots, Not Sticks: A Historical Analysis of Beijing's Economic Statecraft Towards Hong Kong." *Journal of Current Chinese Affairs* 50, no. 3 (2021): 422–37.

Suzuki, Shogo. "Economic Statecraft, Interdependence, and Sino-Japanese 'Rivalry'." *The Pacific Review* 35, no. 5 (2022): 971–94.

Tang, Shiping. "China and the Future International Order (S)." *Ethics & International Affairs* 32, no. 1 (2018): 31–43.

República Argentina. Resolución 760/2013: acuerdo de crédito. Aprobación, 2013. www.argentina.gob.ar/normativa/nacional/resoluci%C3%B3n-760-2013-218673.

Reuters. "China's Cosco to Build $2 Billion Shipping Port in Peru: Ambassador." News release, June 1, 2018, www.reuters.com/article/us-peru-china-idUSKCN1IX5WW.

Richardson, Neil R., Charles W. Kegley, and Ann C. Agnew. "Symmetry and Reciprocity in Dyadic Foreign Policy Behavior." *Social Science Quarterly* 62, no. 1 (1981): 128.

Rodrigues, Jorge Fernando. "Frente Nacional dos Prefeitos: não disputamos com o governo a compra de vacinas." *CNN Brasil*, March 2, 2021. www.cnnbrasil.com.br/saude/frente-nacional-dos-prefeitos-nao-disputamos-com-o-governo-a-compra-de-vacinas.

Rollo, Stuart. *Terminus: Westward Expansion, China, and the End of American Empire*. John Hopkins University Press, 2023.

Rosenberg, Emily. *Spreading the American Dream: American Economic and Cultural Expansion, 1890-1945*. Hill and Wang, 1982.

Rühlig, Tim Nicholas. *China's Foreign Policy Contradictions: Lessons from China's R2P, Hong Kong, and WTO Policy*. Oxford University Press, 2021.

Rüland, Jürgen. "The Rise of 'Diminished Multilateralism': East Asian and European Forum Shopping in Global Governance." *Asia Europe Journal* 9, no. 2–4 (2012): 255–70.

Sagasti, Francisco. "A Conversation with President Francisco Sagasti of Peru." Interview by Benjamin Gedan and Cynthia Arnson. *Latin American Program*. Wilson Center. February 18, 2021. www.wilsoncenter.org/event/conversation-president-francisco-sagasti-peru.

Saldinger, Adva. "What Is Dfc's Mandate? Debate over a Bill Turns Up Many Answers." *Devex*, July 27, 2021. www.devex.com/news/what-is-dfc-s-mandate-debate-over-a-bill-turns-up-many-answers-100460.

Samuels, David. *Ambition, Federalism, and Legislative Politics in Brazil*. Cambridge University Press, 2003.

SASAC. "Directory." 2023, http://en.sasac.gov.cn/n_688_4.htm.

Scartascini, Carlos, Cesi Cruz, and Philip Keefer. "The Database of Political Institutions 2020 (Dpi2020)." Inter-American Development Bank, 2021. https://publications.iadb.org/en/database-political-institutions-2020-dpi2020.

Sceats, Sonya and Shaun Breslin. *China and the International Human Rights System*. Chatham house, 2012.

Schweller, Randall L. and Xiaoyu Pu. "After Unipolarity: China's Visions of International Order in an Era of Us Decline." *International Security* 36, no. 1 (2011): 41–72.

Scissors, Derek. *China Global Investment Tracker*. Washington, DC: The Heritage Foundation, 2011. www.aei.org/china-global-investment-tracker/

Seah, Sharon, Joanne Lin, Melinda Martinus, et al. *The State of Southeast Asia: 2024 Survey Report*. ISEAS – Yusof Ishak Institute, 2024. www.iseas.edu.sg/wp-content/uploads/2024/03/The-State-of-SEA-2024.pdf.

Sequeira, Aarón, Natasha Cambronero, and Esteban Oviedo. "Gobierno de China es el que más financia viajes de diputados." *Nacion*, October 9, 2023.

www.nacion.com/el-pais/politica/gobierno-de-china-es-el-que-mas-financia-viajes-de/RN6Q5YY2LVCLFARNSCT7WUFFEY/story/.

Serbín, Andrés and Andrei Serbin Pont. "The Foreign Policy of the Bolivarian Republic of Venezuela: The Role and Legacy of Hugo Chávez." *Latin American Policy* 8, no. 2 (2017): 232–48.

Shambaugh, David. "Assessing the US 'Pivot' to Asia." *Strategic Studies Quarterly* 7, no. 2 (2013): 10–19.

Shambaugh, David. "Containment or Engagement of China?: Calculating Beijing's Responses." *International Security* 21, no. 2 (1996): 180–209.

Smith, Peter H. *Talons of the Eagle: Dynamics of US-Latin American Relations.* Oxford University Press, 1996.

Soulé, Folashadé. "'Africa+ 1' Summit Diplomacy and the 'New Scramble' Narrative: Recentering African Agency." *African Affairs* 119, no. 477 (2020): 633–46.

Soulé-Kohndou, Folashadé. "Bureaucratic Agency and Power Asymmetry in Benin–China Relations." In *New Directions in Africa–China Studies*, edited by Chris Alden and Daniel Large, 189–204. Routledge, 2018.

Stallings, Barbara. *Dependency in the Twenty-First Century?: The Political Economy of China-Latin America Relations.* Cambridge University Press, 2020.

Starrs, Sean. "American Economic Power Hasn't Declined – It Globalized! Summoning the Data and Taking Globalization Seriously." *International Studies Quarterly* 57, no. 4 (2013): 817–30.

State Department. "Growth in the Americas." News release, 2019, https://2017-2021.state.gov/growth-in-the-americas/.

Steil, Benn. *The Marshall Plan: Dawn of the Cold War.* Oxford University Press, 2018.

Stone, Randall W., Yu Wang, and Shu Yu. "Chinese Power and the State-Owned Enterprise." *International Organization* 76, no. 1 (2022): 229–50.

Strange, Austin. *Chinese Global Infrastructure: Elements in Global China.* Cambridge University Press, 2024.

Strange, Susan. *States and Markets.* Bloomsbury Publishing, [1988] 2015.

Strüver, Georg. "What Friends Are Made Of: Bilateral Linkages and Domestic Drivers of Foreign Policy Alignment with China." *Foreign Policy Analysis* 12, no. 2 (2016): 170–91.

Stuenkel, Oliver. "América Latina en el mundo post-occidental." In *El no alineamiento activo y América Latina: una doctrina para el nuevo siglo*, edited by Carlos Fortin, Jorge Heine and Carlos Ominami, 180. Catalonia, 2021.

Summers, Tim. "China's 'New Silk Roads': Sub-National Regions and Networks of Global Political Economy." *Third World Quarterly* 37, no. 9 (September 1, 2016): 1628–43.

Summers, Tim. "Carrots, Not Sticks: A Historical Analysis of Beijing's Economic Statecraft Towards Hong Kong." *Journal of Current Chinese Affairs* 50, no. 3 (2021): 422–37.

Suzuki, Shogo. "Economic Statecraft, Interdependence, and Sino-Japanese 'Rivalry'." *The Pacific Review* 35, no. 5 (2022): 971–94.

Tang, Shiping. "China and the Future International Order (S)." *Ethics & International Affairs* 32, no. 1 (2018): 31–43.

Tang, Xiaoyang. *Coevolutionary Pragmatism: Approaches and Impacts of China-Africa Economic Cooperation*. Cambridge University Press, 2021.

Telam. "Fernández afirmó que 'no quiere un mundo bipolar' y que son 'bienvenidas' todas las inversiones." December 7, 2022. www.telam.com.ar/notas/202212/613549-fernandez-inversiones-china-estados-unidos.html.

Telias, Diego and Francisco Urdinez. "China's Foreign Aid Political Drivers: Lessons from a Novel Dataset of Mask Diplomacy in Latin America during the Covid-19 Pandemic." *Journal of Current Chinese Affairs* 51, no. 1 (2022): 108–36.

The Economist. "Github: Theeconomist / Graphic-Detail-Data." *The Economist*, October 27, 2018. https://github.com/TheEconomist/graphic-detail-data/tree/master/data/2018-10-27_chinese-century.

The Economist. "The Chinese Century Is Well under Way." *The Economist*, October 27, 2018. https://github.com/TheEconomist/graphic-detail-data/tree/master/data/2018-10-27_chinese-century.

Tian, Nan, Diego Lopes da Silva, Xiao Liang, and Lorenzo Scarazzato. *Trends in World Military Expenditure, 2023*. Stockholm International Peace Research Institute, 2024. www.sipri.org/sites/default/files/2024-04/2404_fs_milex_2023.pdf.

Times Higher Education "World University Rankings 2023." (2023). www.timeshighereducation.com/world-university-rankings/2023/world-ranking.

Toettoe, Benjamin and Richard Turcsanyi. "National Dependence and Public Perceptions: Understanding the Economic Determinants of Foreign Policy Preferences toward China." *International Interactions* 50, no. 6 (2024): 941–74.

Tokatlian, Juan Gabriel. "Estados Unidos-América Latina: Por Una Diplomacia De Equidistancia." In *El No Alineamiento Activo Y América Latina: Una Doctrina Para El Nuevo Siglo*, edited by Carlos Fortin, Jorge Heine, and Carlos Ominami, 61–82. Catalonia, 2021.

Toosi, Nahal. "'Frustrated and Powerless': In Fight with China for Global Influence, Diplomacy Is America's Biggest Weakness." *Politico*, October 23, 2022. www.politico.com/news/2022/10/23/china-diplomacy-panama-00062828.

Trucco, Florencia. "Instituto Butantan en Brasil dice que vacuna de Sinovac tiene eficacia 'superior al mínimo recomendado por la OMS'." *CNN*, December 24, 2020. https://cnnespanol.cnn.com/2020/12/24/instituto-butantan-en-brasil-dice-que-vacuna-de-sinovac-tiene-eficacia-superior-al-minimo-recomendado-por-la-oms.

UNCTAD. "Unctad Commodity Price Index, Annual (2015=100)." December 14, 2023. https://unctadstat.unctad.org/datacentre/reportInfo/US.CommodityPriceIndices_A.

United Nations. "Comtrade Database." November 15, 2023. https://comtrade.un.org/.

Urdinez, Francisco. "The Accession of Latin American Countries to the Asian Infrastructure Investment Bank: Lessons from Brazil and Chile." *Asian Education and Development Studies* 10, no. 3 (2021): 374–85.

Urdinez, Francisco. "'They Own Our Country!' Voter Reaction to Anti-China Rhetoric: The Case of the Presidential Election in Brazil in 2018." *Electoral Studies* 86 (2023): 102708.

Urdinez, Francisco. "Undermining Us Reputation: Chinese Vaccines and Aid and the Alternative Provision of Public Goods During Covid-19." *The Review of International Organizations* 19, no. 2 (2024): 243–68.

Urdinez, Francisco and Margaret Myers. "Regional Repository of Chinese Investments in Latin America." ICLAC and Inter-American Dialogue, 2024. https://china-latam-iclac.netlify.app https://iclac.cl/mapa-repositorio-regional-de-inversiones-chinas/.

Urdinez, Francisco, Camilo López Burian, and Amâncio Jorge de Oliveira. "Mercosur and the Brazilian Leadership Challenge in the Era of Chinese Growth: A Uruguayan Foreign Policy Perspective." *New Global Studies* 10, no. 1 (2016): 1–25.

Urdinez, Francisco, Jan Knoerich, and Pedro Feliú Ribeiro. "Don't Cry for Me 'Argenchina': Unraveling Political Views of China through Legislative Debates in Argentina." *Journal of Chinese Political Science* 23, no. 2 (2018): 235–56.

Urdinez, Francisco, Fernando Mouron, Luis L. Schenoni, and Amâncio J. de Oliveira. "Chinese Economic Statecraft and US Hegemony in Latin America: An Empirical Analysis, 2003–2014." *Latin American Politics and Society* 58, no. 4 (2016): 3–30.

US Bureau of Economic Analysis. "Direct Investment by Country and Industry." 2023. www.bea.gov/data/intl-trade-investment/direct-investment-country-and-industry.

Valor Soja. "Mato Grosso es grosso: el mayor estado agrícola de Brasil es también el que tiene el mayor PIB per cápita." *Bichos de Campo*, December 19, 2023. https://bichosdecampo.com/mato-grosso-es-grosso-el-mayor-estado-agricola-de-brasil-es-tambien-el-que-tiene-el-mayor-pib-per-capita/.

Villalobos, Alejandro. "Argentina rechazó el proyecto chino en Tierra del Fuego." *Loginews*, June 26, 2023. https://noticiaslogisticaytransporte.com/general/26/06/2023/argentina-rechazo-el-proyecto-chino-en-tierra-del-fuego/185100.html.

Voeten, Erik. *Ideology and International Institutions*. Princeton University Press, 2021.

Voeten, Erik. "Resisting the Lonely Superpower: Responses of States in the United Nations to Us Dominance." *The Journal of Politics* 66, no. 3 (2004): 729–54.

Voeten, Erik, Anton Strezhnev, and Michael Bailey. "United Nations General Assembly Voting Data." edited by Erik Voeten. V18Harvard Dataverse, 2009. https://doi.org/10.7910/DVN/LEJUQZ.

Volcan. "Hechos de importancia." News release, March 28, 2023, www.moneycontroller.es/noticias-de-la-bolsa-espa%C3%B1ola/volcan-compania-minera-saa/otros-hechos-de-importancia-1242383.

Volcan. "Memoria Anual 2021." News release, 2021, www.volcan.com.pe/wp-content/uploads/2021/03/Memoria-Anual-2021-vJOA.pdf.

Volcan. "Operaciones en energía." News release, 2021, www.volcan.com.pe/operaciones/energia/.

Volcan. "Volcan firma convenio con Cosco Shipping Ports Limited para construcción del terminal portuario de Chancay." News release, May 14, 2019, www.volcan.com.pe/volcan-firma-convenio-con-cosco-shipping-ports-limited/.

Wang, Yuan. "Executive Agency and State Capacity in Development: Comparing Sino-African Railways in Kenya and Ethiopia." *Comparative Politics* 54, no. 2 (2022): 349–77.
Weiss, Jessica Chen and Jeremy L. Wallace. "Domestic Politics, China's Rise, and the Future of the Liberal International Order." *International Organization* 75, no. 2 (2021): 635–64.
Weiss, Linda and Elizabeth Thurbon. "Developmental State or Economic Statecraft? Where, Why and How the Difference Matters." *New Political Economy* 26, no. 3 (2021): 472–89.
Westad, Odd Arne. *The Global Cold War: Third World Interventions and the Making of Our Times*. Cambridge University Press, 2005.
Weymouth, Lally. "Ecuador's President Is Bucking the Latin American Trend." *The Washington Post*, January 25, 2023. www.washingtonpost.com/opinions/2023/01/25/ecuador-president-lasso-economic-reform/.
Wilkerson, John and Andreu Casas. "Large-Scale Computerized Text Analysis in Political Science: Opportunities and Challenges." *Annual Review of Political Science* 20 (2017): 529–44.
Wise, Carol. *Dragonomics*. Yale University Press, 2020.
Wise, Carol and Victoria Chonn Ching. "Conceptualizing China–Latin America Relations in the Twenty-First Century: The Boom, the Bust, and the Aftermath." *The Pacific Review* 31, no. 5 (2018): 553–72.
Wlezien, Christopher. "Patterns of Representation: Dynamics of Public Preferences and Policy." *The Journal of Politics* 66, no. 1 (2004): 1–24.
Wlezien, Christopher. "Public Opinion and Policy Representation: On Conceptualization, Measurement, and Interpretation." *Policy Studies Journal* 45, no. 4 (2017): 561–82.
Wohlforth, William C. "The Challenge of Evaluating Grand Strategy." In *The Oxford Handbook of Grand Strategy*, edited by Thierry Balzacq and Ronald R. Krebs, 575–58. Oxford Academic, 2021.
Wright, Thomas J. *All Measures Short of War: The Contest for the Twenty-First Century and the Future of American Power*. Yale University Press, 2017.
Xie, Zhuan and Xiaobo Zhang. "The Patterns of Patents in China." *China Economic Journal* 8, no. 2 (2015): 122–42.
Yamin, Patricio and Julieta Zelicovich. "Carrots or Sticks? Analyzing the Application of US Economic Statecraft Towards Latin American Engagement with China." *Latin American Engagement with China. Latin American Politics and Society*, 66, no. 4 (2024): 58–77.
Ye, Min. *The Belt Road and Beyond: State-Mobilized Globalization in China: 1998–2018*. Cambridge University Press, 2020.
Zeihan, Peter and Peter Zeihan. *The End of the World Is Just the Beginning: Mapping the Collapse of Globalization*, vol. 14. Harper Business, 2022.
Zhang, Shu Guang. *Beijing's Economic Statecraft During the Cold War, 1949–1991*. Johns Hopkins University Press, 2014.
Zhang, Shu Guang. *Economic Cold War: America's Embargo against China and the Sino-Soviet Alliance, 1949-1963*. Stanford University Press, 2001.
Zhang, Yongjin. "China and Liberal Hierarchies in Global International Society: Power and Negotiation for Normative Change." *International Affairs* 92, no. 4 (2016): 795–816.

Zhang, Yongjin and Barry Buzan. "China and the Global Reach of Human Rights." *The China Quarterly* 241 (2020): 169–90.
Zhao, Suisheng. "The China Model: Can It Replace the Western Model of Modernization?". *Journal of Contemporary China* 19, no. 65 (2010): 419–36.
Zhu, Keren, Ben Mwangi, and Lynn Hu. "Socio-Economic Impact of China's Infrastructure-Led Growth Model in Africa: A Case Study of the Kenyan Standard Gauge Railway." *Journal of International Development* 35, no. 4 (2023): 614–38.
Životić, Aleksandar, and Jovan Čavoški. "On the Road to Belgrade: Yugoslavia, Third World Neutrals, and the Evolution of Global Non-Alignment, 1954–1961." *Journal of Cold War Studies* 18, no. 4 (2016): 79–97.

Index

abandoned markets, 7
Acevedo, Sergio, 83
active non-alignment, 179
"Acuerdo de Cooperación en Materia de Infraestructura de Transporte" (Cooperation Agreement on Transport Infrastructure), 85–86
agency
    of domestic elites, 13
    indirect, 13
Agricultural Bank of China, 3
Aguad, Oscar, 127
alignment with US, decrease, 24
Alliance for Progress, 165–66
    failure to spread a democracy in LAC, 166
    US investments through, 166
alternative economic goods, 7, 9
Americas Partnership for Economic Prosperity, 164, 172
Antofagasta, 60
Aráoz, Mercedes, 93
Araujo, Ernesto, 98
Arévalo, Juan José, 153
Argentina, 40
    Chinese COVID-19 aid, 97
    Chinese dominance due to loss of US influence, 176
    Chinese trade imbalances, 127
    CHINESEACTORS and, 67
    energy infrastructure financing from China, 82
    energy needs, 83
    opposition to US under Kirchnerismo, 124
    Patagonian Dams project, 82–89
    relationship with Brazil, 126
Argentinean legislators
    perception of China as an alternative to US, 126–27
    on shifting to China from the US, 127
    support for Chinese role in economy, 130
    suspicions of China, 127
    themes in Neuquén Space Station arguments, 128–29
Arnson, Cynthia, 171
Asian Infrastructure Investment Bank, 7, 65–66, 134, 164
Assets Supervision and Administration Commission of the State Council (SASAC), 4

Bandung Conference, 179
Bank of America, 3
Bank of China, 3, 85
banking sector, 3
Belgrano Cargas railway project, 85–86, 88
Bell, David E., 166
Belt and Road Initiative (BRI), 4, 12, 65, 164–65
Biden administration, 172
    friend-shoring, 176
    and United Nations Human Rights Council, 145
Blinken, Anthony, 145
BOC, 68

Bolivarian Alliance for the Peoples of Our
    America, 63
Bolsonaro, Jair
    "China threat" rhetoric, 97
    nonideological economic actions, 180
    split loyalties, 98
    Taiwan visit, 97
Boric, Gabriel, 179
Brands, Hal, 40
Brazil
    breakdown of national relationship with
        China, 98, 101
    Chinese COVID-19 aid, 96–102
    Chinese dominance due to increased
        economic weight, 176
    Chinese ownership of niobium mines,
        97, 100
    Chinese trade, 97
    CHINESEACTORS and, 67
    economic weight of US and China,
        52–53
    National Front of Mayors, 100–1
    Northeast Consortium, 100–1
    relationship with Argentina, 126
    role of Congress in foreign policy, 114
    soybeans, 60
    subnational agency and China, 98–100
    and vaccine production, 101
Build Back Better World, 164, 172
Bush, George H. W., 154
    administration, 41
Bush, George W., 45
Butantan Institute, 101

Camargo, Alberto Lleras, 165
Camargo Correa, 83
Carnegie Endowment for International
    Peace, 13
Carrion, Benjamin, 153
Castañeda, Jorge, 177
categories of public or private goods, 9
Central American states
    relationships to Taiwan and China, 62
Chancay Multipurpose Port project (Peru),
    22, 79, 90–96
    COSCO/Volcan partnership, 93–94
    finding investors, 91–94
    infrastructure development needs, 90–91
    Peruvian national government
        attention, 93
    significance of, 94–95

Chase, 3
Chery, 100
Chile
    Chinese COVID-19 aid, 97, 163
    Chinese dominance due to increased
        economic weight, 176
    conjoint experiment, 76–77
    copper, 60, 77
    FDI preference, 77
    Humboldt Cable project, 171
    trade and aid and China, 62
China Communications Construction
    Company (CCCC), 68, 92
China Construction Bank Corporation, 3
China Development Bank (CDB), 60, 85,
    164
China Export & Credit Insurance
    Corporation (Sinosure), 85
China Harbour Engineering Company
    (CHEC), 92, 123
China in international forums, 132–61
    active influence on voting patterns of
        other countries, 147
    characterization of UN over time, 132
    economic influence over voting, 160–61
    participation since WWII, 133–34
    preference for social stability over
        human rights, 146–47
    working within, 133–34
China in LAC
    capital investment 2001–2020, 166
    early 2000s, 65
    geopolitical dimensions of economic
        rise, 66
    investments and loans, 69
    provider of alternate goods, 55
    quantifying influence, 65–70
    quantifying presence of Chinese
        economic actors, 69–70
    strategic positioning, 55–56
China in OAS, 152
China Molybdenum Company (CMOC),
    100
China National Machinery Industry
    Corporation, 68
China National Space Administration
    (CNSA), 122–23
China Parliamentary Groups, 115
China Railway Construction, 68
China Three Gorges Corporation, 68
China–CELAC forum, 63

China–Latin American and Caribbean States Community Forum (2018), 164
China's mobilized globalization, 3
China–US competition
  economic in nature, 7
China–US economic influence in LAC, 5
China–US economic weight and displacement, 6, 48–54
  displacement formula, 49
  by global region, 49
  increased weight without displacement, 52
  in LAC, 49
China–US rivalry
  systemic effects, 19
China–US trade war (2018), 66
Chinese actors in LAC
  non-effects of commodity price cycles, 71
  non-effects of government ideology, 71
Chinese aid
  challenges in collecting, 33
  COVID-19 aid, 7, 11, 13
  in Economic Weight Index, 28
Chinese economic engagement, uniqueness of, 75–77
Chinese economic strength, 7
Chinese foreign policy
  public and private institutions and, 13
Chinese lending in LAC, 27
CHINESEACTORS (proxy variable)
  Argentina and, 67
  average across LAC, 68–69
  Brazil and, 67
  methodology, 67–69
  Mexico and, 67
  by project, 68–69
Cisen Pharmaceutical, 101
Citibank, 44
Citigroup, 3
classical realism school, 16
Codelco, 60
Colombia
  economic displacement, 175
  US economic dominance, 176
commodity boom, 57–65
  as alternate explanation, 57
  and BRI, 63
  and Chinese funding of LAC infrastructure needs, 60
  Chinese need for natural resources, 58–60
  geographical variations, 62

Net Commodity Export Price Index (IMF), 57
  political effects, 60
  temporal contraindications, 61, 63
composite index, 5
Composite Index of National Capability (CINC), 18, 48
Cóndor Cliff, 87
conjoint experiment, Chile, 76–77
containment policy (Kennan), 43
Contreras, Alex, 94
Cooley, Alexander, 56
Cooperation Framework Agreement, 86
Corporación América, 83
COSCO Shipping Ports Chancay Peru consortium, 90
COSCO Shipping Ports Limited, 90, 94
  interest in Peruvian ports, 92–93
Costa, Rui, 99
Costa Rica
  US economic dominance, 176
  COVID-19 aid, 72
COVID-19 aid, Chinese
  across LAC, 7, 11, 33, 97–102, 163
  to Brazil, 13
  Cuba, 97
  government and enterprise aid, 97–98
  to individual countries, 97
COVID-19 mask diplomacy in Brazil, 79, 96–102
  driven by subnational governments, 100–1
  Project S, 101
Cox survival model, 74
Cuba
  Chinese COVID-19 aid, 97
Cuban Revolution, 166

Dahl, Robert, 16
Dato, Alfredo, 126
democracy and economic support in LAC
  failures of, 166
  impetus, 166
Department of Latin American and Caribbean Affairs of the Ministry of Foreign Affairs of China, 115
dependent variable, 27, 35, 55
DFC, 40
domestic developmental needs, 13
Doria, João, 99–101
Dulles, John Foster, 153

economic alignment
  global geopolitical options, 177
economic assistance tied to democratic and human rights performance, 41
economic behavior and strategy, 12
economic center of gravity, 3
Economic Commission for Latin America and the Caribbean (ECLAC), 60
economic displacement
  in the absence of China, 152–57
  active non-alignment, 178–89
  and alignment within OAS, 132
  and alignment within UNGA, 132, 135–45
  and alignment within UNHRC, 132, 145–51
  causes behind US loss, 167–69
  and China's economic influence, 73–75
  Colombia, 175
  continuous, 20
  creation of space for divergence from US influence, 160
  defined, 48–49
  dichotomous, 20
  displacement zone, 180
  effect on domestic policymaking, 107
  effect on Latin American legislator's views on China, 116–17
  effects in international organizations, 131–61
  effects on perceptions of US by LAC citizenry, 107–12
  effects on perceptions of US by LAC political citizenry, 130
  effects on perceptions of US by LAC political elites, 107, 113–30
  effects on public opinion, 105
  effects on voting alignment in United Nations General Assembly, 136, 140–42
  explained, 5, 7, 19–20
  growth of Chinese influence, 23
  impact on preferred trading partner preference, 118
  incremental nature of the shift, 173
  influence on foreign policy priorities of legislators, 117–18
  and international leadership, 173
  in LAC, 15, 108, 111–13
  loss of US influence, 23–24, 112–13
  as operationalizable variable, 53
  Paraguay, 175
  parallels between strategies leading to displacement, 173–74
  Peruvian mining, 91
  political ramifications, 103–93
  regional change in economic weight, 175
  role of private capital, 173
  South America, 175
  temporal lag, 74–75
  US and China in Chile, 20
  of the US by China in LAC, 22, 48–52, 74
  US influence on international organizations, 105
economic influence, China
  commodities, 72
  COVID-19 aid, 72
  and economic displacement, 73–75
  energy, 72
  import of manufactured products, 72
  infrastructure projects, 72, 124
  job creation, 73
  in Mexico, 73
  mining, 72
  South America, 71
economic influence, United States
  Central America, Mexico, and the Caribbean, 71
  humanitarian aid, 72
economic involvement
  US and China, 71–72
economic power
  US control of IFIs, 41
economic robustness of United States
  nineteenth century, 8
economic statecraft
  agency of domestic elites, 13
  American approach, 12
  challenges of US foreign policy, 172
  China, in Southeast Asia, 15
  Chinese approach, 12
  and Germany, 15
  and intentionality, 11–13
  Japan, 12
  Korean approach, 12
  local actors and multi-stakeholder interactions, 13
  in Sri Lanka, 11–13
  US International Development Finance Corporation, 172
economic weight

Index

China's growth of, 20
countries with US predominance, 176
described, 16–17
LAC without South America, 175
South America, 29, 175
and structural power, 17–18
trajectories in LAC, 175–76
economic weight, China, 48, 53, 73
by continent, 27–28
by LAC region, 29–31
trends in LAC, 27
variability of growth across LAC, 55–69
economic weight, United States, 53
causes behind reduction in LAC, 167–69
in LAC, 39–40, 42–43
methodology and limitations, 40–42
retrenchment, 37–38
in Western Africa and Central Asia, 169
Economic Weight Index, China, 25–33
challenges in data collecting, 32–33
Chinese aid, 28
Chinese trade in LAC, 28
exclusion of imports from China, 42
formula, 26
methodological decisions, 25
operationalizable variables, 27
Ecuador
Chinese dominance due to increased economic weight, 176
free trade agreement with China, 167
lack of US interest in a free trade agreement, 167
trade and aid and China, 62
Electroingeniería, 85–86
photo, 85–86
Elites Latinoamericanas project (PELA), use of, 114–29
methodology, 116, 120, 125
use of data in Neuquén Space Station analysis, 116–17
energy infrastructure financing
Chinese, in LAC, 81
Chinese financing, Argentina, 82
Chinese financing, Venezuela, 82
by country, 81–82
US-led agencies, in LAC, 81
Ensuring American Global Leadership and Engagement (EAGLE) Act, 172
environmental clubs, 180
Estremadoyro, Carlos, 93
Eurnekian, Eduardo, 83

Exim Bank, 60, 68
explanatory variables, 55
Exporting Capitalism (Kapstein), 173

Feletti, Roberto, 126
Feng, Huiyun, 179
Fernández, Alberto, 179
Foot, Rosemary, 132
foreign direct investment
data gathering, 32
US in LAC, 46, 165
Fosun, 100
"Framework Agreement of Cooperation in Economic and Investment Matters," 86
free trade agreements
China and Ecuador, 167
China and LAC, 59
and economic displacement, 114
Ecuador-China, 65
and LAC legislatures, 114
NAFTA, 43
Peru and China, 91
trade agreements, 7
Uruguay, 116
Friendship Groups, 115
Frondizi, Arturo, 165

Gallagher, Kevin, 60
geoeconomics, 66
Gezhouba Group, 83, 85
disqualification by World Bank Group, 87
photo, 85–86
Global South, Chinese investment in, 4–5, 8
Going Global policy, 4, 89
Gramsci, Antonio, 163
Growth in the Americas program, 172
Grupo Financiero Banamex Accival, 44
Guide's, Jia, 93

Haley, Nikki, 145
He, Kai, 179
hedging
preferences in LAC, 179, 181
US pressures against, 180
Hirschman, Albert, 13, 65
Huawei, 68
in Latin America, 14–15
and US State Department, 171

Huawei Marine, 171
Humala, Ollanta, 92
human rights
　China's influence on global norms, 144
Humboldt Cable project (Chile)
　overview, 171
　US opposition, 171

Ibrachina, 100
Icazuriaga, Héctor, 83
ICBC, 3, 68
ideological affinities, 58, 63–65
　as alternate explanation, 57
　contraindications, 65
　and the erosion of democracy, 64
　Inter-American Development Bank's
　　Political Institutions Database, 57
ideological competition, 7
Illia, Arturo, 40
IMF, 40–41
Impsa, 83
Industrial and Commercial Bank
　of China, 85
infrastructure projects
　Chinese funding of Argentine
　　railways, 85
intellectual property technology patents, 3
intentionality and statecraft, 11–13
intentionality of displacement, 8
Inter-American Democratic Charter, 154
Inter-American Development Bank, 27,
　40, 164
　Chinese investments through, 168
　Chinese vs. American enterprise tenders,
　　168–69
International Development Finance
　Corporation, 27
International Monetary Fund (IMF), 27
ISEAS-Yusof Ishak Institute, 113

Jacobson, Roberta, 172
Jenkins, Rhys, 60, 66
Jiangsu Hengrui Medicine, 101

Kaplan, Stephen, 60
Kapstein, Ethan, 173
Kastner, Scott, 65
Kennan, George, 43
Kennedy, Bobby, 167
Kennedy administration, 40
Kirchner, Alicia, 83

Kirchner, Cristina, 83
　photo, 85–86
　visits to China, 85
Kirchner, Néstor, 83
　visits to China, 85
Kirchnerismo, 124, 126
Krasner, Stephen, 41
Kroeber, Arthur, 171
Ku, José Gallardo, 92
Kubitschek, Juscelino, 165
Kuczynski, Pedro Pablo, 93
Kuik, Cheng-Chwee, 179

LAC
　China's Cold War lack of engagement
　　with, 43
　Chinese influence in, 9–11
　Chinese interest in, 2000s, 45
　economic dynamics by region, 29–31
　exports, 42
　infrastructure and railway renovation
　　projects, 10
　liberalization of economies, 44
　low or lower-middle income
　　countries, 172
　political landscape, post 2010, 65
　privatization of state-owned
　　corporations, 44
　relations with US, 2001, 42
　and Taiwan, 31–32
　Taiwan recognition and, 177
　US Cold War engagement with, 43
　US retrenchment, 2001–2020, 45–47
　US trade and investment, 1990s, 43
　void left by United States, 71
LAC, relationship between US and Chinese
　power in, 55–69
　China's strategic positioning as US
　　withdrew presence, 55–57
LAC political landscape, early 2000s
　expectation of CCP coalition, 64
　foreign policy analysis, 64
Lasso, Guillermo, 167
Latin American legislators
　economic displacement and views on
　　China and US, 116–29
　foreign economic policy impacts, 114–16
　intermediaries between enterprise and
　　national government, 115
　methodology for analyzing Neuquén
　　discussions, 124–25

perspectives on China and the US, 114–29
role in free trade agreements, 114
Uruguayan view on China, 116
valued by China, 115
Latinobarometer (2015)
LAC trust in US and China for LAC issues, 108–11
Latinobarometer (2023)
LAC trust in US and China for LAC issues, 111
Lipset, Seymour, 166
local agency, 13–15, 22, 78, 102–3
active non-alignment, 179
bottom up cases, 79, 89–102
Chancay Multipurpose Port project (Peru), 90–96
and Chinese economic initiatives, 164–65
COVID-19 mask diplomacy, 96–97
LAC and US economic support, 165
nonideological economic actions, 180–82
Patagonian Dams project (Argentina), 82–89
and shifting economic weights, 177
top down cases, 79–89
logit regression, 110
Long, Tom, 31, 165
López, José, 83
Lozano, Claudio, 127

Macri, Mauricio, 65, 87
Maurer, Noel, 40
McKinsey Global Institute, 4
Medeiros, Evan, 171
Meek, George, 155
methodology, 21–22
economic displacement and political influence, 21
economic weight, 21
Economic Weight Index construction, 25
loss of political influence, 21
US economic weight, 40–42
Mexico
CHINESEACTORS and, 67
US economic dominance, 176
Milei, Javier, 180
military dominance, Chinese lack, 7
Minera Escondida, 60
Monroe Doctrine, 153

multinational corporations
Chinese, 3
Japanese, 3
US, 3
Musso, Mariano, 86

national-level agency, 80–89
Negri, Mario, 127
Nehru, Jawaharlal, 167
Neuquén Space Station, 23
in the Argentine legislature, 122, 124
congressional discussions, 124–25
development, 123
photo, 122–23
Nexon, Daniel, 56
Norris, William, 12, 14
North American Free Trade Agreement (NAFTA), 43

Obama, Barack
on Chinese investment in LAC, 45–47
Obama Doctrine, 46
O'Brien, Thomas, 44
One Belt One Road (OBOR) project, 66
orchestration theory (Norris), 14
Organization of American States
alignment between LAC countries and the US, 132
coding and modeling of 2001–2021 data, 155, 158
domestic resolutions adopted by Permanent Council by roll call vote 2001–2021, 156–58
economic displacement and hemispheric alignment, 155–57
effect of economic displacement on voting, 159
effect of economic displacement within, 152–59
fear of spreading communism, 153
impact of China's economic displacement on alignment with US, 158
influence of United States within, 153–57
Inter-American Development Bank, 154
overview, 152–53
post-Cold War, 154–57
role of China, 152
US influence 1948–1974, 155
Oswaldo Cruz Foundation (Fiocruz), 101

Panama
 Chinese dominance due to loss of US influence, 176
Panama invasion (1989), 154
Paraguay, 31
 economic displacement, 175
passive agents, rejection of, 15
Pastor, Robert, 42, 153, 172
Patagonian Dams project (Argentina), 22, 79, 82–89
 benefits to Santa Cruz, 86
 capacity concerns, 87
 construction status, 87–88
 developing the partnership, 85–86
 environmental concerns, 87
 financing arrangement, 86–88
 origins, 82–84
 political turmoil and, 87
 self-sustaining credit repayment model, 87
 structural power of China and, 88
 winning consortium, 85
Pearson, Margaret, 65
Peralta, Daniel, 83
Perceived value of China–Latin America Free Trade Agreement, 118–20
Perceived value of US–Latin America Free Trade Agreement, 118, 120–21
Peru
 autogolpe (1992), 41
 Chancay Multipurpose Port project, 90–96
 Chinese COVID-19 aid, 97
 Chinese dominance due to increased economic weight, 176
 mining exports to China, 90–91
 Peruvian and Chinese consortial development, 90
Pescarmona, Enrique, 83
PetroChina, 68
Picasso, José, 95
Piñera, Sebastián, 65
Pink Tide, 45, 63–65
Pivot to Asia, 46
policy implications, 169–89
 active competition in provision of goods, 170–74
 division of LAC into two regions, 174–78, 181
political effects, 73
political influence and economic power, 9

political intentionality behind economic means, rejection of, 15
Porzecanski, Roberto, 60
positional power, 16
post-World War II
 European economic recovery, 7
Pou, Luis Lacalle, 65
power
 and economic weight, 17–18
 financial and production pillars, 18
 knowledge pillar, 18
 positional power, 16
 and relationships, 18
 structural power, 16–18
 US dollar and, 18
Power Construction Corporation of China, 68
prestige-infrastructure projects, 80
public and private goods, categorization of, 9–10
public goods as ideal type, 9
pursuit of Chinese goods and investments, 79

Quiñones, Julio César, 115

Ratigan, Kerry, 109
Ray and Myers's database, 33
Reagan administration, 41
Reilly, James, 12–15
relational power, 16
Rocha, Ibaneis, 99
Rocha, Roberto, 99
Rogel, Fabián, 127
Rossi, Araceli, 127
Rostow, Walt Whitman, 166
Rühlig, Nicholas, 13
rule manager, 13
rule monopolist, 13

Sagasti, Francisco, 179
San Martin Train (Argentina), 10
Sancho, Carlos, 83
security externalities, 12
Shaanxi Chemical Industry Group, 115
Shannon, Thomas, 176
Sinopec ZTE Corporation, 68
Sinovac, 11, 101
Smith, Peter, 153, 166
Sociedad Química y Minera de Chile (SQM), 115

soft power
  US decline in, 15
South America
  economic displacement, 175
space station in Patagonia,
    China-controlled
    analysis of parliamentary debate, 107
stability of the hegemonic system
    provision of economic goods, 9
state control theory (Reilly), 14
State Grid, 100
state-owned enterprises (SOEs), 4
  China Railway Construction
    Corporation (CRCC), 10
"*States and Markets*" (Strange), 18
states as global owners and investors, 4
Stefani, Hector Tito, 115
Strange, Austin, 80
Strange, Susan, 16
structural power, 16
  and economic weight, 17
subnational and non-state agency, 89–96
  benefits to Chinese firms, 89–90
  local benefits, 89
Suzuki, Shogo, 12

Taiwan Allies International Protection
    and Enhancement Initiative Act
    (TAIPEI), 177
Taiwan cost, 31
target nation and demand, 15
Three Gorges, 100
three to tango
  described, 15–16
Thurbon, Elizabeth, 12
Tianqi Lithium, 115
Times New Roman "Asia-Pacific Economic
    Cooperation Forum," 179
trade agreements (Chinese)
  Free Trade Agreements (FTAs), 7
Trump administration, 47
  Growth in the Americas program, 172
  Huawei, 171
  on Taiwan in LAC, 171
  and United Nations Human Rights
    Council, 145

UNASUR, 63
"The United Fruit Company"
    (Neruda), 165
United Nations General Assembly
  alignment between LAC countries
    and the US, 132
  China's role in, 134
  Chinese influence within, 136–37
  difference-in-differences analysis of
    economic displacement, 143–44
  economic displacement's negative effect
    on US alignment, 140–42
  effects of economic displacement within,
    140–44
  ideological alignment for LAC
    countries, 140
  LACs voting proximity to China and US,
    138–39
  overview, 135
  resolution types, 138–40
  Voeten, Strezhnev, and Bailey database,
    137–38
  voting alignment and economic
    displacement, 136
  voting convergence trends, 137–38
United Nations Human Rights Council
  alignment between LAC countries and
    the US, 132
  and China, 146–47
  China's role in, 134
  convergence of votes among LAC and
    US, 148
  divergence of votes among LAC and US,
    151
  economic displacement and Latin
    America–US alignment, 148–49
  effects of economic displacement within,
    145–51
  estimated interactive model for voting,
    159–60
  LAC member countries, 148–49
  marginal effect of US economic weight
    conditioned by China's economic
    weight on a country's vote alignment
    with the US, 160
  model for vote analysis, 150
  overview, 145
  Pauselli, Urdinez, and Merke
    database, 148
  resolutions, 149
  and the United States, 145–46
United States as lone superpower,
    43–45, 56
United States' monopoly in private and
    public goods, 9

US displacement of Germany in LAC, 163
US Economic Weight Index, 33–38
  Caribbean, 40
  Central America, 39–40
  by continent, 36
  credits, IMF and World Bank, 39–40
  data sources, 35–36
  exclusion of imports from the US, 42
  formula, 34–35
  inclusion of exports to the US, 42
  and the LAC, 36
  operationalizable variables, 35
  overview, 34–35
  South America, 39–40
US Export-Import Bank, 8
US in LAC
  challenges of private sector mobilization, 172
  contraction of influence, 39
  decline of economic influence, 55–56
  early twentieth century, 8
  environmental compliance measures, 180
  reactive foreign policy, 165–67
  shift away from capital to human issues, 47, 55
US International Development Finance Corporation, 167, 172
US investment in LAC
  1897–1953, 163–64
  post-WWII assistance programs, 164
US retrenchment, 4, 45–47
US role in world
  and Trump administration, 38
USAID, 166
USAID assistance programs, 41

US–China economic weight and displacement, 6, 48–49, 52–54

Venezuela
  Chinese dominance due to loss of US influence, 176
  trade and aid and China, 62
Voeten, Erik, 132, 135
Volcan Compañía Minera, 90
  benefits of COSCO partnership, 94–95
  controversies regarding, 92
  involvement with Chancay Multipurpose Port project, 91–93

Wang, Yuan, 80
Wang Yi, 164
Washington Consensus, 34, 44–45
Wei, Zhang, 95
Weiss, Linda, 12
Westad, Odd Arne, 47
Western Development Program, 4
Westphalian principles, 147
"whirlpool effect," 43
Wise, Carol, 60
World Bank, 27, 40–41, 164
  disqualification of Gezhouba, 87
World Trade Organization (WTO), 32
Wuxi Biologic, 101

Xi Jinping, 86, 146

yuan currency swaps, 88

Zhenjiang Xuanju Pharmaceutical, 101
Zoellick, Robert, 162–63

For EU product safety concerns, contact us at Calle de José Abascal, 56–1°,
28003 Madrid, Spain or eugpsr@cambridge.org.

www.ingramcontent.com/pod-product-compliance
Ingram Content Group UK Ltd.
Pitfield, Milton Keynes, MK11 3LW, UK
UKHW041007290326
469448UK00012B/172